THE FUTURE THAT WAS

The Future That Was

A History of Third World Feminism Against Authoritarianism

Durba Mitra

PRINCETON UNIVERSITY PRESS
PRINCETON AND OXFORD

Published by Princeton University Press
41 William Street, Princeton, New Jersey 08540

99 Banbury Road, Oxford OX2 6JX

press.princeton.edu

GPSR Authorized Representative: Easy Access System Europe - tee 50,
10621 Tallinn, Estonia, gpsr.requests@easproject.com

ISBN 9780691233604
ISBN (e-book) 9780691233628

Library of Congress Control Number: 2025940544

British Library Cataloging-in-Publication Data is available
Editorial: Priya Nelson and Emma Wagh
Production Editorial: Theresa Liu
Jacket/Cover Design: Heather Hansen
Production: Erin Suydam
Publicity: Alyssa Sanford and Kathryn Stevens
Copyeditor: Cynthia Buck

Jacket/Cover Credit: *Infinite Woman,* 2019–21. Watercolor, ink, gouache, and gold leaf on paper, 60 × 66 inches, by MacArthur award-winning artist Shahzia Sikander.

This book has been composed in Adobe Text Pro and Gotham.

Printed in the United States of America

10 9 8 7 6 5 4 3 2 1

MIX
Paper | Supporting responsible forestry
FSC® C008955
FSC
www.fsc.org

For my mother, Rupa,
and all women who seek justice through knowledge

CONTENTS

ILLUSTRATIONS

THE FUTURE THAT WAS

Introduction, or What Is the Future We Yearn For?

The Future That Was is about yearning. It is about the yearning of women as a transnational project of knowledge at a time of disillusionment with decolonization in the 1970s and 1980s.[1] As people confronted ongoing crises of neocolonialism, patriarchal authoritarianism, and Cold War militarism, women strove for justice by researching and writing about women's lives and their visions for a different world. *The Future That Was* tells the story of Third World women who ignited a world of research on women's and sexual rights in the 1970s and 1980s and the complex legacy of this vastly unequal knowledge economy.

Third World women catalyzed a momentous expansion of knowledge about women, gender, and sexuality that transformed emancipatory politics across the world. I illuminate this history by exploring the study of women in the decolonizing world, with a focus on South Asia and the many women's networks that stretched from South Asia to the African continent, the Caribbean, the United States, and beyond. As people confronted the failures of new democracies and the fractured promises of constitutional equality, women saw in radical acts of research and writing the opportunity to argue for their place as citizens against patriarchal norms. They created research networks that reached beyond borders, built organizations to promote the training of women in wide-ranging fields, supported transnational women's research projects, and advocated for women's rights at the national and international levels. They staged public protests to argue for research on women's lives and equitable policy for women. These long-lasting networks, organizations, and social and political movements championed transnational research on women for decades.

Third World feminism was a reinvention of the Third World.[2] Over the course of this book, I argue that the very idea of the Third World was made anew by women who saw transnational solidarity as a potent tool against neocolonialism and patriarchal nationalism in the fractured global politics of the 1970s and 1980s. These researchers self-identified as Third World women and reimagined Third World internationalism as a critical alliance against authoritarianism.[3] In doing so, they claimed a collective feminist politics that reached across geographies intimately linked through global histories of colonization and enslavement and fought against enduring systems of neocolonialism, inequality, and militarism perpetuated by the Cold War.[4] The women who animated this world of research included a wide range of intellectuals from South Asia, the African continent, the Caribbean, the Middle East, and the United States. These highly educated urban women were often from dominant classes, ethnicities, and castes. They were trained in wide-ranging fields of research as economists, sociologists, political scientists, lawyers and legal scholars, civil servants, writers, editors, publishers, and activists.

In contrast with traditional accounts of decolonization, development, and human rights, *The Future That Was* recasts the history of decolonization through a genealogy of feminist knowledge production. I follow in the long tradition of anti-colonial thought at the intersection of intellectual history and political theory, centering Third World feminism in the history of twentieth-century political thought. Research on the world's women expanded rapidly, revolutionizing everything from foundational measures of economic and social development to frameworks of international law and citizenship and the very definition of human rights. Yet feminist research took many trajectories in an era when the failures of self-determination and economic sovereignty fed rising authoritarian movements. While many in the decolonizing world led massive revolutionary protests against patriarchal state repression, women also collaborated with the state, international organizations, and private foundations to expand research that fortified carceral governance through policies focused on the protection of women.[5]

Women seized the means of knowledge production, critiquing postcolonial inequality and rising authoritarianism around the world and theorizing radically just visions of the future. Women pursued the work of writing and publishing on women and gender at a scale never seen before.[6] They created new infrastructures for research that centered women and the pursuit of gender justice and argued for equal rights and political autonomy for women in the present and in the future. Women were writing feminism into being as they led movements, created women's studies programs, and established women and gender as legitimate subjects of scholarship. The organizational and personal papers, oral histories, and scholarship produced by Third World women form the primary archives of this book.

The Future That Was is the first comprehensive history of the United Nations (UN) Year and Decade for Women (1975–1985). It reveals the paradoxical dependence of international women's research on the growing infrastructures of nongovernmental organizations (NGOs), private foundations, and international governance that defined a new politics of women and gender from the 1970s until today. International and transnational research projects sponsored by the UN, aid programs, national policy initiatives, and international foundations became the primary way for Third World women to pursue their aspirations to create knowledge yet also delimited the research that they produced. Women engaged the domain of development research while also at points critiquing and subverting the limits of international funding structures. I recast standard depictions of Third World women and reimagine the seemingly sterile records of women and development by bringing together wide-ranging archives that include thousands of pages of international conference proceedings, state and NGO policy reports to feminist anthologies, women's oral histories, feminist journals, speeches, memoirs, and poetry.

This is a history powered by jet travel and new forms of communication and archived through the popular technologies of the photocopier, the handheld camera, and the camcorder. Feminist ideas traveled across languages, lexicons, and borders. Women moved between geographies to be in community with one another, gathered at international conferences around the world, crowded together in classrooms and auditoriums, and wrote and published in multiple languages. This period from the 1970s through the early 1990s saw the unprecedented expansion of feminist exchange around the globe, with women gathering together in geographies spanning from Mexico City, Copenhagen, and Nairobi to Delhi, Cairo, Lahore, London, New York, Boston, Kingston, Colombo, Ulaanbaatar, Algiers, Dakar, and Beijing.

As they moved across borders and disciplines, Third World women pursued the decolonization of knowledge itself. This history unfolds in chapters organized around critical sites and genres that have defined the trajectory of feminist research: the conference, the report, the organization, the book, and the protest. Through the rise of these now dominant forms and genres, I analyze the promises, challenges, and failures of feminist thought in the decolonizing world, reflecting on a generation of researchers who wrote women into existence in the face of persistent threats of violence.

The Future That Wasn't

I write this history fifty years after the rapid expansion of aspirational international feminist research that reached across geographies, policymaking, and funding networks. The texts, organizations, and mass movements that resulted from the expansive study of women have defined not only how we think about women and sexual minorities around the world but the very measures we use to assess development, human rights, and democratic governance. What has this history of ideas created, and how are we to understand the massive expansion of women's writing and thinking in this moment? To reflect on the life of feminist thought now is a monumental project. It requires collective thinking on what genres, research infrastructures, and institutions have been monumentalized through the study of women and gender, and what structures must *fall*.

To write this account I went to the past to understand a world of women's writings about their present crises and future aspirations. But I also looked to the future. Or rather, I looked to my own present to better understand the eventual future that followed this moment of international feminist research of the 1970s and 1980s.

The futures that Third World women worked toward in the 1970s and 1980s have now been replaced by the reality of our present. It is a cruel reality. It is a present where hard-earned protections for reproductive rights have been wholly demolished in the United States and in the many US foreign policies and aid packages that dictate reproduction and health around the world. Where the most promising radical anti-colonial constitutional democracies of their times—first India, then South Africa—face endemic issues of majoritarian nationalism, exclusionary citizenship, and gendered violence manifest in cultures of xenophobic mob violence and rape that target women and minorities who dissent. Where homosexuality is condemned again and again in the postcolonial world as a foreign import, just as feminism has been dismissed by reactionary political movements for decades as alien and dangerous to society. Where claims that women's, queer, and trans rights are outside of "tradition" serve as the primary justification for virulent anti-women and anti-LGBTQ legislation in Asia, Africa, and the Caribbean. Where anti-trans legislation and policy sweeping the United States, the United Kingdom, and the rest of the world, justified through biological determinist arguments about state protection for women and children, threatens the very survival of trans and nonbinary people.

It is a present where unfolding crises of war, colonial occupation, and state-enforced famine decried by Third World women fifty years ago now produce some of the most horrifying scenes of war and genocide, with suffering and scales of visible death at levels that the world has not experienced in a century. Where people are forced to migrate as a result of global inequality and climate catastrophes wrought by greed. Where people die by the thousands crossing treacherous borderlands, suffering preventable diseases in emergency camps, and drowning in makeshift vessels in the sea, uncounted in life and death.

This is not the radically just world imagined by a generation of women who worked tirelessly to build different possibilities for women in the future. They wrote, dreamed, organized, researched, compiled, edited, published, gathered together, danced, recited poetry, chanted slogans, fought, protested, and wrote still more to build a world where research and writing would produce real, substantive gains for women and minoritized communities. Their imagined future is not our present.

It is hard not to critically assess where we are now, more than half a century after the global research on women that made possible transnational and national agendas, policies, institutions, and research that transformed the way we think and write, not only about women, gender, and sexuality but about the effects of everything from development to democratic politics. There is no question that feminist advocacy and research have transformed many measurable policies for women and sexual minorities and created a visible politics of international sexual rights today. Across languages and geographies, there are countless research centers, women's studies programs and curricula, national commissions and bureaus, and laws and policies committed to the study of women and gender. There are now standardized social scientific genres of state and NGO research utilized by feminist, queer, and trans rights organizations that work to translate the lives and worth of women and sexual minorities into measurable forms for international organizations, nation-states, donors, and a broader public.

Yet, despite the massive incitement to knowledge about women and gender made possible by new policies, laws, and educational institutions, research has often had a limited effect on substantive social and political change in much of the world. The inconsistent impact of feminist research on the lives of women in the decolonizing world is largely attributable to a total lack of will and enforcement from many states that have stifled any possibility of justice and equality for women in and beyond policy and law. With the expansion of international institutions that assess states through a rubric of women's development but offer few enforcement mechanisms, women's and gender rights have been co-opted by postcolonial democracies and authoritarian states alike. The widespread proliferation of women's bureaus, commissions, and gender research centers has allowed most postcolonial states with little interest in advancing women's rights to use them as an alibi signaling state compliance with international norms of gender equality and women's rights. And under new attacks in the present, many international aid programs and states have rapidly dismantled and defunded research infrastructures focused on women and sexual minorities.

Today the lives of most girls and women of the world remain precarious. In many places, despite dozens of laws, national commissions, and reports, women's lives are measurably worse than they were decades ago. The goals of justice and freedom for women have been undermined by twenty-first-century politics that claim to protect the interests of women while reasserting patriarchal domination over the bodies and lives of women and sexual minorities. Authorities traffic ideas of the protection of women as a justification for the expansion of the security state, the adoption of surveillance technologies, and the enactment of anti-queer and anti-trans legislation.[7]

For the past twenty-five years, as a result of the ongoing global war on terror, the domain of gender research and sexual rights has been dominated by increasingly militarized and securitized states, neoliberal funding structures, and influential right-wing religious networks that have perversely deployed the language of gender and women's rights to expand carceral structures directed at women and sexual minorities.[8] Especially since the 1990s, Third World women's research has been increasingly marginalized and privatized through a model of funding based on donors, creating dependencies for the work of women's research that have often emptied these projects of their radical political potential.[9] States deploy neoliberal ideas of women's empowerment on behalf of projects of racialized and caste-ist policing, war, and debt programs that encourage women to take on debt in the form of "microloans" that often create endless cycles of dependency.[10]

Even as *The Future That Was* accounts for the possibilities and limits of Third World feminist movements and intellectual projects, I do not subscribe to a simple diagnostic assessment of success or failure. Such didactic thinking has become a primary way in which many scholarly frameworks assess the value of social and political movements for civil rights during the twentieth century. This binary paradigm has limited how we understand radically democratic imaginaries of women and minorities with ambitious goals of achieving self-determination and global economic redistribution.[11] Diagnostic assessments of social movements too often attribute failure to the ideological basis of liberatory theories and actions while not taking seriously the *content* of these complex ideas and organizations, nor accounting for the many ways dominant states and private industries suppressed, co-opted, defunded, and massively bureaucratized these movements. Evaluations of the failure of feminist projects often do not offer systemic analysis of the structural and material conditions that made the work of Third World feminist researchers fragile and dependent on the whims of national planning commissions, donors, and international priorities, often compromising their radical ideas. Such frameworks overlook the remarkable intellectual labor of women who defied and subverted these challenging conditions to build a world of feminist research and writing despite all the odds against them.

The deployment of an empty rhetoric of rights by both liberal democratic and increasingly authoritarian states today offers a stark contrast to Third World women's visions of anti-colonial self-determination, bodily autonomy, and radical freedom for all fifty years ago. For much of the twentieth century, networks of women pursued radically democratic visions of their societies by innovating frameworks of universal civil rights and justice through focused research on women's lives. They did so with full knowledge of the uncertainty and danger that resulted from writing about the complex political and social struggles of women. Women faced very real threats to their lives for expressing dissent under increasingly dangerous neocolonial structures of knowledge and power. Despite the many risks, women theorized a world free of authoritarianism at every level, linking women's liberation in the home and community to democratic rights in the state and international society.

Yet *The Future That Was* also reckons with the hierarchies and exclusions that shaped the feminist pursuit of emancipatory knowledge. I reveal the many asymmetries in geographies, disciplines, and forms of expertise perpetuated by women who claimed to represent the Third World. Class domination, caste supremacy, racism, and biological determinism shaped the trajectories of Third World feminist thought in the 1970s and 1980s. Exclusions defined the limits of the earliest domains of international research on the world's women, shaping later debates about gender, racism, and caste supremacy on the international stage in the 1990s and early 2000s.[12] There were many foreclosed paths for research and unrealized visions of freedom as women collectively strategized to transform the trajectory of decolonization.

Decolonization and the Crisis of Authoritarianism

On September 21, 2001, the feminist network Women Living Under Muslim Laws released an urgent statement begging for caution in response to the events of September 11, as the United States threatened revenge and war against the people of Afghanistan. "Vengeance is not justice," the women declared as they warned of the long-term effects of the US war for women around the world.[13] The bold statement of a transnational collective of women pierced the deafening silence following the catastrophic events that had unfolded at the World Trade Center in New York just ten days before. Women Living Under Muslim Laws decried the costs of terrorism, warned of a loss of democratic rights, and condemned the rapid growth of patriarchal religious fundamentalisms in the region. The statement powerfully declared that "violence cannot eradicate terrorism" and warned that retaliatory acts of militarism by the United States would only wreak further havoc on the most vulnerable people in societies around the world. Rather, the collective insisted that the solution to global discontent and extremist antagonism had to be based in the ideas and needs of the most powerless people in times of conflict.[14] Retaliatory war would have profound consequences for "women in Muslim countries and communities in particular" that would suffer unspeakable consequences from military action, while ultimately the "space for alternative positions will vanish" under the impossible conditions of war.[15]

Women Living Under Muslim Laws is a transnational research collective of Third World women that was founded in 1984, more than twenty-five years before 9/11. For decades before 2001, the organization had been producing research and writing on the problem of religious fundamentalism that foregrounded the perspectives of women and insisted that women's equality was at the heart of the struggle for self-determination. By the early 1990s, Women Living Under Muslim Laws boasted an extensive research network with thousands of active women in over forty countries.[16] Their fears about military retaliation by the United States and an unfolding catastrophe that could lead to total democratic impossibility in Muslim societies in Asia, Africa, and the Middle East became a tragic reality.

The September 11 attacks took place during my first week of college at a university in America's heartland. While public discourse in the United States was dominated by fervent patriotism, many worked to envision an anti-war movement for the twenty-first century. As a student, I, like so many, looked to histories of war, ideologies of colonialism, and critical theories of anti-colonial liberation and decolonization to try to understand this world-changing event. I have distinct memories in the days that followed September 11, 2001, of witnessing the power of dissenting statements, like the bold words of Women Living Under Muslim Laws, that countered patriotic calls for indiscriminate war. In the face of dangerous ideologies of racism and religious prejudice and the total suspension of critique of the US government, this transnational collective of women insisted that the most vulnerable people of the world had the right to survive and pursue democratic sovereignty. Feminism, against calls for retribution and vengeance, asserted an ethics of the living in the face of fear.

Decolonization, as was clear in that moment in 2001, never ended.[17] The second half of the twentieth century saw a world emerging from the horrors of World War II, nuclear devastation, and the violence of border-making partitions. As global powers reorganized themselves into what would be a decades-long Cold War, people around the world began to push for emancipation and decolonization with new claims to sovereignty and self-determination. Despite the promises of liberation, the coercion, violence, and oppression of erstwhile imperial regimes did not disappear at the formal end of colonialism. New regimes of domination emerged based in the global reorganization of economic inequality and ongoing systems of colonial domination.

A rapid succession of decisive events accelerated long-standing anti-colonial resistance and movements for decolonization. In the 1940s, the world had ruptured with the dramatic partitioning and restructuring of states across the postcolonial world and Europe. What resulted were seeds of violence and conflict that would grow in the decades to come in multiple partitions, new economic dependencies, and the novel state technologies of apartheid. By the early 1950s, the promise of anti-colonial liberation had swept the colonized world, as fervent struggles for self-determination emerged in rapid succession.[18] The landmark 1955 Bandung Conference and Afro-Asian solidarity conferences that followed powerfully declared a transnational commitment to postcolonial sovereignty grounded in democratic ideas of self-determination "based on the will of the people," in the language of political theorist and historian Partha Chatterjee.[19]

Democracy and self-determination for people—for *all* people—was totally new in this moment, and it was a revelation. These pivotal events introduced the first real possibility of formal citizenship for all. By the early 1960s, people around the world were gaining access to the vote, building independent governments, and creating new alliances between decolonizing states, from the paradigm-shifting civil rights struggle in the United States to global movements for decolonization. These novel experiments with universal rights marked the first time democratic citizenship could be claimed by the darker peoples and nations of the world.[20]

Throughout this book, I use the phrase "the decolonizing world" to refer to regions in Asia, the Middle East, the African continent, and the Caribbean undergoing formal and active processes of decolonization following the decline of European colonial powers after World War II. But it is also a critical reframing of the world as a *whole* in the moment of decolonization, away from the standard historiographic framing of "the Cold War" to center the history of decolonization in the postwar period. The concept reflects ongoing efforts by most people of the world to subvert and fight against formal colonial structures of power that had spread from the late eighteenth century, with a particular focus on the former British Empire, regions in Asia, Africa, and the Caribbean, and territories increasingly under the control of the US empire in the twentieth century. The term "the decolonizing world" further encompasses ongoing struggles against the enduring residues of coloniality in the postcolony: ongoing movements against the authoritarian nation-states that sustained their power through neocolonial dependencies.

Women took on critical roles in early anti-colonial movements and nation-building projects, organizing major movements and transnational conferences for women between the 1920s and 1940s.[21] However, women's rights were often on the periphery of the formal global politics of decolonization that followed in non-alliance and the internationalism of self-determination in the 1950s and 1960s as many postcolonial leaders worked to erase women's contributions to anti-colonial liberation struggles. The "Final Communiqué"—the official declarations for freedom and independence for all colonized peoples that resulted from the Bandung Conference—outlined areas where all people would participate in broad liberatory projects of self-determination.[22] However, the statement and the conference proceedings offered no specifics about the conditions or rights of women, nor did it treat women as a distinct political class despite decades of political organizing for women's issues during the anti-colonial struggle, although Bandung would come to have a profound influence on women's movements that followed.[23] Yet, in these early decades of decolonization, women's rights were to be perpetually subordinate to the broader nationalist project and the reorganization of the global alliances.[24]

Just as people called for national self-determination and democratic citizenship as non-alignment politics gained momentum, the United Nations became a critical site for a new world-making politics of economic and political self-determination and radical redistribution for decolonizing states, as conceptualized by political theorist Adom Getachew.[25] But these novel experiments at the UN were quickly replaced by the reality of global development priorities that were far from the radical ideas of redistribution of many anti-colonial thinkers.[26] By 1960, the UN had declared its first-ever major theme for a decade, the first official Decade of Development, from 1960 to 1970.[27] This declaration of the theme of development would shape the UN priority areas related to women, with "development" as one of three key themes in the International Women's Year (1975) and Decade for Women (1976–1985) that followed.

The Cold War shifted the trajectory of global decolonization away from the radical redistributive goals of formerly colonized people. New states in the decolonizing world, largely ruled by an educated elite, looked to profit from the tug-of-war between the United States and the Soviet Union by promoting nationalisms and desperately working to modernize their states and economies. Under the guise of development, postcolonial states deployed new technologies that centered women as key measures, including the increasingly powerful disciplines of demography, population studies, and development economics to govern, surveil, aggregate, and often exploit people newly constituted as the population-citizenry.

By the 1970s, the dream of self-determination and true democratic citizenship had been replaced by the nightmare of neocolonialism, economic dependency, and unending political insecurity.[28] Global relationships of dependency created more inequality in an already profoundly unequal world through new development programs and infrastructures of debt in the creation of the World Bank and International Monetary Fund (IMF). And in 1979, the Iranian Revolution and the Soviet invasion of Afghanistan shocked the world and inaugurated a new era of reactionary religious populist movements that stretched from regions in the Middle East to South Asia to the African continent.[29] The authoritarian states that resulted deployed a rhetoric of anti-colonial sovereignty while implementing emergency laws that suspended civil liberties alongside authoritarian patriarchal laws and policies that denied women access to basic citizenship and systematically dispossessed women.[30]

In 1981, political theorist Eqbal Ahmad brilliantly diagnosed the crisis of authoritarianism in the Third World in foundational essays on the fracture of postcolony states, what he named the "pathology of power" fostered by neocolonialism and postcolonial authoritarian politics.[31] He argued that the dramatic shift from the promise of constitutional democracy to autocracy resulted in the global rise of perverse hybrid states that merged enduring colonial structures of governance with a new global technocratic elite that profited from exploitative flows of global capital. These authoritarian postcolonial states mimicked but undermined democratic governance.[32] The crisis of authoritarianism plagued states in Asia, Africa, and Latin America that promised true democracy and development. Yet, paradoxically, global development and modernization programs did little to help most of the people of the world. For Ahmad, neocolonial structures of global domination and their regional puppet neofascist states kept most people subordinate in systems of governance built without their consent and ruled by an elite that profited from militarism, carcerality, and economic exploitation.

It was in this moment of insecurity and cascading crises of global inequality that women's issues, two decades after the Bandung Conference, achieved formal visibility on the international stage at an unprecedented scale with the official UN International Women's Year and Decade for Women. As the politics of non-alignment and self-determination fractured in global conflicts over oil and religious nationalism, this moment fomented the rise of international women's movements in the 1970s. Ultimately, it was the declaration of the first International Women's Year in 1975, followed by the declaration of the UN Decade for Women between 1975 and 1985, that served as the single most important catalyst for the massive expansion of research and writing on global women.[33] Were it not for the UN Year and Decade for Women and the subsequent global conference on women in Beijing, international research on women as we know it would not exist.

The formalization of three central themes for International Women's Year and the Decade for Women—development, equality, and peace—extended the long-standing UN commitment to development to the domain of women's rights. The International Women's Year and Decade for Women intersected with the second UN Decade of Development between 1970 and 1980, an overlap that was critical for the trajectory of international research on women in the decolonizing world; in its first decade, that research had been focused almost entirely on questions of development. In this moment, Soviet influence began to recede from the domain of international women's research, although Soviet alliances remained significant for the final Afro-Asian women's conferences and the 1985 conference of non-aligned states on women and development. By the late 1980s, international research on women was primarily dominated by foreign policy priorities and foundations in the United States and northern and western Europe.

The widespread emphasis on development led to a critical epistemic shift in which the metrics of development were inextricably tied to the study of women, converging under the umbrella infrastructure of women and development (WAD). As women and gender came to have global prominence through the new paradigm of WAD, it was reframed quickly as women *in* development (WID), and later the paradigm was broadened under the policy umbrella of gender and development (GAD).[34] In the late 1980s, women's internationalism expanded from its singular focus on women's economic development to gender and human rights, most notably through the rise of international debates about violence against women.[35]

With the rapid expansion of women's internationalism, the idea of gender transformed from being a seemingly benign term treated as synonymous with "women" to an increasingly politicized concept that signified the potential reorganization of modern societies based in the critiques of patriarchy and heterosexual reproduction.[36] By the early 1990s, as scholars and activists reimagined social and political life in new theories and policy initiatives focused on gender, the idea came to symbolize everything from women's economic independence to sexual rights to critiques of gendered violence. By the Beijing Women's Conference in 1995, the priorities of the organization UN Women were dominated by expansive ideas of gender empowerment and novel claims to women's human rights through the mandates of international law.[37]

While feminist internationalism expanded from the 1970s, women faced growing authoritarian repression at home. In wide-ranging postcolonial spaces, from South Asia to Africa, the most marginalized communities were sterilized and forcibly displaced in programs of development and planning, everything from books to public assembly was banned, and protesters were policed, jailed, and disappeared. Those who dissented were labeled as anti-national, traitorous, blasphemous, dangerously feminist, and a threat to the state. And perhaps no dissent was as visible as that of women, who refused the impossible conditions of silence by writing about the urgency of women's freedom and taking to the streets.

The Feminist Reinvention of the Third World

When I set out to write a book on the history of Third World feminist thought, I imagined a utopian moment of autonomous women's movements that came long before the powerful reach of the acronyms of development, international NGO networks, and later neoliberal funding structures could be felt. I aspired to uncover a lost history of ideas of women's freedom at the center of Third World ideas of solidarity from the 1950s before the overwhelming dominance of development. Yet the early period of decolonization was largely dominated by men. This moment saw the rise of utopian movements that culminated in the nationalist cause, which deferred fulfillment of the promise of women's liberation until sovereignty was fully realized.

But something extraordinary happened in the decades that *followed* the early period of decolonization and non-alliance. By the early 1970s, Third World women had mobilized in the face of increasing crises in response to and in spite of the fractures of the utopianism of solidarity and developmental nationalism that characterized an earlier moment of Third Worldism. As the postcolonial state faltered, women insisted on leading internationalist movements and creating usable knowledge that could solve the problems of their time.

In focusing at length on the 1970s and 1980s, I turn away from the utopianism and recuperative romance that has dominated much of the scholarship on solidarity, Afro-Asia, and Third Worldism during the 1950s and 1960s. Instead, I foreground this later period to understand how women resuscitated transnational solidarity and created a new vision of Third Worldism in the face of widespread disillusionment and despair. What are the visions of politics for people whose dreams of freedom went unfulfilled with formal decolonization, despite the granting of legal sovereignty to the darker peoples and nations of the world? How did women argue for their freedom when the very liberatory framings of anti-colonialism were co-opted and perversely deployed by authoritarian states to enforce patriarchal ideas of tradition that systematically dispossessed women? How was such freedom to be achieved in the crisis of their authoritarian present?

Third World women reinvigorated Third Worldism through novel critiques of neocolonialism and authoritarianism. By the time women were gathering at international conferences and in transnational research collectives in the 1970s, the dreams of global redistributive plans, unified Afro-Asian political alliances, and secular ideas of radically democratic internationalism had faded into the nightmare of famine, war, and global debt. In response to these crises, women looked to grounded research on women to organize against and critique the cruel effects of increasing global inequality.

By *Third World women* and *Third World feminism* I refer to concepts that originated in wide-ranging radical movements for decolonization in many parts of the world and women of color feminisms in the First World during the late 1960s and early 1970s. One of the earliest uses of the term "Third World women" can be found in the Third World Women's Alliance (TWWA), an internationalist collective based in New York and California. Emerging from Black women's political organizing and the women's wing of the Student Nonviolent Coordinating Committee (SNCC) for civil rights in the United States, the TWWA was perhaps the first organization to conceptualize the term "Third World women."[38] The idea of Third World women was critical for Black feminist thought that followed, notably in the early work of Third World feminist philosopher and activist Angela Yvonne Davis and in the foundational statement of the Combahee River Collective.[39] Other genealogies of the idea are found in early uses of complementary terms of solidarity among women intimately involved in anti-colonial movements who claimed a defiant solidarity politics among women through Afro-Asianism and Third Worldism in the aftermath of the Bandung Conference. Many iterations of the project that followed expanded the use of the term to Third World feminism.

Yet in the ten years after the Third World Women's Alliance made its powerful assertions of Third Worldism in the early 1970s, the designation "Third World women" was often reduced to a developmental descriptor and pejorative term, especially by US development programs and in research conducted by American women.[40] As early as 1984, in her field-defining study, self-declared Third World feminist Chandra Talpade Mohanty offered a devastating critique of the objectification of women of the so-called developing world through the idea of Third World women, which had by then been reframed as a patronizing category in First World research on women's development.[41] For Mohanty, the proliferation of development studies reflected the epistemic domination of Western women researchers through their racist objectification of other women.

While the term was used disparagingly in development circles, intellectuals defiantly claimed the concepts of Third World women and Third World feminism as a collective liberatory politics through novel interventions in critical theory, particularly Black women, women of color, and feminist internationalists.[42] Third World women and feminism became key ideas for the thousands of women engaged in the work of research who produced new theories of solidarity against the exploitation of women and gendered oppression in diverse postcolonial geographies.[43] Expansive and geographically promiscuous ideas of Third World women and Third World feminism were invoked by women around the world, including intellectuals and activists in the decolonizing world and American women of color organizing under a wide range of categories including women of color, Black, Latinx/Chicanx, Asian American, Arab American, and postcolonial feminist.[44] These visions of feminist solidarity beyond borders directly shaped the emerging concept of *transnational feminisms* after 1989 with the end of the Cold War, an idea that conceptualized alliance against the tumultuous politics of economic liberalization and neoliberal NGO-ization.[45]

Perhaps no idea was as significant in catalyzing this domain of Third World feminist research as *neocolonialism*. As conceptualized by Third World women in the 1970s and 1980s, neocolonialism was powerfully framed as a critique of the domination of knowledge. As Ghanaian political theorist, politician, and revolutionary Kwame Nkrumah declared in his landmark 1965 text, *Neo-Colonialism: The Last Stage of Imperialism*, neocolonialism created a facade of newly independent states that were economically and politically subjugated to Western power, with no true sovereignty.[46] Third World women reconceptualized neocolonialism as primarily a form of *epistemic* domination that resulted from the continued dependency of decolonizing states. Women from the decolonizing world diagnosed the paradoxes of incomplete and failed processes of decolonization by linking neocolonial domination to rising authoritarianism, which created the cruel conditions of patriarchy and poverty that women faced every day. The critical feminist concept of neocolonialism as epistemic domination remains, I believe, one of the most potent, if underutilized, ideas in contemporary critical and feminist theory, one that denaturalizes the unequal structures of knowledge that continue to shape how we study postcolonial societies.

Through these critiques of neocolonialism and the perversion of sovereignty in postcolonial authoritarianism, Third World women confronted the reality of their present: new global systems of violence and exploitation increasingly threatened the lives of women and their children. The first generation of Third World researchers with access to higher education felt it was their duty to record and account for the cruel conditions of scarcity and gendered subordination that defined the experiences of most of the women in the world. Third World feminism centered women and the realities they faced, insisting that bearing witness to women's subjugation was critical to the reform and flourishing of postcolonial societies.

Third World women committed themselves to seeking grounded, comparative, *situated* knowledge based in empirical research produced in diverse geographies. For this generation of women, empirical research based in the detailed study of the lives and livelihoods of women was essential to combat the discontent of an increasingly fractured world. These transnational theories looked to similar conditions among women across geographies to identify the failures of the nation-state and the neocolonial policies that perpetuated women's subordination. Women acutely diagnosed how militarism, displacement, and deprivation created impossible conditions for people, and they emphasized that it was primarily women and children who suffered the immeasurable harms that resulted. The agenda of Third World feminist research addressed but extended far beyond narrow understandings of "women's issues" focused on women's work and reproduction. Women insisted on situated, systemic forms of research that linked the conditions of women to global economic inequality, problems of food insecurity and famine, access to health care, the violence of war and border-making, and the cruel conditions of forced migration and displacement.

But the work of feminist research was always constrained. In a world dominated by foundation capital and the priorities of development, there was little possibility of truly autonomous feminist research for Third World women. Women's research and writing in the decolonizing world was rarely free from the mandates of the dominant research paradigms of development and the unequal material infrastructures of internationalism.

Examples abound of early Third World women's intellectual endeavors in the 1970s that had to fit the narrow paradigms of development to gain access to basic funds. We might look to the experience of early women's research in Bangladesh. As people fought a devastating war and genocide in Bangladesh in 1971, the Ford Foundation was already on the ground funding the first research projects on Bangladeshi women.[47] Indeed, there is no way to write the history of feminist ideas without acknowledging the central place of the Ford Foundation in the establishment of women's studies as a field of inquiry around the world.[48] Ford provided the seed funding for almost all major centers, institutes, and departments dedicated to the study of women in Asia, Africa, Latin America, and the United States, including the first women's studies program at Spelman College, the renowned historically Black women's liberal arts college. Minoritized women in poorer nations and communities had little choice but to create research organizations at the interstices of funding for food aid, development conferences, and the shifting priorities of international philanthropy.

In response to this massive expansion of women in development studies, Third World women took advantage of the resources made available to build infrastructures for research while simultaneously making substantive critiques of the neocolonial nature of development studies. They created research methods and asked novel questions about women's lives and labor, insisting on the unique perspective of Third World women who had directly experienced ongoing exploitation and violence. Many women pursued state-based feminist research with the hope that their ideas would be realized through policy reforms and laws impacting women in newly established postcolonial states. Other women, including those aligned with socialist Third Worldism, organized research in direct opposition to state policy with the goal of revolutionizing the very ways in which women became legible as political and economic subjects. As intellectuals working both in and against the state, Third World feminists demanded alternative approaches to women's rights, insisting on the importance of women's own ideas about radical equality and self-determination.[49]

A History without Prophets

Third World feminists, it is often said, understood what was to come. These visionaries knew what would go wrong. They warned about the world's future ills.

Scholars and activists have often framed the lives and works of Third World women and feminisms as prophetic. The prophetic status of Third World feminisms is reflected in the way that contemporary movements cite their ideas as the height of revolutionary potential and valorize their intellectual labor and lives. Indeed, in my own search for a moment of Third World feminisms free of development and the empiricism of UN internationalism, I had hoped to recoup a truly autonomous domain of Third World feminist research from fifty years ago to help me better cope with the despair of the present.

Yet, too often contemporary scholars and activists idealize Third World feminism as a sign of moral certitude from the past that stands as a measure of today's political actions against crisis. Romantic renderings of women of color and Third World women's thought can blunt the complexity of their ideas, reducing their value to simple measures of ideological purity.[50] Despite the regular citation and exaltation of Third World feminist "foremothers," few historical studies have seriously engaged at length with the actual content and histories of the promises and limits of the global Third World feminist project. Those idealized accounts of Third World women, which function as a relative measure for our own political present, preclude critical reflection on the material and political realities that they faced in building infrastructures for the study of women in the 1970s and 1980s.

The reality is that women's research and writing was differentially shaped by structures of power and access. Many of the women in this book accessed privileges of color, class, caste supremacy, education, location, urbanity, familial status and descent, and gender identity—structures of hierarchy and domination that defined the work that many women did yet often went unacknowledged. And as self-declared Third World women produced Third World women and feminism as political categories, many objectified other subaltern women as their research objects and obfuscated social hierarchies in their own societies, reproducing epistemological problems of power and knowledge that they themselves critiqued. These researchers were profoundly influential in internationalist domains of women and development.

The reality is also that Third World women's research on the world's women was often arduous, precarious, and risky—a result of the economic, political, and social insecurity that defined much feminist intellectual work in the decolonizing world outside of the First World academy. Women engaged in extensive unremunerated labor on behalf of movements, organizations, and feminist publications. They often worked on the periphery of secure employment in the traditional academy, committed their own personal funds to research and publishing, and served in contingent and precarious positions—all while also doing the unpaid reproductive and household labor that women are expected to do. As a result of long-term stress, economic difficulties, and social and political exile, many suffered from chronic and life-threatening diseases. Some were dispossessed from property and long-term security by their own families. Many women died early as a result of these conditions. And with the passing of this pathbreaking generation of women, so, too, go the unpreserved and discarded personal papers and privately held materials that documented a world of research and writing on the world's women.

I offer this cautionary note against elevating Third World and women of color feminisms to a place outside of history and critique to suggest that we gain much more from histories that attend to the extraordinary life and labor of Third World feminist ideas *and* to the epistemological and material limits of these projects. It is my goal in carefully engaging these histories to better understand the diverse forms of situated knowledge that women produced and to account for contradictory postcolonial politics and the tenuous material conditions that shaped Third World feminist research. In the chapters of this book, we bear witness again and again to how quickly entire infrastructures of knowledge for the study of women could be, and have been, totally disassembled, defunded, and destroyed as a result of the changing whims of NGOs, international aid priorities, private foundations, and right-wing religious and neo-imperial knowledge projects.

By unburdening women of ethical certitude in every word that they produced, we can take seriously the many innovations of Third World women's thought while critically reflecting on the epistemological limits and fragile material foundations of Third World feminist research. Rather than prophesizing for our contemporary predicaments, Third World women were diagnosing their present and working to change their worlds.

It is a tragedy that the political turmoil and uncertainty that defined the present for Third World women in the 1970s and 1980s—majoritarian violence, expanding militarism, and neocolonial authoritarianism—so closely resemble and shape the problems of our present fifty years later. From these histories of Third World feminist thought, we find not only novel theories of life-making despite crises but also cautionary tales about the unfulfilled promises, conceptual limits, and material constraints of global research on women. There is much to be learned from the achievements, inadequacies, and vulnerabilities of their epistemological projects.

As I trace women's research consultancies, reports, and policy publications, I account for the domination of empirical social scientific research in the proliferation of research on the world's women in spaces of the Third World. This book cautions against the normalization of social science research by liberal internationalism and the wholesale reliance on comparative global measures in the late twentieth century, which has dominated research on women for decades.[51] Researchers increasingly exalted global metrics of women's social and economic subordination in emancipatory projects on the international stage. In the decades that followed the UN Decade for Women, the widespread dependence on narrow measures of gender and development made women and sexual minorities particularly vulnerable to authoritarian attacks on social scientific expertise. What is made possible, and what is lost, when women take up the project of empirical social science to try to realize their visions of justice and equality?

The descriptive argument for rights, "women make up half of the world," based in biologically deterministic arguments about women as a demographic monolith, has served as a primary justification for Third World feminist politics for the past fifty years. Women have built and relied on an unequal knowledge economy that utilizes demographic proof of sexual difference to prove women's worth. These knowledge structures have established a novel mode of understanding social life that M. Murphy has powerfully diagnosed as the "economization of life."[52] There is a troubling biological determinism in international feminism from this moment that resulted from the dominance of social science research on women. Multiple ideologies of domination crept into these domains of research, including naturalized ideas of biological womanhood, caste subjection, racial supremacy, elite urban hierarchies, and class domination. These issues plagued women researchers and delimited the trajectories of research on women for decades after.

Feminist researchers looked to demography as destiny. Through careful engagements with feminist conferencing, publishing, and report writing, I critically engage wide-ranging researchers from the decolonizing world who participated in the development and replicated social scientific epistemologies of family planning, development economics, population research, quantitative metrics, and indices of development.[53] I suggest that Third World women invested in empirical approaches to the study of women to prove the worth of women in a liberatory framework of rights and to have demonstrable "evidence" of the everyday subjugation of women. Yet the exaltation of empiricist methods in women's research produced an almost total reliance on narrow social science measures as the singular approach to the study of women in the decolonizing world. I reveal the marginalization of humanistic and theoretical approaches to the study of women in the decolonizing world and the near-total absence of infrastructural or material support to study literary, philosophical, and theoretical frameworks in international women's studies curricula and programs.

International women's development transformed the priorities of research and policymaking through a new quantifiable social science of womanhood that has defined modern rights and international development agendas from the 1970s until today. These domains of research have often subsumed questions of women's liberation, sexual autonomy, and bodily choice through the seemingly neutral framework of quantitative demographics, the logic of sex ratios, and the language of economic development. A new lexicon of keywords in women and development obfuscated women's political struggles through the technocratic language of poverty eradication, obscuring ongoing movements against class exploitation and caste subjection as well as global movements against racism, histories of enslavement, and racial difference.[54] Terminology like "the status of women," "women's empowerment," "population measures," and "development indices" masked systems of domination and subordination and reduced these critical sites of politics to descriptors that functioned in service of social scientific empiricism. This conceptual obfuscation was compounded and replicated by Third World researchers who were employed in the machinery of research on women and development.

Third World feminist research was not monolithic, and its variations reflected the vexed geopolitics of internationalism and changing global hierarchies of domination and subordination that marked this moment. Over the course of this book, I document the *asymmetry of Third World feminism*, particularly the dominance of women with access to English-language higher education in the new world of research built through the machinery of the UN. India in particular dominated as the key exemplar of the developing world in the emerging domains of women and development and Third World feminisms in the 1970s. Upper-caste elite Indian women engaged in women and development research were highly visible on the global stage and had access to epistemic and political authority in the space of law, development, and research on women.[55] This asymmetry became more exaggerated over the 1970s and 1980s as development economics from India came to dominate the domain of global development and key Indian women took prominent roles in shaping international women's studies at international diplomatic and scholarly conferences and gained access to US publishing venues.[56] This difference in access was the direct outcome of elite women's access to education as a result of a long history of robust educational institutions in India. Whereas, for example, the establishment of the African university was a key project of decolonization from the 1960s to the 1980s, colonial and then postcolonial India had decades of formal structures for women's education from the early twentieth century as well as institutionalized elite women's movements from the late nineteenth century that had long shaped international norms of women's rights.[57] Women of the decolonizing world who inherited long-standing English-language educational and organizational infrastructures came to have more prominent roles during the UN Year and Decade for Women.

As a history of ideas and knowledge production, this book is not a history of Third World women's *movements*, although many social and political movements are critical sites for the rapid expansion of feminist research and appear throughout the chapters that follow.[58] Nor do the many diverse texts and publications that form the primary archives of this book represent *all* forms of writing produced by Third World women, particularly proliferative writings like the political pamphlets that women have authored as part of social movements and political parties. Feminist research has taken many diverse forms, often extending far beyond the printed page. My hope is that this historical account becomes one among many that take seriously that women seized the means of knowledge production and shaped an epistemological revolution for women's rights and liberation in the late twentieth century.

Nor do I claim to have written the comprehensive history of *all* Third World women or to have represented every aspect of Third World feminist research around the world. In its primary focus on transnational feminist research projects that reached from South Asia to the African continent, the Caribbean, and the United States, this book does not chronicle at length the histories of Third World women's research in spaces like Latin America and Southeast Asia. Yet *The Future That Was*, in its focus on intellectual histories and research infrastructures, offers key lessons for comparative fields and transregional histories in which women have pushed back against authoritarianism using the tools of knowledge production.[59] We urgently need more studies from diverse geographies and languages that center the momentous rise of transnational feminist research and writing in the history of ideas in the twentieth century.

Today the lives and life-worlds of these researchers are endangered in fragile and decaying archives that are again under threat amid a new wave of rising authoritarian states. Their powerful transnational work has been reduced at many points to a stream of acronyms that appear in official state and NGO documents. And the decades-long efforts of women to create a proliferative future for feminist research has been overshadowed by the rapid decline of the authority of international law and international human rights, the increasing dominance of private donor expectations, and demanding managerial norms placed on feminist workers and women's organizations that undermine the independence of women's research.[60]

The Future That Was

Women in saris, salwar kameez, and shirts and jeans sit and stand close to one another. Taken at a monthlong workshop on "Women and Development" in Koitta, (Manikganj) Bangladesh, held in March and April 1986, two consecutive photographs reveal shifting moments from a scene of a

FIGURE I.1. **Upper and lower**: Women and Development Workshop, March and April 1986, Koitta, Bangladesh. Applied Socio-economic Research (ASR)/Nighat Said Khan Archival Collection.

group of women posing for a photo. Looking at the two photographs, the viewer gets a clear sense of the animated space of the workshop. There are shifting positions between the photos, with changing glances, expressions, and radiant smiles. Women move in and out of the frame. A few women hold papers, but most just hold each other.

The intimacy of the group is undeniable. Women casually drape their arms around each other, touch hands, embrace one another. Looking at these two photographs, one can imagine in the way hands and bodies shift between shutter clicks the lively interactions that shaped the workshop. Perhaps these relationships developed over the course of the monthlong gathering. Surely, because of the geographical distances and national borders that define the fractured worlds of the subcontinent, many had not met before the workshop. Maybe over a matter of days, women went from unfamiliar nods and distant hellos to intimate laughter and hand-holding, their bodies coming closer and closer together.[61] Like so many workshops from this period, there may have been passionate debates and disagreements as participants asked what development was and whether aid would actually change the lives of women. Perhaps unspoken and unacknowledged hierarchies of caste, status, education, and touch shaped relationships between international workshop participants and the local working women who served food and cleaned the workshop venue. No doubt, women experienced shared histories of border-making, gendered violence, genocide, war, and famine that defined the shattered lives and geographies of the subcontinent. Women who were once strangers as a result of national divisions no longer were.

We might contrast the intimacy of these group photographs with those well-known official photographs of the many formal political meetings and conferences of postcolonial men that shaped twentieth-century nonalignment and Third World internationalism. In archetypal images of international conferences and diplomatic meetings, like the images of the famous Asian-African conference at Bandung in 1955, notable politicians and delegates are centered in the frame. Sometimes these men sit formally at an official conference table, with their names and titles in view. Or they stand formally, shaking hands. In contrast, the photos from the 1986 workshop in Bangladesh were taken inside, without a formal table and chairs. There are no clear distinctions between those who are seated and those who are standing. They evoke the familiar vintage sensibility of many 1980s amateur images: bright colors, sepia skin tones, and fluorescent lighting, with some areas of the image slightly out of focus. Nor is there any indication of where and who these women are—no signs memorialize the conference, and no placards within the frame formally record the event for posterity.

The photographs are carefully preserved in the extraordinary archives of Applied Socio-economic Research (ASR), a feminist organization in Lahore, Pakistan, that thrived for over forty years; it is one of many research collectives I explore in the chapters that follow. This rich collection of photographs and informal video footage taken over decades gives us a glimpse of the worlds of women's gatherings in South Asia, particularly in Lahore through the 1980s and 1990s. These image archives reveal a world of women who built feminist research and writing across borders.

We learn about the particular workshop in Bangladesh in 1986 from the photo caption, added years later by ASR archivists. The captions note that the workshop was convened by two organizations represented by the acronyms FAO and FFHC—the Food and Agriculture Organization of the UN and the Freedom From Hunger Campaign. By the 1980s, Third World feminists had reframed agricultural development and food aid as essential women's issues. The monthlong workshop brought together women working at the intersection of women and development from across South Asia. The names are incomplete, but from those named, we get a sense of the reach of this experiment under the umbrella themes of "women in development," "food aid," and "hunger." The photograph includes Pakistani feminist sociologist Nighat Said Khan, the director of ASR and an important archivist of women's movements who saved and labeled all photographs from this and many other workshops. Among the participants pictured are key thinkers, including Bangladeshi feminist activist, intellectual, and environmentalist Khushi Kabir; Indian feminist scholar Amrita Chhachhi; Sri Lankan feminist and human rights activist Kumudini Samuel; Indian feminist writer and activist Kamla Bhasin; and Bangladeshi lawyer and human rights activist Sultana Kamal.

At workshops like the one held in Bangladesh in 1986, women collaborated to design new measures of women's economic life by gendering concepts like the "informal economy" and defining women's housework and unrecognized agricultural labor *as* work. They invented potent legal categories of domestic and sexual violence and advocated for legal reforms against gender-based violence in national and international law. They radically reformed definitions of rape, dowry murder, and child marriage and contested patriarchal customary laws and colonial structures of inheritance. Women came together to reimagine the relationship of religion to women's democratic rights and fought against fundamentalism across communities.

Women's organizations devised new frameworks to understand poverty and created sustainable development programs based in the perspectives of women. At international meetings and conferences, Third World women insisted on a feminist politics of location, arguing that the agendas of First World feminists obscured long histories of underdevelopment. They traveled across six continents to collaborate together. And they protested, protested, protested. They stood against dictators, were attacked by the police with batons, and were jailed for writing in public about political and legal equality for women. They demanded real and lasting decolonization.

The chapters that follow are organized around these key genres and sites of Third World feminist knowledge production: the conference, the report, the organization, the book, and the protest. These forms and genres for research on women were in formation in the 1970s and 1980s, but today they are naturalized as the dominant approach to global research on women. These structures, from the women's conference to the policy report on the status of women, came to have normative status in research and writing on women for decades to follow. Each chapter is framed through a question that reflects the dreams of Third World women as they worked to build feminist community, produce research for radical policy reform, and take to the streets in protests for women's fundamental rights.

What is the future that was, the future that Third World women imagined?[62]

In that future, women would be free. They would have real access to democratic rights and citizenship. It would be a world where women would be free of authoritarianism at every scale, from the home to the state. Where all women had access to literacy and education. Where the many networks, institutions, and publishers that women built in the 1970s and 1980s would flourish and continue to sustain the study of women and gender. Where women's research would transform law, and policy reform would affect real change for the most marginalized. Where women would come together to laugh and dance and perform plays that enacted their liberation. Where the household was not a site of violence, but a space organized around choice and familial support. In the future, women would have the right to work with dignity and fair compensation, and the work of women, including their reproductive labor, would be recognized *as* work. In Third World women's visions, people would reverse environmental degradation and confront climate crises that disproportionately affected women. The future would be free of perpetual war, and no people would live under occupation or in senseless incarceration. Women's sexuality would not be a site of violence and familial policing, but a source of freedom and power. People would not be forced to migrate or flee because of deprivation and violence. In the future, women would build a sustainable collective across difference based not only in comparative empirical data and indices but in shared aspirations for a different future.

Today their sense of yearning persists. This yearning can be found in the aspirations and movements that reimagine feminist action in the twenty-first century. We see it in the undeniable aspirations of political mobilizations that cite Third World feminism as foundational to new ideas of freedom and pursue transnational research to contest authoritarianism and endless war. Movements today work to undo an authoritarian biopolitics of life and death, to reimagine a feminism for living in the twenty-first century.[63]

In the future, survival would no longer be in question.

1

The Conference, or What if Gathering Together Liberated Us?

"One problem of the women of the Third World, it is colonialism," the woman at the mic says. "We are half of the population of the world that still lives under colonialism. Beware of colonialism." She is speaking with determination. She has traveled a great distance, from Puerto Rico to Nairobi, to be there with fellow Third World women.

Here, at the Third World Women Speak Out session, the hundreds of people sitting close together are buzzing, while women line up in the aisles waiting intently for their turn to speak at the microphone. Next, an Indian woman in a sari approaches the microphone; she calmly declares that the most significant problems facing Third World women are poverty and illiteracy. Another woman speaks, identifying herself as Marjorie Mbilinyi from Tanzania. She passionately decries the continued subjection of the African continent under neocolonialism based in the "increasing financial conquest of Africa, which has taken place since independence in the early sixties and . . . financial bondage, which is led by the World Bank and the IMF." Next in line for the mic is a Black woman from the United States. She begins tentatively but quickly gains momentum from the energetic support of the audience. She provokes cheers and applause as she exclaims, "We have got to just take power and say no, enough of that. You don't tell me what I want. I am what

I am. I am a woman. I am Black or dark or whatever. I am proud, and I am going to seize the opportunity and fight you every way down the line."[1]

It is the summer of 1985. From the auditorium windows, participants can see the sunny open grounds of the University of Nairobi, as well as the crowds of many of the over twelve thousand people gathered at the NGO Forum for the Third World Conference on the status of women.[2] The auditorium is packed: all the seats are filled, with more people standing in the wings. Gathered here are women from around the world, many of them listening intently to the translation of speakers on conference headsets. The speakers are sharing structural critiques about urgent issues that shape the everyday lives of women across the world.

Many in the audience are veteran activists who have been to dozens of international conferences, including the previous UN women's conferences in Mexico City and Copenhagen. Others are experiencing the collective energy of the room and finding a common language for the struggles of Third World women for the first time. The anticipation and excitement are palpable as people look around to see who is in attendance. Women of different races are clothed in every color—red and green saris, orange and yellow kaftans and boubous, white and blue Catholic habits, multicolored kangas, blue nursing uniforms, peach 1980s skirt suits—styled with every shade and shape of hair, hijab, scarf, and headdress.

But what was the impact of this session on Third World women? Framed as an event with women "speaking out," the session featured women passionately critiquing state policy and international inequality, yet the audience was primarily like-minded people who identified as Third World women. The session was less a platform for speaking *out* to states and governments and more an occasion for Third World women speaking *among* themselves.

After all, "Third World Women Speak Out" was, by design, sequestered from the formal space of UN high politics. That is, the "Speak Out" session was the culmination of panels, discussions, workshops, and conversations staged as part of the NGO Forum at the 1985 conference, the "World Conference to Review and Appraise the Achievements of the UN Decade for Women." But the forum, held at the University of Nairobi, was a thirty-minute walk away from the official space of the official UN conference. That diplomatic conference, with official UN delegates, took place at the iconic Kenyatta International Convention Center (KICC), whose vast pavilion and dramatic buildings sit right in the heart of Nairobi's business district. KICC, designed by Norwegian architect Karl Henrik Nøstvik and commissioned by Kenya's first president, Jomo Kenyatta, was the quintessential representation

FIGURE 1.1. The University of Nairobi pavilion. From IWTC, *Images of Nairobi: Reflections and Follow Up*, 5. IWTC collection at Smith College Special Collections.

of African modernist architecture, built just a decade before the UN women's conference. Powerfully illustrating the contradictions of women's issues in a time of decolonization, the official diplomatic meeting site, with its high modernist forms, symbolized the tensions between global inequality, development, and modernization.

The nineteen hundred official delegates at the final UN Decade for Women conference filled the spaces at KICC, from the tall tower to the convention area designed to be a facsimile of a traditional hut.[3] Just over a mile away, at the NGO Forum, participants moved across the vast pavilion and concrete-walled classrooms of the African university, which was overflowing with women from all the nations represented. The green areas of both the Jomo Kenyatta conference center and the University of Nairobi were filled with booths, bold posters, colorful banners, and women from around the world.[4]

FIGURE 1.2. Tower of Babel illustration of the 1985 Nairobi Conference. From IWTC, *Images of Nairobi: Reflections and Follow Up*, 15. Adapted by IWTC from *Xilonen*, IWY Tribune, Mexico City, 1975. IWTC collection at Smith College Special Collections.

The "Speak Out" session at the NGO Forum was, by design, segregated from the formal space of UN high politics. While the women in the university auditorium delivered powerful political speeches against patriarchy, neocolonialism, debt programs, and the persistence of gendered violence, the formal diplomatic meeting ultimately adopted resolutions that went against the sentiment of the NGO Forum's Third World session. The two events happened in parallel but were driven by vastly different politics.

The final document produced by the diplomatic meeting, "Nairobi Forward-Looking Strategies for the Advancement of Women," compiled the official resolutions, which were framed within the largely neutral language of "promoting women's participation" through the conference themes of development, peace, and equality. The "forward-looking strategies" of 1985 eliminated the contentious language that had animated previous UN women's conferences. The seemingly endless list of resolutions blunted the critical edge of Third World critiques of neocolonial systems of indebtedness, the destruction of ongoing wars and Cold War militarism, and colonial occupation.

The massive proliferation of international conferences on women transformed the research and writing on Third World women. In this chapter, I argue that transnational conferences on women served as pivotal events that catalyzed an epistemic revolution in research by Third World women. Yet, over time, these events increasingly marginalized the potent politics of Third World women against colonialism, global debt, and authoritarianism. I analyze which epistemological projects were made possible and which forms of knowledge were foreclosed at the global gatherings on women that started in the 1950s and flourished in the 1970s and 1980s, culminating in the visible and widely celebrated UN conference on women in Nairobi. Ten years later, in 1995, the UN Decade for Women was followed by a massive UN conference in Beijing.

With the sudden proliferation of international conferences on women in the 1970s and 1980s, women across the political spectrum learned of and invested in the modern social scientific study of women, in which the empirical study of women was linked to liberatory possibilities within states and on the international stage. At the non-aligned Afro-Asian women's conferences of the 1960s and 1970s, academic and scholarly conferences on women, and the UN women's conferences, research became a contentious site for women.

"The Conference" charts how Third World feminists centered geopolitics in their work at international conferences, foregrounding the place of feminism in contesting enduring epistemologies of colonialism and economic exploitation. I analyze a series of emblematic conferences that focused on women in the decolonizing world, from the Afro-Asian women's conferences of the 1950s through the 1970s to the official diplomatic and academic conferences spurred by the UN International Women's Year and Decade for Women between 1975 and 1985. Women's internationalism was transformed over this period, from a project of women's patriotic participation in the postcolonial national project of non-aligned states in the 1950s and 1960s to a novel Third World feminist internationalism shaped by opposition to jingoistic nationalism.

These women were marginalized at home in the domain of nationalist politics but also on the international stage. Ultimately, this chapter contends with the paradox that Third World women continuously invested and reinvested in internationalism despite the inadequacy of these frameworks for addressing Third World women's priorities. I account for the way women, with full knowledge that scholarly and diplomatic conferences often excluded the expertise of Third World women, continued to seek out international forums for research and writing. For these women, the new spaces of feminist internationalism, especially the many domains of the UN, offered a rare platform for articulating a politics against virulent authoritarianism, fundamentalism, and nationalism at home. Although women from spaces across Asia, the Middle East, Latin America, the Caribbean, and the African continent critiqued and condemned international conferences for their racism, ethnocentrism, and narrow visions of women's rights, they returned again and again to the international conferences to argue for a feminist geopolitics based in Third World perspectives, despite the seeming futility of their efforts.

Nairobi was to be the culmination of a wave of Third World feminist efforts to shape UN internationalism. There, women articulated devastating critiques of the global status quo, including unequal structures of capital and war. But few listened. The past decade had seen the expanding influence of opposing forces who consolidated their power at Nairobi and decisively excluded these critiques from formal conversations. By the end of the Decade of Women in 1985, American feminists as well as key powers in the United Nations characterized Third World feminist critiques as too "political" and beyond the limited bounds of "women's issues." Women, it was argued, could be empowered through capitalist development, legal reforms, and individual rights. Third World women spoke up and spoke out. But the many networks they built and the research they pursued in the first flush of conferences were, after years of retrenchment, dismissed with little consequence.

The Women's Conference and the Segregation of Third World Women

Third World feminism was a geopolitical alliance for survival against crisis.

The Third World feminism staged at UN conferences for women in the 1970s and 1980s was not, as it has often been characterized, a utopian project. Gone were the lofty, optimistic dreams of the Third Worldism of the 1950s and 1960s that invested in nationalist visions of equality and alliances for more egalitarian futures.[5] Rather than yield to the widespread disenchantment of comrades with the failure of postcolonial states, women insisted that there was no time to dwell in the melancholy of lost promises and national collapse. Instead, women turned to research and writing in a realist politics that would assess the crisis of the present.

In embracing a new realist politics, they argued that women bore the brunt of the material consequences of the systemic failures of states, warmongering, and global inequalities, and they demanded action to address the cruel realities that women faced. They called for action against the cruel circumstances that resulted from the First World imposition of structural adjustment; the realities of apartheid, occupation, and authoritarianism; and the gendered violence of forced migrations. To achieve an understanding of these crises, women championed comprehensive empirical research on women.

The UN conferences on women, unlike any previous international UN conferences, featured massive parallel gatherings authorized by the UN that served as official spaces for popular participation. These sites of popular participation appeared first under the label "NGO Tribune" at the first UN women's conference in Mexico City in 1975 and then as the "NGO Forum" at the subsequent conferences through Beijing in 1995. The NGO Forum at Nairobi in 1985, like those that came before, was placed at a figurative and physical distance from the main stage of the official diplomatic conference and its formal processes for debating and adopting UN resolutions. The UN reframed women's popular politics through the domesticating language of the NGO, a neutralizing designation that sequestered women's issues within the domain of social life. For a moment, the formal diplomatic meetings of the UN Decade for Women reflected the sudden influence of the Third World on global women's movements.

Yet the official UN conference in Nairobi in 1985 ultimately proved the enduring dominance of the United States and its power to suppress the anti-colonial, anti-war, and anti–structural adjustment viewpoints of women from across the globe. At a remove from the official conference in Nairobi, the NGO Forum overflowed with thousands of participants who vehemently critiqued state policies oppressing women, rising militarism, and international debt programs that produced conditions of perpetual deprivation. With a "peace tent" at its center, the NGO Forum staged sessions on consciousness-raising and women's improvement and promoted an agenda centered on frameworks of social reform, technical skill building, and the promise of solidarity. Third World women spoke loudly and with fervor, but far from the putative stage of high politics.

International women's conferences across the decolonizing world had long shaped the trajectory and infrastructure for research and writing on and by women. Yet there was no question that the UN's International Women's

Year and Decade for Women catalyzed a massive expansion of women's internationalism through the infrastructure of UN women's conferences and the national machineries of women's bureaus and commissions launched as a result. Over the course of the second half of the twentieth century, a wide range of international conferences on women brought together thousands of people from around the world, most notably at the four high-profile UN world conferences on women in Mexico City in 1975, Copenhagen in 1980, Nairobi in 1985, and Beijing in 1995.[6] The UN conferences were unprecedented events, the largest gatherings of women recorded in human history. They came together by the thousands to engage with one another about the struggles and rights of women.

International women's conferences expanded rapidly in the second half of the twentieth century, creating solidarities between women of newly independent and decolonizing spaces. Yet, as they grew in importance and stature with the formalization of the Decade for Women, international conferences became the primary stage for coordinated efforts by First World women to dominate global research on women and depoliticize Third World women's theories of neocolonialism, authoritarianism, and global economic inequality. First World women, particularly American women working in government and academia, had vastly different plans for the platform of international women's rights. Insisting that women's issues were distinct from global geopolitics, they marginalized general critiques of colonialism and global political inequality at workshops and conferences, blunting the potency of Third World women's critiques. Conference organizers and leaders argued that critiques of neocolonialism, global debt dependency, and authoritarianism exceeded the domain of international women's rights. Third World women argued that conference organizers and leaders dismissed the intellectual labor and interventions of women from independent and decolonizing spaces in Asia, Africa, Latin America, and the Caribbean, falsely separating them from problems of global inequality and economic exploitation.

Over the course of the Decade for Women, the dismissal and marginalization of Third World research on women was achieved through the conceptual and spatial relegation of Third World women's ideas to spaces outside the domain of formal rights and politics. Organizers physically segregated conferences and delimited Third World women's issues to themes of social service, individual empowerment, and technical skill building. Despite the conceptual and physical segregation that was increasingly built into international women's conferences, Third World women flooded international events and created sophisticated transnational intellectual networks, hoping to build a different future for radically equitable feminist research and organizing. Yet, even as international conferences on women proliferated and Third World attendance increased dramatically during the 1970s and 1980s, Third World women's perspectives were increasingly marginalized, isolated, and condemned for being too political and separated from the mainstream concerns of women's research, writing, and policymaking. By the 1990s, international organizations and global funders based in the First World successfully dominated the format and structure of international conferences and defined the trajectory of global research on women.

Afro-Asian Women's Conferences and the Promise of National Liberation

The politics of non-alliance set the stage for novel coalitions and networks of Asian, African, and Middle Eastern women in the mid-twentieth century. As historian Stephen Legg has argued in the context of early twentieth-century international roundtable conferences for colonial India and the League of Nations, the conference was foundational in the making of twentieth-century internationalism.[7] The event of the conference was especially critical for the development of women's internationalism as a novel place for the exchange of research, ideas, and strategies for women's rights.

The infrastructure of women's transregional and international conferences expanded rapidly from the 1930s through the early 1970s, before and after the visible Asian-African conference at Bandung, Indonesia, a watershed moment in the making of transnational epistemologies that reimagined the global order. In 1931, the All-Asian Women's Conference was held in Lahore, British India, with an explicit vision of women's international solidarity across colonial spaces during the interwar period as anti-colonial nationalist movements gained momentum.[8] The 1947 Asian Relations Conference held in Delhi, India, built a platform for pan-Asian women's collaboration, with explicit resolutions from delegates to pursue women's legal, economic, and social equity in newly independent states in Asia, and created the cross-regional Association of Asian Women.[9] As feminist scholar Elisabeth Armstrong shows in her work on the "Women in Asia" conference in Beijing, China, in 1949, women inaugurated a new era of internationalism as Asian states fought for decolonization. The 1949 conference brought together distinct strands that were critical for the transnational conferences for women in the decolonizing world, including social reform projects, state feminism that pursued formal equality in postcolonial nation-states, and a left revolutionary politics based in mass labor movements, especially among women peasants.[10]

These wide-ranging concerns of the early transnational women's conferences, including equality before the law and agrarian labor exploitation, shaped the Afro-Asian women's international conferences that followed in the 1950s, 1960s, and 1970s. These gatherings created a unique body of knowledge as they carefully documented archives of conference proceedings and built expansive networks of non-alliance across geographies.[11] The Afro-Asian conferences were foundational for knowledge infrastructures across genres, including research and writing on state sovereignty and policymaking, Afro-Asian literature and film, and multilingual social and political tracts on national liberation that targeted a broader public.

By 1958, in Colombo, Ceylon (present-day Sri Lanka), African and Asian women held their own conference, one that envisioned solidarity across the two continents organized by women's organizations in Asia from Indonesia, India, Pakistan, Burma, and Ceylon, with additional representatives from Ghana.[12] The gathering followed the highly anticipated conference of twenty-nine countries at Bandung, Indonesia, in 1955; the solidarity conferences of the Afro-Asian People's Solidarity Organization (AAPSO) in 1957 and 1958; and the first Afro-Asian writers' conference in 1958.[13] In 1961, the first official Afro-Asian women's conference was held in Cairo, Egypt; with thirty-seven member states in attendance, the event was a massive expansion compared to previous conferences. Many regions were participating in an international meeting as independent states for the first time.[14] The second Afro-Asian women's conference was held in 1972 in Ulaanbaatar, Mongolia, and a third conference featuring social science research on the social development of Afro-Asian women took place in Alexandria in March 1975, in anticipation of the first UN world conference for women in Mexico City in the summer of 1975.[15]

Consider the opening statement at Cairo. "The questions of women" must be understood "vis-à-vis world problems," stated Bahia Karam, an Egyptian feminist and head of the Women and Children Section of the Afro-Asian People's Solidarity Organization. And these problems, Karam warned, included political ones, like the banning of nuclear arms and the demand for peace.[16] Moreover, here at the outset of the conference, Karam placed women's movements at the heart of the newly independent nation, where women "assumed their rightful part in the world" as "active workers and fighters" in the nationalist movement.[17] Echoing this sentiment were the official messages sent to the Cairo conference from leaders of non-aligned countries, from Ghana's Kwame Nkrumah to Indonesia's Sukarno to Algeria's Ferhat Abbas. Across continents, then, there was consensus that women could be political in relation to gendered roles in the nationalist project.[18]

But other conclusions were drawn from these events, too. Embedded among the delegates from non-aligned states at the Cairo conference was a spy from the US Central Intelligence Agency (CIA). The CIA, reporting on the "communist activities" of the AAPSO in 1961, asserted that the Afro-Asian women's conference was explicitly communist in nature, and that as an overtly political project with only left political aims, it was not really a conference on women's issues.[19] It was, according to the CIA, "a strictly political affair," a gathering where "plans to concentrate on the economic, social, and cultural problems of women had been thwarted."[20] For the CIA, the Afro-Asian women's conference was a puppet of Third World politics, "indistinguishable from the usual anti-imperialist, anti-neo-colonialist statements," with resolutions that demanded an end to foreign interventions in Patrice Lumumba's Congo as well as in Laos, Cambodia, and Vietnam.[21]

Clearly, the CIA balked at the idea that women cared about global geopolitics as it described the event in a tone of condemnation. But the report was accurate in its summary of the 1961 conference: the Afro-Asian women's alliance was, at its heart, "anti-west, anti-imperialist, and anti-neocolonialist."[22]

Eleven years after the first Afro-Asian women's conference, a massively expanded second conference took place with representatives from more than sixty independent states, occupied territories, and dominions, as well as from multiple transnational women's organizations, such as the All-Arab Women's Federation, the All-African Women's Conference, and the Women's International Democratic Federation. The conference had multiple goals: to understand the "Afro-Asian women's mass movements in the fight against neo-colonialism and for the consolidation of the non-capitalist way of development" in pursuit of the "transformation of society and in defence of people's gains and rights."[23] By 1972, over eighty sovereign states had been created in the decolonizing world, and in a matter of just a few years, billions of people—indeed, most of the people of the world—had gained access to democratic governance and sovereignty.

To achieve this goal, the 1972 Afro-Asian women's conference offered a comprehensive theory of neocolonialism that linked women's political consciousness in the nation-state to the continued exploitation and perpetuation of economic dependence of newly independent states on the West. The opening remarks for the conference acknowledged socialist state power and the place of the Soviet Union in decolonization and national liberation. Yet Afro-Asian participants, in asserting that the independence of the new postcolonial states was theirs alone, preserved the unique place of non-aligned politics in the context of Cold War divisions. The conference publication also boldly argued for the anti-imperial, anti-occupation stance of Afro-Asian women against apartheid in South Africa and the massive expansion of American imperialism in its wars on Vietnam, Laos, and Cambodia and its collusion with the military state of Israel in the oppression of Palestinians. For the Afro-Asian women's alliance, women were at the heart of independent nations and had a patriotic duty to support national independence and progress.[24]

The conference featured key resolutions that linked women to nationalist projects of the state and development, highlighting "the participation of Asian and African women in the struggle for liberation, independence, and peace" and "the contribution of Afro-Asian women in the economic, social, and cultural development." The opening resolution on liberation explicitly linked women's issues to the anti-colonial struggles: "Asian and African women are realising more and more the inter-connection between the problems of the status of women and the general struggle of the peoples for independence, democracy, peace, and social progress."[25]

The conference organizers declared that the rights of women were inextricably tied to the project of national liberation, with a resolution explicitly stating that "equal rights and emancipation of women is a foregone conclusion and should be included in the national programs of all liberation movements and independent governments and new progressive legislature should be promulgated forthwith."[26] Participants from states across Africa and Asia argued that, despite legislation, discrimination against women persisted in employment and wages, education, and professional life, and thus national liberation was insufficient to achieve true rights for women.[27] They centered women's rights to "family planning" and "fully paid maternity leave" as essential to the project of women's liberation in Africa and Asia.[28] Postcolonial liberation was contingent on ending the subjugation of women in marriage through polygamy, patriarchal dowry systems, and child marriage.[29] Over the course of the proceedings, conference speakers argued that women required full franchise and complete economic, political, and social equality to achieve true liberation.

Just three years later, the AAPSO held its third and final conference of Afro-Asian women, the Afro-Asian Symposium on Social Development of Women, in Alexandria from March 8 to 14, 1975. Opening on the sixty-fifth anniversary of International Women's Day—March 8, 1975—the conference brought together visible women leaders of Afro-Asia, state officials, and

AAPSO members across geographies, highlighting contemporary research on women across the decolonizing world. The conference participants reflected the complicated destiny of national liberation movements, with key "first ladies" of postcolonial Afro-Asia in attendance, including the first lady of the Philippines, Imelda Marcos, and Egypt's first lady, Jehan Sadat, who symbolized the women of their nations. This was a moment of promise and increasingly tenuous postcolonial democracies, before the assassinations and increasingly draconian nationalist authoritarian projects that emerged across Afro-Asia.

Just as she had done fourteen years before at the Cairo gathering, Bahia Karam welcomed the audience to the third conference of Afro-Asian women. She marked the convergence of two historic events: International Women's Day and the first-ever International Women's Year declared by the UN.[30] The symposium was devoted to highlighting the work of the International Women's Year and outlining the priorities of Afro-Asian women on the global stage ahead of the first UN conference for women in Mexico City in June and July 1975 and the socialist Internationalist Democratic Women's Federation conference in Berlin in October of that year. Moreover, the general report to the conference linked the International Women's Year in 1975 to the end of fascism thirty years earlier in 1945 and argued that women were critical to the fight against fascism not just in the past but in the liberation movements of Vietnamese, Palestinian, and African women in the present.[31]

Women's issues must not be isolated from political struggles, declared the conference organizers, as both women's and national liberation required the protection of independent states from "colonialism, neo-colonialism, racism, Zionism, Fascism."[32] The general report aligned the work of the Afro-Asian women's section with the causes of liberation, with a focus on "Palestinian people's right to self-determination." Organizers also expressed support for independence movements in the Persian Gulf; across Africa, including the Somali coast, Eritrea, and Morocco; and in the newly independent state of Bangladesh. The proceedings expressed support for "the victories against imperialist America" in Vietnam, Cambodia, Laos, and South Korea, as well as across Latin America.

The published conference proceedings featured extensive research on women across member states of Afro-Asia. The publication included almost four hundred pages of detailed social scientific research reports from regions across the African continent, Asia, the socialist states of Poland and Bulgaria, and Cuba. The third Afro-Asian women's publication reflected the dramatic rise of research on the status of women presented at international conferences by the middle of the 1970s.[33]

Ultimately, the social scientific research papers on "women's status" were the central feature of the third conference of Afro-Asian women and reflected the main focus of the symposium: the expansion of comparative research on women. The featured research on the status of women was wide-ranging, focusing on topics such as the position of rural women in Sri Lanka, women and the liberation of Angola, the role of women in personal law in the Arab world, the subjection of women in apartheid South Africa, and racial discrimination against Palestinian women in the occupied territories. Researchers addressed a diversity of critical themes, including illiteracy among women, law, women and socialist societies, rural women, juvenile delinquency, and women and unions.

Across the 1960s and 1970s, from the early transregional Asian conferences to the expansive Afro-Asian women's conferences, women's freedom was tied directly to the project of nationalist liberation and sovereignty. In this framework, the work of women in the decolonizing world was solely for the broader nationalist cause. While women's issues were framed as complementary to the cause of the nation, Afro-Asian women sought to reshape what that nationalist cause could be by demanding that true citizenship for women, as promised by national liberation, required an international alliance of Afro-Asian women. They argued that the nationalist cause was served by laws protecting reproductive autonomy, parental leave support and childcare, and equal rights in marriage, divorce, and work.

Most significantly, the project of transnational alliance across women in Afro-Asia from the 1950s extended beyond women's issues; it was explicitly invested in a geopolitics against imperialism and authoritarianism. Women increasingly argued that social scientific research on women was critical to the project of liberation. Through research on everything from law to work, coalitions of prominent Afro-Asian delegates developed broad critiques of economic and military imperialism in which they insisted that the liberation of the nation and the liberation of women were one and the same—a liberation to be achieved through research, publications, and the power of the collective conference.

The Wellesley Conference and the Problem of Neocolonial Research

While conferences on women in the 1950s and early 1960s featured key themes of women and national liberation in Afro-Asia, the 1970s and 1980s inaugurated a new era of Third World women's internationalism. The Third

Worldism of women in the 1970s and 1980s was distinct from the utopian visions that were staged so dramatically at the paradigmatic Bandung and Afro-Asian conferences in the 1950s and 1960s and that created alliances across state leaders, writers, and women. Earlier aspirations for Third World solidarity at the height of formal decolonization, based in nationalist ideas of world-making, were short-lived.

By the 1970s and 1980s, the romantic vision of Afro-Asian sovereignty had ceded ground to a growing politics of discord, disillusionment, and grief in the face of state failure, global economic inequality, and the perpetual threat of war.[34] In the wake of utopian imaginations of decolonization and unity in non-alliance, a series of promising leaders were tragically lost and a never-ending pessimism—about the neocolonial decline of postcolonial nations, the failure of economic redistribution and reform, and the unfulfilled promise of democratic governance in the face of militarism and authoritarianism—emerged.

But Third World women refused the dark mood of the late 1970s and 1980s. For women previously involved in Afro-Asian solidarity networks, the expansion of women's internationalism through the UN International Women's Year and Decade for Women provided a key platform from which to openly confront the harsh realities of the authoritarian present and create new cross-border coalitions for building a different future. As postcolonial states fractured, women created a novel domain of international organizations, movements, and collectives that critiqued the false pretense to sovereignty and gender inequality resulting from anti-colonial nationalism, laying bare the unfulfillment of promises made to women in patriarchal nationalist movements.

Women increasingly self-identified as Third World women and as Third World feminists with a distinct political platform that defied the patriarchal nationalist cause. They radically redefined ideas by creating new alliances at global conferences based in their opposition to neocolonialism as well as the rise of patriarchal legal regimes and the policies of postcolonial authoritarian states. Third World feminisms offered a language with which to critique the systemic global issues of economic underdevelopment, resource extraction, and puppet military governance common to newly independent and decolonizing states. Third World feminists placed local women at the center of a revitalized Third Worldism. For these women researchers, this era of coalition-building against global inequality required novel approaches to empirical research, direct actions for legal reforms, and collective knowledge-making about economic and social policies that would better sustain life for the most vulnerable in society.

In December 1972, the UN proclaimed 1975 the first year dedicated to the theme of women, to be marked with an international conference in 1975 in Mexico City, known as the World Conference of the International Women's Year.[35] The first conference was held for two weeks in the summer, from June 19 to July 2. Originally imagined as a stand-alone event for the International Women's Year, it would be the first of four official UN international conferences on women after delegates declared 1975–1985 the Decade for Women. It also led to the proliferation of parallel conferences and meetings, publications, and research initiatives focused on the themes of equality, women, and development. As historian Jocelyn Olcott describes the 1975 women's conference in her study of Mexico City, key conflicts between American women and women of the so-called developing world took place, but the conference also laid the foundation for new relationships between First and Third World women.[36] As historian Joanne Meyerowitz suggests, the Mexico City conference revealed an increasing sense of mistrust from Third World women who felt that US programs on women in development disregarded their expertise.[37]

The resurgent internationalism of Third World women emerged with the rise of women's international conferences. A striking example of women's conferences occurred in 1976 at Wellesley College. Spurred directly by the UN declaration of the first International Women's Year, the college held the ambitious International Conference on Women and Development. The Wellesley conference was a pivotal event for global feminist critiques of the dominance of American women's studies, and it would be foundational for the trajectory of Third World feminist alliances.

The Wellesley conference is not as well known as the famous Barnard Conference on Sexuality in 1982, which staged American debates about the "sex wars" and reflected tensions between feminist activists and academic feminists. Yet the Wellesley conference was no less controversial and pivotal in the history of feminist ideas, particularly with respect to the enduring critique of feminism's unequal knowledge production about the world's women. The event demonstrated that US academic research on global women treated these issues solely through the domain of policymaking and the social science of development.[38] The "Women and Development" project and its limitations and failures changed the course of international feminist research and reflected US academia's equation of global feminist research with policymaking.

Wellesley College scholars and administrators founded the Center for Research on Women in 1974; it was among the very first institutional centers for women's research at colleges and universities in the United States.[39] The center held the highly anticipated International Conference on Women and Development, featuring 117 women from 32 countries, two years after it was established. It was the most ambitious international academic conference on the global issues of women in any part of the world to date. The planning committee for the Wellesley conference featured eleven white American women who conducted research on different regions of the world, including Asia, Africa, and Latin America, and additional American scholars from Middle Eastern studies were consulted.[40] In the planning committee's fundraising prospectus for the International Women and Development Conference, the event was described as a "follow-up to the United Nations conference in Mexico City" with scholars who were studying women in Africa, Asia, Latin America, and the Middle East.[41]

The charge of the conference was broadly defined as exploring "women's participation in development and its impact on their status in society." The thesis of the conference used keywords that had shaped the Mexico City conference: "women," treated as a self-evident category, was used alongside the term "development," as linked to women's "status" and the social world. Development, according to conference organizers, was to be "construed broadly, to include not only economic development" but also "familial roles, participation in the social polity, etc.," in addition to the socioeconomic roles of women.[42]

The conference organizers had two major goals. The first goal was to develop a "professional field" of research on women around the world, while the second was to develop "effective public policy related to women." For conference organizers, the makers of public policy were scholars of the First World who needed local researchers to gain access to datasets and help American scholars succeed in reaching their own research goals. This approach to research is described directly in the planning document circulated prior to the conference, in which organizers stated that the intent was to create "intellectual exchange with scholars in the countries we are studying in defining problem areas as well as in testing our models and generating data." The "we" of this statement referred to Americans studying other parts of the world. Ultimately, what was at stake was the expansion of research on women from local studies to the broad comparative study of women around the world, which would allow First World researchers to develop broad theoretical models.[43]

With the support of Wellesley College, the Ford Foundation, and the Office of Women in Development at the US Agency for International Development (USAID), international scholars traveled to Wellesley College to engage with scholars from the United States working on the rest of the world.[44] According to the conference prospectus, scholars from the so-called developing world would offer their data and experience from local contexts while learning from theoretical models designed by their Western colleagues. The four-day conference featured panels on rural women, the place of women in production, women and changing family structures, women's education, women and migration, women's informal organizations, women and the law, and women and urban labor. The final day focused on development policy actions, with a focus on research action and policy recommendations.[45] The conference proceedings and select research presentations were published as a special issue of the recently established feminist publication *Signs: Journal of Women in Culture and Society*.[46]

The conference funding was telling and reflected the increasing involvement of foundations in academic feminism on issues of international development. Conference organizers received funding from the Rockefellers' Agricultural Development Council, the Ford Foundation, the Johnson Foundation, the Lilly Endowment, Pathfinder International, the Rockefeller Foundation, and the Tinker Foundation, as well as national area studies professional associations.[47] The projected budget for the conference was approximately US$26,200 in 1976, equivalent to about $143,700 in 2024. As a collaboration across the academy, the US government, and private philanthropies, the Wellesley conference reflected the increasing entrenchment of funding from the US state and private foundations in the project of scholarly research on women. The conference featured many prominent scholars conducting international research on women, gender, and development with positions and close links to organizations like the Ford Foundation, USAID, and the UN.

A glimpse at the program shows the wide range of expertise at the conference. Among the hundreds of women scholars and program officers at the conference were Bangladeshi feminist Rounaq Jahan, American social scientist Hanna Papanek, American women's studies founder Jean Fox O'Barr, Ethiopian feminist sociologist Zenebework Tadesse, American anthropologist Ann Stoler, Kenyan feminist scholar Marjorie Mbilinyi (who took the mic a decade later at Nairobi), Ford Foundation officer Adrienne Germain, Moroccan feminist sociologist Fatima Mernissi, Thai feminist sociologist and political scientist Mallica Vajrathon, Indian feminist sociologist Vina Mazumdar, Indian legal scholar Lotika Sarkar, Sierra Leonian anthropologist Filomina Steady, Nigerian poet and feminist scholar Omolara Ogundipe-Leslie, and world-famous Danish economist Ester Boserup. The International Conference on Women and Development was a who's who of elite research on women. Indeed, Boserup's work influenced the declaration of the UN International Women's Year and the Decade for Women, while Adrienne Germain was pivotal in shaping the Ford Foundation's funding for women for the next decade, and many went on to hold high-ranking positions and advisory roles in the UN.

What unfolded at the Wellesley conference was dramatically different from what American organizers had imagined. Jam-packed with panels dominated by American academics, the conference schedule allowed little time for discussion, debate, or input from Third World participants, who felt silenced in session after session.

By the end of the first day, dissatisfied Third World researchers from Asia, the Middle East, and the African continent decided to form their own *counter*-conference. This "underground" conference, held over many nights at the conference hotel, was not framed by the formal ideas of "women" and "development" but focused instead on questions of the legal subordination of women in customary law, neocolonial governance, and authoritarianism. These political similarities across the postcolonial world made the cause of Third World feminist research more urgent than ever. Conversations linked feminist research across regions in the decolonizing world as participants addressed the comparative analysis of the legal subordination of women in religious customary law, the problems of structural adjustment programs for women, and the subordination of women under postcolonial governance.

The Third World women's counter-conference at Wellesley ran late into the night as researchers carved out space for their own research priorities, which centered the urgency of geopolitics for feminist thought. Feminist researchers compared and contrasted parallel economic, political, and social challenges that shaped the condition of girls and women in their countries. Indian feminists Vina Mazumdar and Lotika Sarkar circulated their new social scientific report on the status of women in India, *Towards Equality*, promoting it as a model for other Third World research on women.[48] As Filomina Steady recounted, the fierce criticisms of the conference by Indian feminists made waves among researchers from the African continent and Latin America, who similarly condemned the limited methods and research exploitation of First World research. Women from the African continent, including Steady, Fatima Mernissi, and Egyptian physician and writer Nawal El Saadawi, among others, representing regions across the African subcontinent and North Africa, came together to discuss the beginning of the first pan-African feminist research organization, the Association of African Women for Research and Development (AAWORD).[49]

The archives of the 1976 International Women and Development Conference, which are held in the Wellesley College Archives, tell a triumphant story of the conference, offering essentially no evidence of the scathing critique and dissent by women of the decolonizing world. However, accounts aired immediately after the event make clear the profound dismay and anger of participants. Third World commentators reflecting on the conference did not mince words, condemning the conference organizers for treating Third World women as objects of research and "native informants" while refusing to take seriously their trenchant structural critiques of neocolonialism, knowledge inequality, and extractive debt.[50]

Following the conference, a collective of African women quickly published a statement of condemnation, "African Women Take a Stand."[51] They opened their statement by laying out the stakes of the African feminist critique: "We wish to register here our deep objection to the language used in dialogue with us by some of the conference conveners, which ranged from the patronizing to the insulting." As African participants at Wellesley made clear, while American women might have secured funding for an international conference, that did not give them the right to "exploit the presence" of Third World women without giving them an equal voice in the organizing and publication of the research from the conference. The economics of the global women's conference betrayed the profound economic inequality at the heart of the American global feminist project: "We would like to remind the conveners of this particular conference that much of the wealth which allows for the funding of conferences such as this is derived from the exploitation of the regions from which we come. Therefore, the question of gratitude for having been invited, or charity on the part of the hosts, does not arise."[52]

The statement offered trenchant criticisms of the conference and more broadly the paradigm of women and development. The collective of African feminists indicted organizers for holding a conference on the "developing world" in the United States while offering no critique of the condition of American women, particularly the subjugation of women of color. The article condemned the conference for having no Africans or people of African descent on the planning committee and for failing to make space for African and African diasporic perspectives in the panels or the publication plan. African women registered their dissent on the uncritical view of "development" taken by conference organizers and American panelists, as well as the complete and total failure of the conference to offer any critique of First World developmental projects that exploited Asia and Africa. As they took a stand on the failure of the intellectual work of the conference, they insisted that the *Signs* special issue accurately reflect the criticisms of the Wellesley conference, which ultimately it did not. And the statement definitively declared that "the primary reality of our societies today is unquestionably that of neocolonialism which presents severe obstacles to us as African peoples, as women and as researchers, and which is *the* major obstacle to development in its human and broadest sense."[53]

Alongside colleagues who collectively took a stand as African women, prominent feminists from across North Africa and Southeast Asia, including Nawal El Saadawi, Fatima Mernissi, and Mallica Vajrathon, came together and published a transnational collective statement that also condemned the International Women and Development Conference.[54] Years later, this critical statement against the Wellesley conference served as a foundational citation for Chandra Talpade Mohanty's widely popular 1984 critique of the objectification of Third World women in First World feminist research, "Under Western Eyes."[55]

For El Saadawi, Mernissi, and Vajrathon, the stakes of the Wellesley conference were high. Third World women had been forced into yet another international event after the UN conference in Mexico City, which had been dominated by white American women. Their statement offered an urgent call for change, and it was their charge "to make sure that we shall never have to face the same situation that we faced in Wellesley," as the American organizers had once again created an environment that silenced and disregarded the concerns of Third World women—a repeat of their experience at Mexico City. The statement put the terms of their critique starkly: "We want to explain the feelings of third world women who have to confront one of the latest developments of neo-colonialism: Maternalism."[56] American women had created an entirely new form of neocolonial domination based in the exploitation of the knowledge and expertise of Third World women.

Yet these viewpoints were not shared by American participants. As Joanne Meyerowitz demonstrates, American observers from USAID and the Ford Foundation had a very different understanding of the events that unfolded at Wellesley. A USAID participant described the poor technical quality of the presentations from Third World women, and Ford officer Elinor Barber expressed regret that, for Third World women suspicious of First World researchers, the conference, an academic gathering, had become a political event.[57]

Ultimately, what was at stake for Third World participants was the very meaning of the category of women and the place of an anti-colonial politics in international research on women. As Third World women argued, white women from the First World who wished to perpetuate imperial knowledge projects in the name of women's rights promoted a false vision of global unity through some self-evident idea of women's issues. As El Saadawi, Mernissi, and Vajrathon contended, "We want to destroy the myth that the mere fact of being women will unite us all and that women are not political beings; that political discussions at women's meetings mean 'diverting from the women's issues.'" They argued that the Third World women's dissent not only was necessary but was the *only* reason the conference was historically significant: "We want to emphasize the fact that 'explosions,' 'conflicts' and 'disruptions' which occur in conferences, such as the one at Wellesley, are healthy; and because of them we believe the conference was a success."[58]

The authors broke down the many ways in which the conference failed in its structure and execution and suppressed, silenced, and exploited the ideas and critiques of Third World women at every stage. It was, in their characterization, exclusionary in everything from the initial organization to the very panel topics that organized women into the binary of "developed" and "developing." But they insisted that, in the face of the failure of networks of anticolonial movements, women were the only people who continued to actively pursue internationalism in a period of increasing disillusionment and fear.

Clearly, Third World women at Wellesley were disenchanted with this transnational project of research on women. Yet, even so, they felt an even more urgent need to create international solidarity. For women dismayed by early efforts at international research collaborations, the promise of real change at international conferences on global women remained, despite the failures and racialized exploitation that pervaded the Wellesley conference. Hope persisted among the many Third World women invested in the liberatory promise of feminist research.

The optimism of Third World women was most palpable at the highly visible UN conferences held during the International Women's Year and the Decade for Women. Perhaps, as the UN Decade for Women promised, the international conferences would better fulfill the needs of the world's women.

The UN Decade for Women and the Expansion of Knowledge Infrastructures

In the middle of the 1970s, as the promising Afro-Asian nationalist coalitions were increasingly fractured by rising authoritarian movements and military power, women of the decolonizing world looked to the expanding universe of UN conferences on women to recast women's internationalism outside of failed nationalist projects. And it was true—the UN women's conferences offered an extraordinary platform for women of the world. Conferences for the International Women's Year and the Decade for Women were held across the world. The first conference for International Women's Year took place in Mexico City in 1975. Contentious debates from Mexico City spilled over into the wide-ranging international meetings and conferences on women that quickly followed, like the counter-conference at Wellesley.

The second conference in the middle of the UN Decade for Women was held in Copenhagen in 1980. Again, it was marked by fractious political differences between First and Third World women, at both the diplomatic conference and the first official NGO Forum. The first conference in Mexico City was held between June 19 and July 2, 1975; with participants from 133 member nations, it was the largest ever supplemental conference for NGOs at a UN conference. (The first supplemental NGO conference had been held at the UN population conference a year before.) The NGO event was first called the NGO Tribune and was later renamed the NGO Forum at the conferences that followed.[59]

In her study of the conflicts and conversations that unfolded at Mexico City, feminist historian Jocelyn Olcott argues that the International Women's Year conference was "a launch pad for an array of global feminisms."[60] For Olcott, the conference was not solely about the conflict between First and Third World women; it also served, she noted, as a critical turning point for feminist exchange and networks between First World women and highly educated elite women from other parts of the world. Resolution 3520, passed after the Mexico City conference, expanded International Women's Year to a full Decade for Women, to be focused on the themes of equality, development, and peace and dedicated to implementing the World Plan of Action.[61]

The second conference marking the midpoint of the UN Decade for Women was held from July 14 to July 30, 1980, in Copenhagen, Denmark.[62] Originally, the mid-decade conference was to take place in Tehran, Iran, yet by the late 1970s, officials were uneasy about the political upheaval there. Conference organizers shifted gears and moved the gathering to Copenhagen, staging the events at smaller universities and conference areas, leading to what many women later complained was a disjointed conference scattered across a racially exclusive European city. Still, the Copenhagen conference had 145 delegations at the official conference, which opened with the official signing of the Convention on the Elimination of All Forms of Discrimination Against Women, the first and most significant international "bill of rights" for women.

The final conference of the UN Decade for Women was held in the center of Nairobi from July 15 to July 26, 1985. The Nairobi conference produced the "Nairobi Forward-Looking Strategies for the Advancement of Women," a document that set forth goals for the advancement of women by the year 2000.[63] Ten years after the official end of the Decade for Women, the Beijing conference was held to assess progress toward meeting the Nairobi strategies. Held September 4 to September 15, 1995, with the NGO Forum held in Huairou, a town forty-five minutes outside of Beijing, the conference had 189 member nations in attendance, with approximately 17,000 official delegates and a massive NGO Forum attended by approximately 35,000 people from around the world.[64]

As declared in 1972, the UN's International Women's Year would have three primary goals: the promotion of equality between men and women, the integration of women into the project of global development, and the recognition of women as important for international relations and world peace.[65] The three themes of equality, development, and peace framed the International Women's Year conference and the subsequent UN Decade for Women through broad and ambitious concepts that were flexible and largely undefined in terms of their political implications. These keywords would become the signature concepts for all UN women's events following the Mexico City conference. They would also shape the priorities of wide-ranging events that used the UN's International Women's Year as a platform to hold conferences and build networks for international women's research.

The UN poster for the first women's conference depicted the themes of the conference and the research infrastructures shaped by the decade in an enduring emblem that has symbolized the UN theme of women since the 1970s: a stylized dove. Embedded within the dove is an equal sign and the Linnaean symbol for woman. The dove represented peace and progress, broadly symbolizing development according to official documents, with the equal sign representing the dream of women's equality with men. Also inscribed within the dove was the Linnaean pictogram of the female sex. The Linnaean "biological symbol" for woman would be a critical part of UN iconography, appearing as sun rays, as waves, and as the bodies of masses of people across the visual iconography of the UN conferences. Designed by American graphic designer Valerie Pettis, the image would endure and become the primary symbol for the UN International Women's Year and the Decade for Women; it is still used as the icon for the organization UN Women.

The declaration of the UN's International Women's Year produced massive funding streams committed to creating new metrics of women, new

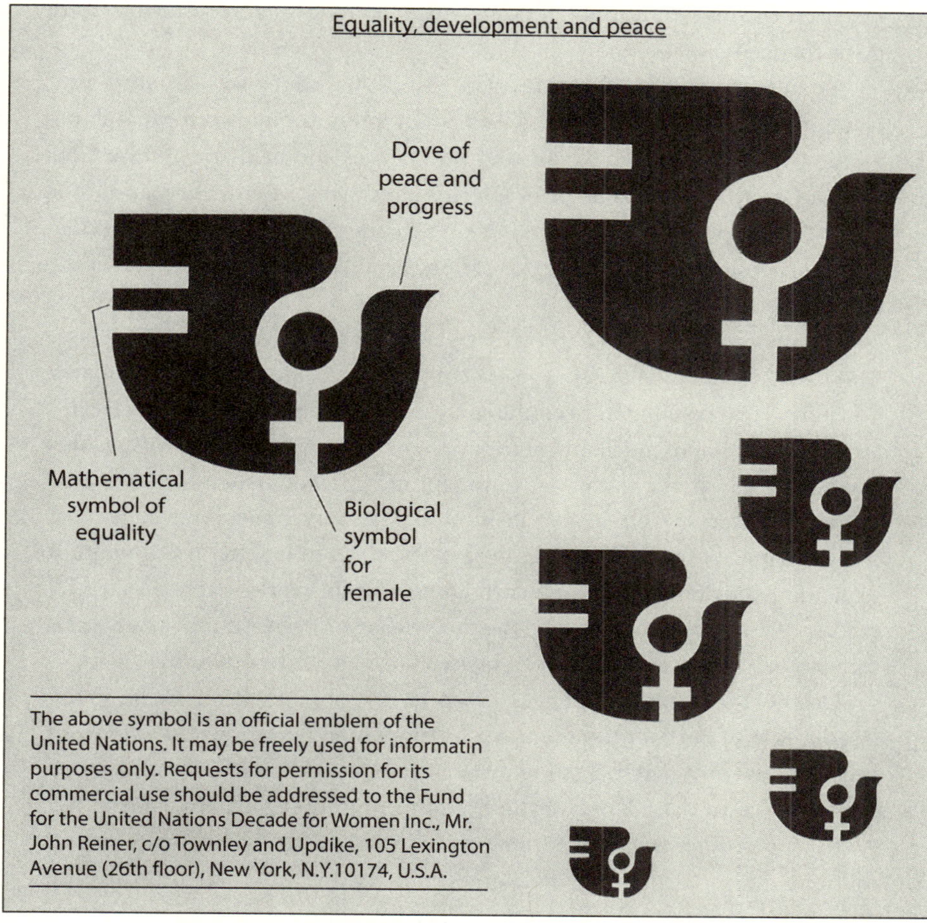

FIGURE 1.3. Official UN document with explanation of the symbolic dove used to promote the United Nations Decade for Women: Equality, Development, Peace (1976–1985) by the Branch for the Advancement of Women, Centre for Social Development and Humanitarian Affairs, UN (Vienna). Distributed at the Third World Conference in Nairobi and preserved in the personal papers of Robin Morgan, Schlesinger Library on the History of Women in America.

international infrastructures of knowledge, and novel research networks dedicated to studying women around the world. The UN produced both quantitative and qualitative moral diagnostics to assess and combat gender inequality across nations. Its research machine became the primary evaluative mechanism for developmental progress based in the comparative study of the status of women. The UN catalyzed new domains and methods of research through hundreds of conference declarations, resolutions, and goals focused on women.

As such, from the 1970s through the 1990s, there was a paradigm-changing focus on women in the domain of internationalism. Research on women was to be organized around the themes and priorities of the UN, focused on the conference principles of development, equality, and, to a lesser extent, peace. These themes were extended to encompass new initiatives and policies on women's education, legal access, citizenship, health, and access to work.

UN conferences served as primary sites for women's internationalism. These events reflected the complicated effects of the international mandates and norms that resulted from conference meetings. Ultimately, the UN lacked strong enforcement mechanisms for implementing and upholding its resolutions and goals, particularly with powerful and influential member states like the United States. Still, despite its limited power over sovereign states as a nongoverning body, the UN emerged as profoundly influential in defining and expanding the domain of women's rights around the world. In particular, UN priority areas for women shaped the massive flow of private and state capital to women's research and service organizations around the world.

Despite the sudden influence of women on the international stage in the last decades of the twentieth century, historians have inadequately theorized how the rise of the global study of women has transformed the trajectory of global politics and late twentieth-century internationalism.[66] From the 1970s, the project of internationalism—in terms of the domains of development and the expanding discourses of human rights—was dramatically *feminized*.[67]

By *feminization* I mean the expansion of the labor of people who identified as women in the project of internationalism in the domain of the UN, global research institutions, and the thousands of internationalist NGOs, as well as the shift in policies and global priorities that focused on women's social and economic lives. I also use the concept of feminization to comprehend the sudden importance of research on women in the 1970s and 1980s and the rise of new measures of women's life and work—everything from the education of girls to maternal health to women's informal labor to sexual violence—to comprehend the success and failure of virtually all aspects of international development and rights.

Women's rights, staged at UN international conferences, became critical to an expansive knowledge project that constituted indices and measurements of national progress. And this social scientific knowledge project defined a new ethical order, which centered the gender of development and women's rights in UN internationalism. It is striking that women's issues become a critical site for the expansion of the domain of development and human rights just as the UN was increasingly losing status and influence on the international stage, where the UN was feminized in all the diminutive meanings of the term.

Yet the UN Decade for Women, with its initiatives for research on women, was not simply a foreign imposition on Third World women's movements. While the UN expanded the domain of international women's rights, Third World women also looked to the UN to gain access to resources and build the capacity to train women, conduct research, and write and publish about women. These women understood that with the International Women's Year and the Decade for Women, they gained access to a rare opening for institutional support for their own liberatory research projects. For a generation of women mobilized by increasingly powerful global women's movements, the UN emerged as the primary domain in which to access material support for education, publication, and advocacy.

Moreover, the UN conferences served as a visible platform on which to question patriarchal structures of authority in postcolonial states. Third World women invested in UN women's internationalism to build a project of dissent against authoritarian postcolonial states that increasingly threatened women's access to equal rights and subjugated women through draconian laws enacted by patriarchal religious nationalist movements. Third World women looked to the infrastructure of the UN as a site for reinvesting in the promise of liberal principles of equality and rights in opposition to authoritarian postcolonial and settler states.

Nowhere is this mutual investment in women's internationalism by the machinery of the UN and Third World researchers clearer than in the massive expansion of research infrastructures on women.

The very first resolution of the International Women's Year in 1975 focused on research and training for women in Africa with a call to expand infrastructures of research on the African continent.[68] The UN Plan of Action adopted at the Mexico City conference articulated thirty priority areas and mandated the creation and fortification of "instruments and programmes" that would assess the "status of women" in order to achieve the goals of the International Women's Year, primarily through a focus on research and education.[69] The plan offered guidelines to all member states for implementing an apparatus of actions and institutions based on the recruitment and training of women for research on women. The principles and goals of the plan were directed at national governments as well as public and private institutions, women's and children's organizations, unions, media, political parties, and NGOs.[70]

Most significantly, the first UN Plan of Action for women recommended that nation-states set up national machinery that would employ local women researchers to measure the development of women in priority areas. This research infrastructure, based in an "interdisciplinary and multisectoral machinery" created through national commissions on women, women's bureaus, and women's research centers, would be the charge of the state.[71] These national women's commissions and bureaus would measure the status of women under the law, economic policy, and social life.

The Mexico City Plan of Action stated that, at a minimum, member states had to be able demonstrate within five years significant changes in law and policies for women by massively expanding mechanisms of research on women. The first five-year goals focused on research and education—specifically, increased literacy and civic education for women, technical and vocational research, and training for women in industrial and agricultural labor; greater access to education for women; new forms of research and measures for everything related to women, including health, sanitation, nutrition, and family planning; increased research and education on the legal inequality of women; and the promotion of women's education institutions.[72]

Importantly, the Plan of Action included significant financial incentives for all Third World states, from democratic to authoritarian governments, to participate in the new infrastructure of women's research, whether or not doing so was a true state priority. "Developing countries" would receive support and resources from the UN fund for the International Women's Year and the UN Economic and Social Council to set up and run this research and reporting machinery.[73] The material support for research institutions focused on women's issues would be further fortified with dedicated research training institutes for women organized by a new arm of the UN.

For Third World women involved in UN projects, conferences were followed by more and more conferences. Training institutes for UN-trained researchers were followed by international meetings, regional seminars, adjacent agency convenings like UNESCO (UN Educational, Scientific, and Cultural Organization) workshops, and international conferences. Women traveled around the world for the project of women's rights, representing a particular region and research object across the domains of the UN, from geographies of research in "Asia" or "Africa" to thematic research on "rural women" and "child health." The labor of feminist research was increasingly dominated by the work of global conferencing: serving as representatives of regions, presenting specific research case studies, and engaging in vast comparative projects with novel global measures that linked women and gender to markers of development.

The UN created an international architecture for training in doing social scientific research on women, conducting this research, and distributing it globally. This architecture was institutionalized in the establishment in 1976 of the UN's International Research and Training Institute for the Advancement of Women (INSTRAW), then adopted officially by the General Assembly following discussions at Mexico City on the implementation of the Plan of Action as a research training and output priority for the "developing world."[74] INSTRAW remained a discrete institution within the UN until 2011, when it was converted into the UN Women's Training Centre as part of a new unit, UN Women.[75] The three goals of the institute were training, research, and the dissemination of information.

For the founders of INSTRAW, there were two reasons for the creation of sustained research and training centers for women. The first goal was to create knowledge in the face of a near-total absence of social scientific research and quantifiable data, which UN officials argued was necessary for the inclusion of women in development programs for the second UN Decade of Development. The second purpose of INSTRAW was to train women, particularly those from the Third World with little access to educational infrastructure, so they could participate in the regional women's research institutes set up by the UN.[76]

By the end of 1976, officials had decided that INSTRAW would have central offices in Tehran, which was also the designated host for the second World Conference on Women in 1980.[77] Iran, under the direction of the shah's sister, Princess Ashraf Pahlavi, had pledged US$1 million for the research center (equivalent to approximately $5.4 million in 2023), along with a state-of-the-art library of materials on research on women and administrative support.[78] Additional support would come from other states, including Mauritius, Turkey, the Philippines, and the Netherlands.[79] However, with political unrest leading to the overthrow of the shah and the founding of the Islamic Republic of Iran, everything changed. The new government of Iran quickly withdrew from all promises to support women's issues, both at the UN and domestically. The second Decade for Women conference was eventually moved to Copenhagen, and more than five years later, INSTRAW finally found an institutional home in Santo Domingo in the Dominican Republic.

Throughout the 1980s and 1990s, the UN built an expansive global architecture for the training in, research on, and distribution of social scientific research on women. This arm of the UN focused on developing "statistics, indicators, and other data on women," and research focused primarily on development goals as they related to women, including women's labor and the economy, water and sanitation, and renewable energy.[80] INSTRAW held seminars and trainings around the world with thousands of women, training Third World women to become development planners and social science researchers as part of new women's organizations. The research training and types of quantitative measures of development and data collection methods remained unchanged throughout the decades of the UN training institute for women, ensuring the global implementation of development indicators as essentially the sole standard in the global study of women. The UN further commissioned filmmakers to create a documentary TV series called *Women and Development* that would disseminate research on women to a broad audience with episodes about "sex roles," work, and the legal struggles of women across the world.[81]

Yet perhaps nothing shaped the trajectory of Third World women's participation in internationalism more than the vast UN sponsorship of the research consultancies associated with the women's conferences. For Third World women, these relationships of support for individual researchers transformed the foundational conditions for research. The research consultancy was a system for institutional research through which researchers in the "developing" world received direct funding for projects.

In the consultancy system, the UN capitalized on the first generation of women from the decolonizing world, particularly in the spaces of South Asia and East Africa, who gained access to higher education in foreign master's and PhD programs that newly focused on development studies. While many of these women faced profound barriers to accessing disciplinary doctoral programs in economics and political science, they soon found some access to development programs. Despite limited access, they continued to face profound challenges in conducting advanced research, from the demands of reproductive labor to professional barriers imposed through sexual harassment and violence committed by prominent development economists—as described, for instance, by Devaki Jain in recounting her experience of being assaulted by world-famous economist and sociologist Gunnar Myrdal.[82]

Before meetings and conferences, women researchers from around the world would conduct technical research and prepare detailed reports on regions across the Third World with quantifiable, comparable datasets that were then employed in a large-scale research infrastructure of global indicators on gender and women. The UN, in collaboration with private foundations, would cover the salaries and research expenses of Third World women during the research period, as well as their travel and room and board expenses at the UN and UN-related conferences.[83] Through the consultancy system, global women's conferences offered social and economic mobility to the first generation of Third World women researchers with access to postgraduate education. Many women built their own careers as international gender experts, first through UN consultation and then in official positions in the UN for women's initiatives based in regional and comparative social scientific expertise.

Multiple arms of the UN sponsored training, research, and publications on women around the world for conferences during and after the decade. Between 1975 and 1985, INSTRAW produced dozens of publications on women's economic roles, sanitation, women and food production, and women in development planning. INSTRAW publications included training manuals for researchers doing quantitative social science research. The publication, *Training Users and Producers in Compiling Statistics and Indicators on Women in Development*, offered replicable strategies for producing data on women for researchers in the so-called developing world. INSTRAW's "how-to" manuals complemented the many datasets being produced by other powerful arms of the UN.[84] The Population Division of the UN's Department of International Economic and Social Affairs produced dozens of comprehensive global comparative studies of fertility levels, population, sex ratios, and marriage rates for women and children. The UN's Statistical Office conducted extensive household and labor surveys of women, expanding publications on new domains of economic research, particularly the study of the "informal sector" and the place of women's work in new global measures of labor. The Statistical Office further refined methods and statistical measures of women in terms of demography and economic indicators of women's work. Alongside the demographic and statistical divisions, various regional economic commissions produced comprehensive datasets and studies of women and development by region. The Economic Commission for Africa published wide-ranging studies of African women and development, while the Economic and Social Commission for Western Asia had produced its own journal on women and development in Arabic by 1985.[85]

Indeed, when it came to women, multiple UN agencies functioned as research institutes producing social scientific data about measurable conditions of women and children in preparation for the women's conferences.

The UN Children's Fund (UNICEF) produced extensive research on women in relation to child development in the 1970s and 1980s, with case studies and comparative global research on the role of women in the survival of children. The International Labour Organization (ILO), in collaboration with INSTRAW, published key studies on women and economic activity and "women at work."[86] As feminist historian Eileen Boris demonstrates in her landmark study, the ILO was a massive machine of internationalist knowledge production on women.[87] The ILO framed Third World womanhood primarily through the question of labor. By the 1970s, the ILO's extensive catalog of research studies on labor and development focused on women and work in the developing world, creating a massive body of knowledge about women's labor in the Third World.

These studies were complemented by the research work of the UN Food and Agriculture Organization, which produced research and publications on women's labor in agriculture, with a focus on rural women. It also published detailed training manuals for rural women to increase production and develop women's skills in management. The UN Industrial Development Organization further produced extensive research on women's labor, focused on industrial and manufacturing labor.[88]

Finally, the UN's own designated research and publication organization, UNESCO, had pivoted to the comprehensive study of women by the mid-1970s with special issues of its journal, the *UNESCO Courier*, dedicated to the women's conferences. It did so by publishing a special issue for every UN conference on women. The first special issue on International Women's Year was published in March 1975, with a follow-up issue in September 1975 on the Mexico City conference as the "Turning Point for Women." The next special issue on "The Invisible Woman," on the occasion of the Copenhagen conference, was published in July 1980, and a special issue on "Women: Tradition and Change" appeared in April 1985 in anticipation of the Nairobi conference. Finally, the last special issue, "Women: One Half of Heaven," was published in September 1995 in anticipation of the fourth conference in Beijing. UNESCO also held its own research conferences on women and social science around the Third World to promote research on women in association with the UN world conferences for women.[89]

Multiple additional publications resulted from UNESCO conferences detailing the rise of women's studies and the social sciences across spaces like Asia and the Arab world. Other UNESCO studies focused on women's development indicators and the participation of Third World women in research and development focused on Africa. In preparation for the Nairobi conference,

UNESCO created its own plan for the advancement of women. UNESCO conference publications ranged from research on rural women's production in the Third World to technical education for women, women's education, and science and technology for women.[90]

The many conferences held during the UN Decade for Women catalyzed knowledge production and publications on women at a scale never known before. In just a few years, and spurred by the UN conference theme of development and two UN decades dedicated to Third World development, women of the "developing world" became the primary object of research and writing in modern internationalist research projects, defined by and through an expanding world of social scientific indicators based in the disciplines of statistics and demography. In preparation for regional planning meetings and the international conferences on women, multiple organizations under the UN sponsored study after study linking women to every measure of development.

These conferences and workshops not only produced a vast terrain of knowledge defined almost exclusively by the social science of developing women but also generated a vast network of global women consultants and researchers in the "developing world" who were trained and sponsored by the UN. These Third World women would serve the goals of UN international research and become critical to the new apparatus of UN women.

UN Resolutions and the Occupation of Knowledge

Between 1947 and 1975, the UN added eighty-seven states as new members, including dozens of Third World nation-states, making the "developing world" the majority in the UN membership. With this expansion came a dramatic shift in the political concerns that defined UN internationalism, including pressure from most of the world's member states to condemn First World economic exploitation, Cold War militarism, and ongoing imperial and settler colonial policies. In the 1950s, as Adom Getachew explores in the work of global men committed to Black liberation, the UN shifted from primarily allied imperial nations to the central platform for utopian visions of global redistribution and justice.[91] By the 1970s, with American interests increasingly threatened by the rising dominance of non-aligned states, the UN had become marked by tense divisions between the United States and US allies and most of the world.

At the same time, by the mid-1970s, the UN had become the primary platform for Third World feminist research. The 1975 Afro-Asian women's symposium in Alexandria, convened just before the first UN women's conference, framed the work of Afro-Asian women through the new focus on women at the UN and foregrounded translatable social scientific research on women to advocate for a politics of anti-colonialism, anti-apartheid, and anti-Zionism in Mexico City a few months later. With the International Women's Year and the Decade for Women, Third World women pursued opportunities for education and training through UN research institutes, built research networks across borders at international conferences, and gained access to essential funding and institutional resources as UN research consultants.

The thirty-five resolutions and decisions adopted at the 1975 International Women's Year Conference would come to define the domain of research on women for decades to follow. The resolutions addressed wide-ranging themes related to women, including women's, maternal, and child health; women's employment; protections for elderly and disabled women; the role of the UN in population research on women; and the implementation of a UN Plan of Action.

Global geopolitics was also a critical part of the International Women's Year resolutions, including debates about the "status of women" in southern Africa under apartheid, the oppression of people during canal construction in Panama, aid to women in Vietnam in the context of proxy wars, the violation of human rights in Chile, and the oppressed status of women amid the Israeli occupation of Palestinian territories. Resolution 3, on the status of women under apartheid, made an explicit conceptual link between women's rights, the Universal Declaration of Human Rights, and the 1972 General Assembly resolution for action to combat racism, apartheid, and racial discrimination.[92] Specifically, Resolution 3 condemned the apartheid state for its contempt for the principles of the UN and cited the principle of women's dignity in opposition to apartheid. This conceptual link between the Universal Declaration of Human Rights; the General Assembly resolutions against racism, apartheid, and racial discrimination; and the status of women would be critical to another resolution at the conference, Resolution 32.

That resolution, one of thirty-five adopted resolutions, critiqued Zionism for its negative effect on the status of Palestinian women. The adoption of the resolution was a turning point in UN geopolitics and a signal moment in knowledge production at international women's conferences. Resolution 32 was the first resolution passed at any UN conference to condemn and call for the elimination of Zionism, spurring what would be an all-consuming debate about the question of Zionism at the UN in years to come, starting with the meeting of the General Assembly just a few months after the women's conference in Mexico City. Resolutions 3 and 32 were critically linked through a dual framing that placed racism and discrimination alongside the condition of women, citing the broad objectives and goals of the International Women's Year and the stated goals of women's equality, development, and peace.[93] It would also mark one of the first articulations of a key feminist argument linking apartheid and Zionism, both conceptually and materially.[94]

At stake in Resolution 32 were the *conditions* of Palestinian women under occupation. As the resolution declares, the World Conference of the International Women's Year was "deeply concerned about the prevailing conditions—political, social, demographic, and economic—of the Palestinian people, and in particular the conditions under which the Palestinian woman lives, and recognizing the close relationship between such conditions and the question of Palestine."[95] With the expressed concern about "prevailing conditions," the resolution affirmed the equality of human beings for people who suffered "under the yoke of colonialism." It explicitly paralleled earlier resolutions from the conferences of Afro-Asian women against colonialism, Zionism, and apartheid, in language that had been used throughout the 1960s and early 1970s. Indeed, it was this phrasing by Afro-Asian women that the CIA had marked as suspicious and politically volatile more than a decade before the International Women's Year.

The language in Resolution 32 was bold. In placing Zionism alongside racism and apartheid in a series of oppressive conditions that defined the condition of women, it would become among the most visible and contentious resolutions during and after Mexico City. The resolution further declared that national sovereignty and liberation mandated the complete end of Zionism: "Considering that international co-operation and peace require national independence and liberation, the elimination of colonialism, neo-colonialism, fascism, zionism, apartheid and foreign occupation, alien domination and racial discrimination in all of its forms and also respect for human rights."[96] It cited a range of UN resolutions on rights, from the economic rights and duties of states to fundamental human rights.

What is striking is the resolution's stance calling for the solidarity of all women with Palestinian women and people against the "flagrant violations of fundamental human rights committed by Israel in the occupied territories." It linked the idea of women's human rights to an internationalist anti-carceral politics staged at the UN, appealing for women of the world to "take the necessary measures to secure the release of thousands of persons, fighters for the cause of self-determination, liberation and independence, held arbitrarily in the prison of the forces of occupation." The resolution called on all states and international organizations to give assistance, both "moral and material," to Palestinian women in their struggle. Specifically, it outlined the Palestinian right to return home against continued displacement. Lastly, the resolution requested that the UN in particular offer its infrastructure of organizations and *research* to address the needs of Palestinian women.[97]

The adoption of a resolution that called for the equality of women through the elimination of Zionism alongside apartheid, racism, and colonialism at the International Women's Year conference was a signal event in the history of the UN: it was the first UN declaration to condemn Zionism and frame it as a violation of human rights. By the fall of 1975, the General Assembly, spurred by actions at the Mexico City conference for International Women' Year, took up the question of Zionism and passed Resolution 3379, which stated that Zionism was "a form of racism and racial discrimination"; this resolution was officially revoked more than fifteen years later, in 1991.[98] Contentions about Israeli policies of cultural assimilation in the occupied territories also animated debates and conflicts about cultural heritage and research at international UNESCO meetings in the mid-1970s.

At Mexico City's conference on women, the Israeli delegation had expressed its dismay at the inclusion of the Palestine Liberation Organization (PLO) at the conference in an inflammatory anti-PLO statement.[99] Even as they registered their discontent, the cause of Palestinian women received widespread support from large Third World delegations at the official diplomatic meeting. These actions including a massive walkout by allied delegations when the first lady of Israel, Leah Rabin, took the stage.[100]

These actions caught the attention of the United States. Just before delegates convened for the conference on women in Mexico City at the end of June 1975, US President Gerald Ford had designated a new permanent US representative to the UN, none other than Daniel Patrick Moynihan. Moynihan had built his career in government ten years earlier through the publication of his landmark social scientific report, *The Negro Family: The Case for National Action*.[101] Commonly known as the Moynihan Report, it would become notorious for its troubling depictions of the pathologies of the Black family, specifically prejudicial understandings of Black women. Moynihan's study was an important object of critique for Third World and Black feminist thought; Angela Davis condemned the report as blatantly racist and sexist as early as 1971 in her groundbreaking study "Reflections on the Black Woman's Role in the Community of Slaves," published while

Moynihan served as US ambassador to India.[102] Davis's critique was published a few years prior to Moynihan's appointment as the permanent representative to the UN.[103]

Moynihan, like other policymakers such as Henry Kissinger, looked to war as effective foreign policy. He felt that the UN, with its sudden expansion of membership of states with the darker peoples of the world and its advocacy for women, had come to represent the dangerous contagion of the Third World. He resented the shift in rhetorical power in UN internationalism away from US-dominated diplomacy.

Moynihan, taking on a new role as the official US representative to the UN, felt it was time for UN member states to be fearful of the presence of the United States.[104] Moynihan took a hardline approach to US diplomacy, which he felt was passive, impotent, and too bleeding-heart liberal toward the Third World when it came to UN internationalism. In his language, it was high time that the "Third World feeds itself."[105] He expressed irritation at the adoption of Resolution 32; just a few months later, he would argue at the General Assembly that any language critical of Zionism and in favor of Palestinian rights was tantamount to antisemitism.[106] The *New York Times* reported in December 1975 that just after the vote on Resolution 32, Moynihan's wife described how "Pat" had mocked the Third World member states at the UN, proclaiming that "the lunatics were taking over the asylum."[107]

There was no question that Third World delegations—the so-called lunatics in Moynihan's troubling depiction—were taking over, and they were doing so through the research and writing infrastructures of the UN.

This takeover, then, was perhaps the most remarkable and overlooked consequence of Resolution 32: it created an incitement to knowledge by centering the *study* of the conditions of Palestinian women. Third World member states seized the means of knowledge production for the women of the decolonizing world. When Third World delegations argued that what was missing from understandings of the deleterious effects of occupation and colonialism for women was comprehensive information about the condition of women in currently and formerly colonized spaces, the UN mandated a research project that would illuminate these conditions. The question of Palestine was less contentious at the first UN conference in Mexico City, but after resolution and debate across subsequent UN General Assembly conferences, the politics of resolutions and research on Palestinian women pervaded the conference at Copenhagen five years later.

What could be known with quantitative and qualitative research on the condition of women in the occupied territories? And who had the right to write about the conditions of the Palestinian woman on the international stage? With the adoption of Resolution 32 as part of the Mexico City Plan of Action in 1975, the Economic Commission for Western Asia (ECWA, now the Economic and Social Commission for Western Asia), founded just two years earlier as the youngest of five regional councils representing regions of the world, argued that it was the ECWA's responsibility, and it set out to produce a comprehensive research report on Palestinian women. The ECWA's regional conferences in 1976 and 1977 called upon the UN to identify, through research projects and proposed plans of action, the needs of Palestinian people. These resolutions at regional conferences calling for research and policy on Palestinians, alongside resolutions at UNESCO conferences and those adopted by associated organizations like the World Health Organization, spurred the ECWA to initiate a massive data-gathering research project on the condition of Palestinian women. At the ECWA preparatory meeting in 1979 during the lead-up to the 1980 Decade for Women conference in Copenhagen, the council created a research study and a plan of action.

What resulted was a research report on Palestinian women that was officially submitted by the ECWA to the UN at the Copenhagen conference in 1980.[108] The ECWA's report on Palestinian women served as a call to institutionalize research on women through centers for research and data collection, training for researchers and statisticians, and organizational expansion in the territories in order to gather basic information about the condition of Palestinian women.[109] It was framed through the official themes of the UN Decade for Women: equality, development, and peace. As the ECWA argued, it was impossible to use these key organizing UN themes to understand Palestinian women because the themes of the Decade for Women had assumed national liberation and sovereignty—principles unavailable to the women of the occupied territories.[110]

At stake was the total lack of available research about the specific condition of Palestinian women, which, the ECWA argued, made the work of policymaking impossible. As the report laid out, there were critical obstacles to improving the conditions of women in Palestinian territories because of the lack of good research and the "difficulty of obtaining additional information about the Palestinian people, in general, the Palestinian woman, in particular, and the occupied territories." The information about women in occupied territories that did exist was insufficient for writing even a basic report about Palestinian women's lives, because statistics did not assess issues like work and labor in relation to sex. There was a total lack of research infrastructure in the territories, and "the Palestinian social, economic and planning institutions lack[ed] sufficient data," particularly with regard to data specific to women, which was essential for making any policy for women in the region.[111]

Although good social scientific research on women in the spaces of the Third World was generally lacking, the ECWA argued that the total absence of substantial data about Palestinian women was uniquely concerning and "a result of the special condition of the Palestinian people and their dispersion."[112] What was required, the ECWA argued in its report, were diverse studies to combat the total lack of research infrastructure. The absence of usable information required immediate intervention by the UN to build a substantial database about Palestinian women through research, including sample surveys to amass statistics about women, immersive studies of the place of Palestinian women in society, psychological studies of the experience of women in the occupied territories, research on the effect of the forced migration of men on women's lives and livelihoods, and studies of the condition of Palestinian women in Israeli prisons.

The ECWA report set out critical areas for research on women, including education, legal structures, family services and health care, media, and the role of regional women's and international organizations in promoting the equality of women. In each area of research and policy development, the report outlined the challenges that Palestinian women faced as a result of the conditions of limited access to education; the struggles of migrant work; the restricted access of women and children to basic health care; the need for extensive improvements in the training of all educated people in the region, including teachers, nurses, and doctors; and recommendations for organizational support and training for women leaders in women's organizations. It offered a detailed program of action for each area of research and policy on women.

For example, to understand the impact of legal regulations in the territories on women, the report suggested that the UN take action to study the laws related to the movement of Palestinians and identify the effects of law on Palestinian women. It recommended studies to understand the conditions of Palestinian women incarcerated in prisons. It further asked that international organizations apply the ILO's conventions on work conditions and the protection of workers, as well as maternal leave policies and other labor policies specific to women.[113] For health care and family services, the report recommended that the UN support the study of health care access in the territories and establish childcare centers and maternal health centers, with a specific focus on nutrition services.[114] The report asked that international organizations create women-specific datasets for Palestinian women and offer opportunities to Palestinians to participate in international research training workshops and international conferences.[115]

The ECWA report was prepared and officially submitted in time for the 1980 UN women's conference in Copenhagen. The question of the inclusion of Zionism in official resolutions would animate divisive debates at both the 1980 official conference and the NGO Forum. Israel vehemently contested the UN's inclusion of the report among the documents for the Copenhagen conference, questioning the legitimacy of the regional coalition of ECWA because of its inclusion of the PLO among its members.[116] The Israeli delegation held a press conference and protest during the conference to accuse the UN of "vicious attacks on Israel" based on the inclusion of the research report.[117] For Yehuda Z. Blum, Israeli ambassador to the UN, the ECWA report on Palestinian women, with its recommendation to expand the infrastructures of research in the occupied territories, was an "attempt to manipulate the means and machinery of the UN" and a "distasteful and vicious scheme" that went against the principles of UN women's rights.[118] The letter expressed regret that the report had been submitted as an official supplemental document to the Copenhagen conference.[119]

Nevertheless, following a contentious ten-hour session that ended at 2:35 a.m., the Copenhagen conference adopted a 218-paragraph program of action for the second half of the Decade for Women, with ninety-four votes in favor, including almost all the Third World states, and four dissenting votes from Australia, Canada, Israel, and the United States. There were twenty-two abstentions, including most of the states in western and northern Europe.[120] While many Third World states insisted that the resolution was critical to the theme of peace as it related to women, dissenting states like the United States emphasized that the resolution took away from the "real" matters related to women, and that the geopolitics of colonialism, apartheid, Zionism, and racism were separate from women's issues, the focus of the conference.[121]

In the 1980 Copenhagen action plan, there were two major changes from the Mexico City plan. First, and most significant, was the addition of an introductory paragraph for the conference plan that repurposed language from Resolution 32, which had focused specifically on Palestinian women. Now the language, as the framing terms for the *entire* program of action in the introduction of the 1980 Plan of Action, insisted that "without peace and stability there can be no development." It tied the strengthening of peace, one of the three themes of the decade, to the elimination of "imperialism, colonialism, neocolonialism, zionism, racism, racial discrimination, apartheid, hegemonism, and foreign occupation, domination and oppression," insisting that these issues were about "fundamental freedoms and human rights."[122] No longer a specialized resolution, the conference resolution placed the elimination of these conditions at the heart of the goals of the UN women's decade.

The other major shift in the program of action in 1980 was catalyzed by a proposal of the official delegate from India, Ambassador T.C.A. Rangachari, who composed a carefully revised official resolution on aid to Palestinian women in response to the ECWA report.[123] The Indian proposal was successful, and the second UN women's conference adopted resolutions that directly supported UN efforts to expand research and publications on the conditions of Palestinian women. The resolution for research and training for Palestinian women conceptually linked it to the UN mandate to assist the women of southern Africa under apartheid.[124] The resolution, "Assistance to the Palestinian Women Inside and Outside the Occupied Territories," called for special measures of assistance at the international level to establish a special fund for research and policy related to Palestinian women. Specifically, it mandated that the UN "undertake studies and research pertinent to the social and economic conditions of the Palestinian women with a view to identifying their specific needs." According to this resolution, research was required to identify the basic needs and resources required for women in the region. It further called for the UN to "establish, expand, and diversify educational and training programmes for Palestinian women."[125]

Directly following recommendations from the comprehensive report of the ECWA, the resolution adopted at the Copenhagen conference called for the elimination of restrictive legal measures that hindered Palestinian women, especially in their role as workers. The resolution also followed key recommendations from the report, recommending that the UN assist and train women in women's organizations, implement and train professionals for health and nutrition programs, and collect data and information about the social and economic conditions of Palestinian women who were displaced or restricted in their access to rights under continued occupation.[126] The program of action recommended by the research report on Palestinian women, despite Israeli and US objections, had a profound effect on the Third World states at the Copenhagen conference and its outcomes.

In 1985, during the lead-up to the final UN conference for the Decade for Women in Nairobi, the eighth official conference of non-aligned and developing states took place, the first official state conference of non-aligned states that focused entirely on women. Women were no longer a quarantined subject, separated in conferences on Afro-Asian women, but now were centered in the politics of non-alignment. The convening, held in New Delhi, India, in April 1985 ahead of the third UN conference on women that was to take place in July, brought together around sixty Third World states for a conference titled "Non-Aligned and Other Developing Countries on the Role of Women in Development," or the Non-Aligned Women and Development Conference. The ambassador of India submitted the official report from this convening to the UN for the World Conference of the UN Decade for Women.[127] The report, a critical review of the UN decade and goals from the perspective of the Third World, ran more than four hundred pages. It assessed the status of women in the developing world, named critical obstacles that impeded the objectives of the UN Decade for Women, and argued for the central role of "developing countries" in internationalism related to women at the UN. And the report reinforced the demands of the resolution for the study of the condition of Palestinian women and children.

It also took the opportunity to assert key tenets of non-alignment itself. In a definitive statement, the Non-Aligned Women and Development Conference reiterated the key tenets of non-alignment, arguing that non-alignment, in its original principles, was about "the struggle against imperialism, colonialism, neocolonialism, apartheid, racism, zionism and all forms of foreign aggression, occupation, domination, interference of hegemony as well as against great power and bloc policies" and linking the question of non-alignment to the status of women.[128] The language was almost exactly the same as the fifth paragraph of the official 1980 Copenhagen Plan of Action, and intentionally so. The report of the Non-Aligned Women and Development Conference highlighted the central role of Third World states in redefining the question of women on the global stage: "The intervention by non-aligned and other developing nations in the global debate on women's equality, development and peace has introduced new dimensions, giving to the debate a political, international and developmental character in place of the earlier approaches which viewed issues surrounding women's status as essentially a social and cultural phenomenon."[129]

The redeployment of the official UN resolution from the Copenhagen conference as the core philosophy of non-alignment revealed the transformative role of the many states of the Third World in shaping the framing of women's rights at the UN women's conferences. For a moment, the non-aligned and "developing" world had indeed taken over the UN. Well, at least when it came to the question of women.

By the Nairobi conference, however, Israel had prepared its own research report on the condition of women so as to contest research reports like the ECWA's and a revised 1984 report on Palestinian women. The report, titled "Arab Women and Children under Israel's Administration: A Paper in Rebuttal of Document A/CONF.116/6," was submitted to Leticia Shahani, a Philippine feminist and secretary-general of the Nairobi conference, in March 1985.[130] It was not included in the conference documents because of the technical rules of submission and review; still, it was widely circulated among officials and registered and archived among official correspondences for the conference. Israel's 1985 report offered a general defense of all aspects of the Israeli state policies regarding Palestinian women and rebuttals of claims that Palestinian women and children faced restricted access to education, health, or legal rights as a result of occupation. The rebuttal report, citing general statistics on demographic change in Israel and the expansion of gross domestic product in Israel, argued that there had been significant improvements in health and education institutions for Palestinians. It offered a divergent perspective on themes of development, education, and welfare, arguing that occupation by Israel was a benevolent project that had benefited women and led to progress and improvement of the condition of women and children in the occupied territories and generally asserting that Palestinian women lived in better conditions than women in other parts of the Arab world.

Like the ECWA report five years earlier, the rebuttal from Israel on women in the occupied territories described general social scientific data with *no* specific data on women. Instead, the rebuttal report offered general statistical information from the Israeli Central Bureau on issues like agricultural output, farmer income, household sanitation, hospital capacity in the territories, and birth rate and infant mortality.[131] The report's authors conceded that there was no social scientific research available specific to "Arab women" in relation to questions of work and health. Yet, unlike the ECWA report, it stopped short of recommending that any additional research be done on the conditions of Palestinian women. Ultimately, the March 1985 report was not included among the official documents of the conference, owing to the technicalities of timing and process for filing reports at the UN. Yet, while not an official submission, the report was widely circulated and influenced the events that would unfold at the third UN women's conference six months later.

At the 1985 Decade for Women conference in Nairobi, the "Third World Women Speak Out" session at the NGO Forum was animated by condemnations of neocolonialism and colonial occupation. Women fervently

THE PEACE TENT

The 3 striped tents that formed the centrally located complex known as The Peace Tent, were an important feature of FORUM '85. They were a safety valve and focal point for some of the more hotly contested and difficult global issues under discussion in Nairobi, and for many, became symbols of the spirit of the FORUM itself. The grassy area around the tents also served as a place for groups to gather, and the oversized patchwork globe at the entrance to the main tent set the tone with its declaration: "As a woman I have no country. My country is the whole world."

For more information on The Peace Tent and any future actions planned, contact:

Feminists International for Peace and Food (FIPF)
c/o F. Farenthold
2100 Travis Street
Suite 1203
Houston, TX 77002, USA

FIGURE 1.4. The Peace Tent in the International Women's Tribune Centre. IWTC, *Images of Nairobi*, 8. IWTC collection at Smith College Special Collections.

expressed solidarity with Palestinian women and with women living under conditions of apartheid in southern Africa.

But such speech was firmly kept in the margins of the official meeting. UN officials, anticipating heated discussion of the occupied territories and apartheid after what took place at the Copenhagen conference, placed a giant "Peace Tent" in the center of the grounds of the NGO Forum to pacify conflicts between the thousands of women in attendance—specifically conflicts between women on the question of Israel and Palestine.

Still, women of the NGO Forum worked to push their priorities into the decision-making at the official meeting. The participants called for a mass march to make a statement that the thousands of women at the NGO Forum should have a voice in the official governance. They planned the demonstration at the official UN diplomatic conference at the Kenyatta International Convention Center to tell "the government people" at the diplomatic meeting who held the real power in Nairobi "what *we* have said and decided."[132] But although initially imagined as a march that would take to the streets from the University of Nairobi campus to KICC, Kenyan authorities did not give the women permission for the march.

Rebuffed and denied entry to KICC, the organizers called on thousands of women to fill the grounds of the University of Nairobi with a massive rally at which they would publicly state their perspectives for the official UN meeting. At the gathering, Nawal El Saadawi, an Egyptian physician, feminist writer, and key dissenter at Wellesley's International Conference on Women and Development, told the thousands of women in the crowd to stand against all forms of apartheid and colonialism. As the crowd cheered, El Saadawi exclaimed, "There is no peace without justice, no development without justice. In the Third World we cannot develop because we are exploited by neo-colonial powers."[133]

Yet El Saadawi's words and the anti-colonial perspectives of the marchers had little place in the official proceedings of the UN meeting, marking a dramatic shift from previous UN women's conferences.

Symbolically at least, locating the final UN women's conference on the African continent in the visible city of Nairobi represented a triumphant imagination of decolonization and dreams of national sovereignty. The conference elected as president of the proceedings the women's rights activist Margaret Wambui Kenyatta, daughter of Kenyan liberation leader Jomo Kenyatta, the country's first prime minister and president.[134] And this time when the representative from Israel took the stage, some delegates did stage a walkout, though it was smaller in scale (primarily involving the Arab and Palestinian delegates).[135]

But many Third World delegations found themselves in the difficult position of feeling compelled to be reluctantly deferential to First World demands, especially those of the US delegation, headed by President Ronald Reagan's daughter, Maureen Reagan. The US delegation, alongside Israel, demanded that the resolutions remove geopolitical claims about Zionism and Palestinian women and neutralize the politics of non-alignment through the language of women's development and rights. Ultimately, the United States communicated that the resolution calling for the elimination of Zionism would have significant consequences for dependent Third World states, and it was dramatically removed from the adopted resolution and Nairobi Plan of Action.

The US delegation's plan, beginning long ahead of the actual conference, was to prevent another Plan of Action like that of the Copenhagen conference. In the months leading up to Nairobi, Maureen Reagan had petitioned for the conference Plan of Action to pass only if the delegate vote in favor was unanimous. Reagan emphasized that only a unanimously passed plan would gain status as a plan of "international significance."[136] Reagan's efforts to ensure US domination of the Plan of Action for women through a unanimous vote did not come to fruition but effectively set the stage for a shift in the Nairobi conference proceedings.

At the conference, the paragraph up for consideration linked the advancement of women to the elimination of Zionism along with "racism, Apartheid, and exploitation" as well as "all forms and manifestations of foreign occupation, domination and hegemony."[137] This paragraph was officially submitted by the Soviet bloc and offered the same language adopted at Copenhagen in 1980 and at the non-aligned conference that had just taken place months before in 1985. In response, the US delegation went to work to fracture alliances through a series of backroom diplomatic meetings, with a proposal to remove Zionism in session. The Soviet bloc and Arab states did not have enough votes to override the revision.[138] Finally, in a complicated collusion between the United States and dependent states, Zionism was removed from the adopted resolution. Even then, this change was made only after the US-led contingent threatened to veto the entire Plan of Action for the conference and Israel and the United States threatened to walk out of the conference and pull their delegations from the event.

Strikingly, it was Margaret Kenyatta who ultimately brokered the deal that led to the removal of Zionism from the official resolution of the conference. Fearing that the final event of the Decade for Women would be a total failure, Kenyatta introduced revised language that eliminated the term "Zionism" from the resolution, replacing it with "all other forms of racism and racial discrimination."[139] In the end, the resolution adopted at the conference eliminated language on Zionism. It was instead reframed in a neutralizing language of "obstacles" to the achievement of women's rights as outlined by the UN. These obstacles included "imperialism, colonialism, neo-colonialism, expansionism, apartheid and all other forms of racism and racial discrimination, exploitation, policies of force and all forms of manifestations of foreign occupation, domination and hegemony," a framing that offered little structural analysis of who caused the obstacles.[140]

The radical Third World project that sought the total transformation of the conditions of women's structural oppression by states through an explicit demand for the *elimination* of colonialism, neocolonialism, Zionism, apartheid, and racism had now been reframed through the far more tentative and apolitical language of "obstacles" that women generally faced. There was no reference to the possible causes of these impediments, and the states or structures that were agents of impeded equality for women were not named.

The conference did pass a resolution on Palestinian women and children, a revision of initial resolutions to conduct research into the condition of Palestinian women. Under the theme of "peace," the conference Plan of Action's resolution in paragraph 260 on "Palestinian Women and Children" was no longer framed in the language of research for aid, as it had been in the Copenhagen Plan of Action, but simply noted the "difficult living conditions" of Palestinian women, their imprisonment, and what most delegates resolved was Israel's violation of the Geneva Convention regarding the displacement of Palestinian women from land. Yet, unlike the mandates for knowledge acquisition in previous conference plans, rather than specifically calling for action with regard to research on women and children, the paragraph made no such mention of research or writing. Instead, it suggested that women coordinate efforts with the General Assembly's Programme of Action for the Achievement of Palestinian Rights.

There was one vote against this paragraph. The United States cited "its strong objection to the introduction of tendentious and unnecessary elements into the Forward-looking Strategies document which have only a nominal connection with the unique concerns of women."[141] Again, the United States declared in its opposition that the question of the rights of women was totally separate from the geopolitics of colonialism and occupation.[142]

The United States, led by Maureen Reagan, cast votes against two other major resolutions in the official Nairobi Plan of Action. First, it cast the only "no" vote against paragraphs in the resolution that demanded the condemnation and end of the "abhorrent apartheid system" and called for sanctions against the South African government. In the official document of the Nairobi conference, an asterisk to paragraph 44 on apartheid noted the US objection, stating that "the United States reserved its position on paragraph 44 because it did not agree that the obstacles should be considered the main reasons for the inequality of women in most countries."[143]

The second "no" vote from the United States was prompted by its objection to a paragraph on global wealth redistribution. The passage asserted that an "obstacle" to women's equality was profound economic inequality, and it called for the mass restructuring of the economic order "on a just and democratic basis."[144] Again, the United States objected to these paragraphs under the claim of a commitment to women's rights, by asserting that these resolutions were not about women.

For the first time since 1975—when a resolution was first adopted at the women's conference in Mexico City and subsequently at the 1975 General Assembly—the United States and Israel successfully eliminated Zionism from an official document of the UN. This triumphant win for the Americans foreshadowed the increasing dominance of the coalition of the United States, its allies and protectorates, and the state of Israel at UN conferences. The final conference of the UN Decade for Women shifted away from the mandates of previous UN women's conferences, which had mandated that states conduct research and build infrastructures to support research, training, and writing on the conditions of Palestinian women and children. These institutional calls for the expansion of research were also abandoned, after a decade of contention over who had the right to create knowledge about the specific conditions of Palestinian women.

After exhausting deliberations, conflicts, and threats of walkouts and failure, Margaret Kenyatta, at around 4:00 a.m. on the final day of the conference, pounded her gavel and declared the Nairobi conference, the final conference for the UN Decade for Women, over. So, too, were the initiatives led by Third World delegations that had looked to the UN to generate a research apparatus on women and the gendered effects of policy in the occupied territories.

Ten years later, at the fourth UN conference, held in Beijing, China, there were no resolutions on Zionism and no mandates related to UN-supported research on the conditions of Palestinian women. Such geopolitical issues were no longer the direct purview of the world's women.

The Afterlives of the Conference

Over fifty years of women's international conferences made possible extraordinary new alliances of women built across geographies beyond the nation-state. They shaped Third World women's critiques of the epistemic neocolonialism and led to new initiatives to create new methods and transnational approaches from Third World women. They institutionalized the modern social scientific study of women in much of the world and created the foundations for the global study of women, gender, and sexuality as we know it today.

These international conferences staged a new vision of emancipatory, participatory politics for women from the newly decolonized world who framed the promise of liberal rights through new visions of internationalism. By the 1970s, women from across most of the world had begun to forge a new lexicon of Third Worldism, one based in Third World women's rights against the pitfalls of patriarchal nationalism. And the International Women's Year and the Decade for Women conferences inaugurated an entire infrastructure of research and writing through training institutes, research consultancies, and publishing made possible through the UN.

And yet, despite their symbolic roles as the public conveners and secretaries of UN conferences and the NGO Forums, Third World women never controlled UN conference organizing or the politics of the diplomatic meetings. The travel to, attendance at, and participation in international conferences for most women in the world was almost entirely dependent on international foundation funding and UN research priorities, especially for those who served as research consultants.

Moreover, Third World women's alliances, research initiatives, and political visions staged at UN conferences were often sequestered from the formal domain of politics. The momentum for these efforts was short-lived, and many institutions built during the time of UN women's conferences were fragile. The projects that women envisioned were often under-resourced and limited, highly dependent on institutional prioritization of quantitative demography and statistical research and comparative indicators over any other forms of research.

In my 2021 interview with Sierra Leonian feminist scholar Filomina Steady, she described in detail her experiences at the official diplomatic meeting at Nairobi. Steady attended multiple UN women's conferences, formed Third World alliances as a dissenting participant at the Wellesley International Women and Development Conference, and later worked as a research consultant, special adviser, and deputy director for women's issues at the UN through the 1980s and 1990s. While she had attended the NGO Forums at previous women's conferences, the Nairobi conference was Steady's first opportunity to serve as an official delegate for the diplomatic gathering. Unlike the convivial atmosphere of like-minded women at the NGO Forum, the official space of the diplomatic meeting was tense, according to Steady. As she immersed herself in the KICC meeting, Steady witnessed the mundane experience of resolution after resolution passing over the course of hours and days. She felt dismay at the inequality of the debates, especially in the many hours and days of diplomatic meetings and animated contention over apartheid and Zionism.

After days of nonstop speeches and disagreements, Steady said, all the official resolutions were drafted and finalized, typed, compiled, and circulated to official delegates across the auditorium for their records when they returned to their home governments. It was a time without internet, email, or easy access to UN files, and the documents produced at the Nairobi conference were a critical resource for member states on international goals for women.

When the conference ended, the delegates, exhausted from hours of irresolution, quickly filed out of the auditorium and left the venue. As they rushed out, Steady looked around the room. The floor of the venue was covered with paper scattered under the seats. The hundreds of draft and final resolutions circulated throughout the conference were now indistinguishable from one another on the ground, discarded without care.

A *Los Angeles Times* report on the Nairobi women's conference corroborated Steady's account: "The floor was a sea of trampled resolutions, documents, and scribbled notes. The tables were littered with Coke bottles and candy wrappers, overflowing ash trays, souvenirs of Nairobi or the conference, defunct earphones and headsets for translation and more draft versions of documents suddenly not worth the paper they were printed on."[145] For Steady, the delegates' total disregard for the documents of debate and resolution symbolized the painful truth of the official UN women's conferences: the member states' lack of real commitment to or care for the survival and rights of women.

As Steady said to me, she was hit by the reality of the Nairobi conference's limited impact. With all its colorful pageantry, complicated diplomacy, and neutral resolutions, the conference, she realized, would have little effect on the actual lives of women in most of the world. This event, with its complicated formalities, dozens of resolutions, and spatial segregation, was not enough to realize Third World women's geopolitical goals.

Despite her dismay, Steady and other Third World women continued to invest in and work directly for UN internationalism, and they returned again and again to dozens of international UN-sponsored conferences, workshops, and panels on women. Although these gatherings were often disappointing, most women had little choice but to attend and actively participate: international conferences were indispensable sites for research and advocacy related to Third World women. Ten years later, Steady, alongside thousands of women from the NGO Forum, took a long journey in hundreds of buses to stand outside the official UN conference in the rain, surrounded by fences and the Chinese army at the fourth UN conference on women in Beijing.[146] They had traveled to listen to Hillary Rodham Clinton, then first lady of the United States, who declared, “If there is one message that echoes forth from this conference, let it be that human rights are women’s rights, and women’s rights are human rights, once and for all.” Just a few years later, in Laura Bush’s speech to the UN on International Women’s Day, women’s rights as human rights would become a primary justification for the US invasion of Iraq and Afghanistan.[147]

2

The Report, or Whatever Happened to Third World Feminist Theory?

A collective of women bears witness to the empirical quantification of their lives in the form of a data visualization on the declining status of women. This striking image frames the cover of the 1977 study *Critical Issues on the Status of Women*—a summary of the paradigm-shifting Indian report *Towards Equality*, published in 1974.[1] The cover features a familiar-looking graph with lines visualizing the declining place of women in India (figure 2.1). A white line stands in stark contrast with the graph's intricate black grid, which charts decline from 1901 to 1971 and beyond. Superimposed on the empty space below the graph is a sea of white outlines of the backs of heads, no faces in view.

From afar, the eye is pulled from the white line to the corresponding sketches of anonymous heads turned away.[2] One can infer that these outlines are the abstract forms of the subject of the study—Indian women, whose hair buns populate the crowd. In the bottom-right corner, in bold black letters, stands the acronym ICSSR, the Indian Council of Social Science Research, the young government agency that funded many of the earliest studies on women in postcolonial India.

The vertical and horizontal axes of the graph are unnamed. The reader knows only that there is urgency in this measure—an aggregate decline that is to be appraised, mapped across time, and placed on display. It is as if this

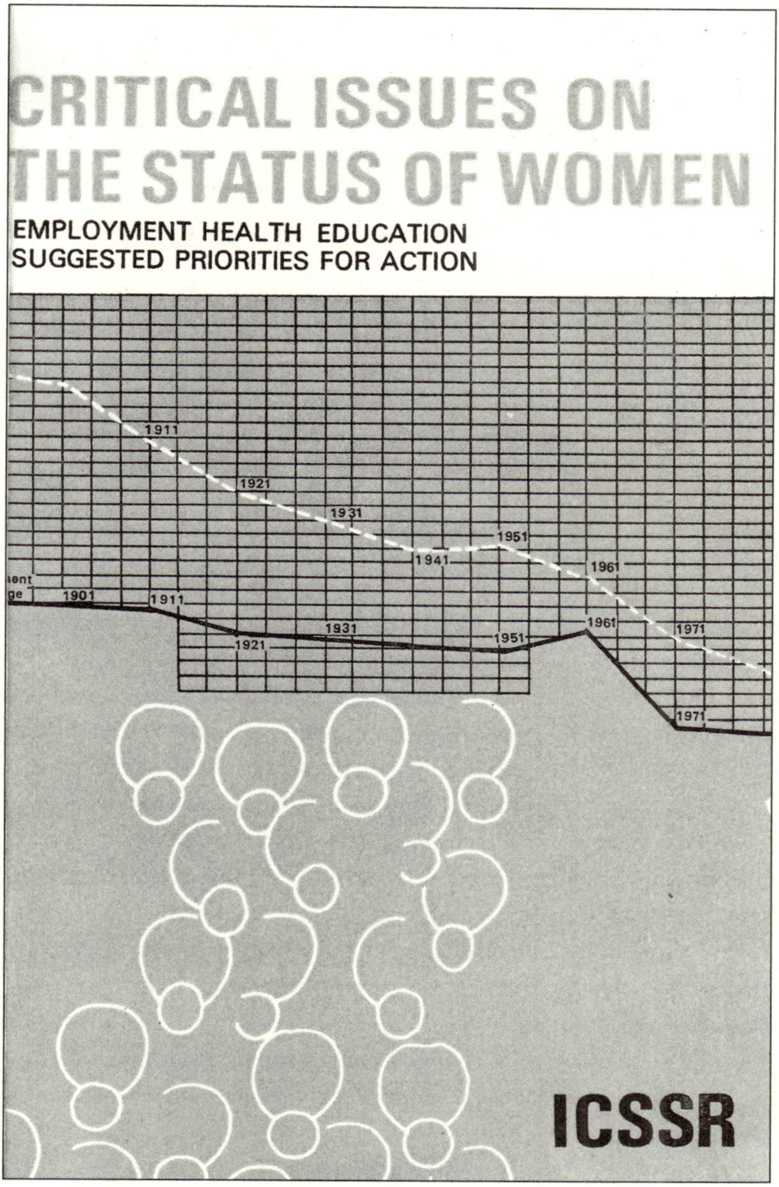

FIGURE 2.1. Cover of the 1977 summary of the India status of women report. Indian Council of Social Science Research, *Critical Issues on the Status of Women.*

collective of women is watching in anticipation of a future that is to come, a future of women's quantification through the expanding domain of the social scientific reports that have dominated the study of women in much of the world since the 1970s.

This chapter offers an account of and a reckoning with the promises and limits of the social scientific report on women through an analysis of the archives of the "status of women." Rather than attempt a comprehensive analysis of all reports from around the world with their thousands of pages of aggregate data, charts, and descriptions, I analyze the rise of the *idea* of the status of women report in the decolonizing world.[3] What forms of knowledge came under the rubric of the "status of women"? What ways of knowing have been institutionalized in the novel field of knowledge created by these reports on women, and who and what has been left out?

The archives of the status of women report reveal a paradoxical history of the promises of women's rights in a time of formal decolonization and the limits of state-sponsored social science to fulfill dreams of Third World women's liberation. Through an analysis of key early reports, women's memoirs, and oral histories with surviving women researchers, I develop a critical hermeneutic for the paradigm-shifting genre of the social scientific report on the status of women. I argue that we must confront the overwhelming dominance of the empirical report on the status of women by NGOs, states, and international organizations in much of the world and ask what has been lost in the institutionalization of empirical research on women.

The expansive political economy of research sponsored by states and international foundations became a self-perpetuating genre, confining the great majority of researchers studying global issues of women, gender, and sexuality to policy-oriented social science. As status of women reports proliferated, researchers naturalized biologically determinist notions of sexual difference that sutured the domain of women's rights to increasingly powerful fields of research like demography and population studies. The knowledge economy of the status of women report marginalized other ways of knowing and theorizing in the decolonizing world, particularly humanistic approaches to the study of women and gender.

At the heart of this chapter is an epistemological concern with what it means to know and to write women through the archives of status of women reports, which today constitute one of the most abundant sources on the world's women.

In assembling these archives, I reflect on the emancipatory promise and failures of the social sciences of women. If "description is not liberation," as

Black feminist geographer Katherine McKittrick argues with poetic repetition, then how are we to understand women researchers in the decolonizing world who saw in the description of women's status the potential for liberation?[4] Black feminist and Third World women thinkers from the 1970s and 1980s cautioned against policy research that perpetuated rhetorical fictions of the pathological deficiencies of Black, Indigenous, and Third World women.[5] Angela Davis, in her field-defining 1971 essay "Reflections on the Black Woman's Role in the Community of Slaves," critiques the premise of the "tangle of pathology" of Black women and the Black family in the 1965 Moynihan Report.[6] For Hortense Spillers, the genre of the report, epitomized by the Moynihan Report, marked women through the "powerful stillness" of reductive categories of people condemned in prescriptive typologies.[7] For Chandra Talpade Mohanty, the homogenizing impulses of First World social science on the Third World woman discursively colonized knowledge about women in most of the world.[8]

There are seemingly endless policy reports on women. Yet critical scholarship has offered little reflection on the extraordinary rise of the genre of the social science report as *the* defining form of social research on women for much of the second half of the twentieth century, especially for women of color in the First World and formerly colonized women across Asia, Africa, the Middle East, and Latin America. This chapter denaturalizes the social science report on status as a dominant form of knowledge about women and grapples with the paradoxical and sometimes uncomfortable genealogies of Third World women who personally invested in the genre of the report in their politics and labor. This generation of intellectuals were never solely anti-state, utopian, or revolutionary, even as they dissented from and protested against the state. These women critiqued yet invested in state-sponsored social scientific research and worked within and against the domain of the state in pursuit of equality and full citizenship. Through focused study on the history of the status of women reports, I explore the material and epistemological effects of the dominant genre of the study of women for "most of the world."[9]

Disciplinary Knowledge as Emancipatory Politics?

Transnational research on the status of women emerged with fervor amid the rise of Cold War–era state-sponsored social science in the spaces of Asian, African, and Caribbean decolonization.[10] In the decades of Asian and African anti-colonialism, international discourses had moved from the "woman question" of the nineteenth century to the "status of women"—that is, from the comparative assessment of civilizations to the quantified comparison of developing societies.[11] The first UN Decade of Development, in the 1960s, the rise of women's movements in the early 1970s, and the declaration of the UN International Women's Year in 1975 together spurred a veritable revolution of knowledge by and about women and a massive proliferation of social scientific studies focused on women across the decolonizing world.[12]

These policy reports, written by NGOs, nation-states, and international foundations, produced new gendered norms of citizenship and development in the 1970s and 1980s and defined what a proper woman subject in a developed nation should be and do. The early status of women reports in the 1960s and 1970s featured wide-ranging approaches to the study of women—including illustrations, engaged qualitative research, and close textual exegesis of religious texts. Yet by the late 1980s, the status of women report had been standardized with genre conventions that prioritized quantitative survey methods of demography and comparative aggregate description, conventions that soon came to dominate a vast knowledge industry on "women in development"—an ever-expanding domain of state-sponsored research and policymaking conducted by thousands of researchers and institutionalized by local women's groups, NGOs, national governments, and international organizations and foundations.

The ideas and genre conventions introduced by the expanding apparatus of the social science report on the status of women produced long-lasting legacies for women's rights and more broadly the domain of sexual rights in much of the world.[13] For newly independent governments, women's NGOs, and international foundations, the status of women report had multiple functions, serving as a descriptive assessment of the place of women in newly decolonizing societies, a reporting structure for donors, and an argument for continued funding for international and national programs. The UN deployed the report as an international metric in making new norms of rights in the comparative study of member nation-states. As I explored through the reports on Palestinian women in chapter 1, reports on women's status also became powerful sites of political contestation and contentious claims to sovereignty over knowledge.

This novel project of knowledge about women's status was framed as "action research" by leading Indian feminist Vina Mazumdar, a primary architect of the Indian status of women report, a founding figure in women's studies in India, and the first head of the ICSSR's Programme of Women's Studies.[14] For Mazumdar, action research was a novel enterprise of participatory social research that focused on the past and present condition of women in the service of new policy directives for the future. This utilitarian view of knowledge framed any and all research on women in the decolonizing world as research with a *purpose*. In this framework, the primary justification for research on women's lives was its function as a catalyst for policies that addressed women's rights and as a reparative response to the deficiencies of policy research that until the 1960s had solely focused on men. The research was to produce "immediate results" that would "solve urgent needs of women in a new nation," in the language of Bangladeshi feminist political scientist Rounaq Jahan.[15]

Thus, for Mazumdar, Jahan, and others, the study of women was not solely about scholarly inquiry. Rather, research on the status of women emerged in the Third World at a moment of feminist mobilization that sought high-impact policy change in the 1970s. Social scientific methods of documentation, sociological description, comparative classification, empirical generalization, and demographic quantification were inextricably linked to what Caribbean feminist economist Peggy Antrobus describes as the commitment of a generation of women who saw promises for feminist futures in the "cause of development" in the aftermath of colonialism around the world.[16]

For many women intellectuals in the decolonizing world, the report on women offered proof of women's presence and worth. Perhaps even more importantly, the report provided data that were essential for feminist movements fighting for the rights of women as equal citizens in decolonizing nations. The status of women reports in the 1960s and 1970s created an originary lexicon of women's rights based in the constitutional protections of equality that shaped the rise of state-sponsored feminisms.[17] The early status of women reports offer insights into feminist investments in the state prior to the formalization of relationships that have been characterized as "governance feminism," particularly the central role of social science in the making of state feminisms.[18] In many parts of the decolonizing world, the status of women reports laid the epistemological foundations for later state governance on women and gender, relationships that expanded rapidly in the decades following the UN International Women's Year.

Yet what becomes clear through the history of the report is that governance feminist priorities were limited in their impact. Although women participated in state institutions in the form of research projects and legal reforms, few policies were enforced by the state, and there was little change in the lives of most women. Today much of the intellectual work of women researchers inside and outside the academy in the decolonizing world is dedicated to writing policy reports on women for governments, NGOs, and international organizations, a contemporary reality that is difficult for many feminists.[19] This vexed history of policy research on women has shaped, and often constrained, the terrain of women's scholarly production and the institutionalization of women's studies in much of the world as we know it.

Researchers were often highly educated women from dominant classes, ethnicities, races, and castes in the Third World—women who eventually gained access to powerful international networks, resources, and ideas. These researchers self-identified as Third World women. As Mohanty argues, the often-pejorative concept of the Third World was subversively reframed by women of color around the world as a claim of solidarity between minoritized women in the First World and "the colonized, neocolonized, or decolonized countries (of Asia, Africa, and Latin America) whose economic and political structures have been deformed within the colonial process."[20] The term "Third World women" reflects the enduring power of this idea reclaimed by women in the 1970s as a feminist project of self-determination against gender inequality, racial discrimination, and economic exploitation in the aftermath of colonialism and enslavement.

The new action research on the status of women was not simply about developing new policies for Third World women. Rather, over the course of the 1970s and early 1980s, the quantification of women through empirical research on their status was deemed necessary as a new measure of the domain of life itself. These measures of development transformed the global comparative project of empirical knowledge.

Women's status was the gold standard in a new universalist calculus of economic development by postcolonial nation-states and international agencies that measured industry growth, law, employment, population, public health, and education through the aggregate study of women. Through claims of true objectivity in the dictum "statistics never lie," modern social scientists claimed to be the sole proprietors of expert knowledge that assessed and predicted the use value of the labor, health, poverty, and reproduction of most of the women of the world. By the late 1980s, scholars and policymakers declared the status of a nation's women, particularly their economic roles and labor contribution, to be the primary index of "capability" in a new lexicon of development economics that took as its central object the quantification of women and their offspring in the new social sciences of "women in development."

For development economist Amartya Sen, the concept of capability was "substantive" freedom, primarily measured by and through the status of women.[21] Free market development economics deployed concepts of "freedom" to argue for new measures of economic value. Sen, and economists who followed him, produced a widely influential economic calculus of development that exalted human productivity as the sole avenue to freedom. The line of thinking in development economics that followed, particularly in policy circles, framed women's freedom as a social good through the promotion of women's labor. This vision stood in stark contrast to Black, women of color, and decolonial feminist theories of gendered unfreedom, which argued that the bonded reproductive and productive work of women was foundational for systems of slavery and colonialism.

The quantification of women's productivity, or lack thereof—in terms of work, reproductive capacity, poverty, and death—functioned as the essential indicator of a postcolonial nation's economic development. The field of political economy, with its idealization of economic choice as the key to human agency and freedom, gained an almost mythical power in the twentieth century as the triumphant solution for every problem in social and political life.[22] The argument by development economists by the end of the century that development was freedom itself placed women at the center of a new economic calculus of liberation. And who needed freedom more than the Third World woman?

A New Global Information Order

The reports on women's legal, economic, and social status constitute one of the largest archives for research on women in the decolonizing world in the second half of the twentieth century. Comprehensive research on women was initiated around the world during the buildup to the UN International Women's Year in 1975, the event that historian Jocelyn Olcott, in her study of the first UN women's conference in Mexico City, argues was the "launch pad for an array of global feminisms."[23] Reports on women proliferated in the decades following that pivotal conference, particularly in newly independent nations eager to prove their equal status as UN member states. Soon, the status of women became the primary genre of reporting during the UN Decade for Women from 1975 to 1985 and in the years leading up to the largest UN conference on women in Beijing in 1995. By the 1980s, commissions on women and status of women reports became a norm of governance, especially for postcolonial states across Asia, Africa, Latin America, and the Caribbean.

By then, the expansive genre of the status of women report had become the primary mode of knowledge generated at a time of postcolonial internationalisms that established a "new information order." At least, that is how Peggy Antrobus described this moment in a lecture that, delivered with optimism in the middle of the UN Decade for Women, assessed the success of the decade.[24] Antrobus, the first head of the women's bureau in Jamaica, a founding member of the Third World women's research collective DAWN, a leading Caribbean feminist at the UN women's conferences, and a chronicler of the global women's movement, saw the study of women in this information order as critical for the new economic order and the new international development strategy of global development and structural adjustment programs, which sought to massively reorder social, political, and economic life in Asia, Africa, the Caribbean, and Latin America.[25]

The sudden and rapid rise of quantitative, policy-oriented social science transformed the global study of women as new domains of "women in development" emerged in the 1970s. The knowledge economy of international reports, created alongside the expansion of global conferences, as explored in chapter 1, produced enduring entanglements between national governments, women's NGOs, and international institutions of the UN and its social science apparatus—the UN Educational, Scientific and Cultural Organization (UNESCO), the UN's International Labour Organization (ILO), and the former UN Fund for Population Activities (UNFPA)—alongside international philanthropies such as the Ford Foundation.

This new social scientific language—of indices and measures of value and development for women—closely resembled an older paradigm of colonial social science. The colonial paradigm of research on women had assessed the status of women in heterosexual marriage and reproduction as the primary measure of the comparative evolution of civilizations.[26] M. Murphy has theorized that the rise of a new discourse of the "economization of life" during the Cold War in the 1960s, initiated through intertwined epistemologies of political economy and population, was built on deep histories of colonial technologies of quantification like the census.[27]

As historian Joanne Meyerowitz demonstrates, women had become the primary objects of international development programs by the 1980s, when global women emerged as the "deserving poor" in US-led microcredit programs that paradoxically reframed debt as development in emerging 1980s "gender and development" paradigms.[28] New economic, educational, and political initiatives in what First World governments and international agencies designated as the developing world resulted in massive investment in research and policy on girls and women.[29] Productive womanhood became a discrete object of knowledge in increasingly powerful fields of knowledge that shaped policymaking, including sociology, demography, family planning, economics, political science, and law.

The framework of the status of women reflected an early internationalist imaginary based in comparative legal status and hierarchies of citizenship built on an alliance of imperial nations. The call for the study of the status of women emerged as early as the 1930s in the League of Nations, though with little success in its early stages.[30] The Commission on the Status of Women, founded in June 1946 under the auspices of the UN Economic and Social Council, was subject to a new standard of international rights that emerged with the creation of the UN. Framed by the 1945 UN Charter as asserting equal rights for men and women, the commission introduced a new era of international women's rights.[31] In its first decade, the commission produced the first comprehensive data and analysis of women under the law of key European and North American UN member states. The commission initiated wide-scale research and survey projects in the 1950s, sending questionnaires to member states on country-specific data related to the status of women under the law, women's education, and women's work.[32]

In the 1950s, the Commission on the Status of Women mobilized the research capacity of UNESCO and the ILO to conduct research on women's political rights and access to education.[33] In a major meeting in Calcutta in 1958, UNESCO brought together international social scientists to discuss the importance of modern social science to documenting rapid changes at a time of nation-building and decolonization around the world. The UNESCO-sponsored social scientists identified the "status of women—politically, economically, socially, and educationally"—as a primary area of research for the agency. The Calcutta meeting resulted in one of the first comprehensive studies of the status of women anywhere in the world, *Women in the New Asia*.[34] It was followed in 1964 by a special issue of the *UNESCO Courier*, that body's official journal, comprising studies that spanned eleven countries in South and Southeast Asia. By 1967, UNESCO and the Social Development Section of the Economic Commission for Africa had produced the first comprehensive status of women report for Africa, *The Status and Role of Women in East Africa*, a comprehensive study of the status of women in six newly independent countries in east Africa.[35]

By the 1960s, the status of women was linked to an expanding domain of family planning programs under the UN. In 1968, Helvi Sipilä, representative from Finland, became the special rapporteur for the Status of Women and Family Planning Project under the UN, the first position of its kind.[36] Under this project, Sipilä would sponsor numerous research studies and initiatives that culminated in a comprehensive large-scale, multi-country comparative study during the lead-up to the 1975 International Women's Year conference. In the 1970s, the UNFPA, with the support of international foundations, including Rockefeller and Ford, funded twenty-six "Law and Population" projects in the "developing world" on the status of women in laws pertaining to "family planning."[37] These reports were produced primarily by international social scientists based in universities and research institutes in the United States and Europe.

Status of women commissions began proliferating around the world. The first national studies were convened by the United States, the United Kingdom, Poland, Denmark, China (Taiwan), and Afghanistan, with special government sections set up to study the status of women in Argentina, Australia, Austria, Canada, Japan, Libya, and Norway.[38] The first and most visible national government status of women report was produced in 1963 under President John F. Kennedy, with the publication of *American Women*. The report was the result of a presidential commission, first led by Eleanor Roosevelt, whose twenty-eight members included cabinet members, senators, social scientists, and leaders of social organizations representing African American, Jewish, and Catholic women. The final report was relatively short, fewer than seventy-five pages, with brief sections on achieving equality through the domains of women's education, home life, employment, and legal status.

The next large-scale report was produced in Canada in 1970. The Canadian report, in contrast with the US report, was nearly 500 pages long; its ten chapters covered women's status in everything from their place in society to the economy, education, the family, childcare, public life, citizenship, and criminal law; the report also presented a plan of action to achieve women's equality. The Royal Commission on the Status of Women in Canada collected information from researchers, activists, and people across Canada in the form of 468 briefs and over 1,000 opinion letters, and 890 people were consulted by the commission in town halls and meetings held in fourteen cities.[39] Ireland's Commission on the Status of Women, convened in 1970, published a preliminary status of women report in 1971 that focused on the issue of equal pay in relation to women's employment and included a section on marriage laws.[40]

Ireland's report was quickly followed by India's in 1974 and Trinidad and Tobago's in 1975. The Canadian status of women commissioner served as a guiding expert for the latter, much to the chagrin of some women researchers in Trinidad and Tobago who had very different goals for their report.[41]

In preparation for the UN conference for the International Women's Year, the government of Ghana established the National Council on Women and Development in February 1975. The organization's mandate was to conduct research on women and to advise the government on new development policies related to women. From 1975, the Ghanaian government sponsored a number of research studies on women's status in the domains of politics, education, and gender inequality under the law and in society.

These groundbreaking status reports set key standards for what was to be contained in an inquiry into the status of women. The domain of the study expanded exponentially in the years that followed, particularly in those conducted by nation-states across the decolonizing world, which utilized reports to measure international development goals and access essential international funding under new funding streams of the UN, UN partners, and private foundations. By 1979, Sri Lanka, Nepal, and Barbados, among many others, had published their own comprehensive national status of women reports.

But the single most important catalyst for the generation of knowledge in the novel genre of the status of women report was the official decision to declare the first UN International Women's Year in 1975.[42] In 1968, during the lead-up to the Mexico City conference, the UN Commission on the Status of Women initiated an international survey of its member states. By the 1970s, the language of the "status of women" had been established as a key marker of international development in debates about women's rights in most of the world. This knowledge project about women was initiated across domains, from the studies of small women-led NGOs and labor cooperative networks to the national governments of UNESCO and UNFPA member states and international foundations.

The Ford Foundation would come to play a vital role in the creation of the status of women as a distinct object of inquiry, and it would become a key patron of Third World women researchers. With new UN initiatives building research on women, the Ford Foundation abruptly shifted from funding small programs on women's "home economics" to making massive investments in empirical social scientific research on women's status under new initiatives on "women in development" over the course of the 1970s. Ford Foundation program officers such as Elinor Barber and Adrienne Germain produced reports on the "status" of women across decolonizing spaces in Asia and North and East Africa, including India, Pakistan, Nepal, Bangladesh, Indonesia, Thailand, the Philippines, Egypt, Ghana, and Kenya, and directed funds to local researchers to conduct social scientific studies on women's status and women in development.[43]

In a 1974 Ford memorandum, "Poor Women: A New-Feminist View," Germain argued that Third World women were foundational for reaching international aid and development goals. For Germain, who had traveled widely to report on women's status, the study of women in the "developing world" was essential because "women's roles, their status, and their life conditions are not just a symptom of underdevelopment but a cause."[44] Germain's argument—that women were key to Third World development—would become commonplace by the late 1970s, providing a primary justification for expanding the empirical study of women.

In a meeting in December 1979, the Ford Foundation's trustees made a pivotal shift in their funding priorities toward programs that funded research on and outreach to women to "eliminate sex discrimination" and "integrating a concern for women's status and roles" into existing Ford-funded programs.[45] The foundation created a special working group to focus on programs and funding related to women; it was led by Barber, Germain, and program officers Mariam Chamberlain, who used Ford funding to develop women's studies in American universities, and Terry Saario, who committed resources to women's education programs. The Ford Foundation also began to fund key publications authored by Third World women researchers on women's status, including key reports by scholar Soha Abdel Kader on the status of women in Egypt and by political scientist Rounaq Jahan on the condition of women in the newly independent nation of Bangladesh.[46]

Over the course of the 1970s, numerous national, UN, and foundation-sponsored reports on the status of women were published. Ford funded the travel and participation of Third World women as well as women of color from the United States to attend the UN international conferences on women beginning in 1975 in Mexico City, throughout the UN Decade for Women, and until the 1995 UN women's conference in Beijing. Ford also became a key source of funding for a wide range of the earliest women's studies programs and centers throughout the 1980s and 1990s in Asia, Africa, the Caribbean, and Latin America and among historically Black colleges and universities in the United States.[47]

The Status of Comparison

What kind of information can be found in the early status of women reports? The policy report is so commonplace that most people have some familiarity with the genre. Status of women reports often list an agency or commission as the author without any individual names. These reports include a uniform table of contents and introduction that give a broad overview of the study, feature chapters that succinctly summarize key findings of research, and end with policy recommendations.

Yet, as I explore next, there was little standardization of status of women reports in the range of areas researched. What was standard was the premise of the study: a universal idea of integration-based equality under the law in "women's status" in relation to an unspoken comparison to the status of men. From their inception, national and comparative multi-country status of women reports included little reflection on the use of a universal category of "woman" and offered no parameters for what constituted the domain of "status." Women were to be equated, made commensurate, and analogized across time and geographies, a project of universal comparison that traveled from the narrow domain of legal status and women's equality before the law to encompass all aspects of political, social, and economic life. These self-evident categories of "equality," "women," and "status" were taken as the foundations for a comparative project of international rights based in the newly enshrined constitutional rights of universal equality in new democracies around the world.

In 1974, in advance of the International Women's Year, the UN initiated its largest project of comparative studies of the status of women in independent member states, focusing on women's legal status across geographies where "law" was defined broadly as all aspects of government policy related to women. The results of these studies were published, to much fanfare, in a single volume in English in 1976 in the *Columbia Human Rights Law Review*. With a congratulatory preface by Helvi Sipilä, who was then serving as the UN secretary-general of the International Women's Year and assistant secretary-general for social development and humanitarian affairs, the issue featured monographs on the status of women by scholars on location in fifteen countries: Brazil, Egypt, France, Ghana, India, Indonesia, Iran, Jamaica, Kenya, Peru, the Philippines, Sweden, Togo, the United States, and Yugoslavia. National scholars with expertise in law, political science, and the broad field of "population studies" were commissioned across these regions to produce reports on the legal status of women during the lead-up to the International Women's Year conference, which was the "needed impetus to research on the status of women," according to Sipilä.[48]

Such a comparative study of the legal status of women was imagined as a project essential for women's equality. Women's equality, for the UN, required the freeing of women from "bondage" in systems of patriarchy in the Third World, but the problems of population growth and "family planning" also needed to be addressed. For Luke T. Lee, executive secretary of the International Advisory Committee on Population and Law, the purpose of comparative cross-sectional studies of the status of women was the pursuit of total equality, where an ideal system of law would free women from the bondage of cultural "tradition." In his introduction to the issue, Lee asks, "Is it possible to alter these traditional approaches so that women will be neither enslaved nor caged, but accorded complete equality with men, in law and in fact?"[49] The *fact* of women's status, when released from the "enslavement" of their subordination to men, was to be measured in country reports produced through the joint research ventures of the UN and NGOs.

The fifteen detailed studies of women and the law published in the *Columbia Human Rights Law Review* demonstrate that the principle of equality defined the comparative study of the status of women and yet led to very different descriptions of women's status. The legal status of women was to be researched across geographies as a discrete domain of knowledge, produced as a set of commensurate data points, and assimilated into a list of concrete policy recommendations. "Legal status" was generalized to encompass all legal, social, and economic policies that defined women's lives in and beyond the formal domain of the law in sovereign states. Reflecting the dominant presence of population studies in the international study of women, the category of "women" in these studies appears as a self-evident biological classification, a given demographic category for half of the population rather than a political idea or socially constituted category.

The table of contents sought to produce consistency across the reports, with each country study offering data in the same order: general problems related to women and the law, political and civil rights, penal law (including laws against rape, abortion, and, in some reports, homosexuality), health and family planning, education, employment, policy recommendations, and a historical timeline of laws. The objects of inquiry were static across the country reports: "women" was a biological given, "legal status" was any kind of government policy that could be linked to women, and the domains of law, from criminal and civil law to economic policy, were comparable across nation-states despite their vastly different legal structures and codes.

The volume offered uniform content and fixed key terms for each chapter, but individual case studies offered very different information to explain the status of women in their countries. While Sweden proclaimed that Swedish women were always-already equal and had been "held in high esteem" in Sweden from 800 to 900 CE onward, the timelines for postcolonial nations tell a drastically different story.[50] In postcolonial reports, colonialism caused a violent fracturing of colonized societies through homogenizing laws that forced heterosexual monogamous marriage and patriarchal property regimes on diverse and plural communities that practiced a wide range of kin relations, from matriarchy to polygamy.

Country studies from Brazil, Ghana, Indonesia, Kenya, Peru, the Philippines, and Togo begin with the problem of the inheritance of multiple colonial legal structures that led to women's continued subordination through "household servitude" and "procreational servitude," in the language of Véronique Dagadzi, a magistrate in Togo and the author of that country's status of women report.[51] For Yaa Luckham, a faculty member at the University of Dar es Salaam and the author of Ghana's report, the study of the status of women exposed the "social stresses and conflicts in a post-colonial pluralistic society" in the wake of British colonialism.[52] Irene Cortes, the first woman to serve as dean of the University of the Philippines College of Law and the author of the Philippines report, attributed the subordinated status of women to colonial structures of law: "Filipino women have never been forced to hide themselves behind veils, to have bound feet, or to walk several paces behind their male companions. But under the Civil Code introduced by Spain, married women were classified with incompetents like the insane, the deaf mutes, the civilly interdicted and minors."[53] The study of the status of women became fertile ground to launch a substantive critique of inherited colonial structures of law and the dangers of incomplete processes of decolonization.

The reports and their recommendations also expressed unrealized visions for women's legal rights across geographies from the 1970s. The promise of equality for women in a decolonizing world was near, and the comparative assessment of the status of women was critical to ensuring that promised future. Reports utilized the language of women "caged," in "servitude," in conditions of the "enslaved" under patriarchy, in contrast with the "freedom" promised by the new constitutional rights for women as full citizen subjects introduced over the twentieth century. With women's suffrage and legal equality came the possibility of freedom. For Shahnaz Sadjadi and Marianne Hedin-Pourghasemi, research associates at the Pahlavi Population Center in Shiraz, Iran, women had achieved near-equality under the law in Iran by 1976.[54] Published three years before the Iranian Revolution in 1979, their extensive study of the status of women in Iran imagines a vastly different trajectory for women's equal status under the law than what was to come.

The special issue of the *Columbia Human Rights Law Review* was among the first of many large-scale comparative status of women projects that followed. Ambiguity in the definitions of "status" and "women" served the comparative internationalist project well, as universalist terms could be widely applied as standards across geographies to use the new research on women to assess the progress of nation-states. This project of equivalence, based in comparative indicators, was critical for a growing internationalist infrastructure that placed women at the center of a global project of commensurability.[55]

The Status of Equality

At a moment of rising authoritarianism and conservative populist movements across regions in West and South Asia and sub-Saharan Africa in the late 1970s, as women writers worked both within and against the postcolonial state, the international report became critical for articulating priority areas for emerging local and national women's movements. India's aptly named *Towards Equality* report was published in December 1974, more than ten years after the first status of women report in the United States.[56] The Status of Women Commission in India was created by the government of India in September 1971. The production of the final report was risky, and its publication shrouded in secrecy, as it revealed stunning failures of the Indian government to address women's inequality in postcolonial India.[57] The report circulated widely, and in the decades that followed it was proclaimed to be a "founding document" of the priorities of the Indian women's movement that set the agenda for one of the most significant Third World women's movements.[58]

The report was authored by ten prominent women leaders and activists with expertise in social science and the law, none of whom held formal government office. The report built on a long tradition of data-gathering on women in fact-finding missions dating back to women's movements in late colonial India. Including supplemental materials, *Towards Equality* was almost five hundred pages long, including multiple appendices and bibliographic references. It had nine chapters, with numerous subsections on a wide range of subjects. Women's equality was the framing concept for the study, while the breadth of the areas that constituted women's equality was vast, reaching far beyond the country reports of the UN studies of legal status. The report featured sections on demography, sex ratios, fertility and "family planning"; detailed the composition of religious traditions, including Hinduism, Islam, Christianity, Buddhism, Jainism, Sikhism, Bhakti traditions, tribal religions, Zoroastrianism, and Veerasaivism; and offered descriptions of marriage forms, Indian matrilineal versus patrilineal systems, and commentary about women engaged in prostitution, unmarried mothers, elderly women and widows, and women in prisons. *Towards Equality* addressed issues of adoption, inheritance, customary personal laws, spousal support, unorganized labor, agricultural labor, wage employment, service labor and the professions, and women's education.

The *Towards Equality report* is a dense artifact that testifies to the complex history of the politics of social research in an increasingly technocratic postcolonial state and offers a partial glimpse of complex social and political worlds translated into the language of seemingly neutral descriptions of women's inequality and palatable policy recommendations. The commission carried out nationwide surveys and collected government studies conducted at the local and national levels related to all aspects of women's lives to that point. The introduction offers a summary of the wide-ranging research methods undertaken to produce the report: "The intention of the Committee was to interview a cross section of women from different walks of life, in the distinctive regions of each State. . . . On an average the Committee met about 500 women belonging to different categories in each State. These tours were of immense value, for acquiring an understanding of the conditions of women in different parts of the country, as well as for clarifying the Committee's approach to its task."[59] The cross-country "tour" of women became the primary framework for the assessment of women's status. Members of the committee traveled to every state in India, meeting around twenty thousand women across India in less than two years. They worked closely with the newly formed ICSSR to produce comprehensive demographic studies of women. The committee held thirty-one meetings over sixty-five days and completed the report in less than fourteen months.[60]

We learn from *Towards Equality* that many methods were used to produce the final report. Research methods included oral interviews, focus groups, collective gatherings, demographic surveys, and statistical analysis. In the process of producing the report, the commission created its own archives of qualitative and quantitative data and condensed this information. The research for the project was conducted at a scale never seen before; it was undoubtedly the largest research undertaking on Indian women to date.

Yet, despite the vast terrains traveled to collect information, *Towards Equality* does not include other forms and genres that may have been part of these social and political lives at the time of researchers' cross-country visits: songs, poems, chants, or any narratives that troubled the category of "women" or accounted for caste subordination and religious differences enforced in eating, touching, and cleaning that may have shaped these focus group encounters. Any details about the affective life of research are instead found in the rare memoir, oral history, or personal essays of prominent women.[61] Nor does anything remain of the diverse textual and research material that forms the citational apparatus of the status of women reports, including the hundreds of letters submitted to commissions, petitions from women's groups, and empirical sociological and demographic studies from a wide range of fields commissioned by the ICSSR. The absence of narratives, affective expressions, and quotidian details about social life in a policy report is perhaps unsurprising in this genre of action research, which promised social scientific objectivity in aggregate organized around abstract principles of measurable equality.

Still, the key archive that remains of the report is the report itself, and the many written forms, genres, and perspectives that it took to constitute the document have largely disappeared into history.

The guiding concept for the report was the equality of the sexes, much like the fifteen country reports in the *Columbia Human Rights Law Review*. Indeed, the twentieth-century constitutional imaginary of secular equality was a defining principle in many new postcolonial constitutions and became an important feature of the status of women reports. Equality for the decolonizing world was newly enshrined as a right for women under new and progressive constitutions. Yet the authors of *Towards Equality* emphasized that the constitutional principle of equality of men and women had little meaning on the ground in a society like India, where equality was not a universal value in the face of a deeply unequal "traditional society": "Equality is an article of faith in our Constitution and guaranteed by specific articles. We could, therefore, treat this as a settled fact, for which no discussion was necessary. Our investigation, however, proved that there was still considerable ambiguity as well as ambivalence in the general understanding of the need and implications of sex equality in our country."[62] These critical interventions addressing women's equality defined womanhood primarily through the position of women as wives and mothers and continued to define the priorities of a dominant lineage of the women's movement primarily through heterosexual reproduction.

Equality for women could not simply be enshrined as a principle in the constitution. The authors of *Towards Equality* declared that this required a wide range of special policies that would address the subordination of women: "We believe . . . that if our society is to move in the direction of the goal set by the Constitution, then special temporary measures will be necessary to transform *de jure* into *de facto* equality."[63] The elusive goal of women's equality mandated inquiries into the status of women in and beyond the law, across domains that would result in special policies for women in everything from education to labor. In this view, the study of women's status was a key mode to political justice in the lives of women.

Perhaps the most striking feature of *Towards Equality* appears at the end of the report: a powerful note of dissent from two of its well-known authors, Lotika Sarkar and Vina Mazumdar.[64] Sarkar and Mazumdar argued that women required reserved seats for political office, in opposition to the view of other authors of the *Towards Equality* report and in contrast to the position of Indian feminists of an earlier generation who did not believe in any special provisions for reservations for women in government. Their dissent pointed out the failures of formal equality before the law when the social world was so profoundly unequal for women and prevented them from accessing their basic rights: "Our reasons for dissenting on this matter are consistent with the findings, that run throughout the Report, that despite progressive legal changes, the actual condition of life of the mass of Indian women has not changed much."[65]

Strikingly, Sarkar and Mazumdar's dissent was published at a moment when India had its first woman prime minister, Indira Gandhi. Gandhi's place as a woman leader was no doubt vexed for the growing women's movement, which argued for the need to have women in office yet insisted on the inadequacy of powerful women like Gandhi, who did not represent the views of progressive Indian feminists. On June 25, 1975, just six months after the publication of *Towards Equality*, and in the middle of the UN women's conference in Mexico City, Gandhi declared a period of emergency law, later called "the Emergency." During the Emergency, Gandhi installed a set of authoritarian measures that suspended civil liberties to secure her power and violated a wide range of human rights, including a forced sterilization campaign for "population control."[66]

The struggle to gather data on women was not unique to India but a phenomenon that many feminists from South Asia argued required substantive innovation for the social study of women, particularly because the social conditions of women's seclusion created unique challenges for researchers in the region. For political scientist Rounaq Jahan, in her 1975 study of women's status in Bangladesh conducted as part of the collective research group Women for Women, the absence of knowledge was a failure of knowledge and methods in understanding social life. Jahan begins her report on the status of women in Bangladesh with a similar declaration about the struggle to write about the status of women: "It is difficult to write about women in Bangladesh. Little published material is available on women. . . . The vast majority of Bangladesh's 35 million women live in *purdah*, and little is being said or written about their problems." As Jahan notes, the lack of women researchers made accessing and compiling statistical and qualitative data on women more challenging, as "the lack of data on women" resulted from the extensive "difficulties researchers (usually male) face in studying women in a purdah dominated society."[67]

Yet the real problem was that women's issues were completely unrecognized in research as a premise for research. Besides the lack of data, the failure of male-dominated research methods to address the isolation of women compounded a problem that made research on women difficult even for local women researchers of the same communities. The problems faced by women living in *purdah* persisted: "The fact that nothing is being written about the problems of women in Bangladesh does not mean that the problems do not exist. Indeed, women of Bangladesh are one of the most oppressed in the world."[68] The social seclusion of women was reflected in the statistical seclusion of women. It was the work of the Third World woman researcher, according to Jahan, to "draw attention" to the conditions of women and make them a legitimate object of study. Then only would the problem of women's oppression be visible and actionable by the state.

The challenge of data collection on women was a common concern mentioned in status reports across geographies. Like Jahan, Nepali scholar Meena Acharya, a feminist development economist and the lead author of an ambitious 1979 report on the status of women in Nepal, expressed frustration at the difficulties that women researchers faced amid the absence of good data about women: "The task of drawing a truly representative statistical profile of Nepalese women is a difficult one. . . . Existing statistical sources and research studies in Nepal do not offer enough information on these and many other aspects of women's lives."[69] The absence of data and the inability to classify women's work and social roles led to a lack of political will to change the condition of women.

In the face of political inaction, the international momentum for comprehensive status of women reports created an opening for innovation in methods and approaches to studying and disseminating knowledge about women. Acharya recognized this opportunity, calling for a direct link between the Nepal status of women research project and a comprehensive national plan of action for women in Nepal. Acharya, alongside a team of expert researchers, began an expansive status of women project that resulted in a years-long process of research and writing on the status of women through detailed sociological and economic studies of different ethnic groups in Nepal. The first report, a statistical survey of women, was published in 1979 by Acharya. The second part of the project spanned multiple studies of ethnography "field studies" on women's status in eight different ethnic groups published in 1981.

Compared to contemporaneous reports from South Asia that are entirely text, the Nepal status of women report is unusual in its inclusion of visuals. It features an extensive number of photographs of women and children as part of its studies on women's status. On the cover of volume 1 of the first report authored by Acharya, *The Status of Women in Nepal*, the viewer sees a collage of photographs of Nepali women and children in a classic ethnographic "development studies" style, including a hand applying *sindoor* to a woman's face during the marriage ceremony, a smiling young girl with a lesson book on her lap, a woman breastfeeding an infant, and a determined-looking woman walking with a child holding her hand.[70]

The photographs are credited to Ane Haaland, a social scientist who coauthored the 1976 UN Children's Fund (UNICEF) report, *Communicating with Pictures in Nepal*, which argued for simplified line drawings for pamphlets because development programs were particularly challenging to implement among the largely "illiterate population," which, for the authors, required a communication style akin to picture books for children.[71] Many of the Indigenous communities of the region had long been subject to colonial ethnographic research, including ethnographic photography. The text of UNICEF's *Pictures* report promoted broad UN recommendations for communication styles in "the developing world" in the 1960s and 1970s. UNICEF's promotion of the use of stereotypical images and photographs followed in the long tradition of colonial ethnographic photography, prioritizing a kind of pedagogy of the masses through typological photographs and stereotypical line drawing images of common women in status reports.

The predominance of photographic images and drawings in Nepal's status of women reports, along with the publication of extensive regional field studies of women of distinct ethnic communities, distinguished the project from contemporaneous status reports from other states in the decolonizing world that had no photography or images besides data visualizations in graphs and charts.[72] The emphasis on photography and drawings and ethnicity-based regional study in Nepal's status project extended decades-long ethnographic studies of Nepal's multi-ethnic and largely rural village society. Yet Nepal's report also reflected a broader emphasis on visual forms in status studies and the ubiquitous use of photographs of unnamed subjects in social scientific development studies of Third World women from the early 1980s onward.

The status of women report was a novel genre that generated new methods of collecting data and visualizing women, spurring an entire infrastructure to support an expanding knowledge economy focused on women. The study of the status of women led directly to the institutionalization of social scientific study in the study of women—most importantly the creation and institutionalization of women's studies across the Third World in the 1970s and 1980s. The authors of the country reports in the *Columbia Human Rights Law Review* were prominent legal scholars, magistrates, and researchers who went on to write national status of women reports, attend UN conferences on women, and found women's studies departments, institutes, and centers. The authors of India's *Towards Equality* report, including Neera Desai, Vina Mazumdar, and Lotika Sarkar, would go on to create the women's studies program at SNDT Women's University in Bombay and build the Center for Women in Developing Societies in Delhi, the first centers and institutes dedicated to the study of women in India.[73] The report also led to Mazumdar's employment as the first head of women's studies under the newly formed Indian Institute of Social Science Research, the single largest national funder of social research in India. Bangladeshi feminist Rounaq Jahan built the Women for Women research collective in Bangladesh, one of the first Third World research networks, and, like others, she went on to hold key positions at the UN. Meena Acharya, who led the groundbreaking project in Nepal, would later work for the World Bank and serve as a long-term consultant for the UN on women.

Following the first status of women reports, women's studies as a social science enterprise was institutionalized across the decolonizing world in the form of university departments, centers, and government institutes. These institutions, dedicated to the social scientific study of women and development, were funded by national governments, the UN, and foundations like Ford.[74] Early reports on women's status, which set out to prove the very existence of women, were critical to the expanding legitimacy of the social scientific study of women for women's rights in the decolonizing world in the 1970s and 1980s.[75]

A return to this moment demonstrates that the status of women report made palatable a politics of women's rights and equality built on the resources of the state. The authors of the reports saw in the genre a means to claim subversive, sometimes radical politics against patriarchal power in the language of seemingly neutral bureaucratic change, an approach that significantly differed from movements that saw their goals as primarily anti-state and anti-capitalist.[76] For the women who authored the status of women reports, claims for women's equal status and social rights were strategically placed in the domains of the "social" and "economic," a seemingly neutral language used to avoid direct confrontations with a sensitive postcolonial state on the brink of becoming an emergency authoritarian regime and under increasing pressures from the international aid community.[77] This history reveals how early feminist researchers invested in the genre of the social science report to launch substantive critiques of law in the aftermath of colonialism and produce potentially transformative policy reforms for women.

Yet it also demonstrates how quickly the domain of feminist politics was assimilated into the policy-oriented language of the postcolonial state and comparative international rights. The archives of Third World women reveal that Third World women expended extensive intellectual labor on state projects and translated visions for women's liberation into the quantitative, demographic genre of the status of women report. For these researchers, the knowledge project was the first step toward a radical shift in the condition of women. Yet these histories demonstrate the vexed history of Third World feminist politics that worked both in tandem with and against the state. The postcolonial state, with its expansive bureaucratic technologies of social scientific research, was a promising if limited and limiting tool of women's emancipation.

The Suppression of Status

What of the many reports that never came into being? A history of suppressed reports and performative government commissions on women highlights the contradictory role of the status of women report in the history of women's rights in the decolonizing world at a time of rising authoritarian regimes in the decades after formal decolonization. Government reports on women were offered on the international stage as proof of good governance by authoritarian regimes in postcolonial spaces. States claimed political legitimacy by convening numerous commissions in the name of women's rights. Yet postcolonial governments often quickly suppressed the research and policy recommendations that resulted from these commissions.

The example of postcolonial Pakistan's suppressed status of women reports offers a stark contrast with the publication and triumphant legacy of India's *Towards Equality* report, which was heralded as a founding moment in the women's movement in 1970s India. From the 1970s on, the Pakistani state produced multiple "status of women" reports, a history that reveals the paradoxical role of women's rights in postcolonial spaces in a new global economic order. The status of women, as reported, reflected the will of the government in power; despite the presentation of objectivity in research, the report was never a neutral object. Every stage of writing and publishing the report was political, from information-gathering to empirical description to data analysis and policy development. For the Pakistani state, the threat of women's equality was acute, as it again and again redacted, suppressed, and disappeared reports on women.

In 1976, one year after India's report was spurred by the UN women's conference in Mexico City, the first commission on women in Pakistan authored a government-sponsored report on the status of women. Created after the ratification of the new 1973 Pakistani constitution, which guaranteed equality of the sexes, the commission set out to conduct the first comprehensive study of women in postcolonial Pakistan.[78] The commission's mandate was to conduct research that would ameliorate women's "social, legal and economic conditions" in Pakistan in the aftermath of constitutional crises and wars, including the national crisis and violent suppression of an independence movement that ultimately resulted in the creation of Bangladesh in 1971.[79] The commission produced a detailed report on the status of women in Pakistan; initially presented to the Commission of Law Reforms, the report was immediately suppressed by the government under Zulfikar Ali Bhutto and was never publicly released or implemented in policy.

Soon after, in 1977, Bhutto was overthrown in a military coup that brought General Muhammad Zia-ul-Haq to power. The report of this first commission on the status of women was permanently disappeared in the aftermath of the coup. The ambitious 182-page report from 1976 set forth a radical agenda for women's equality before the law and beyond in Pakistan and was only made available after Zia's death. The report's two major parts paralleled other country reports from the 1970s, particularly the India report. Addressing the legal status of women, the first part provided wide-ranging analysis of ways to improve women's status in family law, employment law, criminal codes and procedure, and laws related to political parties. The report recommended that a law be passed to establish a permanent commission on the status of women in Pakistan. The second half of the report explored other major aspects of women's status, from their social status to their education and textbooks and their employment and working conditions, and it also reported on women's professions, health, and experiences of discrimination.[80]

After officially dismissing the 1976 report, Zia swiftly implemented the Hudood Ordinances in 1979, draconian laws that claimed to adhere to Sharia law and limited women's access to citizenship, bodily autonomy, and legal rights. These laws resembled other stringent legal regimes passed across the Muslim world following the rise of Islamic movements from 1979 onward. In response, there were numerous public protests by visible women's groups fighting the repression and subordination of women under the Hudood Ordinances. This moment of military authoritarianism and Islamization under Zia spurred a new wave of women's movements and the growth of women's rights organizations by the early 1980s.

With the forced suppression of the 1976 report from the policies of all state ministries and the new code of the Hudood Ordinances, Zia faced a growing outcry from women against their oppression under Muslim law. In response to women's opposition to draconian laws and mass mobilization against the government, Zia convened his own Commission on the Status of Women in 1983, which published a very different report in 1985.[81] According to this report, the Commission on the Status of Women was formed with intentions very different from those of the 1976 commission, which was committed to secular rights. Zia's commission was based in a stated intention to "Islamicise society" and "safeguard the rights of women as provided by the Holy Quran and the Sunnah," while also responding to increasing demands from NGOs and women's organizations.[82]

Zia's institutionalization of his own bureau on the status of women and commissioning of a report was symbolic of the performative nature of women's rights at a time of postcolonial authoritarianism. The status of women commission and report functioned as critical tools for postcolonial dictators to demonstrate their commitment to internationalism. Seeking continuity in the loans from the International Monetary Fund and the World Bank that made their wealth possible, leaders like Zia, among other authoritarian leaders in Asia and Africa, utilized women's bureaus and status of women reports to perform their adherence to democratic internationalism on the global stage, all the while enforcing authoritarian rule through patriarchal religious laws at home.

And yet, even as Zia tried to manipulate international norms for an authoritarian state project based in the subjugation of women, the second status of women commission boldly went against his intended aims. This second report was, at its heart, an anti-authoritarian statement of feminist dissent against the Hudood Ordinances of Zia's Pakistan. The second report was composed by twenty-five women. While it was officially authorized by

Zia to demonstrate his compliance with international norms and mandates on women's issues, the report offered a bold reformulation of the genre of the status of women report by and through a feminist hermeneutical interpretation of Muslim law.

The report shifted the study of women's status from the assessment of secular laws that promised equality for women under postcolonial constitutionalism toward a textual exegesis of Muslim religious texts, arguing for women's equality under the logic of Muslim law, in opposition to the discrimination against women under Zia's Hudood Ordinances. One of the authors of the suppressed report from 1976, Begum Zari Sarfaraz, a social worker, advocate for women's rights, and leading public health expert, was appointed chair of the new Status of Women Commission under Zia. Yet, like the 1976 report, this report was suppressed by Zia's government, in this case because it offered a vehement critique of the legal subordination of women based in textual interpretations of the Qur'an. Zia imagined a commission that would justify his draconian Hudood Ordinances, but instead he received a powerful articulation of dissent in the language of Muslim law.

The 1985 report reflected the way the framework of the status of women could be used to make an argument for women's equality under Muslim law rather than secular constitutionalism based in principles of abstract equality. Following Zia's assassination, newly installed prime minister Benazir Bhutto made the key political move of finally publishing the report in 1989. Bhutto understood the power of the report's critique during Zia's reign and knew that releasing it would expose women's staunch criticisms of his gender-discriminatory, patriarchal interpretations of Sharia law. The delayed publication of the disappeared report also revealed conflict inside the 1985 commission: in a dissent written in Urdu (unlike the main report, which was written in English) conservative religious scholar Begum Nisar Fatima insisted that Islamic law did not guarantee women's equality and that women were subordinate to men.

In 1997, the government of Pakistan successfully published an official status of women report, the first such report not to be suppressed immediately upon production. This report was published two decades after the 1976 study on the status of women was produced and disappeared, more than a decade after the 1985 report and its suppression under Zia, and almost ten years before the passage of the Women's Protection Bill of 2006, which finally overturned the Hudood Ordinances. The authors of this report included Asma Jahangir, a premier feminist leader and human rights lawyer who had been arrested and jailed during Zia's regime. Her participation in the democratic state feminist project of Pakistan's third status of women commission and report, coming after decades of her radical opposition to authoritarianism, spoke to the complex and shifting terrain of feminist engagements with and in opposition to the state. The report signified a concerted effort by Pakistani feminists to turn away from the patriarchal institutions and laws brought by Islamization under Zia and return to the constitutional promises of secular equality.

To further the circulation of ideas on the published status of women report, Shirkat Gah Women's Resource Centre, a women's organization created in the 1970s in opposition to the Zia government, produced a summary of the 1997 commission report titled *Towards a Better Tomorrow: The Report of the Commission of Inquiry for Women*. This text, like the ICSSR's summary of *Towards Equality* produced twenty years earlier in India, condensed and translated key ideas and recommendations from the commission on women report for wide distribution. For a new generation of Pakistani feminists in the 1990s, it was imperative that the new status of women report not be suppressed like those that had come before. Its publication was urgent: "The main purpose behind this Simplified Version is to bring this dream of a better tomorrow to a wider group of people—men and women, students and teachers, bureaucrats and politicians, activists and idealists. By doing this, Shirkat Gah hopes that the Commission of Inquiry Report will not suffer the same fate as previous reports on women's status, which gathered dust on the shelves of government offices."[83] As with the use of the term "towards" in India's *Towards Equality* report, Shirkat Gah argued that the status of women was about aspirations *toward* a better future, a promise of a "better tomorrow."

The cover of Shirkat Gah's 1997 summary report on the status of women in Pakistan, like that of the 1977 India report, features a powerful image that frames the study (figure 2.2). In the center is a woman, embodied through the Linnaean symbol for woman. She is outside of the household, a working woman, with the door of her home appearing in the distance behind her. The cross-sectional element of the symbol is transformed into the arms of an abstract woman in a balancing act, walking a tightrope suspended in the air. On one side, a man lounges upon her right arm, his head the symbol of man. On the woman's other arm hangs a balance of duties: cooking, hanging clothes to dry, and taking care of small children. A thought bubble appears to the right of the woman's head with two equal signs of the sexes. As all things hang in the balance, we see her unrealized dream of equality between men and women.

FIGURE 2.2. Cover image by Feica of Shirkat Gah Women's Resource Centre's 1997 report, *Towards a Better Tomorrow*.

Throughout Shirkat Gah's summary report, we see multiple artistic representations like the one featured on the cover by the artist Feica, a newspaper cartoon illustrator who visualized the "status" of Pakistani women's unequal burdens. These images stand in stark contrast with the written contents of the 1997 report, which, like other secular international reports, offers dense descriptions about the constitutional right to equality, the rights of women to political participation, women's access to citizenship, the demographics of women, and continued gender inequality in the domains of family law, labor law, criminal law, and employment. Feica's illustrations, embedded between bullet points, section headings, and abstract descriptions of legal and social status, bring to life a different view of that struggle and dream of women's equality. Feica's images of faceless and nameless women imprisoned in the home and burdened by care labor are in excess of the utilitarian genre of the report. Almost out of place, the images are intimately linked to the promise of that future as offered in bullet points on laws, demographic descriptions, and policy recommendations.

The framework of absence serves as a powerful hermeneutic to reflect not only on studies that were suppressed but on reports that were successfully published and circulated. The archives of early status of women reports reveal a history of research questions not asked and concepts and information left unmarked. These absences formed the basis of a wide range of critiques of women's movements that emerged in the 1980s and 1990s from racial and ethnic minorities to working-class feminist movements and international LGBTQ movements that were often in tension with earlier feminist movements.

As a form, the status of women report was framed around the question of legal equality and did not accommodate the diverse and diverging perspectives and grassroots movements of women from different races, castes, classes, and ethnicities. The India report, for example, elides key questions that animated political debates of the time, including the oppression of low-class and low-caste communities, tensions between Hindus and religious minorities, gendered violence, and the separatist tensions that defined national politics through the 1970s and 1980s. Like colonial and postcolonial reports that came before, caste, similar to the concept of women, was depoliticized and minimized to a demographic measure rather than a political ideology. Later, Vina Mazumdar argued that the absence in India's report of overtly political questions like the gendered subordination of low-caste and Dalit women, Hindu upper-caste majoritarianism, and gendered violence could be explained by the focus on *equality* as its overriding theme rather than the theme of difference, which Mazumdar suggested would have produced a different report.[84] From the collected comparative international reports of the legal status of women across the world to early national reports from Canada, Trinidad and Tobago, India, and Nepal, few reports overtly engaged with the political questions brought to the fore by social movements that stood in opposition to the state.

The Standardization of Status

The status of women reports were not a site of revolutionary politics, nor did they purport to be. After all, the report was to be "actionable" by state and state-affiliated governing agencies in pursuit of normative goals of economic and social development. Third World feminist researchers, in their desire to demonstrate the worth of women as research subjects, exalted the language of demography and quantitative measures in their claims to social scientific authority on the status of women. In doing so, they naturalized sexual difference and posited aggregate descriptions of women as the preferred form of action research in the project of women's rights.

Although Third World women researchers engaged diverse communities and languages, they offered little critical engagement with the complexities of social life that would undo that aggregate picture of a uniform idea of "women" as demographic description. Reports offered little analysis of long histories of class hierarchy, racial difference, caste violence, gender nonconformity, and state violence against minorities. These dynamic forms of oppression and conflict in postcolonial spaces shaped the very meaning of "status" and "women." Perhaps most strikingly, no status of women report offered any comprehensive data or recommendations that directly addressed women's desires or same-sex sexualities, particularly those desires that exceeded the domain of heterosexual reproduction. Instead, feminized sexuality and women's desires were disappeared through a lexicon of demography and an economics of reproduction in measures of marriages, birth rates, and sex ratios. If these reports were to be the founding documents of a wide array of postcolonial feminist movements, what types of movements did they found?

Even the most normative versions of the status of women report would at points exceed the norms of mandated frameworks of empiricism and aggregation. Early reports offered novel research about women's general conditions in the domains of the economy, work, and religious and secular law. Most strikingly, the visuals on the covers of summary reports from

FIGURE 2.3. Uniform covers of UNESCO status of women reports published in the 1980s.

India and Pakistan provide a very different narrative imaginary for women, picturing collectives of women invested in witnessing women's status and feminist dreams of the future in the balancing act of everyday life. These excesses in the archive of reports undo seemingly sterile archives of reports to offer other ways of knowing beyond the tyranny of the measurable index of women's capacity that dominated the analytical framework of gender research in most of the world in the decades that followed.

By the late 1980s, the status of women report had been formally standardized and promoted by UNESCO—as epitomized in another extensive multi-country status of women project almost fifteen years after Sipilä's special issue in the *Columbia Human Rights Law Review*. UNESCO's project used the analytic of the status of women to compare development across states that had not yet published extensive national status reports in Asia, including Afghanistan, the People's Republic of China, the Lao People's Democratic Republic, the Maldives, Mongolia, Thailand, and the Socialist Republic of Vietnam. The studies were released from 1989 through 1991 in a fully standardized format, with parallel tables of contents and covers with the same image in different colors to distinguish the publications from one another. On the cover, the viewer sees an artistic rendering of the now-iconic UN dove representing peace (see figure 2.3). Inside the dove is a photograph of a little girl's face, a representation of the paradigmatic girl-child of Asia. Underneath the dove, the viewer sees the iconic Greek temple symbol that is UNESCO's logo.

Yogesh Atal, an Indian sociologist of village society, the general editor of UNESCO publications and the principal director of UNESCO's Division of Social Science for more than two decades, offered framing prefatory remarks for all of the status volumes. Atal situated the UNESCO project in relation to the UN International Women's Year and the Decade for Women, which had centered women's problems in the modern social sciences. Atal mapped the transformation that had taken place since the beginning of the decade: "national machineries" had been set up in some countries, while other governments "established special ministries for Women's Development." More than a decade after the first women's conference, there was now a "sizeable literature, and a growing community of scholars interested in research on women." Yet, for Atal and UNESCO, the study of women lacked standardization, as "such researches and studies are scattered and have not been utilized in an effective way for policy-making and for raising awareness on women's issues amongst the general public."[85] For Atal, the time had come for a comprehensive review of the Decade for Women's status of women projects and to write reports for states that had not yet produced country-specific research on the status of women.

UNESCO thus embarked on a multi-country survey of the status of women across these seven countries to create comprehensive standard reports, carrying on a long tradition of reports from colonial states and international organizations that looked to the survey to create comprehensive and comparable datasets across states and regions. The standard contents of the UNESCO status reports responded to UNESCO Secretariat questions about the history of country-specific policies toward women, the country demographic profile, a question on the role of women in public life, and any special issues faced by women and children. Each survey then asked the respondent to offer a summary conclusion and possible recommendations.

The reports of the UNESCO multi-country status of women project, as a collection of survey reports, offer highly standardized reflections on issues across very different regions of Asia, with little space for discussions of the impact of geopolitical crisis, war, and economic issues on the status of women. The sections on demographics and laws across all seven country reports are standard and offer little commentary on the politics shaping women's status in each country. Yet the reader does learn—in brief sections on the history of the country in relation to the status of women—of different pro-government stances for the equality of women from the report authors.

For example, the author of the Afghanistan status of women report, Kabul University professor Wali M. Rahimi, had previously published a study of the social sciences in Afghanistan for UNESCO in 1977.[86] In his 1977 report, Rahimi critiqued the lack of infrastructure to support social science research in Afghanistan, but he also noted the promising inclusion of women in higher education at Kabul University and the commissioning of an official status of women report on Afghanistan by the central government in the mid-1970s. Political turmoil and upheaval would prevent that 1970s status report—which was to report the findings of one of the earliest status of women commissions in Afghanistan in the early 1970s—from ever coming into being. More than ten years later, Rahimi took up the project for UNESCO under very different circumstances of revolutionary change amid Soviet occupation, which he does not mention in his 1989 report. In the 1991 status of women report, Rahimi offers little commentary on the rapid political changes happening on the ground in Afghanistan except for his citation of "progressive" policies for equal rights for women under the current ruling government of the People's Democratic Party of Afghanistan.[87] Instead, he focuses on the feudal patriarchy of peasantry, as well as the standard survey questions of the demographic, occupational, and cultural differences between men and women in the country.

Like Rahimi, the authors of other reports argued for continued efforts to improve the conditions of women under current national governments. Strikingly, the 1989 UNESCO status project included several socialist states that had not previously produced reports in the 1970s and early 1980s. The author of the Vietnam report, Ngo Ba Thanh, was herself part of the government of the Socialist Republic of Vietnam as a deputy president of the Legislative Commission and vice president of the Viet Nam Women's Union. In the Vietnam report, she endorses current government policies toward women in the aftermath of the Vietnam War, but provides little commentary on the effects of war on the status of women except to celebrate women's participation in revolutionary resistance and women's long-standing commitment to anti-war, anti-US military efforts in the region.[88] Ultimately, the Vietnam report calls for the continued development of the country to help women out of the impoverished conditions of peasant subsistence.

The author of the China report, Wei Zhangling, a professor at the Chinese Academy of Social Sciences, briefly analyzes changes enacted by the post-1949 government in China. She argues for improving the condition of women through the implementation of a new constitution and marriage law. Zhangling, like Rahimi on Afghanistan and Ba Thanh on Vietnam, attributed the continued oppression of women to former feudal social structures and the problem of a patriarchal peasantry.[89]

Yet, despite such salient asides, the standardized mandates of the genre of the status of women were clear. Over the hundreds of pages of these reports, the status of women could at most offer brief and general commentaries on histories of transformative political change, revolutions, and the aftermath of the ravages of war. Ultimately, the status of women was about demographics and the cultural and social participation of women in the present and had little to do with what came before.

The Afterlives of the Report

Empirical reports on women came to constitute most of the intellectual labor done by women researchers in much of the world in the decades that followed the rise of status reports. Almost fifty years after the initiation of the UN International Women's Year, there is an excess of archives of policy reports, but implementation and enforcement of policies on women have been limited. As a result of this hegemonic knowledge economy, many women researchers in the Third World could make a living and put their research training to work only while constrained within the strict genre of policy reports for NGOs or international foundations. A vast number of words produced by women researchers went into the multinational knowledge industry of UN, governmental, and NGO reports. And as women researchers labored, writing report after report, perhaps fewer words were left to write otherwise and in other genres, less time was available to ask different questions, and little institutional space or material support was available for exploring alternative ways of knowing outside of the language of development measures and indices.

As Antrobus lamented in an interview with me in 2021, perhaps the goals for research on women would have looked different if Third World feminists had known "how fragile all of our struggles for progress could be, and how swiftly they would be reversed in a moment."[90] Despite half a century of social scientific research, an abundance of reports, and legal mandates, the economic, social, and political lives of many women in the world remain unequal and unchanged in the twenty-first century.

This history reveals the vastly unequal allocation of resources and the failure to create sustainable shifts in the everyday lives of women by a massive and expanding political economy of global government and NGO status of women reports. Reports reflected naturalized biologically determinist notions of sexual difference in demographic data and framed global feminist politics through gender essentialist arguments for women's equality. Fifty years later, the international infrastructure of research on women, gender, and sexuality, funded by governments, international organizations, and foundations like Ford, has been rapidly dismantled by authoritarian states that condemn foreign funding for women and for queer and trans people as neocolonial and antithetical to nationalist values.

We cannot see the faces of the many women illustrated on the covers of reports on the status of women in India and Pakistan. Eventually, the only face that we see is standardized through the paradigmatic symbol of the girl-child across the UNESCO reports. As people bear witness to endless data visualizations and studies that co-opt the language of women's freedom through the dominance of a lexicon of economic indices, the expressions and dreams of women remain largely hidden from view.

3

The Organization, or What if We Collaborate across Borders?

"Today the world is in crisis."[1]

So declared a pan-African collective of women in the "Nairobi Manifesto" composed and presented at the final United Nations conference of the UN Decade for Women. Written by three pathbreaking transnational Third World women's research organizations—AAWORD (Association of African Women for Research and Development), WIN (Women in Nigeria), and ZARD (Zambia Association for Research and Development)—the statement was released to the international press on July 13, 1985.[2] The manifesto criticized the limitations of the UN Decade for Women and insisted on an alternative vision of development that centered knowledge created by Third World women's organizations.

The manifesto was a declaration of dissent as well as an agenda for the future. The organizations argued for women's political action in five critical areas to ensure the future of the continent in a time of uncertainty. They declared the voices of a pan-African collective of women critical to exposing the injustice of apartheid across the continent. They insisted that feminists had unique insights into the cruel monetary exploitation of Third World people by the World Bank and the International Monetary Fund (IMF). The statement decried the burden of famine and food insecurity and the unending displacement of peoples in a growing global refugee crisis, insisting that

FIGURE 3.1. Kanga marking the 1985 UN Decade for Women Conference in Nairobi. Schlesinger Library on the History of Women in America. Photograph by Durba Mitra.

displacement and deprivation were key feminist concerns. The collective condemned postcolonial religious fundamentalisms that oppressed women while masquerading as anti-colonial claims to sovereignty. This coalition of African feminist organizations argued that women offered unique insights into these dangerous and persistent threats—of segregation, starvation, forced migration, religious authoritarianism, and neocolonial exploitation—for these issues were a matter of life and death for women and the social worlds that they sustained.

Significantly, the Nairobi Manifesto proclaimed that the true emancipation of colonized people required the decolonization of research on women. For this alliance of African women's researchers, women's issues were fundamentally political, and organizing across geographies was necessary to create novel epistemological foundations for freedom in a neocolonial world. As the manifesto declared, governments too often relegated women's issues to "isolated projects" in the limited domain of "social welfare." The women's bureaus and divisions that postcolonial governments established were primarily performative gestures, inadequate infrastructures of "national machinery" rather than empowered institutions.[3]

But it was women who were "most adversely affected by existing development strategies" that perpetuated global inequality. "Africans should insist on their right to define and implement an autonomous development strategy," the manifesto declared, and it was African women and their collective networks who were "at the forefront" of that defining project. The emancipation of the continent could only be achieved through the "creative energy" of women, who were essential for "a new self-reliant and people-centered development."[4]

The most extraordinary aspect of this manifesto was its proposition that women-centered research, led by feminist research organizations from the Third World, could undo the authoritarian present. The manifesto proposed an agenda for radical change based on the "creative" force that women could bring to building "alternative visions."[5] Effective political transformation required new definitions of the continent based in women's original ideas and research, and that definitional work could happen only when women had sovereignty over their own ideas. Material struggles against food shortage, forced displacement, and authoritarian right-wing patriarchy could be addressed only through an aspirational project that centered the epistemological visions of African women.

In the face of a failing project of decolonization, the world was in a crisis that threatened its very survival. It was women's autonomous research networks and organizations that would create the intellectual framework for imagining a truly sustainable life.

As the last two chapters have shown, knowledge-making about the condition of women was, at its heart, a project of dissent. For almost two decades, feminist researchers defied the constraints of the national project and came together to collectively imagine different futures through critiques of patriarchal nationalism and authoritarianism. They sought out new domains of women's internationalism to create new epistemological infrastructures, from Afro-Asian women's networks to development workshops to UN initiatives like the women's conferences and status of women commissions.

In this chapter, I theorize the feminist organization—like the organizations that authored the Nairobi Manifesto—as a key site of epistemic making and unmaking for and about women. I focus on one unique and powerful version of the organizational form: the Third World women's research organization (TWWRO), which shaped a vast knowledge economy by and about women in decolonizing spaces, including Asia, the African continent, and the Caribbean. I argue that the Third World research organization inaugurated a new era of democratic politics based in the transnational institutionalization of the study of women.

Over the course of the chapter, I follow an overlapping cast of women intellectuals who animated these projects across multiple transregional research collaborations. This group of prominent feminist intellectuals collaborating across many organizations included, among others, Senegalese feminist Marie-Angélique Savané, Ethiopian sociologist Zenebework Tadesse, Indian political scientist Vina Mazumdar, Indian economist Devaki Jain, Jamaican feminist Lucille Mathurin Mair, West Indian economist Peggy Antrobus, Pakistani sociologist Nighat Said Khan, Pakistani sociologist Farida Shaheed, and feminist editor Florence Howe. Their alliances and collective projects resulted from an extraordinary moment of unprecedented access to higher education for a class of upwardly mobile Third World women. And these interconnections were made against a backdrop of postcolonial women's solidarity, which fostered the global movement of ideas and collaboration of women across borders at a scale never seen before.

TWWROs grew rapidly in the 1970s and flourished in the 1980s across decolonizing spaces, but this remarkable moment of solidarity had ended by the late 1990s and early 2000s. By then, the domain of autonomous women's and gender research had been repurposed by technocratic nation-states to fit into narrowly quantified measures of global indicators—the primary currency for international and national state machineries.

The Rise of the Nongovernmental Organization

Looking back before the pivotal moment of the UN Decade for Women, it is as if women had not existed in postcolonial policymaking—at least not as a primary reason for institution-building. Of course, women had been a key object of state intervention and legal reforms long before. Colonized women had long been an obsession of colonial policies and the primary justification for racist colonial ideologies that perpetuated the myth of colonies as backward because of the subordination of colonized girls and women. Women's movements across the colonial world and the decolonizing world had for decades pushed progressive agendas for women's suffrage, women's legal rights under family law, and social work as an integral part of the anticolonial struggle.[6]

Yet from the 1970s onward, women took on new visibility as the primary subject of state intervention in social and economic life. Between the UN International Women's Year in 1975, the subsequent UN Decade for Women, and the lead-up to the Beijing women's conference in 1995, women emerged as the primary focus of an expanding infrastructure of international administration and national technocratic expertise that claimed the domain of social life as its object through categories of women and gender.

In so doing, women's rights became an indispensable idea. This vision propelled the liberatory visions of women's movements and organizations, but it also soon served as the key justification for a multinational infrastructure of governance over social and economic life that moved from local organizations to international governing bodies. In this moment, women became critical in the proliferation of a concept that seemed infinitely malleable: the nongovernmental organization (NGO).

A glance at any national or international register for the years between 1975 and 1995 immediately reveals the proliferating number of organizations dedicated to women's issues. This vast and diverse terrain of women's organizations was structurally outside the domain of the government, lumped together under the term "nongovernmental organization," yet these groups were never fully autonomous. They supplemented and were supplemented by state research projects and national development programs that utilized the new apparatus of women's NGOs to outsource state welfare projects and increasingly privatize the domain of aid for women and children.

But what is the NGO? It may be best understood as a moving signifier.

NGOs extended far beyond the domain of women's social welfare organizations, bringing together international capital and postcolonial state structures in novel administrative forms that mediated and transformed the terrain of democratic governance. Women were at the heart of the institutionalization of these paragovernmental structures, as both the figurative subjects of intervention and the literal agents of transformation. Third World women invested in developmentalist agendas and human rights and built organizations that assembled civil society into interest groups and advocacy areas.

The institutionalization of the women's NGO created durable infrastructures of biopolitical governance that privatized welfare policies while bureaucratizing the most intimate domains of corporeal, social, and economic life. This infrastructure was built and sustained by a complex of international funding, postcolonial bureaucracies, and a new domain of Third World organizational workers, overwhelmingly based in an emerging class of educated women with specialized expertise.

The NGO is a vexed, often-maligned idea in the history of women, gender, and sexuality in the twentieth and twenty-first centuries. Feminist and queer studies scholars have reflected on the meteoric rise of NGOs through the "NGO-ization" of women's and sexual rights movements across the Global South, particularly with the end of the Cold War and the rapid expansion of neoliberal economic policies focused on women and sexual minorities in the 1990s.[7] Feminist scholarship on NGO-ization has critically assessed the contradictory place of these institutions in the landscape of women's rights.

Yet, despite numerous studies that employ this idea, "NGO-ization" remains a term with ambiguous signification. Few historical studies have tracked empirically, in sheer numbers and size, the vast terrain of national and global women's organizations that emerged across the decolonizing world during the 1970s, 1980s, and 1990s and focused on issues such as legal and social advocacy, health and family planning, women's labor, and gender violence.[8] Alongside the growth of this novel institutional form, feminist histories have rarely theorized how NGOs reshaped the trajectory of electoral politics and the very workings of postcolonial democracy, even as these organizations, often totally unaccountable to the public and wholly outside the domain of democratic politics, quickly came to mediate almost every aspect of civil engagement and social and economic welfare, particularly in relation to gender and sexual minorities.[9]

To comprehend and critique these rapid changes in governance and organizing, a generation of Third World women—themselves critical participants in this tectonic organizational shift—created their own infrastructure of research and writing. Women's research organizations were one of many NGO forms to emerge in this moment, but their focus on the production of knowledge and self-reflexive approach to organizing made them distinct. They focused their organizational efforts on the inadequacy of Third World research and launched scathing critiques of extractive First World academic research and exploitative research conducted by NGOs.

Funded by international philanthropies like the Ford and Rockefeller Foundations, the social science machinery of national governments, as well as by a massive investment in Third World research by Nordic countries following the International Women's Year, TWWROs carved out a domain of research collectives of women focused on the lives of women in the Third World. These organizations flourished across newly established nation-states, diverse spaces that shared common histories of colonial structures of governance under the former British and French Empires, including South and Southeast Asia, North Africa and the Middle East, the African continent, and the Caribbean. These transnational spaces shaped postwar debates about equality and development in the UN and became key spaces of contestation and investment in research on women. Many organizations extended transnational feminist networks beyond the newly decolonizing world to Latin America, bringing together regions from across the Third World.

Despite rightful skepticism today from feminist activists and scholars about the NGO knowledge economy and the dependencies created by NGO aid networks, organized research on women and gender for development and rights was not always pursued toward nefarious ends. For Third World women researchers in the 1970s and early 1980s, the autonomous research organization was, at its heart, an *ethical* project that mobilized the knowledge of people on the ground to counter neocolonialist epistemologies. Women, like the organizations that penned the Nairobi Manifesto, argued that creating usable knowledge that could be used across geographies by women with common struggles was a project with transformative potential.

In this logic, Third World scholars would build infrastructures that innovated methods that were comparative and collective across decolonizing geographies. The radical politics of transnational research could be used to subvert increasingly authoritarian ideas of women's subordination in postcolonial nation-states. The project was both deeply local in terms of the ethics of research and necessarily transnational. To use language that would have dangerous political implications decades later, these research organizations, in their deep criticism of the failures of the nation-state, were often "antinational" projects that centered the needs and ideas of minoritized people.

In this way, transnational research on women's lives was a politics in and of itself. Rather than serving as the supporting material for women's movements on the ground, research was the primary means for an epistemic revolution. These organizational networks created new priorities and methods that saw empirical research as intimately linked to policymaking, with profound effects on the trajectory of research on women and gender for decades to come in the form of institutes, centers, and organizations dedicated to the social science of women and development. The goal? The decolonization of research.

Even as these organizations have played a pivotal role in the history of global feminist politics, the archives of research collectives and their members are scattered and most often unpreserved. These histories suffer from a lack of institutional and public support for, and often outright opposition to, the conservation and safeguarding of archives of women, gender, and sexuality. The survival of these organizational archives becomes more precarious with the loss of a generation of feminists who built these collectives and visions for feminist researchers. Unlike prominent women in the United

States, the personal papers of Third World women from the decolonizing world are almost never preserved for use by researchers and students.

Yet the women protagonists of this story worked to create their own record of research through research publications and conference proceedings. As women organized transnational research centers and conferences, they preserved records of their research and insisted that women take over all dimensions of knowledge production, from research notes and papers to the self-publication of text. Their work offers a record of the radical ideas and research frameworks that shaped the proliferation of feminist research in the 1970s and 1980s.

The archives of published papers and meeting notes offer only a partial glimpse into the rich worlds of women organizing novel research collectives. Few tensions or differences between feminist researchers about the stakes of their work are recorded in the vast majority of the materials preserved in libraries and organizational offices that form the formal archives of published papers and conference proceedings of these Third World women's organizations. Although some recollections of feminists give us a sense of the debates between women about politics and strategy, in the absence of Third World women's personal papers, sources that portray the impassioned differences that shaped and at points fractured these organizations are scanty at best. Traces of these women's intimate interactions, differences in method, and friendships can be found between the lines in the citations of white papers, in the thanks offered in conference presentations, in the acknowledgment sections of research publications, in the photographs of meetings, and in the retrospective public conversations on social media decades later that document both the solidarity and differences among feminist organizations. Third World women's calls to action, organizational founding statements, research papers and anthologies, and recollections of their earlier lives form the primary archives for the epistemic revolution made possible by women's research collectives.

The Decolonization of Research

"Research is part of the process of liberation," declared Filomina Steady, feminist researcher from Sierra Leone and founding member of AAWORD, at the 1980 NGO Forum at the second UN conference on women at Copenhagen. For AAWORD's founding member and organizational president, Marie-Angélique Savané, a Senegalese researcher, research was an "essential need," not some "luxury that Africans cannot afford."[10]

Six years later, at a meeting of vice chancellors of African universities in Harare, Zimbabwe, the World Bank insidiously subverted Savané's language by declaring that higher education in Africa was a luxury. This statement, reported by political theorist Mahmood Mamdani who witnessed the World Bank declaration in Harare, symbolized the new mandate for mass divestment in research and education enforced by the World Bank and IMF that would gut the world of feminist research and the African university more broadly.[11]

But in 1980 there was still hope. Scholars and practitioners from around the world gathered to discuss how to organize and institutionalize a new domain of international study: women's studies. The workshops at Copenhagen were brimming with excitement. Scholars seeking to build connections and networks crowded into classrooms in a small university center to listen to the work of women's research organizations on the ground in Asia, Africa, the Middle East, and Latin America. For participants, the new domain called "women's studies" was not simply research *on* women, but a unique field of knowledge that could shape a new organizational politics based in the study of women *by* Third World women.

In this section, I reconstruct the rise of transnational TWWROs, focusing on two organizations in the domain of Third World feminist research that held signal importance for decades: the pan-Africanist organization AAWORD, founded in 1977, and Development Alternatives with Women for a New Era (DAWN), founded in 1984 as a pan-national organization bringing together women from across Latin America, the Caribbean, South and Southeast Asia, and the African continent. Through an analysis of the early history and subsequent development of these organizations, I argue that women exalted feminist social science research as a means to fight patriarchal nationalisms, the rising military authoritarianism of the postcolonial nation-state, and international development and structural adjustment programs that deprived women of the ability to meet their basic needs.

Even before the International Conference on Women and Development at Wellesley College in 1976 (see chapter 1), new collectives of leading feminist researchers contended that materialist social scientific methods and transnational comparative projects would counter long-standing racist understandings of colonized societies. For these women, the nationalist project had proven itself to be insufficient for the needs of women. Neocolonial development programs and international debt systems had subjected people in the postcolonial world, and women especially, to a global system of perpetual poverty, violence, and labor exploitation across postcolonial geographies.

AAWORD's founders created the transnational organization in response to the dissatisfaction of women scholars from Africa with the ongoing failures of what they again and again identified as "Western research"—disciplinary knowledge produced in Europe and the United States that assessed the rest of the world. The Wellesley conference played a pivotal, if tumultuous, role in this story. Frustrated with the colonial and neocolonial attitudes of their colleagues, the Third World women held a shadow conference that centered the research of women from the decolonizing world. The result of those urgent conversations and critiques was the first transnational women's research collective in the Third World, the pan-Africanist research collective AAWORD, which served as the basis for a range of transnational feminist research collectives that emerged in the next decade.[12] AAWORD's mission was clear: "In its research policy, AAWORD is to promote the decolonization of research in Africa."[13] The organization's Africa-wide focus was to be on women who sought to create novel methodologies for research to transform the lives of African women and Africa more broadly.

Many African women intellectuals had already begun collective agitations against the biased social science projects of Western researchers before Wellesley. The previous year, researchers had gathered in Zambia after the UN conference for International Women's Year to discuss the possibility of an African women's research center. In Zambia, the heart of the liberation movements of southern Africa during the 1970s and 1980s, women scholars from all over the continent witnessed firsthand the violence of apartheid systems and neocolonial systems of extraction in increasingly powerful debt programs. One year later, at Wellesley, Third World women protested the ubiquity of Western women conducting extractive research on the so-called developing world.

By late 1976, AAWORD had been founded with around twenty members, a membership that rapidly expanded as women established local and regional chapters for research. With funding from the Swedish Agency for Research Cooperation with Developing Countries, the first two organizational meetings defined the mission and vision of the new pan-African collective. The members in attendance in Lusaka, Zambia, in 1976 and Dakar, Senegal, in 1977 called for innovation in the very methods and concepts that shaped the social sciences of Africa. In these early mobilizations of the collective, women called for autonomous research opportunities through AAWORD and demanded a wholly independent network of women for women, separate from governmental or international organizations. As an autonomous network, the organization was to create liaisons and offer material support for research in regions across the continent without any interference from the state.

For Zenebework Tadesse, AAWORD was founded to meet the collective desire by women from across regions to do research surrounded by others who understood the plight of the isolated feminist researcher:

> You also begin to feel you are not alone. Sometimes when you're in your own given space, it looks almost hopeless, it's so difficult, but when you see larger numbers of people experiencing the same things or overcoming some of the difficulties that you thought were unimaginable, then it sort of nurtures your hope that with time and more energy, change will come.[14]

AAWORD offered respite and solidarity for women who experienced alienation and threats in increasingly authoritarian spaces in postcolonial Africa. Unlike the precarious national machinery on women and development, which continued to be dominated by men, AAWORD was to be a *sovereign* organization—an alternative, pan-African vision of feminist epistemologies. It was a space of hope and possibility for real, sustainable change, led by the first generations of educated women across decolonizing spaces on the continent.

Tadesse, AAWORD's first secretary, grew up in Ethiopia and left as a young woman at a time of profound tumult. After moving to Chicago for college, she became involved in African diasporic movements in support of the Ethiopian student movement. Like other diasporic Africans in the United States during the civil rights era, Tadesse soon joined the Black Liberation struggle in the United States, working in collaboration with the Black Panther Party in Chicago. After taking up her post in AAWORD in the late 1970s, Tadesse played important roles in several TWWROs, including the Council for the Development of Social Science Research in Africa (CODESRIA), DAWN, and Sisterhood Is Global. In the 1990s, she returned to Ethiopia to start a research center in the aftermath of authoritarian rule.

To achieve this transnational sovereignty over ideas, AAWORD instituted a flexible organizational structure that was able, in theory, to adapt to the changing terrain of development research and collaborate with other women's research organizations from across the continent and beyond. The organizational structure of AAWORD created a pan-African framework for governance, participation, and publication in three parts: a general assembly for all members; a bureau that housed administrative positions like president, secretary, and treasurer; and an editing committee, which edited member publications for AAWORD. AAWORD, in other words, was a research organization, an editorial collective, and a publisher.

The democratic, pan-Africanist structure created a flexible infrastructure for AAWORD members to make a mark at international events like UN conferences. AAWORD sustained alliances across disciplines, pooled material resources to support research, and pursued methodological innovation while sustaining regional expertise.

This multidimensional approach, in turn, furthered AAWORD's continuing break with Western researchers, which had been simmering for years and finally broke out into the open at the Wellesley conference. AAWORD particularly objected to the vast and influential literature on women and development in Africa that perpetrated ethnocentric understandings of African societies. In a 1982 special issue of *Development Dialogue* based on a research conference held in 1982 in Dakar, AAWORD outlined its radical vision for "another development," protesting that the "predominant type of most of the social science research carried out on women in Africa, particularly in the last decade, has been that of Western women academics." There was a straight line from colonialist knowledge and Western feminist research, as "historically, 'research' on Africa was conducted by merchants, missionaries, colonialists, and anthropologists," but was now being done under the guise of feminist research. The research that resulted was a form of extractive colonial capitalism that recapitulated racist ideas of "native cultures and practices."[15]

AAWORD objected not only to who was doing development research but also to what that research looked like. AAWORD questioned the methods deployed by Western researchers to gain access to information and represent African societies. In 1983, AAWORD held a workshop titled "Research on African Women: What Kind of Methodology?" at which researchers from across the continent offered critiques of the methodological deficiencies of research on African women. During the workshop, AAWORD researchers offered wide-ranging indictments of the exploitative lexicon of development research and the limited concepts that organized the priorities of Western research on women. Filomina Steady put the critique in stark terms: "The exploitation of Africa was not restricted to mineral and vegetable resources or the cheap labour and markets. Research also had an exploitative commercial function. Raw data became part of the 'cargo' extracted from Africa for processing and expropriation in the West."[16]

In particular, Steady and other AAWORD members critiqued the hypocrisy of Western women conducting research on Third World women under claims of universalist feminism. An African feminist view of development required a critique of Western women's standpoint and ongoing intimate relationships with dominance: "Western women," Steady observed, "are a relatively new addition to male dominated research institutes and funding opportunities. Like all newcomers, they are very protective and defensive of their newly gained access." Steady critiqued the "useless data" collected from decades of research in Africa and the "inadequacy of the dominant research methodology" that had been used to obscure histories of colonial domination and patriarchal violence in Africa.[17] Steady rejected the "dichotomous models" so popular among "Western" social scientists, arguing that imposed binaries like "rural/urban, formal/informal, public/private, traditional/modern, developed/developing" had fundamentally bifurcated the organically integrated social and economic worlds of African societies.[18]

These colonial binaries perpetuated violent inequality and Western domination of Africa through a false ideology of development that imposed social difference as the organizing principle of funding. It was a "scientific colonialism," in Steady's words, one that would continue unabated unless and until African women intellectuals could foreground the domination of Africa by the West and the central place of women in creating structural change. Yet these inequalities could be dismantled if sovereign African feminist research projects focused on the question of power and researched the material living conditions of people who could barely subsist. Only by rejecting these false ideologies could a true consciousness-raising about the neocolonial exploitation of African women be achieved.[19]

The work of AAWORD centered the intellectual models and innovative methods of African women to foreground their unique insights into the lives of women and to counter accusations by men that feminist research was a foreign import. Marie-Angélique Savané vehemently defended the work of feminist intellectuals and the need for women-centered research based in Africa. A founder and the first president of AAWORD, Savané was a fierce advocate for feminist intellectuals. She held multiple roles in the UN during the 1990s and 2000s and later emerged as a controversial figure in Senegalese politics. In a tense interview on feminist responses to the rise of Islamic fundamentalism in Senegal in the mid-1980s, Savané defended the work of feminists to advocate for legal codes that would defend the rights of women against new patriarchal codes that sought to overturn the family codes in favor of dogmatic Sharia laws:

> The accusation that feminists here are merely imitating foreign lifestyles is simply groundless. The development and propagation of social theories has always and everywhere been the business of intellectuals. Look at history. You will observe that the prophets were marginal figures in their own societies. The feminist is no exception to that rule. It is only logical that those women best placed to compare their situation with that of their mother's generation happen to be intellectuals. Intellectuals are equipped to think of theoretical models and to fight for change on the basis of a more or less thorough critical analysis of ideas.[20]

The feminist intellectual was, in Savané's vision, a logical and rational progression from earlier generations of women who had fought for national independence. Despite being condemned and marginalized by postcolonial men, the woman intellectual would, in Savané's telling, prove to be the *primary* harbinger of radical social and political change.

This was a claim for a politics of knowledge beyond representation: here and elsewhere, Savané argued that it was the philosophical and theoretical innovation of feminism that made its vision of change so potent. Still, representing women was the start of any such revolutionary politics of knowledge, one far ahead of the current moment.

Indeed, AAWORD argued that contemporary social science research had largely overlooked women. To the extent that contemporary social science had considered the status of women on the continent, it replicated its colonialist roots by offering narrow understandings of abstract social modeling based in African failure. These Western models had stripped Africans of history, agency, and capacity for social change based on the age-old developmentalist logic of primitivity.

To contradict ethnocentric accounts of women without agency in an unchanging, "primitive" Africa, AAWORD researchers insisted on the proof of data-oriented social science to account for the *present* conditions of African women, with a primary focus on the material conditions that shaped the work and livelihoods of women. In the language of AAWORD, African women needed data that reflected "the Now." They had *real* research to do to account for the dynamic material lives of women.

AAWORD members argued against ahistorical colonialist studies of tribal structure, suggesting instead that social scientific studies conducted by African women offered critical insight into women's economic lives, dramatically changing roles within urban and rural social movements, and labor. The study of African societies and African women could not be delimited to the domain of culture and tribe, as women did multiple forms of modern labor, from agrarian to reproductive work, and defied any singular view of culture or tradition. AAWORD researchers insisted that, contrary to the "tribal" stasis of Western social scientific studies of Africa, African women lived fully within the domain of modern colonial capital. Indeed, women were the most vulnerable to the pains of neocolonial modernization policies, as AAWORD publications again and again centered the ways in which women were disproportionately affected by the crushing power of global structural adjustment programs and violent state policies built on gendered violence, ranging from apartheid to rising religious fundamentalisms.

The decision of Third World women researchers to elevate the policy-oriented social science of the present as the primary decolonizing knowledge project had complicated and far-reaching consequences for research on women, gender, and sexuality in the African social sciences through the 1980s and early 2000s.[21] AAWORD's early workshops saw the first collaboration with CODESRIA, the leading pan-African social science organization. At the time of its founding in the early 1970s, CODESRIA was heavily dominated by men.[22] In the priorities of CODESRIA, "gender" emerged as a focus area of social science research in response to AAWORD member critiques of CODESRIA's neglect of social scientific research on women and gender.

By 1994, members of AAWORD and prominent African feminist social scientists, including Fatou Sow, Ayesha Imam, and Amina Mama, had built the CODESRIA Gender Institute, which soon became the best-resourced space in which to do critical research on women on the continent. These pan-African institutes on women and gender continue to offer a critical space for research and publications on gender and social science on the continent. Yet, while CODESRIA endured with independent funding from the Swedish government, AAWORD and other smaller research organizations struggled under challenging conditions of donor dependency and the massive defunding of research and education that accompanied the structural adjustment programs.[23]

By the late 1980s, funders had divested from the education sector at the national and international levels, and so AAWORD fought to find consistent material support. In 1990, AAWORD member and Nigerian feminist Ayesha Imam argued that researchers would have to publish more to create a knowledge infrastructure for feminist research in the face of mass cutbacks to education and research training in Africa. Yet, in anticipation of the decade to come, Imam expressed anxiety that there was "little hope for improvement," as "the acceptance of IMF type conditionalities continues to mean cutbacks in education" and would prevent the few women who had any access to education from accessing any training or conducting research in the years to come.[24]

Reflecting on the work of AAWORD and other African research efforts more than twenty years after its founding, Senegalese feminist economist and member Yassine Fall critiqued the painfully unequal infrastructure of research that AAWORD pushed against from its formation. As she explained, "Within the context of African and world crises in the 1970s and 1980s African and Third World women became an important stake in the geopolitics of globalization and in view of maintaining multinational corporations' hegemony on the peripheries of world capitalism."[25] The push for multinational neocolonial capitalism in the 1980s had created almost impossible conditions for Third World women's research, such that projects were delimited to "administrative research" conducted by First World–funded researchers who sought to profit from new research that exploited women "in the unequal international division of labor and for capital accumulation." By the 1990s, these pro-capitalist forms of research on Third World women created conditions where "indigenous research and donor driven research" were "on a collision course."[26]

Even so, the studies of AAWORD through the 1990s and 2000s demonstrate the organization's lasting reach across a range of subjects. These publications reflect the changing funding landscape for research and publication during this period, when much of the funding came from the UN research wings. AAWORD publications of this period were funded in collaboration with the Ford Foundation, Oxfam America, and the UN Development Fund for Women (UNIFEM), part of the initiatives of UN Women. These organizations supported AAWORD's work, including workshops, working groups, and subsequent edited collections of transregional research. Moreover, AAWORD's impact on social science research for women in Africa is reflected in its diverse array of projects: women and reproduction, women and the mass media, HIV/AIDs in Africa, perceptions of sex equality in Africa, women's movements in different regions of the continent, democratic change and women's participation in politics, gendered violence, and economic and social change at the turn of the century.[27]

AAWORD's early networks built on a critical idea that has been a signal contribution of African feminist thought to critical theory: the situated critique of neocolonialism. In highlighting how AAWORD theorized neocolonialism, I am reflecting on one of the most potent critiques of the nature of failed democratic state power in the twentieth century. As Kwame Nkrumah declared in his landmark text on neocolonialism, neocolonialism represented African states as independent with "all the outward trappings of international sovereignty."[28] Yet, even as they feigned independence, they were economically and politically subjugated.

AAWORD feminists precisely diagnosed this paradox of decolonization. African feminists directly critiqued the false pretense to sovereignty in neocolonialism, issuing indictments of everything from puppet governments and military dictatorships to apartheid and apartheid-like governance structures, the perverse euphemism of "structural adjustment" programs, and the violent workings of religious nationalism through systems of patriarchal Muslim law that swept across the continent in the 1980s.

Eight years after the founding of AAWORD, another research organization was created in its image. In 1984, the research organization Development Alternatives with Women for a New Era was founded as a grassroots transnational network of Third World women from Asia, Africa, Latin America, and the Caribbean. The research network, which remains active today, initially focused on the place of Third World researchers in development. As prominent Indian feminist economist and founding member Devaki Jain recounted, DAWN's founders were inspired by AAWORD to create a new organization that would center women's critical perspectives on development *across* the wide-ranging geographies of the Third World beyond a particular region.[29]

Organized in anticipation of the last conference for the UN Decade for Women in Nairobi, DAWN united Third World women in a common project of scholarship, activism, and policymaking. At an early meeting in Bangalore, India, DAWN was by far the most international in scope of any of the TWWROs, uniting researchers from Pakistan, India, Bangladesh, Sri Lanka, the Philippines, Malaysia, Senegal, Brazil, Jamaica, and Barbados. DAWN members held multiple memberships in well-known feminist networks, became national leaders for women's rights, and produced groundbreaking feminist scholarship. Its members included Moroccan feminist sociologist Fatima Mernissi, leading Caribbean feminists Lucille Mathurin Mair and Peggy Antrobus, Indian feminists Devaki Jain and Gita Sen, and African feminists and founding members of AAWORD Zenebework Tadesse and Marie-Angélique Savané.

The founding of DAWN, like AAWORD, was based on the insistence that critical feminist engagement with the state developmentalist project at the international and national levels would dramatically shift the trajectory of postcolonial indebtedness and dependency. As recounted by Gita Sen, a founding member of DAWN and a prominent feminist economist and public health expert from India, DAWN was founded as an explicitly Marxist feminist organization whose members produced regional research on the crisis of survival in the form of debt relief and access to food. DAWN feminists argued for policies that addressed the nexus of "production-reproduction," based in "the critique of the state and a continued belief in the necessity (if not the promise) of the developmental state."[30] For Sen and other founding members of DAWN, Marxist feminist approaches to development were not solely based in the critique and condemnation of the developmental state. Rather, Marxist feminist goals could be achieved only through the ongoing involvement of feminist intellectuals who would not only critique but also improve the workings of nation-states and the UN. The hope was that recognizing women's work *as* work would make development programs more potent and radically equal.

DAWN enshrined the principle of commonality across geographies because the inequalities inflicted on the Third World through internationalist development and debt programs had created commonality across the Third World. Explicitly transnational in reach, DAWN connected feminist issues from Brazil and India to Barbados and Senegal. Founding members insisted on the potential for liberation through feminist scholarship that took on everything from local and national policymaking to the global governing structures of the UN and the IMF.

In DAWN's pathbreaking founding document, *Development, Crises, and Alternative Visions: Third World Women's Perspectives*, Gita Sen and Caren Grown articulated a politics of solidarity through a common epistemology of the Third World, claiming organic links between women's issues across geographies: "Our knowledge of women's experiences with the development process—as researchers, activists, and policymakers—has brought us to a range of common understandings despite different starting points."[31] The draft of the founding text, outlined by Sen and Grown with contributions from the founding members in Bangalore, was a living document, the subject of lively debates and disagreements in the many workshops and conferences attended by DAWN members in the 1980s.

In 1985, DAWN convened a conference in Delhi, India, where participants vehemently debated the founding text. The final report of the conference detailed the debate, ending by declaring that DAWN had created fertile ground for feminist contributions to research: "The fact that so many questions remained unanswered augurs well for the future. For a good question is never answered. It is not a bolt to be tightened into place but a seed to be planted and to bear fruit towards the hope of greening the landscape of ideas."[32]

For Sen and Grown, the UN Decade for Women was a transformative moment, as it was the first time that resources were available for women from different national contexts to meet and find connections across their local circumstances. It was natural, then, that DAWN's members hoped to use the UN conference on women in Nairobi to mark DAWN's entry onto the global stage as the most expansive transnational Third World feminist research organization.

Leading up to the Nairobi conference, at their third international meeting in Bergen, Norway, in March 1985, twenty-four women from sixteen countries strategized about critical areas for DAWN's panel discussions at Nairobi. At the NGO Forum at the Nairobi conference, DAWN carefully choreographed a series of panels that addressed areas for Third World feminist research. An opening statement by Sen and Grown outlined the priorities of Third World researchers, insisting on the necessity of collective work to refine the vast conceptual vocabulary required for Third World feminist research, from reproduction and the sexual division of labor to sexual violence and the gendered oppression of religious fundamentalism.[33] They critically engaged the rapid institutionalization of policies and research on women, calling for wide-ranging women's organizations to become objects of feminist analysis.[34] Their comments formed the genesis of DAWN's founding document.

DAWN's agenda for the NGO Forum at Nairobi demonstrated the ambition of its comparative Third World vision. The day of panels brought together a range of feminist research organizations across the domain of Third World women, linking DAWN's mission to the goals of organizations such as AAWORD, the American National Black Women's Conference on Women for a New World Order, Women in Africa, and Asian Women in Development. Research addressed the themes of crisis and the burden on women, visions for the future, and the critical place of media in shaping consciousness among women. The event brought together Third World women researchers from across regions, including Irene Santiago from the Philippines, as well as African feminists Marie-Angélique Savané and Nawal El Sadaawi (the primary critic at the Wellesley conference and a prominent anti-colonial voice at the UN conferences), Jamaican feminist Lucille Mathurin Mair (introduced in chapter 1 as secretary-general of the Copenhagen UN conference on women), Indian economist Devaki Jain, Pakistani feminist sociologist Nighat Said Khan, Self-Employed Women's Association of India founder and leading Indian economist Ela Bhatt, Bangladeshi feminist and DAWN founding member Hameeda Hossain, and West Indian feminist Peggy Antrobus (featured in chapter 2 on status of women reports).

In taking the organization's message to conferences around the world, DAWN members argued explicitly for the importance of comparative international research on development by Third World women. Jain, one of the most prolific writers among DAWN's founding members, reflected at a 1985 conference in Bangkok, Thailand, on the power of the TWWRO to make a collective response to the predicaments of women. She insisted on DAWN's importance in the development landscape: "We have evaluated, we have reported, we have studied and highlighted. . . . But what is more helpful is to bring out the cross fertilization of experience to warn [each other]."[35]

Mair, the groundbreaking Jamaican feminist, secretary-general of the second UN conference on women in Copenhagen, and founding member of DAWN, argued in *Third World Quarterly* that feminist research organizations like DAWN emerged in response to a "crisis of survival" that defined the Third World in the 1970s and 1980s.[36] At a time of uncertainty and global emergencies of war, famine, and gendered violence, the organizational form of the international feminist research collective issued a siren call for research on all oppressed women. While the UN convened women, it was up to women researchers across regions to set the agenda for Third World feminist knowledge.

The transnational organization catalyzed an epistemic revolution, "creating a new theology and methodology for change," in Mair's words, that would redefine the very founding concepts of development by and through the research of women. DAWN's new philosophy was based not only in the first theme of the UN Decade for Women, development, but also in the third tenet, peace—what Mair dramatized as the issue of "guns and butter," a stance of anti-militarism that argued for basic sustenance for women's survival against the state industrial complex sustaining wars.[37] The struggle for basic survival defined the terrain of a transnational Third World feminism that sought to imagine a radically different future for women's thriving.

DAWN was an ambitious dream of a transnational collective of Third World women, the most geographically diverse Third World feminist research network at the time. The organization has fostered a large and eager global audience seeking alternatives to a dominant development paradigm that failed to improve conditions in the decolonizing world despite two decades of development policy. In its forty years of existence, the organization's focus has shifted alongside rapid transformations in the terrain of women's rights in what Gita Sen, a founding member and long-term leader in the organization, characterizes as its three phases. In the first five years of the organization, DAWN depended on material support from multiple international sources, particularly the Ford Foundation and the Dutch government, and focused on growing a novel network of Third World feminist research on development. The second phase of Third World feminist research took place within an increasingly privatized international gender and development complex following the disappearance of the "Second World" after 1989. Finally, the post-9/11 era was defined by feminist responses to dramatic neoliberal reforms at a time of state retraction from progressive policies while waging a global war on terror. Today the map of DAWN's membership has expanded, but it is less visible on the international stage than it was at the height of global women's rights in the late 1990s. The organization continues to produce international feminist research in different regions on everything from digital justice to vaccine access, reproductive rights, and environmental crises.

The Institutionalization of Research

In December 1984, six months before the closing conference of the UN Decade for Women, Jamaican feminist Lucille Mathurin Mair traveled thousands of miles to Delhi to deliver the distinguished J. P. Naik Memorial Lecture at the Center for Women's Development Studies (CWDS). Founded by Vina Mazumdar and Lotika Sarkar with seed funding from the Indian Council of Social Science Research (ICSSR), CWDS was the first research institute dedicated to the study of women and gender outside a university department in India.[38]

In her CWDS address "International Women's Decade: A Balance Sheet," Mair reflected on the successes and failures of the UN Decade for Women beyond the "simple accounting exercise" of gathering countless diplomats from over 140 member states and producing 506 program points and 75 resolutions. She proclaimed that the decade's greatest accomplishment was a revolution in ideas, led by women.

> [Women] have learned new ways to communicate, to learn, to produce knowledge. . . . Knowledge is one sure path to empowerment. In their

FIGURE 3.2. Lucille Mathurin Mair in New Delhi. Center for Women's Development Studies Collection, Delhi, India.

> growing involvement with the politics of knowledge, women are operating on many fronts, and at many levels. . . . It is, not surprisingly, a woman analyst who neatly put it this way, "In the sixties development was two thirds Utopia, today it is a mess to be empirically studied." And women scholars are doing just that.[39]

By 1984, Mair was already a visible leader among feminists across the Third World at the UN conferences, serving as secretary-general for Copenhagen in 1980. At the invitation of feminist friends whom she had met at conferences across the world, she engaged with CWDS as part of seed conversations for DAWN. In traveling to CWDS, Mair brought her comparative feminist perspective to a premiere research center in the burgeoning field of women's studies in India.

Mair's remarks, which emphasized the knowledge production aspects of the Decade for Women, had a profound effect on members of CWDS and were cited in research papers from CWDS and symposia on women's studies in the years that followed.[40] Mair's address to CWDS conveyed her profound conviction and a shared ethical vision of feminist collaboration, based in an unwavering faith in transnational research for creating systemic change across decolonizing geographies. Transnational feminist research was built through the mobility of women in a signal moment when a prominent feminist could travel all the way from Jamaica to India and stand in solidarity with Indian feminists committed to research on women and gender.

In this section, I feature the institutionalization of research on Third World women in the form of centers and institutes dedicated to the study of women. I engage with research organizations that emerged during and after the decade on women and with collectives based in independent institutes that worked in collaboration with universities to develop a novel field of knowledge in the Third World: women's studies.

Researchers at women's centers and organizations were uniquely positioned as scholars and activists. In writing research in and beyond the university in self-governed TWWROs, these researchers aspired to defy and transgress the obligations of "academic neutrality" that often, they argued, constrained the research of their university counterparts. Women's visions of autonomy in the nongovernmental research organization positioned the women's research center as a site for objective research and programming that had a more direct impact on economic policy, social welfare, and the law.

My goal is not to comprehensively document the institutional history of all of the institutes, research centers, and women's studies departments that emerged in this critical period or to offer in-depth institutional histories of women's research organizations in particular nation-states. Rather, I conceptualize how TWWROs proliferated the project of institution-building for research, teaching, and outreach and created durable domains for building feminist epistemologies through collaborative exchange, programs in pedagogy and education, and an infrastructure for research publication.

CWDS built on the momentum of the publication of India's status of women report, *Towards Equality*, in 1974, which outlined the need for widespread policy to address the extraordinary inequality that women faced in India, including the domain of research on women.[41] As I explore in chapter 2, Mazumdar and Sarkar were coauthors of the *Towards Equality* report and leaders in the burgeoning study of women in India. CWDS was shaped by the earliest women's studies programs in India, especially the pathbreaking Center for Women's Studies at SNDT Women's University in Bombay. That center, in turn, had been founded by a key network of feminists in higher education, most notably the prominent feminist sociologist Neera Desai, another coauthor of *Towards Equality* and a founding member of the Indian Association for Women's Studies.

CWDS had many key collaborators, including Indian feminist economists Devaki Jain and Nirmala Banerjee, who cited the organization as a key influence in their own feminist connections and research work. As a center based in the capital in New Delhi and closely aligned with the Indian government, centers for social science, and national ministries on education and policy, CWDS established women's studies as a field of social science research closely allied with national state initiatives for women and gender.

Mazumdar opened her memoir *Memories of a Rolling Stone* by pondering how to describe her work: "My passport describes me as a social scientist, but very few know me today as one. I am better known as a 'woman activist,' a 'feminist,' a 'troublemaker.'"[42] Without question, Mazumdar was a visionary leader, an unyielding director, and a committed feminist who largely defined the contours of the research priorities and social scientific methods that shaped the first decades of not only CWDS but the broader field of women's studies in India. Mazumdar was the ICSSR's women's studies program director for five years before she and others established CWDS. The ICSSR, the Indian government's primary funding mechanism for national social science research, established a full program on women's studies in 1975 in response to the status of women report.[43] Mazumdar's leadership of this program led to the establishment of both CWDS and the Institute of Social Studies Trust in 1980. ICSSR funding catalyzed the proliferation of women's studies programs focused on the social scientific study of women across institutes and universities in India through the 1980s.

CWDS was the first independent research center dedicated to women outside the university. Its creation was enabled by the 1860 Societies Registration Act, one of a small set of laws used to register NGOs in India.[44] The law, established by the British colonial government, pertained to organizations separated from the domain of formal politics for the promotion of the "diffusion of useful knowledge" in relation to society and charity.[45] Women's research organizations like CWDS registered and claimed official status through the transnational infrastructure of colonial-era laws that created and recognized a class of organizations in the domain of social life and "charity." This legal structure also allowed CWDS and similar research centers to obtain support from international organizations like the Ford Foundation and claim an autonomous domain of research and writing outside of the university.

The founders were among the first generation of elite women in India with broader access to higher education and advanced training in disciplines. These women benefited from their status as well as from Indian constitutional provisions for women's equality. The research priorities of the organization reflected the urban elite status of the women involved in the organization, whose secular feminist perspectives were shaped by their experiences as primarily upper-caste Hindu women with access to education.

The choice of name, the Center for Women's Development Studies, reflected the dominant concept that defined women's issues in the late 1970s and early 1980s: development. The network of feminist scholars who had been involved in the Indian government's status of women commission and report made a deliberate decision to use the language of development, which was easily recognizable in the terrain of international funding for women's issues as a result of the UN Decade for Women and served as the keyword for a growing domain of technocratic research closely linked to governance and policymaking.

The term "development" was everywhere in women's research units, from DAWN and CWDS to the University of the West Indies Gender and Development Institute. In reiterating the term again and again in research publications, founding documents, and organizational names, Third World women expanded its meaning. They claimed the term and positioned women on the ground as leaders for a critical alternative vision to the knowledge industry of development. They made the idea, in all of its ambiguities and significations, do work for their goals of institutionalizing research on women and gender.

CWDS's founding document described it as "a group of research professionals striving for the realisation of women's equality and development in all spheres of life . . . the main objective of the Centre is to help in the promotion, development and dissemination of knowledge, regarding the evolution of women's role in society and trends in social, economic and political organisations which impinge on their lives and status."[46] The program's foundational document outlined two primary goals of the organization. The first was to conduct research on women, specifically in the domains of "socio-economic life and population." The second goal, in the language of Kumud Sharma, CWDS director during the 1990s, was to "reexamine the existing body of knowledge about women and introduce[e] a differentiated approach to the multifaceted and multidimensional problems of women in different socioeconomic groups."[47]

Women's research thus emerged in full force in the late 1970s and early 1980s alongside other transnational intellectual movements that shaped the study of Indian society. The most notable of these was the Subaltern Studies Collective, a group of men situated in the Indian academy and in the United Kingdom and Australia who offered critiques of colonialist, nationalist, and Marxist approaches to the study of India. Born of the moment of disillusionment in the aftermath of Indira Gandhi's Emergency, women's studies established itself as a primarily empirical social scientific field focused both in and out of the domain of academia on actionable, policy-facing research in the present.

The field of women's studies in India, like AAWORD's emphasis on the urgency of social scientific research, was an epistemic politics of the *present* through empirical measures of the realities of women. These epistemological priorities of the study of women, predicated on the qualitative and quantitative measure of the reality of women for the purpose of policymaking and feminist advocacy, stand in stark contrast to the concurrent intellectual movement of the Subaltern Studies Collective and its commitment to reframing India's pasts by theorizing the peasant as the paradigmatic subject of history.

For the founders of CWDS, its status as an independent research organization provided a unique space from which to create and critique knowledge, develop foundational methods for the field, and build a direct relationship between research and social and political action. Unlike scholars housed in university programs or academic departments, researchers affiliated with CWDS made no pretense of separating their research and state-oriented activism. Mazumdar insisted on the power of the independent research organization to effect change:

> Academic-activism, academic interventionism, or academic entrepreneurism may sound questionable terms to many. Unfortunately, in the world after the Second World War the professional need for objectivity in the pursuit of knowledge somehow got mixed up with the notion of academic neutrality. . . . CWDS was founded by a group who did not accept the prevalent ideas about the limited role of academic institutions or the theory of academic neutrality.[48]

As an autonomous feminist research organization outside of the domain of the postcolonial university, CWDS was uniquely situated to do what Mazumdar termed "action research"—that is, research intimately linked to feminist activism that looked to social scientific knowledge to make direct policy arguments for women's rights.

CWDS saw itself as providing the "intellectual arm to the women's movement" by institutionalizing different forms of knowledge production, from workshops and seminars to the publication of journals, white papers, edited collections, and monographs. The center served as the foundation for social scientific research projects on women conducted across India and created workshops and edited collections to create and memorialize these sustained conversations in domains such as law, gendered violence, and microcredit and debt programs. It shaped new social alliances and research collaborations by supporting primarily social science research projects and regularly bringing together communities of feminist scholars in seminars and conferences in Delhi and elsewhere in India.

In 1983, CWDS started publishing the first research journal of women's studies in India, *Samya Shakti*, which in 1994 changed its name to the *Indian Journal of Gender Studies* to reflect shifts in the emphasis of study from women to the broader study of gender. The *Indian Journal of Gender Studies* continues to be the leading research journal on gender studies in India today.[49] Alongside the journal, CWDS published white papers and anthologies featuring the research results of numerous projects conducted with the support of CWDS. Thus, CWDS was a research organization that was also a transregional collective, a convener of workshops and conferences, a publication center for women's studies journals and research papers and books, and a training ground for feminist researchers. Women's knowledge production was explicitly linked to movement work throughout CWDS's founding documents and the many research studies and volumes that followed.

CWDS was also a central player in founding one of the longest-running women's studies organizations in the world. In 1980, CWDS, alongside the program in women's studies at SNDT Women's University and Kanpur University, organized an annual national conference on the theme of women's studies. The first conference of its kind, this national conference led to the formation of the Indian Association for Women's Studies (IAWS), just four years after the founding of the National Women's Studies Association in the United States.[50] The goal of the Indian Association for Women's Studies was not simply to promote the study of women but to create an entire infrastructure of textbooks, curricula, departments and centers, and organizations to sustain, define, and critically revise the field of women's studies in India.

In 1985, CWDS, IAWS, SNDT University, and the Institute of Social Studies Trust, among other organizations, collaborated with the Indian government's University Grants Commission (UGC) to create a new policy priority area. In July 1986, the Indian parliament had adopted the "Programme of Action for National Policy on Education" at the urging of the Ministry of Education. For the first time ever, the national agenda included an entire chapter on "Education for Women's Equality," including strategies for increasing the literacy of girls and women, empowering women through education, and expanding "women's studies" as part of national priorities for research and university education.[51] Between 1986 and 1989, twenty-eight university centers for women's studies were established. By the late 1990s, over sixty women's studies programs had been funded by the UGC; by 2017, UGC was funding more than 165 programs and curricula.

As women's studies expanded in India and abroad, CWDS served as a critical hub in a transnational circuit of women researchers from Third World geographies. In 1985, CWDS held the fourth annual J. P. Naik Memorial Lecture, which followed Mair's address in late 1984. The invited speaker was a woman who had forged a friendship with Vina Mazumdar at international conferences, Yugoslav lawyer and political leader Vida Tomšič.[52] In her lecture, "Women, Development, and the Non-Aligned Movement," Tomšič, like Mair, spoke to her Indian comrades with optimism about the possibilities of transnational institution-building across women's centers and organizations. In particular, Tomšič praised the institutionalization of research into the status of women under the UN's international priorities.[53] Most significantly, Tomšič highlighted the potency of a transnational alliance of women in non-aligned countries in workshops and networks. As an example, she cited the 1985 Non-Aligned Women and Development Conference in Delhi, which critically reflected on the impact of the UN Decade for Women and women's roles in the future. According to Tomšič, the solidarity of non-aligned women demonstrated that women's issues must be put front and center to combat the global economic crisis of the 1980s in pursuit of self-reliance in the Third World. They had "struggled against the tendencies to treat the women's issue as a non-political, humanitarian one."[54] The lecture fortified an idea that ran through these lectures: transnational alliance in pursuit of women's equality was a fundamentally political act.

Mazumdar and CWDS were essential for the growth of women's studies internationally as well. At the second conference for the UN Decade for Women in 1980, a group of researchers from around the world came together to strategize about directions in the burgeoning field of women's studies. At Copenhagen, Mazumdar began a long-term collaboration with renowned feminist editor and convener Florence Howe and launched the idea of a new international network for women's studies and a complementary journal on international women's studies to be published by Howe's US-based feminist publisher, the Feminist Press. This transnational connection led to Howe's lifelong connection to the rich and expanding world of Indian feminism, and she would take several trips to India to collaborate with CWDS. During her 1983 trip, Howe took detailed notes on the first-ever national women's studies conference; these are preserved in her personal papers alongside audio recordings of early CWDS workshops.

Howe and Mazumdar worked closely together to imagine an international agenda for women's studies, and Howe began *Women's Studies International*, a multi-year Network and Educational Project of the Feminist Press. Funded by the Ford Foundation, Howe also worked over the 1980s to support the publication of a comprehensive two-volume collection of Indian women's writings over centuries, *Women Writing in India*.[55] I explore these worlds of feminist publishing further in chapter 4.

In 1994, Howe delivered the tenth J. P. Naik Memorial Lecture at CWDS, as Mair and Tomšič had done almost ten years before. Her lecture, "Promises to Keep: Trends in Women's Studies Worldwide," reflected on a decade of the international institutionalization of women's studies and made a powerful claim: women's studies had been institutionalized in centers like CWDS not simply as a consequence of women's movements over the past decade; instead, the research organizations had been a primary catalyst for nascent feminist movements across the world. Howe declared in her lecture that the logic of social movement spurring women's research had been reversed: "I have not before now understood how women's studies may turn academics and researchers into activists, that women's studies itself may galvanise a movement. . . . I have always thought of women's studies as growing out of movements . . . women's studies in some countries, in Asia and Africa as well as in Eastern Europe has been a strategic force to energise and develop a nascent women's movement."[56] This vision of women's studies as a domain of research that spurred political action was not centered in the nationalist project, but instead was a vision of politics that required transnational connection: "Remember that the future of women's studies is international, which means that beyond the women's history and culture of one's own country, one must begin to teach, to do research and publish cross-culturally."[57]

Women's studies spread like wildfire, and the field's impact was impossible to ignore. Howe reflected on the proliferation over the 1980s of women's studies in the United States and around the world, from China and Korea to Hungary, Uganda, Ghana, South Africa, Peru, Argentina, Turkey, Germany, France, and even post-Soviet Russia. As Howe argued, the field of women's studies was suddenly ubiquitous, for "it is difficult to think of a country without a women's studies centre or an academic women's studies programme of some sort."[58] These organizations and centers conducted research and teaching, supported activist work, and became key sites for feminist publications in the form of journals, white papers, and books.[59]

The researchers at CWDS did just that: they conducted field studies, wrote curricula, and published research papers as well as comprehensive bibliographies and research guides that shaped the direction of feminist activism and movement work in India in the domains of law and economic policy and in the expanding domains of public health and rights work. CWDS produced projects that reached across research areas on women, including land rights, the invisibility of women's industrial labor, women and agricultural production, women and housework, customary law, violence against women, child rights, microcredit, communalism and gender, and women's NGOs.[60] Akin to AAWORD for research on women on the African continent, the published white papers, research articles, and edited collections of CWDS offer some of the most substantial writing on women in India through the 1980s and 1990s.

The research and subsequent policy-oriented activism promoted by CWDS also reflected the organization's oversights and exclusions in feminist commitments, particularly issues related to questions of caste dominance, minoritization, and LGBT advocacy beyond the limited domain of "women's studies." As an organization led by primarily upper-caste Hindu women with key commitments in and proximity to policy and the national government, the organization's areas of research were, like many early studies in the field, exclusionary and hierarchical. Like reports on the status of women, much of the research from CWDS obfuscated the politicization of caste subjection and religious difference by and through the uncritical incorporation of the lexicon of development metrics and, in particular, the language of poverty and rural underdevelopment. The history of CWDS, then, reflects the complicated history of the institutionalization of women's studies in India in framing theory and practice in the field as intimately linked to national state priorities. The work of Vina Mazumdar, Lotika Sarkar, and CWDS as an organization has been widely commemorated and memorialized in reflections from their contemporaries and a later generation of feminist scholars trained and influenced by the organization.[61]

In 1991, India's economy was dramatically reconfigured under pressure from the IMF and the World Bank to promote neoliberal economic policies, bringing to a dramatic halt long-standing structures of government funding for research on women and the field of women's studies inside and outside the university.[62] In spite of these dramatic shifts in the material infrastructures of research on women, CWDS continued to build and thrive in the 1990s and early 2000s. The organization survives today amid ongoing cuts to international funding and the defunding of social science research and education by the Indian government. CWDS also continues to sustain its staffed resource library, which has over several decades preserved the occasional papers and workshop presentations of CWDS and continues to offer students and researchers a vast library of books on women in South Asia and beyond, feminism, and feminist thought.

Research as Anti-Authoritarianism

During the 1970s and 1980s, feminist research organizations focused much of their labor on making knowledge accessible by creating bibliographies, research overviews, and low-cost publications in multiple languages. Feminist research depended on access to national and international publications, and nothing was more important than being able to access books. In the unequal terrain of global publishing, the feminist resource library of the TWWRO was a critical site for feminists building community. For example, in India, the libraries of organizations like CWDS and women's studies archives like the Mumbai-based Sound and Picture Archives for Research on Women (SPARROW), among others, are a testament to decades of workshops, empirical research, instructional syllabi, and vigorous debates in writing and in person made possible by a collective of women who sought not only to institutionalize but also to memorialize the study of women.

Similarly, in 1970s Pakistan, amid growing energy for women's issues, women came together to institutionalize research on women through resource libraries and research collectives. Founded in 1975, Shirkat Gah, a collective of educated women who came together to organize resources and research on women, was officially registered as an NGO in 1976. The group was among the first of many women's organizations that emerged in Pakistan in a moment of revitalized energy for women's collective movements for equal rights, and the first self-declared "feminist organization" that went beyond the domain of women's issues.[63] Shirkat Gah, like CWDS in Delhi, was a research organization that was independent of the government and the university and committed to the gathering of women and the autonomous production and dissemination of research on women and gender issues.

Initiated by seven educated elite women—who were from the first generations of women to access higher education in Pakistan and abroad—Shirkat Gah was shaped by initiatives for women's rights in Pakistan as well as by a rising tide of feminist internationalism.[64] The year 1975 seemed a promising moment for women's rights in Pakistan, with Zulfikar Ali Bhutto's government having created a commission on the status of women in response to the UN's International Women's Year. Many feminists in Pakistan felt a sense of tremendous anticipation about the publication and implementation of the recommendations in the commission's report on women's status, which was expected to be published in 1976. As I explore in chapter 2, that status of women report was subsequently suppressed—labeled as "classified" and disappeared from view—following a military coup by General Muhammad Zia-ul-Haq to power.

With Zia's rise to power, the promise of internationally state-sponsored comparative research on women's issues in Pakistan went unfulfilled. In this hostile environment, where Zia's military authoritarian state colluded with right-wing Islamist movements to secure power, women exalted feminist research and writing as a primary mode of dissent. Shirkat Gah played an essential role in forming the foundational feminist direct action organization Khawateen Mahaz-e-Amal, known in English as the Women's Action Forum (WAF), in 1981 as a direct response to Zia's oppressive policies toward women.[65] Building chapters across Pakistan's cities, WAF soon became the most powerful and popular women's political organization of the 1980s. But before it encouraged direct action against Zia, Shirkat Gah inaugurated a new era of research on women by creating bibliographies, research studies, and resource libraries for researchers.

At the time, few resources existed for research on women, and there were no women's studies centers or programs in Pakistan. In 1978, Shirkat Gah created the first comprehensive bibliography on social scientific studies of women in Pakistan and other "Islamic countries" in order "to provide a basic tool of research required to validate the study of women as a legitimate scholarly pursuit."[66] The bibliography outlined a framework for contemporary and future social scientific research on women in Pakistan and argued that the study of women was most effective as a comparative project with other Muslim societies. Through comparison across geographies and nation-states, researchers could more effectively argue for women's rights at the local and national level.[67]

The Women's Resource Center of Shirkat Gah initiated what would be a decades-long commitment to collecting a comprehensive library of works on women in Pakistan, starting in its libraries in Islamabad and Karachi, and soon in Lahore. Shirkat Gah was joined by multiple organizations founded by WAF members, all of which centered on creating knowledge about women's issues, such as ASR (Applied Socio-economic Research), the Simorgh Women's

Resource and Publication Centre, and the Aurat Foundation. These libraries were open and accessible to researchers, students, and activists.

According to founding members Khawar Mumtaz and Farida Shaheed, Shirkat Gah in its first decade was a voluntary organization that brought together a range of expertise in its membership, including economics, sociology, biology, business, and publishing.[68] The primary goal, according to the organization's founding document, was "consciousness-raising" by promoting women's roles in "social and economic development" and, more broadly, "national development."[69] These efforts to pursue women's equality and development, as well as their consciousness of rights, would be achieved through collective research and publication. Members conducted social scientific research and published in a wide range of areas, including women's health, economic development, labor, and systems of law.

In the late 1980s, the language of women's development was reframed through the language of human rights and began to rely more substantially on external funds. Since then, the emphasis of research on women has migrated from questions surrounding women's status in the domains of economic life and agrarian production to the language of rights and women's empowerment.

From the early 1990s, Shirkat Gah faced a rapidly changing terrain of NGO expansion into Pakistan, which definitively reshaped the material infrastructure and institutional norms of women's organizations. A rapid influx of international funding during the buildup to the UN women's conference in Beijing in 1995, according to founding member and longtime director Shaheed, shifted the study of women to increasingly quantified measures of women's empowerment and human rights. In this moment, Shirkat Gah shifted from a voluntary collective to a full-time employer, with multiple offices, a full-time permanent staff, and a board of directors with a director at its helm.[70]

Still, during the 1990s and 2000s, Shirkat Gah grew as a resource center on women's issues. It continues to conduct research and workshops on a wide range of women's issues. But today, its future survival is tenuous, after the near-total withdrawal of international NGO support and funding. The organization additionally faces ongoing surveillance and orders to leave from the Pakistani government and its military complex.

Across the Third World and over the decades, women's organizations studiously collected reports—as well as thousands of newspaper articles, reports, images, and cartoons on women's issues—to document the everyday oppression of women across regions. No record was more necessary for research on women in decolonizing spaces than the basic documentation of what was occurring in their lives, particularly in authoritarian spaces like 1980s Pakistan, where accurate news about women was hard to come by. These organizations also preserved their own public writings in the form of essays and opinion pieces.

And so, in the archives of groups like Shirkat Gah, one finds carefully curated clippings about everything from cases of violence against girls and women to family inheritance disputes, family law, community punishments, and displacement. Cutting, citing, and arranging these clippings was a meticulous task, a labor of love performed over many years by students, scholars, and activists across organizations. Through the arrangement and compilation of thousands of news articles, images, and documents, these research organizations created an archive that, by indexing the lives, experiences, and deaths of women, entered the everyday lives of women into a permanent record centered on women.

Perhaps no organization created a more abundant archive of materials on women's lives and research in Pakistan than ASR, an independent research organization that encouraged collaboration across borders in South Asia. This organization was founded by a small collective led by Nighat Said Khan, sociologist, feminist activist, and perhaps the greatest archivist (if unexpectedly so) of the last fifty years of women's movements in Pakistan. Khan emphasized that the organization was purposefully given the generic name Applied Socio-economic Research during the height of Zia's authoritarian policies toward women.[71] Under the guise of this seemingly neutral developmentalist name, Khan envisioned a new platform for radical collective feminist thought across interactive workshops, teacher trainings, and interdisciplinary conferences.

From the late 1980s, according to Khan, ASR began to see its work as transnational across South Asia, and distinct from that of other organizations like Shirkat Gah, which was increasingly enmeshed in feminist international networks and funding structures. Certainly, ASR's activities over the next thirty-five years would not only reflect on what constitutes knowledge about women but also create new alliances and solidarities across borders by disseminating knowledge through the independent creation and publication of feminist ideas.[72] Through a series of workshops, research and textbook publications, and sustained partnerships, ASR reimagined how ideas and visions of women's rights could be communicated through text, collective gatherings, and theater performance so as to create a radically democratic future.

Another way TWWROs institutionalized research on women was by regularly convening women in spaces where they could build community around ideas. ASR brought women together in workshops, performances, and panels that cut across class and national hierarchies, regions, and generations. Many of these workshops centered on issues of labor, women, and development, focusing in particular on women's issues in relation to development in rural areas.[73] Other organizations developed textbooks, guidebooks, and curricula in multiple languages, with the goal of teaching women's studies and feminism in rural and urban environments.[74] Key workshops centered the transformative political work of theater and dance for women's rights, bringing radical feminist visions to life for multiple communities across borders in South Asia.[75]

From the mid-1980s, ASR brought together multiple generations of activists, students, and scholars for residential retreats and weeklong workshops that explored women's history, politics, and feminist theory, as well as girls and women from rural and urban Pakistan and from India, Sri Lanka, Bangladesh, the United States, Europe, North Africa, and elsewhere.[76] These gatherings created a world of being in community, together, focused on the dissemination of knowledge, critical debate, and laughter, singing, and dancing in solidarity.

ASR meticulously preserved and cataloged the documents, photographs, and video footage of these workshops. The hundreds of photographs of workshops offer a window into the life of research as feminist collectivity. Consider one striking photograph from ASR's early workshop with the Sindh Rural Workers Cooperative Organization (SRWCO) on women's employment and labor. In this photo, Nighat Said Khan, seated on the floor, looks into the camera as feminist sociologist Ferida Sher lies on her leg, laughing, snacking, and smoking (figure 3.3, upper).

Images of touch, affection, and dancing abound across this archive of feminist research workshops. Among the many photographs from the workshop with SRWCO is another that portrays an ASR member, Mumtaz Begum, sitting on a cot beside an unnamed woman holding a small child (figure 3.3, lower). They look together at documents in Begum's lap as the child playfully lays a hand on top of a page. Perhaps Begum is doing a survey interview, or perhaps they are having a conversation about worker's rights. The clothing drying on a rack that we see in front of the women, out of focus, conveys the sense of living together that defined these workshops.

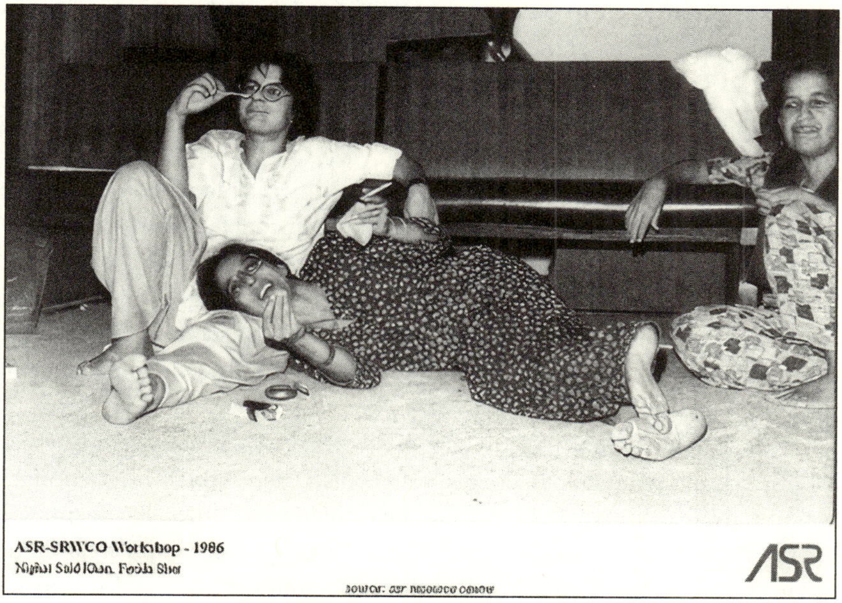

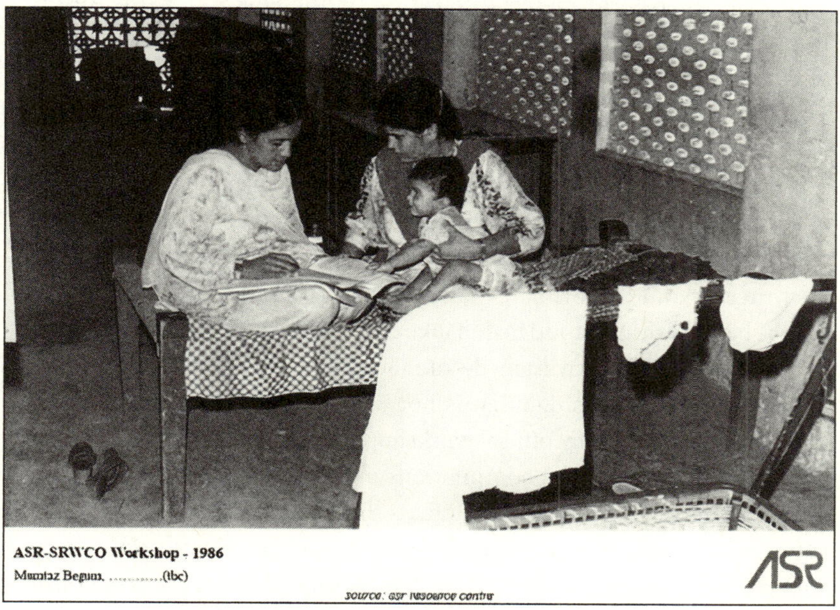

FIGURE 3.3. **Upper:** Nighat Said Khan (left) and Ferida Sher (lying down), ASR-SRWCO workshop, 1986. **Lower:** Mumtaz Begum (left) and unnamed person, ASR-SRWCO workshop, 1986. ASR/Nighat Said Khan Archival Collection, LUMS.

These photos give us but a small glimpse into the rich archives of ASR's visual documentation of the workshops in the 1980s and 1990s. They portray the joy and intimacy of the feminist research and knowledge dissemination project, as well as the many kinds of labor—intellectual, affective, and reproductive—that shaped this work.

What stands out in the extraordinary multimedia records of ASR is the place of friendship, intimacy, and love in the project of feminist knowledge-making.[77] In the late 1970s, Khan traveled from Pakistan to India for the first time and met key feminists who were engaging in struggle and building community.[78] She was just one of dozens of women who traveled across borders to foster cross-national collaboration in South Asia, in defiance of national borders.

Years later, in 1986, Khan joined more than a dozen feminists from across South Asia in a workshop in Bangladesh, as discussed in the Introduction. In a photograph of the feminist participants laughing together, Khan appears alongside Indian feminist sociologist Kamla Bhasin, Indian feminist development scholar Amrita Chhachhi, Bangladeshi feminist Khushi Kabir, and Sri Lankan feminist performer, cultural critic, and activist Sunila Abeysekera.[79] At the workshop, Khan was said to have offered an oral apology, on behalf of Pakistani feminists, for the atrocities committed in 1971 by Pakistan.[80]

That conference was among many of the long-standing interactions between Khan and Bhasin that led to their long friendship and a series of transnational workshops and publications. These transnational projects symbolized an ethic of solidarity across borders. Their alliance, achieved through collective thinking on issues of teaching and writing women's studies, feminist theater and performance, and visions of South Asia–wide feminist research and writing, stood in defiance of the priorities of the nation-state.[81]

This alliance was not without debate and differences in ideas and approaches to the work of feminism. What is not often preserved in the archives of TWWROs—in the many official workshop schedules, conference programs, piles of photographs, and compilations of research papers—are the many debates, tensions, and political conflicts that shaped engagements between impassioned and fiery women. In reflections years later, women active in these feminist organizations portray and continue to engage in complex relationships and debates that shaped the work of feminist research and organizing.[82]

With the opening and relative easing of border restrictions between India and Pakistan in the 1990s came an efflorescence of feminist research, writing, and thinking across the border. Much feminist research across borders was influenced by the efforts of ASR and its priority of cross-border collaboration, including the work of feminist editors and authors Urvashi

Butalia and Ritu Menon on the 1947 partition of British India. These visions of South Asian feminist research across borders (in the form of workshops, edited collections, and feminist writings) were built through collaboration across borders and communities. They offer, and embody, a vision of radically democratic futures for a society pulled apart as a result of colonialism and then brought together again through the collaboration of women in Pakistan, India, Bangladesh, Sri Lanka, and Nepal.

In March 2001, ASR, along with other feminist organizations in Lahore, gathered feminists together at "A Making of Meaning." This transdisciplinary women's studies conference included feminist scholars and publishers from India, Bangladesh, Sri Lanka, Nepal, and Pakistan. The workshop was multidimensional, including formal research presentations, singing and performance, dance, and an exhibition of feminist art. Presenters represent a vast array of geographical and disciplinary expertise, including Latvian social scientist Alice Thorner, ASR founding member Nighat Said Khan, Bangladeshi feminist political scientist Amena Mohsin, Sri Lankan feminist scholar Rohini Weerasinghe, Nepali feminist economist Meena Acharya, Indian political scientist Zoya Hasan, Pakistani feminist scholar Huma Haq, Pakistani feminist lawyer Hina Jilani, Indian feminist historian Ratnabali Chatterjee, Pakistani theater scholar Asma Mundrawala, Bangladeshi artist Nazlee Laila Mansur, Pakistani artist and principal of the National College of the Arts Nazish Attaullah, Pakistani literature scholar Neelam Hussain, Indian literature scholar and oral historian Kavita Panjabi, Indian feminist publisher Urvashi Butalia, and many others.

On the last day of the convening, outside on a rooftop terrace, Pakistani women offered a formal apology for the atrocities committed against the people of Bangladesh in 1971. This was an apology first offered by WAF, in alliance with other Pakistani women's collectives, several years earlier in 1996 (which itself resonated with the expressions of feminist repair offered in 1986 at the workshop in Bangladesh). Feminist historian Uma Chakravarti, who was present that day at the conference, recounts that, as the reparative statement of apology to the people of Bangladesh was spoken, women embraced, crying, overcome by emotion in the moment.[83] According to Khan, no one knew the statement was coming, for its organizers had kept it under wraps for fear of state interference.

What resulted was a moment of reckoning and mourning in solidarity. It was the culmination of decades of alliance across borders by women who sought to research and write a different world.

In her talk at the March 2001 ASR conference, Farida Shaheed, an ASR founding member and the longtime director of Shirkat Gah, declared that feminist research and organizing was not about gaining access in an existing system. Instead, it was about transforming the system through an internationalist project. "We are not just talking about changing Pakistan, South Asia," declared Shaheed. "We are really talking about changing the entire world."[84]

The solidarity and promise of these conferences were made all the more poignant because of how swiftly events changed just after this collective act of mourning. Just months later, the terrorist attacks on September 11, 2001, dramatically changed the course of history, as well as movement across the India-Pakistan border. Since then, the movement of women across the border between Pakistan and India has been largely prohibited and made impossible through bureaucratic delays and visa denials. Indian women who seek to travel to Pakistan undergo unending scrutiny at the border, and visa regimes and citizenship laws restrict and lead to scrutiny for people traveling from Bangladesh to India.

Two decades later, the possibility of such feminist collectivity happening again has been foreclosed, both by increasingly restricted borders and by an inward turn in feminist organizing. That shared South Asia–wide feminist vision for democratic futures, based in alliance across partitions, is largely unavailable for a new generation of feminists. Lost, too, is the insistently transnational project of feminist research against nationalism in the work of organizations like ASR, which sought to undermine the dangers of majoritarian, jingoistic nationalism and state violence through feminist knowledge-making across borders.

Research as Subversion

On September 21, 2001—just ten days after the attacks on the World Trade Center in New York City—the feminist research organization Women Living Under Muslim Laws (WLUML) released "In Search of Justice, Human Rights, and a Just Peace." As I describe briefly in the introduction to the book, WLUML's statement condemned the September 11 attacks in solidarity with women's movements across the world while expressing the profound sorrow of women living in the Muslim world who knew the devastation of religious violence firsthand. The statement decried "the human cost of terrorism" perpetuated on a global scale, declaring that women who lived under these regressive regimes had intimately experienced the loss and destruction caused by acts of violence.[85]

Even so, for WLUML, "vengeance is not justice," and retaliatory acts of militarism by the United States would only wreak further havoc on the most vulnerable people in Muslim societies. The statement declared that "violence cannot eradicate terrorism" and that the solution to the profound discontent and extremist antagonism was the fight against global inequality.[86] The collective of women powerfully insisted that "Bin Laden and the Taliban are not Afghanistan." Retaliatory war would have profound consequences for "women in Muslim countries and communities in particular"; they would suffer unspeakable consequences from military action, while ultimately the "space for alternative positions will vanish."[87]

Women Living Under Muslim Laws had been created seventeen years earlier, in July 1984, when Farida Shaheed of Shirkat Gah connected with women from eight countries in the Muslim world.[88] WLUML was a novel research organization founded by a network of women from Algeria, Bangladesh, Iran, Mauritius, Morocco, Pakistan, Sudan, and Tanzania. It was the first of several women's organizations to build a transnational feminist network for Muslim women and other women living under Muslim states. Early members included Shaheed, Algerian feminist Marieme Helie Lucas, Nigerian feminist sociologist and member of AAWORD Ayesha Imam, Bangladeshi feminist scholar Salma Sobhan, Yugoslav journalist Cassandra Balchin, and Sri Lankan feminist Faizun Zackariya.

WLUML was the dream of Helie Lucas, a feminist sociologist who taught social science in Algeria. She would serve as a key guiding thinker in the organization in its first years. Alarmed by the story of three Algerian women who had been imprisoned for discussing a proposal for a new family code, Helie Lucas joined feminist scholars in other regions to research the global shifts that linked regressive legal movements against women in Algeria with a new era of women's subordination, justified through new codes for family and criminal law. These controversies included political debates about Algerian custody rights, draconian laws of evidence against women in Pakistan, the complicated politics of the equal rights of women and their struggles under minority customary law in India, and the cruel punishment of a woman in Abu Dhabi who was stoned to death by the state on adultery charges two months after giving birth.[89] WLUML's central mission was to create and share knowledge about women's issues under the law across these spaces, especially in the aftermath of the Iranian Revolution in 1979, the passing of the Hudood Ordinances in Pakistan in 1979, and ongoing attempts to pass stringently patriarchal laws across Asia and the African continent in the late 1970s and early 1980s. The "much wider problem confronting women in the Muslim world," argued WLUML founding member and Shirkat Gah director Shaheed, was the rise of new regimes in the Muslim world that passed "legal, social, or administrative measures justified by reference to Islam that militate against women's autonomy and self-actualization."[90]

For the early network of feminists who built WLUML, transnational knowledge production was necessary to subvert the increasingly powerful presence of regressive, authoritarian states that used the language of Islam to justify the subordination and erasure of women as political subjects. The organization was necessarily transnational in scope, drawing on an internationalist vision for women's rights that saw comparative feminist epistemologies as the primary avenue to contest and undermine a tide of rising Islamic nationalisms. Its objectives were clear: to create networks and connections between women and women's groups within Muslim societies; to produce and disseminate knowledge to increase women's understanding of their own circumstances and comparative situations in other states; and to support the struggle of women for rights through "a network of information and solidarity."[91] The subversion of states built on religious authoritarianism was, at its core, a project of knowledge.

The first planning meeting in 1986, which resulted in a definitive plan of action for the organization, was followed by the release of the first dossier of research on Muslim women around the world. Unlike other international feminist research organizations like DAWN, which had a formal structure and regular convenings, WLUML was at first a loosely organized horizontal network that met every few years to create plans of action and respond to key events and political actions across the world. Like other feminist research organizations, WLUML built its membership and platform through international conferences, notably the last conference of the UN Decade for Women in Nairobi and the 1993 UN World Conference on Human Rights, where women from across the globe mobilized around the increasingly popular language of women's human rights, and the 1994 UN Conference on Population and Development, where internationalist feminists struggled against Christian religious authorities' conservative agenda against gender and reproductive rights.[92] After just ten years in existence, WLUML had over two thousand members in over forty countries.[93]

Shaheed and Helie Lucas articulated a critical transnational feminist politics for people in Muslim societies stretching from the Middle East and Central Asia to North Africa and South and Southeast Asia. The critical organizing principle was women's issues for women in Muslim societies, not Islam. As Shaheed powerfully argued, the choice of the term "Muslim" in the organization's name was intentional and subversive: "Consequently, while it is frequently claimed that any given state, society, is Islamic, it is in fact not

Islamic (i.e., that which is ordained) but *Muslim* (i.e., of those who adhere to Islam) and reflects the prevailing structures, systems, and practices—hence significantly different varieties of Muslim societies that exist today."[94]

Therefore, the focus was on undoing structures and systems that perpetuated women's inequality and oppression under the pretense of adhering to an ordained system of law. As Shaheed outlined, the project of advocating for women living within Muslim societies was necessarily an organizational vision that extended to Muslim women in diasporas across the world, as well as to non-Muslim women who lived as minorities in Muslim-dominant spaces.[95] The category of "Muslim law" referred to the legal structures of Muslim-majority states and "Islamic" republics. It encompassed the broad social and political implications of these new regimes, including the effects of colonial customary and criminal legal structures that delimited minority rights in Muslim-minority spaces, as well as the social and structural laws that governed the experiences of women in the diaspora.

The reach of WLUML went far beyond just "the Muslim world." The transnational impact of the organization is clear in the way its research on legal regimes and the oppression of women became indispensable for immigration asylum cases for Muslim women in Europe and the United States. Colonialism, neocolonialism, and the incomplete processes of decolonization in the postcolonial world had created dangerous conditions for women who faced challenges to their bodily autonomy and basic civil rights under claims of religious authority at every level, from patriarchal communities to neocolonial nation-states.

WLUML produced novel research on women and collated, circulated, and republished research in a range of venues and genres. The organization produced dossiers, carefully curated collections of articles and interviews that assembled the most remarkable research on women living under Muslim laws from across the world. The first dossier, published in 1986, included research on human rights and civil liberties in the Arab world, exiled Iranian women in the diaspora, the new family code in Egypt, the creation of a new solidarity network for Arab women, women's and human rights in Algeria, extracts from a Women in Nigeria publication on women's liberation, and a report on the women's movement in Pakistan.[96] Its publications offered specific and sustainable legal and social strategies to combat new systems of family law and social codes that subordinated women and threatened their lives. Research spanned the African continent, detailing the effects of female genital cutting across vast regions, from Sudan to Kenya to Sierra Leone and Togo.[97] In addition to country reports on feminist readings and critiques of family and criminal legal regimes, the dossiers featured radical original research on women, sexuality, and gender roles in Islam. A striking essay by Farhat Rahman arguing against the control of female sexuality under Islam appeared in the 1988 issue of *WLUML Dossier*.[98] The organization's periodicals and independent publications are still in production today.

The original research curated and circulated by the WLUML dossiers was radical, vehemently feminist, and unflinchingly anti-authoritarian. These dossiers reveal the high stakes of the project of the Third World feminist research organization in defining a feminist politics that was insistently anti-military, anti-war, and anti-patriarchal at a dangerous time. An interview with Algerian feminist Marieme Helie Lucas by Sophie Laws from 1984 represented the radical vision of feminist research. Powerfully titled "Bound and Gagged by the Family Code," the conversation sounded an alarm to feminists around the world about Algerian state violence against women who spoke out against the oppression of women.[99]

What these women saw around the world in the early 1980s was alarming. The global crisis of women being incarcerated in the home and quite literally bound, gagged, and stoned across geographies was called out by feminists who mourned the tragic afterlife of the failed promises of decolonization in spaces reaching from Algeria to Senegal to Pakistan. The crisis of religious nationalisms across the postcolonial world would continue through the 1990s and was intimately known by a network of women who desperately cried out for no more war in September 2001. In the decades that followed, they continued tirelessly in their work researching and writing against the oppression of girls, women, and sexual and religious minorities in spaces like Afghanistan, Pakistan, India, and Nigeria.

Afterlives: The Technocracy of Research

From the early 1990s, feminist researchers faced a rapidly changing landscape of international investment and privatization that undermined Third World feminist research on issues of development, human rights, and the law. The rise of international NGOs and the increasingly dominant paradigm of replicable indices and measurable demonstrations of "capabilities" diminished the radical work of women's research collectivities and the transnational solidarity of the 1970s and 1980s. These new organizations worked in a paradigm of research that defined their deliverables in terms of quantified results on women and gender.

Across spaces of the Caribbean, the African continent, the Middle East, and South and Southeast Asia, these new research mandates created a technocratic agenda for research on women and gender. This agenda was a far cry from the political goals of an earlier generation of Third World women, who saw research as a liberatory project of fighting the crisis of authoritarianism and neocolonialism.

Indeed, by the 1990s, the project of feminist research had been almost wholly co-opted by the state. Postcolonial states deployed the language of women and gender for governance in policing, militarization, and neoliberal policymaking, even while abdicating state responsibility for the basic needs of their citizenry. Established autonomous feminist research collectives, like other educational forms, could barely survive financially in a landscape where the World Bank, the IMF, and increasingly privatized, neoliberal post-colonial governance in the 1990s imposed unequal structural adjustment programs that promoted mass disinvestment in education. The war on terror and mass divestment in women's research beginning in the early 2000s further undermined these radical research organizations.

In an interview in 2013, three decades after founding the first pan-African feminist organization, AAWORD, and later founding DAWN as well, Zenebework Tadesse mourned the radical possibilities of feminist research:

> What I find extremely disappointing about gender research in Africa, is that from a very dynamic, very promising subversive activity, it has become a very technocratic kind of project—for a large number of people, but particularly unfortunately for the young generation—because . . . donors decide what is really critical to fund, OK? For example, there is a huge emphasis on girls' education. So if you are in X African country and you are a gender researcher, you churn out these papers about how education is very important for girls, how many girls are going to school as compared to ten years ago, and make a few types of recommendation, and that's it. So the theoretical autonomy that we hoped for when we set up the organization, the type of original thinking that we wanted to promote about what does feminism in Africa mean, as opposed to another place? What kind of coalition do you form with other groups that are fighting for social justice? For human rights, and so forth. All that has been lost.[100]

The theoretical autonomy and original thinking, the innovative methodologies, the specificity of studying the postcolonized—all was lost in the rise of a technocratic project of gender research. For Tadesse, gender research had shifted from a project of dissent—in the feminist vision—to one that fulfilled only the neocolonial visions of donors. The "theoretical autonomy" of Third World women scholars, their insistence on creating new methods and a new lexicon for research, was lost.

Many TWWROs faced impossible material and political realities and lacked sustainable resources to support the labor of their organization. Several organizations, like Shirkat Gah in Pakistan, eventually became part of the UN machinery, funded by and through their connections with the many research arms of the UN, as well as by private American and European foundations. The changes to the funding landscape, combined with the ongoing assault on civil society by increasingly policing governments, created profoundly constrained conditions. All this laid the groundwork for the neoliberal unmaking of these autonomous organizations over the next two decades.

In the twenty-first century, the autonomous TWWRO faces challenges of unsustainable institutionalization, as well as the complicated needs of a managerial class of women working in women's organizations seeking waged positions. Feminist research looks less and less like an autonomous Third World politics of dissent and more like a standardized language that has little to do with the lives and livelihood of women or feminist politics. Research, and the labor of Third World women researchers, has been entirely subsumed, and now defunded, by the massive international industry of professional social scientific research on women, led by foreign-funded research projects on development economics.

By the 1990s, massive divestment from education at every level, from foreign investment to the nation-state, eroded the material and political conditions from twenty years before, which had made possible the intellectual world-building visions of transnational Third World feminist research organizations. Yet, for a moment, TWWROs tried to imagine the world anew. They worked to revolutionize the means of knowledge production, build overtly anti-colonial social scientific methods that reflected the realities of women's lives and survival in the present, and create a wholly new lexicon for research that centered the ideas of Third World women in the future of decolonizing societies.

Under the duress of the politics of fear after 9/11, women lost that ease of movement, the ability to dwell with one another, to write, laugh, dance, and cry together. The growing domain of security studies wholly overwhelmed the feminist project of knowledge for survival.

4

The Book, or How Can We Seize the Means of Knowledge Production?

"Who are we writing for?" asked Indian writer Vishwapriya Iyengar, denouncing the inequality of feminist publishing in a panel at the second biennial International Feminist Book Fair in Oslo, Norway, in 1986.[1] At the fair, Third World women came together to discuss feminist writing around the world and the inequalities that women of color faced as they tried to publish and circulate their work. Egyptian physician and feminist writer Nawal El Saadawi spoke passionately, calling on Third World women to kill injustice through the pen rather than kill themselves in silence. Ritu Menon, cofounder of the recently established feminist press Kali for Women in India, decried the unequal power of Western publishers that decided what got published and what issue or geography was in style for readers in the First World. For Menon, the global monopoly of North American and European presses had marginalized international women, turning their intellectual work into a fad, while publishing interests in global women shifted geographies like "the fashion industry."[2] Novelist, playwright, and feminist critic Maryse Condé of Guadeloupe expressed her frustration and exhaustion at trying to get work published and the lack of choice that forced her to rely on publishers in Europe and the United States. Speaking from wide-ranging geographies, Third World women insisted that it was time that they controlled the means

FIGURE 4.1: Nawal El Saadawi speaking at the second International Feminist Book Fair, June 1986. Courtesy of Kathy Kaufmann and *Old City Publishing*.

of production themselves rather than fight an unequal political economy of publishing that presumed they had no audience for their words.[3]

For Third World women, writing was a dangerous affair. At a panel on the risks of writing as a profession, women narrated their experiences with persecution and exile. Palestinian novelist and feminist activist Fawzia Hassouna described two assassination attempts on her life after the publication of her feminist fiction. Feminist activist and journal editor Mercedes Sayagues recounted her unending fear of police raids under the military dictatorship in Uruguay. After South African feminist activist and political leader Ellen Kuzwayo spoke of her repression under her country's apartheid regime, the audience stood in applause for her bravery in the face of state and intimate violence.[4] For these women, the pen was a sword that they wielded in a battle against patriarchal violence and state repression.

The International Feminist Book Fair, focused on the publishing potential of women globally, was a novel event in the world of publishing. As countries faced dire economic crises and rising authoritarian governments, women came together for the first International Feminist Book Fair in London in 1984.[5] The fair was billed as a signal event that would create an explicitly transnational project as part of a global movement built on the European and American feminist efforts of the Women in Print movement. Originally envisioned as an event that would take place over a couple of days, the first fair expanded to almost two weeks of panels, displays, and gatherings across London and beyond. Menon recounted how the fair was animated by the politics of Third World women in attendance, including self-declared Third World feminists and allies such as "Alice Walker, Toni Cade Bambara, Buchi Emecheta, Fatima Mernissi, Nawal El Saadawi and Alifa Rifaat, Barbara Smith, Ellen Kuzwayo, Gerd Brantenberg, Suniti Namjoshi, and Madhu Kishwar."[6]

At the London fair, Indian feminist editors Urvashi Butalia and Ritu Menon began to publicize their nascent press and to advocate in earnest for a politics of autonomous feminist publishing in the Third World.[7] Butalia had taken on a leading role at the first fair, coauthoring a catalog highlighting women's books and shaping the event's two stated goals.[8] The primary aspiration was to create a new domain of publishing that would "put feminism, feminist writers, books, and publishers squarely and firmly in the mainstream marketplace, onto the educational curriculum and on library shelves." The second goal was to draw attention away from Europe and North America and toward the rest of the world, to create an infinitely expanding audience for feminist publishing, and "to search out and draw feminists from around the world, particularly developing countries."[9] For Butalia, the future was clear: "Feminist book publishing *will* come to India. . . . The more women write, the stronger will be the desire to publish. If no else will publish them, they will do it themselves."[10]

This chapter tells the story of the urgency of feminist writing and of feminists writing urgently. I argue that this urgency to write permanently transformed the trajectory of Third World feminist movements by foregrounding collective knowledge production as the primary domain of feminist politics for Third World women. And so, over the course of the chapter, I document the ambitious yet fragile world of writing and publication by Third World women, who wrote across genres as they participated in but also exceeded state-based projects of policy-oriented research on women.

The domain of feminist writing and publishing grew rapidly in the 1970s and 1980s as women strove to take over the means of knowledge production. From the late nineteenth century, women in the colonial world had increasingly accessed literacy, writing, and publication, creating new works in genres ranging from essays and social tracts to novels, memoirs, and travelogues. These women not only wrote across forms but laid the groundwork for women's print cultures in multiple languages that took many forms, including journals, magazines, research studies, and books.[11] But the late 1970s were defined by a historic shift that saw the proliferation of almost every conceivable genre of women's writing. Women were researching women and writing and publishing words at an unprecedented pace across decolonizing geographies where most women historically had little access to literacy or formal education. Women sought to inscribe their lives, stories, and ideas in print beyond state mandates for research on women, creating new domains of research and intellectual inquiry from the groundswell of feminist movements around them. They pursued independent forms of writing across genres, building an expansive infrastructure of feminist writing produced by women's organizations, editorial collectives, and new feminist presses. In this moment, the page served as the primary avenue toward collective consciousness for a more liberatory future for women.

Writing was not simply about creating a record of feminist movements as a written trace of women's direct actions and protests. Writing and publishing on women and gender—encompassed in vast and diverse experiments in form and genre—was *itself* a politics.

The unprecedented proliferation of writing on and by the world's women in this moment created an opening in the world of words. The title of this chapter, "The Book," refers to the symbolic power of books for feminist writing during this period. Reframing the paradigmatic idea of "the book" through Third World women's fervor for creating their own canon of sacred texts, this chapter reflects on the mood of this moment—the acute sense of need, the stubborn persistence, the reverence, and women's all-out devotion to the work of research, writing, and publication.

Over the course of this chapter, I reveal the collective conviction of Third World women that writing was a political act essential to the project of decolonization. Women engaged in many forms and genres of feminist writing. Rather than comprehensively describe all the many new forms and genres of writing on women published across these vast geographies, this chapter takes an archaeological approach, linking genres and forms across vast archives of Asian and African women to schematize the constitution of a new world of feminist epistemology in the independent publications of a network of visible and vocal women.

The women featured here have been key players in previous chapters of this book: as organizers of global conferences that built extensive infrastructures for the study of women; as authors and contributors to the massive and self-perpetuating genre of state-sponsored policy reports on the status of women; and as founders of women's research organizations that transformed the use of research and writing to contest increasingly authoritarian structures across the decolonizing world. These genealogies of feminist thought centered collaboration and the shared curation of ideas in and beyond books. I document the work of writing in early white papers and pedagogical handbooks on women, feminist journals, curated anthologies, and women's reflections on research in memoirs. These many forms reveal that the institutionalization of Third World women's research relied on collective labor and authorship—a reflection of the collaborative nature of feminist knowledge politics as well as the precarious material conditions that shaped writing and publication.

Like many unfulfilled aspirations in the global history of feminist writing and publishing, the International Feminist Book Fair was a fleeting dream. Enthusiasm for the event dwindled between 1984 and 1994, and the enterprise ultimately came to an end as feminist presses confronted the rapidly changing conditions of privatization and organizational failure that led to the end of many progressive publishing ventures in the 1990s. Yet, even with the decline of independent publishing in the United States and Europe, Third World women continued to write prolifically and create autonomous domains for writing and publication. Publishers like Kali for Women pushed forward and worked to expand their lists, insisting that there was unrealized potential in the expanding new reading publics of the Third World.

Even so, autonomous feminist writing and publishing in the Third World was on tenuous ground as women relied on a delicate matrix of funding to print and distribute their writings, including private equity and individual patronage, international foundation funding, financing from the UN and affiliated international organizations, and government sponsorship. In this rapidly changing landscape of publication, women continued to write their worlds despite the precarious infrastructures of autonomous research and, for some, direct threats to their lives.

The Pedagogy of Feminist Research

The libraries and archives of 1980s feminist organizations in Asia and Africa are filled with large, dusty stacks of papers and bound volumes, all from the proceedings of dozens of workshops and regional, national, and international conferences. Today, almost fifty years after the founding of many feminist organizations, these research articles and edited volumes are preserved and stored by staff with few resources. The stacks of rare essays and papers are documented in indexes and bibliographies, cataloged with care. The international women's conferences, national machineries for the social science report, and Third World feminist research organizations led to an unprecedented expansion of Third World feminist research across geographies. These research initiatives, collectives, and organizations, initiated during and after the UN conferences, created libraries with rare resources on the study of women that have been essential for the education of multiple generations of researchers.

Most abundant in the archives of women's organizations in much of the world is the independent research study, often referred to as the *white paper* or *occasional paper*. In this section, I analyze the archives of women's research organizations filled with occasional papers and empirical research studies, which formed the bulk of women's autonomous research production in many parts of the decolonizing world, with a primary focus on the well-preserved archives of South Asian research. These position papers were adjacent to and closely linked to the state-sanctioned reports of law, economics, and policy change, yet they were not the same. As the field of women's studies grew in the late 1970s and early 1980s, the audience for these texts expanded from policymakers to a broad domain of intellectual and activist communities focused on women and gender.

These studies and compilations of presentations are the material trace of key seminars, transnational workshops, and countless qualitative and quantitative research projects on the local, national, and international levels, recorded in collections of comparative regional studies, research dossiers, conference proceedings, and newsletters on wide-ranging topics on women. In these pivotal decades, researchers redefined what constituted independent social research on women as they pursued projects that explored wide-ranging topics, including rural women and agrarian labor, urbanization and gender, the limits on women's access to work, women's education, sexual and gendered violence, customary and family laws, the gendered dimensions of majoritarianism and fundamentalism, violence against women, women and the media, and issues in women and children's access to health.

The white paper on women served multiple functions, both as an original work of scholarly research and as a document that offered substantive policy recommendations for use by the state and policymakers. Yet white papers also had a clear role beyond their scholarly content. They served as a deliverable research product for the funders that supported feminist research in the Third World.

For example, in the archives of the Ford Foundation field offices are countless grant files filled with detailed reports of grantees who received funds based on measurable results that were reported regularly to the foundation. These files include detailed curricula vitae of researchers, synopses of large-scale research projects, and grant proposals with budgets for research studies that would result in white papers produced with the foundation's support.[12] Through grants and the information gathered in reports, Ford became a critical coordinator of global research on women. Program officers compared regional grant reports and detailed researcher information from around the world, using grantee information to determine who might be invited to travel to international conferences on women. The grant application and approval forms outlined detailed research and workshop costs distributed to autonomous women's research organizations, classified under US law as the "foreign equivalent" of the 501(c)(3).[13] Budgets for researchers in Asia and Africa included travel, accommodations, material support for the photocopying and dissemination of research papers, and funds for publication.[14] The grantee report included a detailed overview of the research in progress, an accountant-produced budget of expenditures, and reports on papers presented at seminars and conferences completed under the theme funded by Ford.

The predominance of the occasional paper in Third World women's archives reflects the concerted efforts of women to produce research on women with scarce resources. The trajectory of Third World feminist publications was shaped by these intellectual and material investments in research papers as the primary genre for independent social research on women. These studies, published in multiple languages, are abundant in the archives of feminist organizations. Yet many women also had material reasons for focusing on shorter research projects and deliverable publications. Most researchers in Third World spaces did not have the funding, time, or institutional support required to produce extended monographs. Women faced multiple barriers to conducting research, from having to prove the legitimacy of women as an object of knowledge to overcoming barriers to basic resources for these studies. The first generations of women researchers in the 1970s and early 1980s faced challenging circumstances with scant funding and little social support for their work. Women's research was often treated as an illegitimate area of study in the university and a marginal subject by their peers in the fields of economics, sociology, history, and political science. There were few outlets to publish work on women, as university presses and scholarly publishers were unwilling to publish single-author monographs on women and gender.

In the face of widespread disregard for the study of women, the earliest research organizations went to great lengths to produce their own publications with personal funds or to secure some nominal funding from the state or from international organizations like the UN Educational, Scientific, and Cultural Organization (UNESCO), doing so under the auspices of "development studies."

For example, Nighat Said Khan, a Pakistani feminist activist, sociologist, and director of the women's organization Applied Socio-economic Research (ASR), described at length how her organization chose its name so as to elude scrutiny under the military dictatorship of General Muhammad Zia-ul-Haq in Pakistan.[15] The organization could strategically access the resources of development research and funding streams and then direct them toward projects related to the arts, theater and dance, feminist theory and philosophy, and publications for the public. Khan conducted multiple studies funded by the Pakistani government's Women's Division under Zia to secure early funding for her organizational efforts, publishing ASR-generated research in the early 1980s on income generation for rural women in agrarian Punjab, women's employment, women in mining and construction, and the changing conditions of women in Pakistan. These studies were published in English and Urdu to be accessible to a wider readership. This funding was foundational for the development and labor studies produced by ASR, but it was also used to build an entire universe of other activities, including cross-border collaboration across South Asia, seminars on feminist theory, and workshops on theater and performance. ASR's efforts were supplemented by Khan's own personal and household funds, a common practice of elite women who had some access to family money or resources and invested in their own research projects and organizations with whatever meager resources they could muster.[16]

The lack of material support made researchers dependent on the voluntary labor of women and donations for basic print production supplies like paper and ink. For example, in 1992, the Pakistani women's organization Shirkat Gah published an updated version of its bibliography on women from 1978.[17] The updated bibliography was a collective effort and reflected the ongoing struggles of researchers to collect comprehensive resources on Pakistani women in one reference text. The undertaking required substantial effort and resources, including the work of drafting and annotating lists of books, as well as proofreading, formatting, design, and production. Even securing basic resources for printing the bibliography took considerable effort, requiring the donation of paper for the small print run from the well-known Pakistani educational business leader and philanthropist Syed Babar Ali and his packaging company.[18]

Farida Shaheed offers a caveat on the problem of funding feminist research in her introduction to the bibliography, where she asserts that many of the writings on Pakistani women listed there were unavailable or not in circulation. Papers and reports remained unpublished in the stacks of women's centers and were inaccessible to a broader public. As Shaheed declared, "One has to acknowledge that this is the reality of writings on Pakistani women," as few resources were available for the actual publication and circulation of research.[19]

Despite the lack of official publication, the information in unpublished works was too vital to leave out of the bibliography. Shaheed made clear that resources were scarce not simply for publishing these works but also for taking up the very subjects on which women could focus their research: "The very availability (or lack thereof), and the volume of materials on a particular subject reflects . . . the configuration of research funding . . . whereas support is available for development issues, academics (theoretical, analytical, historical, or reflective) have received little attention or institutional support." Shaheed described her hope for an infrastructure of research that would fund the social scientific research priorities of development studies as well as philosophy, history, and creative work, as it was nearly impossible to do humanistic study given the material conditions of the present. As Shaheed dreamed, "One can only hope that in future more analytical and reflective writings will emerge, and that the present publication will help those who undertake this challenging task."[20]

Shaheed was right. While more resources were available for publications on women and development policy, little to no funding was available for philosophical, analytical, theoretical, or creative writing on women. The largest sections of the bibliography highlight research that directly focused on development. Humanistic ways of thinking were completely foreclosed by complicated funding structures that would make the white paper on development and the economics of women's work available for publication by a development agency while other research and publication areas remained unfunded.

Add to these challenges of institutional support the colossal work of the first generation of women researchers, who, if they somehow were able to access research positions or university jobs, most often served in contingent roles or lectureships with heavy teaching loads and little to no research time. Ayesha Imam and Amina Mama argue that the study of women and gender in African gender research and feminist pursuits of academic freedom on the continent were delimited by continuous material barriers to long-term positions, infrastructural access, and key state resources for research.[21] The university, government bureau, and development institute were all defined by patriarchal cultures of social exclusion, unequal resources, and the marginalization and dismissal of women's work. The intellectual labor of research was, in the minds of academics and bureaucrats alike, the work of men. Women researchers faced further challenges in accessing work, as almost all were married in circumstances that mandated marriage for social legitimacy. They had children and carried extensive domestic and caregiving responsibilities for extended family. The first generation of Third World women with access to higher education did their research in stolen moments before and after they had seen to their care and reproductive responsibilities.

These women often came from elite families, and their status and personal resources made possible the research they pursued. The formal work of Third World feminist research was globally disadvantaged, yet in Third World societies it was a privileged domain. The position of researcher was largely accessed by upper-caste and upper-class women from dominant groups. Even as Third World women researchers faced obstacles to conducting research, they benefited from the unequal societies in which they lived. In particular, their intellectual work was made possible by the pervasive presence of low-wage and unremunerated labor inside and outside the household based in hierarchies of servitude. The upper-class elite women who accessed employment and education defined the world of Third World feminist research, an essential element of outsourced productive and reproductive labor that made possible the expansion of women's writings. Most women who pursued research accessed international higher education and networks of urban educated classes with close links to political power and often direct access to the state through family connections or husbands who were bureaucrats or landed elites.

Caste subordination and hierarchies of social class, ethnicity, and mobility were critical to women's research production, just as they had been for centuries for all men who conducted research and wrote books. Women depended on low-wage domestic labor by nannies and maids as well as access to family money to conduct research and travel. Sierra Leonian feminist Filomina Steady told me in an interview that she took up research consultant projects, wrote reports and white papers, and later took on leadership positions in the UN on women in Africa because she had the privilege to hire and travel with a nanny from Sierra Leone.[22] Many upper-class women used their inheritance, other family funds, or familial patrons to hold research meetings and fund research publications. The meetings of the field-defining Bangladeshi women's research collective Women for Women were held in the home of Rounaq Jahan, a prominent and established scholar.[23] That project, like so many feminist efforts, was conceived in her living room over tea and snacks as Jahan simultaneously attended to domestic duties, supported by her own mother and the working people of the household.

Libraries filled with research studies and white papers give only a glimpse of the largely unarchived histories of the lifestyles of the feminist intellectuals who produced research. The desire to publish feminist research reshaped relationships between reproductive labor and hierarchies and women's work, defined social networks, and shaped personal and professional investments. The work of feminist research affected everything from marriage to child-rearing to social and kinship networks.[24]

Feminist research papers were a collective effort. A small number of committed scholars did the time-consuming editorial and curatorial work of workshop planning, hosting, writing, and compiling occasional paper series and proceedings. Those collectives often described their relationships as analogous to familial ties and sisterhood, with all the caring and intimate conflict that defined kin relations.

The Revolutionary Potential of Feminist Writing

Although they made the best of necessity, these women researchers insisted that the collaborative work of feminist research was driven by a moral imperative to improve the conditions of all women through the political potential of knowledge, including the most impoverished women of the Third World. Vina Mazumdar reiterated in her early writings that the publication of independent research on women's issues was more than a project of recuperation or restitution—it was an epistemic revolution. It was "not just compensatory research, to make up for previous neglect" or "complementary research—to fill in gaps of knowledge," but rather, it was essential for democratic societies because it "revealed central questions of society itself and its potential transformation."[25] There was a practical use for feminist study, as the knowledge shaped not only substantive change in governance but also the nature of citizenship and political subjectivity for women.

Thus, feminist research, Mazumdar argued, was "necessary for framing policies that aim to influence the processes of change and for people who want to participate in that change, not as helpless victims, but as *conscious* activists."[26] The commonly known term "conscious" and its variations "consciousness" and "consciousness-raising" dominated the writings of women around the world from the late 1960s onward. It is an idea most often associated with women's movements from the period, a paradigmatic representation of the making of new collectivities through the political subjectivity of womanhood and the shared experiences encompassed in this idea. Consciousness was fundamentally a knowledge project and a pedagogical orientation based in the developmental citizenship of women.

The project of building consciousness through feminist research extended beyond the white paper to many other genres of feminist publication that were funded for their pedagogical value among all classes of literate women. One format that served a critical pedagogical role was the popular manual. These accessible and easy-to-access guides to health, labor, and everyday tasks simplified and translated research on women for the masses into usable knowledge in multiple languages. Many of these manuals were published or funded by the UN Children's Fund (UNICEF) and focused on children's and maternal health, family welfare, and labor skills. Titles from Pakistani women's publications offer a glimpse of the hundreds of pedagogical textbooks and manuals produced by researchers across regions, such as chapbooks on health like *Rahnuma-e Sehat* (Guide to good health) and *Aap Aur Aap Ka Bachha* (You and your child), alongside manuals on skills and work such as *Gharelu Paimaney Per Phalon aur Sabzion ko Shamsi Tawanai Say Khushk Karney kay Tareegay* (Appropriate methods for sun drying fruit and vegetables in the household) and *Rehnumai Tarbiat Barai Hunar* (Directions for skill training).[27]

Yet the pedagogical guide was not written only by urban-based elite researchers. Perhaps most legendary in this history of feminist popular manuals in India is *Sharir ki Jankaari* (Knowing your body); also known as the controversial *Lal Kitab* (Red book), it was published under the powerful title *Apni Kitab* (Your book). This work was first published in Hindi in 1989 by Kali for Women and then translated into multiple Indian languages, including Gujarati, Tamil, and Marathi.[28] As feminist sociologist Jyoti Puri powerfully suggests, *Sharir ki Jankaari* was a key example of a countertext that defied the norms of state-sponsored sex education in India.[29] Conceived, written, and illustrated by hand by a women's collective working as part of the Information Development and Resource Agency under the Mahila Vikas Karyakram (Women's Development Program) of the state health department with funding from UNICEF, the book was the product of development and health funding.

Yet the book was an experiment in content and form. It quickly became a popular guide in many regional languages. As feminist writer, editor, and documentarian Paromita Vohra explains, the text was an illustrated "sex ed" book that sparked a world of controversy and excitement across India.[30] It had been a tricky book for publication, recounted feminist activist and coauthor Indira Pancholi, as illustrations in the initial copy showed women fully naked; rural women critiqued this choice because the resulting controversy would be too great and it would be impossible to openly circulate the book. The author collective came up with a solution designed by Malika Virdi that featured peekaboo access to illustrations of women's bodies: the reader could see a woman fully clothed in traditional clothing and then, by moving a flap, see illustrations of important parts of the body in key moments like menstruation.[31] In an oral history about her life and work as co-editor at Kali for Women, Urvashi Butalia said that the press worked to publish multiple genres, and that the complicated publication technique to create the peekaboo illustrations posed a technical challenge in the publication of *Sharir ki Jankaari*. Eventually the book was hand bound by a women's collective.[32]

Despite the eventual production of a book with illustrations of clothed women, the book remained controversial, being held without distribution in health offices and even burned by officials for being "obscene."[33]

The project of producing accessible and teachable feminist texts extended from the manual for women's health and work to popular textbooks and storybooks. Among these publications were children's rhyme books that reimagined society through the transgression and freedom of girls and the inversion of gender roles and expectations. The children's book was a powerful pedagogical project that reimagined the reach of feminist writings through humorous verses and illustrations.

One such creation resulted from the long-term friendship and collaboration across the Pakistan-India border between Nighat Said Khan and Kamla Bhasin, an Indian feminist development sociologist, activist, and writer who was well known for her work from the late 1990s building Sangat, a feminist network across borders. More than a decade earlier, Khan and Bhasin built an infrastructure of sustained intellectual and artistic engagement between Indian and Pakistani feminists lasting over two decades. Their long-term collaborative work across genres reflects the density and intimacy of the feminist relationships built through the project of collaborative research, planning, and writing. Khan and Bhasin created multiple transnational projects, including jointly authored works on feminist theory, international workshops on feminist theater and dance, and translations of major feminist publications across genres and languages.

The fruits of their intellectual collaboration can be found in the remarkable translation of Bhasin's children's books across the border from 1980s India to Pakistan. Like bell hooks, who later advocated for children's books as essential to the project of knowledge and Black feminist liberation, Bhasin felt that the project of feminist knowledge must center the teaching of imaginative futures to children.

And so, throughout the 1980s in a number of children's books, Bhasin wrote clever songs and rhymes that reimagined gender roles and created a world of possibility for children. In *Ulti Sulti Meeto*, we meet a delightfully transgressive little girl who defies normative ideas of subordinate girlhood.[34] Challenging the norms of everyday dress and behavior, Meeto wears her underwear on her head and her socks on her hands. Everything she does is *ulti*—upside down and topsy-turvy, an inversion of social norms for a young girl. It is through this inversion that we see the transgressive possibility of a girlhood based in freedom and play rather than rules and negativity. *Ulti Sulti Meeto* was first published in Hindi by Kali for Women. Following its publication in India, Khan and ASR, with funding from UNESCO, produced a Pakistani version with Punjabi, Sindhi, and Urdu translations.[35]

The translation and movement of such a children's book across borders, with its radiant illustrations of the defiant little girl, Meeto, drawn by Simran Gill, was itself a mode of anti-authoritarian knowledge-making. The storybook, which tells girls to transgress social expectations and norms, represented a pedagogy of dissent in authoritarian Pakistan, where legal codes and militarism reinforced the state and social subordination of girls and women.

Reflecting on her research among women in rural India, Bhasin noted that she came to understand the importance of verse and song in the project of feminist consciousness-raising through her own communication with her research subjects. In an interview on her feminist work, Bhasin described her epiphany about using the lexicons of folk song and verse to empower women, which transformed her feminist research methods as a sociologist. Over the course of her career as a social scientist and activist, Bhasin increasingly turned to folk idioms and genre-defying feminist writing, as in children's books, to bring ideas of liberation to the public. "Whatever I have to say," Bhasin explained, I say it in song." For instance, Bhasin would add new verses that promoted the rights and power of women to a well-known folk song: "Once you sing that song twice, people remember it . . . in the tunes of the folk songs, I would put my own message."[36]

FIGURE 4.2. **Upper:** Kamla Bhasin's *Ulti Sulti Meeto*. **Lower:** Applied Socio-economic Research's translation of Kamla Bhasin's *Ulti Sulti Meeto* in Urdu, Punjabi, and Sindhi.

At the end of her life, Bhasin was mired in controversy after a lifetime dedicated to feminist causes and the conditions of subaltern women and children across South Asia. She became a complicated public figure who represented larger problems with upper-caste heterosexual women engaged in caste-dominant and queer- and at points trans-exclusionary feminisms. In trans-exclusionary remarks at a conference of her organization in 2021—the year of her death—Bhasin reiterated a narrow definition of the feminist project and asserted that women were the most vulnerable and true victims of patriarchal violence. Activists critiqued Bhasin for dismissing the extensive violence that Dalits and queer and trans communities faced in India and delimiting the feminist cause to the concerns of cis women.[37] Just three months before she died, she apologized for her remarks. Bhasin reflected on her own changing understanding of the terms of feminism. But in some circles, the damage to her reputation had been done. The event reflected ongoing divisions within and condemnations of an early generation of feminists who failed to account for intersectional forms of patriarchal violence, violence against queer and trans people, and state exclusion of oppressed caste communities. Much like government reports on the status of women, the legacy of exclusions and hierarchies of caste, class, and gender politics is a critical part of these complex genealogies of collaboration in independent feminist research and publication.

There is no question that Kamla Bhasin transformed the domain of transnational feminist research and writing through her collaborative projects across borders, her books, songs, and children's books, and her commitment to international feminist collaboration. Her dedication to making feminist knowledge accessible continued until the end of her life. An archive of videos that Bhasin produced and made freely available on YouTube during the first year of the COVID-19 pandemic includes dozens of interviews and self-produced videos of Bhasin reading her own children's books, including *Ulti Sulti Meeto*.[38]

The Curation of Feminist Writing

Feminist writing was an enterprise of sustained and collective curation. The profoundly unequal political economy of research constrained women and often prevented them from accessing the resources and time required to conduct research and write lengthy single-author monographs. In this section, I suggest that the curation of feminist writing across genres was based in an ethics of intellectual labor that centered collectivity.

Moreover, I document how this feminist curatorial project expanded in regional and transnational serial publications, journals, and anthologies. Unlike the single-author study or monograph, edited journals and collective multi-genre anthologies were a far less celebrated intellectual enterprise, particularly at universities, where individual authorship far outweighed institutional recognition for collective intellectual work. Yet in women's publishing, the project of collecting and curating across diverse genres and perspectives was at the heart of Third World feminist epistemologies. Across geographies from the United States to Asia, the Caribbean, and the African subcontinent, self-declared Third World women curated their publications in collaboration across collected issues in journals and multidisciplinary anthologies.

Feminist publication in the decolonizing world in the 1970s and 1980s was defined by the work of the few who took up the challenging and often uncredited intellectual work of editing. As women's research organizations produced scholarly research alongside accessible texts for women, editors of feminist newsletters, circulars, and journals worked to combine research and reports with accessible and creative writing in serial form, engaging multiple genres that reflected the experiences and lives of Third World women. As authors and editors argued, the project of feminist consciousness could be achieved only through knowledge production based in the ongoing writing and publications of diverse women across regions and languages. The journal made that sustained project of curation possible.

The best-known collective of women to first identify as Third World women, the Third World Women's Alliance, was founded in 1971. The American collective produced a landmark serial publication that conceptualized the purpose and goals of Third World women's writing. An independent coalition of Black American women who were originally part of the Black women's caucus of the Student Nonviolent Coordinating Committee came together to work against the oppression of Black women, rooted in long histories of slavery and the subordination of Black women to all men. Their cause extended beyond that of Black women to solidarity with the Third World to form an explicitly transnational collective against oppression across communities of color in the United States and the decolonizing world.[39] The serialized efforts of the Third World Women's Alliance were recorded in its newspaper circular, *Triple Jeopardy*, published between 1971 and 1974. In its newspaper, it promoted anti-colonial and anti-racist political work, linking movement work for racial justice and the geopolitical alliance of the oppressed to the project of creating sustainable forms of knowledge for women. As the alliance declared in its framing statement, published in the first issue of the newspaper, "The third world woman must always be fighting against and exposing her triple exploitation . . . the third world woman consciously aware of the depth of her oppression and willing to fight against it will never give up until all forms of racist, sexist, and economic exploitation [are] eliminated."[40]

The Third World Women's Alliance is credited as an important predecessor for later intersectional feminist organizing in the United States and beyond, yet it is most often treated as a project of political activism rather than an alliance focused on women's research and writing. Strikingly, the alliance centered the production and inscription of knowledge across geopolitical spaces as critical to its mission for the liberation of Third World women. The alliance put forth a comprehensive statement outlining its project of creating a sisterhood in collaboration to engage the larger struggle for racial, class, and sexual liberation. The goals and objectives of the alliance centered ideas in Third World women's organizing, specifically the mandate "to collect, interpret, and distribute information about the Third World, both at home and [abroad], particularly information affecting its women."[41] The alliance argued that the knowledge project was essential as women were historically denied access because of the overlapping triple oppressions of class, race, and gender. It was deprivation from education and access to ideas that prevented women from overcoming their shared oppressions.

Thus, in its ideological platform, the Third World Women's Alliance called for "self-knowledge" so that women could build a future with self-determination and bodily sovereignty. Writing Third World women was a project of personal and political consciousness. Research and writing helped women understand their past and present through sustained study and accessible "knowledge of their bodies."[42]

As women pursued new infrastructures for publication, they faced the ongoing challenges of social, class, and political difference that divided a politics based in the social condition of womanhood. For many women of color and Third World collectives in the 1970s and early 1980s, the curation of multi-author collections on diverse subjects around the world was a way to overcome overlapping social hierarchies through intersectional editorial projects. In these editorial visions, collective publications brought together diverse women's perspectives and would supersede the problem of social and political difference among women within the movement by helping women understand their common experiences of gendered violence and exclusion. Women came together to build a serial publication that might help unite women across difference in *Manushi: A Journal about Women and Society*, under the editorial direction of Madhu Kishwar and Ruth Vanita, two Delhi-based scholars who first imagined the journal while in college at Miranda House, a critical space for Indian feminist movement and intellectual work.

Kishwar and Vanita confronted this challenge of difference in the opening pages of the first issue (December 1978/January 1979) of the journal: "*Manushi* is a journal about women, but is it possible to talk of women as an undifferentiated mass? Isn't life very different for a tribal woman, a Dalit woman in rural India, a factory worker, a clerk, a doctor, a university student, a middle-class or working-class housewife, an air hostess, a nurse, a woman in purdah, or a common prostitute?" The work of the women's journal, according to the editors, was to bring together these different lives, from the most downtrodden "prostitute" to the middle-class housewife, through the political collectivity of women. "Yes, there are a lot of factors dividing women from each other—class, caste, religion, race, education (or the lack of it) . . . yet, if we look at the nature and basis of women's oppression, we discover that our sex determines our common predicament in a very fundamental way."[43]

In an interview conducted almost twenty-five years later, Vanita recounted the clarity of vision for *Manushi* at its inception and the influence of visible and powerful women's movements and international feminist research on the aspirations of the journal editors. Reflecting on the founding of the journal at a time of student feminist activism, Vanita reflected on the powerful presence of women like Vina Mazumdar and the impact of the status of women report among intellectuals and activists at the time.[44] According to Urvashi Butalia, it was Mazumdar who made a room available at the Indian Council of Social Science Research offices for a younger generation of women in need of meeting space. These women had begun organizing around feminist issues like anti-rape law and anti-dowry protests. The conversations at the ICSSR offices were the origins of the journal *Manushi* and planted seeds for the founding of the Kali for Women press.[45] Mazumdar also coordinated a pivotal 1978 visit to India by Feminist Press editor Florence Howe, who spoke of American feminist movements, including lesbian and queer movements, which later became the subject of Vanita's own paradigm-shifting queer studies scholarship.[46]

During its first decade, the journal featured essays and testimonials on diverse aspects of women's lives, from feminist actions to the dangers of dowry murders to actions against rape as well as the struggles of low-class and Muslim women. These political perspectives shifted over the course of the run of *Manushi*, particularly after Vanita's departure from India and Kishwar's explicit entry into far-right politics. By the early 1990s, amid rising anti-Muslim riots and actions, Kishwar had repositioned herself in the women's rights movement, embracing a majoritarian Hindu nationalist vision of India and using the language of women's victimhood and state protection to condemn and exclude Muslim minorities, Dalits, queer and trans communities, and other oppressed groups. Kishwar's homophobia became clearly visible in the 1990s, when Vanita began to identify as a lesbian.[47] More than twenty years after its founding, under Kishwar's later editorial leadership, *Manushi* became a forum for jingoistic nationalist writings on women's issues and reactionary articles that promoted homophobia, dowry, *sati* (widow immolation), patriarchal control over reproduction, caste supremacy, and the exclusion of Muslims and other religious minorities from full Indian citizenship.

Yet, in its early years, the journal was politically progressive and avowedly secular, with a mission to bridge social, economic, and political divisions among women and foster a united politics against the "common predicament" of women's oppression across class, caste, and religion. Ideas about the common ground of womanhood were articulated in *Manushi* in a diversity of genres, including research articles, reports from the field, women's testimonials, poetry, short stories, and letters to the journal. In the first decade, the journal editors were adamant that the journal was to remain an autonomous publication; refusing any government or foundation support, its goal was to sustain the journal entirely through revenue from advertisements that were gender-equitable.

The opening framework in early issues made clear the politics of collectivity and transnational solidarity that defined the work of the journal. The phrase "Consider it yours—ours" appeared in early issues as a collective mandate and goal, with an invitation to diverse readers to recognize themselves in the journal and submit their own writings for publication. *Manushi* was to be a place that recorded the many connections across women's organizations, researchers, creative artists, and activists across class, caste, and geography. The collective was ambitious in how it imagined the journal as a radically democratic forum for every genre of writing women. The journal invited women to "share your experience of being a woman with other women" and to submit writing for publication, from "regular reports" on the struggles and achievements of women across different regions to "articles, interviews, personal accounts, short stories, poems, reviews, paintings, sketches, and photographs."[48]

And women did submit their writings, in diverse forms and across multiple languages, sending thousands of pages to the journal in numbers that made its work urgent but nearly unsustainable. The demand for a forum for women's writing was stunning and overwhelming. Within a year of its founding, *Manushi* editors were making a desperate plea to their readers for more support. In an opening editorial statement, "Sharing Our Problems," they laid bare the difficult and exhausting conditions that defined the work of the women's journal.[49] They apologized for their delay in publishing a journal that was of profound importance for women across India and the world. They detailed problems with the costs and quality of production and the financial weakness of an enterprise based on subscriptions. The journal was truly autonomous, they reminded readers. They refused funding from any government or nongovernment institutions, but now did not have enough money to cover the costs of publishing the journal: "For the first ten months of its existence, *Manushi* was literally 'homeless.' We could not afford to rent an office . . . we had to hold collective meetings in parks, cafés, homes of sympathizers—anywhere possible. And every day we had to carry files and records from one corner of Delhi to another—all this with Delhi's lunatic transport system."[50]

Straining their ability to publish the journal was not only their lack of space for the work but also their lack of basic supplies, infrastructure, and paid staff. It took months to acquire the essentials. Although the editors eventually received donations of a desk and a portable typewriter, they did not have a telephone for basic communication, and calls on the pay phone were expensive. *Manushi*, they declared, had "grown really too big for the less than minimum support-structure" of running it out of a tiny flat with virtually no furniture, using resources that were completely inadequate to keep up with the hundreds of submissions of women's letters, reports, stories, and poems. While they sought ad revenue, the ads being marketed so often objectified women that there was no way to run them in the journal; moreover, they had no phone to receive most queries. Yet somehow, with a loyal and strong following, *Manushi* managed to survive these difficult early years and become one of the most circulated and longest-running Third World women's journals in the world.

The first decade of *Manushi*'s publication offers one of the most significant archives of women's movements and collective actions across India during this critical period, with detailed regional reports and testimonials placed alongside key reporting on international women's movements. The first issues of the journal resembled an edited anthology, containing diverse elements that defined its unique offerings, including reports on regional issues as well as women's issues around the world, poetry, short stories, testimonials, and exposés about low-caste and low-class women and their work. One poem from the journal's first year laid bare the stakes of the project of women writing their own worlds.

My Book

I too have written a book
Born of a woman's pain,
Of a man's hunger.

People did not read my book.
Perhaps they didn't find time to
Read it.
Perhaps they felt
No need to keep it
In their libraries
And reading rooms.

Rejected, discarded,
My book has recorded
Man's hunger
For food,
For sex.

When he hungers for food,
I prepare it.
When he hungers for sex,
I offer myself.
I become his food.

After all, is he not Humanity
Who will fight the good fight?
And so is it not his lawful right
To consume me
To satisfy his hunger?

Is it not his right
To burn my book
In celebration of his "literary
writings"?

And yet
I keep writing this book.

Again and again,
I resurrect it from its ashes.

From brothels,
From orphanages,
Protective homes, prisons,
I gather grief, pain.

I struggle
To assert the humanity
Of woman,
To make place in this world.
For my book.

—MANIMALA (TRANSLATED FROM HINDI BY *MANUSHI*)[51]

The author writes evocatively of the right of women to use the book to survive, to claim "the humanity of woman" in the face of erasure, censorship, and forced social and sexual submission, even if only in words. "My Book" epitomizes the objective of *Manushi* as an interdisciplinary venue for political and linguistic translation across feminist writing, a translation of words, ideas, and circumstance, to create a political ethics based in the struggles of women across people and places.

The letters to the editors from around the world, published at the end of each early issue, reveal how powerful this work of translation, linguistic and geographic, was for women around the world. Readers responded enthusiastically, taken by the political promise and diverse perspectives and genres offered in the pages of *Manushi*. As one letter from Kiran in Patna declared, "The publication of *Manushi* has been like the breaking of stifling silence."[52] Khawar Mumtaz of Pakistan, a feminist intellectual and activist and later the chair of the National Commission on the Status of Women, wrote in 1980 to congratulate the editors for their "forceful" work to advocate against the common conditions of the oppression of Third World women. The same issue included the letter "Reaching Out to Our Sisters" from American feminist poet and essayist Adrienne Rich. Rich reflected on being profoundly affected by the research she read in the first issues of *Manushi* and addressed what she described as the unspeakable oppression of women garment workers in India who toiled in difficult conditions to produce the fast fashion clothing sold in far-off America: "I shall never look at a rack of such clothing again without thinking of that reality."[53] In the first years of *Manushi*, women wrote to the journal from all over the world, from Pakistan and Kenya to Scotland and the United States. Considering that the journal was produced out of a small flat with a donated typewriter, no paid staff, and little funding for printing, its circulation and impact around the world was stunning.

In a letter to *Manushi*, editors from the Kenyan publication *Viva: The Magazine for Kenyan Women* expressed their excitement and solidarity with the cause of women's publishing in India and their hope to republish research articles addressing comparative women's issues for a Kenyan audience.[54] The republication of essays from around the world is but one trace of a world of transnational exchange across women in the decolonizing world that expanded the reach and impact of Third World feminist writings.

Viva was itself a remarkable publication. Founded in 1974 as the first women's magazine in East Africa, it was published until the early 1990s. In its early years, it was primarily a venue for writings on subjects such as fashion, skin care, and serialized stories, but it was always imagined as more—as a venue for women's voice and expression.[55] By the late 1970s, *Viva* had gone beyond its initial charge of covering beauty and fashion and emerged as a key venue for writing on politics for East African women. Appearing in its pages was writing on everything from the position of women in the new marriage laws to women's right to divorce and an anti-colonial semiotics of gender. It also published serialized short stories, poetry, and visual art. Popular magazines and periodicals were followed by scholarly feminist periodicals like the South African feminist journal *Agenda* (founded in 1987), the first feminist journal on the continent, which preceded the pancontinental gender studies journal *Feminist Africa* (established in 2001).[56]

In one of the most widely circulated writings from *Viva*, " 'Call Us Ms.,' " Zarina Patel wrote on the language politics of patriarchy across languages in postcolonial Kenya, from Kiswahili and Kikuyu to Gujarati.[57] Patel, an avid reader of *Manushi*, asked its editors to expand their circulation to East Africans. In her essay in *Viva*, Patel called for a change in the terms used for women, arguing against the use of diminutive terms like "girl" and "child," which reinforced colonial-era patriarchal kinship across ethnic groups. She held that there was a whole new lexicon of freedom based in the liberatory visions of anti-colonialism and Third Worldism, which reached across geographies: "It is not a matter of accident that words such as solidarity, black power, alienation, zombie, feminist, and mass action have evolved this century. They fittingly describe prominent phenomena prevalent in the era of capitalism and imperialism."[58] Whether in India or East Africa, it was the work of women across the spectrum to write their worlds and create a common vocabulary for liberation against residual colonial lexicons that dominated and subjugated people through patriarchal cultures and languages.

Interactions between national and regional women's journals and their international readers reveal the unrelenting demand for transnational connection and collaboration among women across geographies. A truly transnational enterprise, however, required a venue for sustained global conversations. Official venues for feminist publishing had largely centered the lives and work of Euro-American women, and few spaces existed for truly international exchange in writing. Precipitated by the UN International Women's Year and the declaration of a global Decade for Women in the 1970s, American journals, founded by American women and largely reflective of US feminist debates, quickly began to incorporate articles on international issues, often written by First World researchers.

The turn toward the global in American feminist publishing reflected the growing importance of global ideas of women's studies and reflected the reach of transnational feminist thought. The best-known publications in this history of feminist publishing were the popular scholarly journals that proliferated in the United States in the 1970s, including journals like *Women's Studies Quarterly*, founded in 1972 and published by the Feminist Press, and *Signs: Journal of Women in Culture and Society*. Founded in 1975, *Signs*—which would become the leading journal for the field of women's studies in the United States—published its first issue with international feminist research articles in 1977. The special issue featured pieces and reflections from the 1976 International Women and Development Conference at Wellesley College.

In 1979, ahead of the second UN conference in Copenhagen, Florence Howe, the founder and editor of the Feminist Press, initiated conversations with Indian feminist scholar Vina Mazumdar about a collaborative workshop and potential long-term publishing project on the international dimensions of the new field of women's studies.[59] With funding from Mariam Chamberlain of the Ford Foundation, and collaborating with the National Women's Studies Association, the Simone de Beauvoir Institute at Concordia University, SNDT Women's University in Bombay, and UNESCO, the eighteen roundtables, panels, and events at Copenhagen laid out the work of women's studies practitioners and public policy related to women across South Asia, Africa, the Caribbean, and North America and the United States. The opening seminar, "Research: Developing a Body of Knowledge about Women—For Women," set out a plan of action for exploring the possibilities of a world of feminist research and publishing.[60] Women's studies practitioners, in Howe's language, shared resources with scholars from across geographies, from course syllabi to children's books to feminist newsletters and textbooks for everything from primary school instruction to university teaching.[61]

The program at Copenhagen and the resulting journal, *Women's Studies International,* became the basis of a network of scholars who published full issues as supplements in the pages of *Women's Studies Quarterly* from 1981 to 1984. *Women's Studies International* covered multiple areas of women's studies on a global comparative scale, from research articles to essays to teaching aids for women's studies instructors to institutional analysis of women's studies graduate education and the professionalization of the field. As part of the project, feminist scholars traveled to the United States to visit the offices of the Feminist Press from India, Brazil, Japan, New Zealand, Australia, Peru, Bangladesh, Lebanon, Spain, Portugal, Ireland, and elsewhere. As part of these efforts to create a transnational collective of research on women, particularly with perspectives that *centered* the Third World, Howe and Mazumdar expanded the *Women's Studies International* network to more than a thousand people from sixty countries who were working in fields that broadly focused on "teaching and research about women."[62]

Women's Studies International featured both regional case studies and broad comparative studies of women's and gender issues. Ultimately, Howe and Mazumdar hoped to move beyond the serialized journal to publish full monographs on international women's studies by the Feminist Press, a goal that mostly went unrealized because of the material and staffing constraints of the press and the challenges of sustaining the volunteer editorial work of Mazumdar and others. Much like the response to other women's journals, the outpouring of writing for the enterprise of *Women's Studies International* was overwhelming. Yet the commitment of Howe and Mazumdar to the work of editing across geographies was undeniable: "We have received hundreds of letters, scores of submissions and . . . encouragement to continue our work." The goal of the network and publishing plan was about creating a whole new readership and public for research and writing in international women's studies: "Our . . . work is mainly to disseminate your work, to make news of teaching and research about women accessible . . . to as wide an audience as possible."[63] Howe and Mazumdar's editorial work brought together international voices on women's research and impacted the trajectory of the burgeoning field of women's studies.

The Canonization of Third World Feminism

From the late 1970s through the 1990s, journals featuring global issues on women expanded and circulated rapidly. Perhaps no genre was more significant to the project of women's writing and publishing than the Third World feminist anthology, which came to define the trajectory of research, teaching, and writing on women of color feminisms and global women's studies. The feminist anthology served multiple purposes. It was a critical venue in which to stage debates across political and social differences among feminists, as well as a pedagogical project through which editors carefully curated a range of voices and genres in the growing field of women's studies for the education of students, scholars, and a broader public. Perhaps most significantly, as a usable and movable resource that could be placed in resource centers and libraries around the world, reprinted, photocopied, and circulated widely, the feminist anthology shaped people's access to women's writings.

I argue that these anthologies created a new canon of Third World literary and scholarly texts that became indispensable as the foundation for trajectories of research on women in the decades that followed. The anthology brought key authors of feminist research, literature, and art under the sign of "Third World women." As they prioritized voices and genres that resonated with the causes of Third World women, these anthologies were a usable and accessible resource that brought diverse perspectives into one text.

Early women's anthologies in the decolonizing world brought together general research on topics related to the lives of women in the past and present. These volumes were numerous across regions, and their titles—like *Indian Women*, *The Participation of Women in Kenyan Society*, and *Women in the Caribbean*—reflected the efforts by early researchers on women to create foundational research materials on women in the face of the total lack of any sustained commitment to or infrastructure for the study of women in much of the world. Women's anthologies were editorial projects that served as an overview and guide to the current state of research on women in a region.

For example, as feminists in India worked to put together the comprehensive Indian government–funded status of women report, prominent Indian economist Devaki Jain was editing one of the first anthologies on women in India, *Indian Women*, published in January 1975, just a month after the *Towards Equality* report (discussed at length in chapter 2). Commissioned by the Government of India's Publication Division, the volume featured essays in multiple disciplines that broadly addressed women. In her introduction to the volume, Jain explained why there needed to be a specific volume on women: "The women's liberation movement . . . has created an interest amongst all kinds of people all over the world to find out more about women and the roles they are playing." This interest was reflected, she noted, in "the number of books being written, [and] commissions and committees being appointed to study the status of women."[64]

With leading scholars across the fields of history, politics, demography, literature, and social work featured as contributors, the reach and prominence of *Indian Women* was significant. Jain brought together the writings of feminist leader Kamaladevi Chattopadhyay and other prominent scholars and writers of the time. The volume opened with an essay by acclaimed historian of ancient India Romila Thapar, whom Jain convinced to produce her first significant publication on women in Indian history for the volume. Other featured essays included "A Demographic Profile" on Indian women by Ashish Bose, demographer and director of India's Population Research Center; studies of women in Indian society and kinship and marriage practices in essays on "The Position of Women in Indian Society" and "Marriage among the Hindus" by leading anthropologists André Beteille and Veena Das; an essay, "Women and the Labor Market," by leading Danish economist and founder of the field of women and development Ester Boserup; an account titled "Muslim Women in India" by editor and acclaimed novelist Qurratulain Hyder; and a report on "prostitutes" produced by a rescue home for women. In their examination of the study of women through statistics, economics, philology and structural anthropology, history, literature, law, and testimony, what emerges from these articles is a clear need for more study of women across disciplines and genres.

The ambitions of anthology editors shifted quickly in this period, from general overviews of research on women to political, economic, and social studies of women's experiences, lives, and aspirations. Editors reframed the anthology as a uniquely feminist genre, a critical space of experimentation centered on an editorial commitment to collectivity. The Third World women's anthologies of the 1980s were purposefully unconventional and unruly in terms of genre and form. Editors placed empirical accounts of women's demography and quantitative economic studies of women's work in the same epistemic framework as poetic works of feminist protest and the personal testimonials of Third World women. Editors of volumes focused on US women of color and women in South Asia, the Caribbean, and the African continent insisted that the study of women took every form, from empirical demographics to literary narratives.

Feminist theorists Jennifer Nash and Samantha Pinto argue that women of color and Black feminist anthologies from the 1980s provided an essential foundation for what emerged as a distinct domain of feminisms in the context of US-based movements and fields of women's and gender studies. The anthology was the product of collectivity—in the face of limited access and almost no resources—by the most precarious labor section in intellectual production, women of color. Nash and Pinto suggest that the publication of women of color anthologies was a highly contingent yet strikingly powerful event: "The anthology has been a key vehicle for the production of WOC and transnational feminisms as bodies of thought. It enabled the quick organization of a field dependent on a volunteer and contingent labor force, relying on a moment—unlike now—when university presses were willing to publish anthologies."[65]

The anthologizing of feminist ideas was about assembling a field, and thus the creation of a new epistemic order through the organization of feminist thought under a new rubric of Third World and women of color feminist writing. These editorial experiments produced a distinct canon of feminist thought with enduring influence in the fields of global women's studies and Third World feminism. The anthology uniquely encompassed the vast multidisciplinary forms of research and writing that distinguished the complicated forms and multilingual worlds of Third World women. In volumes spanning Third World geographies, authors and curators demonstrated that feminist thought reached across historical and philological studies, linguistics, creative writing and short stories, letters and correspondence, testimonials, demographic overviews, and economic studies of life and work.

The best-known feminist anthologies were the many edited volumes by American women that expanded the possibilities for the genre at a time of feminist mobilization. Essential in the history of Third World women's and women of color anthologies is the now-classic 1981 anthology *This Bridge Called My Back*, coedited by Gloria Anzaldúa and Cherríe Moraga. It was first published by the independent feminist publisher Persephone Press, reissued in 1983 by Kitchen Table: Women of Color Press, republished by the independent Third Woman Press, and then adapted and translated into Spanish by Moraga with Ana Castillo and Norma Alarcón.[66] The definitive collection of writings by women of color at the time, the *Bridge* anthology represented a new moment in coalitional politics through the many types of writing in its pages, from scholarly essays and criticism to personal testimonials, poetry, and fiction. Although grounded in American women of color feminisms, the editors insisted that *Bridge* was an explicitly transnational project for all Third World women.

Perhaps most striking in this genealogy of feminist writing was the inclusion of a powerful open letter and provocation that paralleled the dramatic invocation to write in Manimala's poem in the pages of *Manushi*. The letter, "Speaking in Tongues: A Letter to Third World Women Writers," was written by the Chicana feminist theorist, poet, writer, and co-editor of the collection, Gloria Anzaldúa. The letter encompassed the commitment of women to anthologizing Third World women's ideas across form and genre. This urgent project, she maintained, was about the very survival of women.

"Why am I compelled to write?" Anzaldúa asked rhetorically.[67] She insisted that she had little choice, nor did the women to whom the letter was addressed: women of color and Third World women from diverse geographies who had long been excluded from the world of the written word. Anzaldúa's letter was a bold demand for Third World women to take up the project of writing and to write like their lives depended on it. In her epistolary plea, Anzaldúa argued that writing was a revolutionary action taken to defend one's basic existence, "because the world I create in the writing compensates for what the real world does not give me." Writing was proof of life for Third World women: "By writing I put order in this world, give it a handle so I can grasp it. . . . I write to record what others erase when I speak, to rewrite the stories others have miswritten about me, about you."[68]

Anzaldúa implored the most oppressed Third World women with access to literacy to write when possible and imagine their liberation through text: "Don't let the pen banish you from yourself. . . . Don't let the censor snuff out the spark, nor the gags muffle your voice. Put your shit on the paper."[69] Anzaldúa demanded that women write themselves in every form, from research and testimonials to poetry, as she did in her own writings. In her framing, Third World women were morally compelled to wield the pen as a weapon against censorship and patriarchal authoritarian structures and states that made and remade women's exclusion and subordination. Writing and anthologizing was a way to make the world anew, in the visions of Third World women, to counter the silencing of oppressed women around the world.

Anzaldúa's revolutionary visions stood in stark contrast with the comprehensive editorial projects focused on policy led by visible American feminists during and after the UN Decade for Women. By the 1980s, with increasing public attention to the UN conferences and global movements, a range of white researchers based in the United States and Europe produced edited collections that compared the oppressed conditions of global and Third World women. They produced an entire library of edited collections that perpetuated pathological understandings of the simultaneous victimhood and cultural failures of Third World women. This critique paralleled what Chandra Talpade Mohanty so devastatingly diagnosed as the continuation of an imperial feminist vision "Under Western Eyes."[70]

Among the most impactful of American forays into the domain of international feminisms were the "sisterhood" collections edited by radical feminist Robin Morgan, culminating in her most ambitious project, *Sisterhood*

Is Global, published by the Feminist Press in 1984. The volume featured a who's who of leading thinkers in international feminist research, with over seventy country studies of women from the intellectuals who appear in events and domains in this book, including Caribbean feminist Peggy Antrobus, Egyptian feminist Nawal El Saadawi, Ghanaian feminist Ama Ata Aidoo, Indian feminist economist Devaki Jain, Senegalese feminist Marie Angélique-Savané, and Thai feminist Mallica Vajrathon, among dozens of other prominent feminist voices from around the world.[71] In contrast with the intellectual experiments of women of color and Third World women's anthologies across genres and form, the edited volumes on sisterhood and Morgan's subsequent institutes and workshops on "global sisterhood" were empiricist and explicitly totalizing. In Morgan's words, her global sisterhood was a "planetary feminist" project.[72]

Despite the disciplinary diversity and range of the prominent contributors from around the world, the chapters of *Sisterhood Is Global* were almost entirely standardized in form and structure. Unlike the multidisciplinary collections of women from around the world that encompassed a diversity of genres and perspectives in a single book, the aspiration of Morgan's *Sisterhood Is Global* was to be universalist and demonstrably authoritative in its quantitative and qualitative analysis of hundreds of national case studies of women. The result was a volume that was purposefully exhaustive in geographic scope and completely standardized, presented as uniformly comparative case studies by country of empirically equivalent measures. Through the accretion and amassing of data across the world, Morgan claimed expertise over all the world's women. In this logic, comprehensive comparison was to be the basis of a global feminist politics. The *Sisterhood Is Global* project represented a moment when the rise of global women created new opportunities for American women to claim epistemic authority over the large-scale aggregate comparative project. Feminist collecting, in this genre of global women, was a totalizing project of commensurability and reductive equivalence of oppression across geographies.[73]

By the late 1980s, the Third World women's anthology had become the norm for the new field of international women's and gender studies, defining major publications in feminist thought across disciplines and regions of the world. Distinct from dominant American volumes like Morgan's global *Sisterhood*, which focused on the oppression of women in the Third World, the Third World and women of color feminist anthology was exploratory in its aims, intentionally open-ended, and assertively anti-universalist.

The genre became the standard for Third World women's publication not only because women's research production and writing was in a precarious condition, but also because anthologies served as the written inscription of women's intellectual convenings in workshops and conferences. The Third World women's anthology was often the only remaining archive of key epistemic events that defined this transformative period in research on women. Numerous volumes were the direct result of the unprecedented expansion of academic and policy workshops and conferences on global and Third World women around the world, on wide-ranging themes of policy, economics, history, health, law, art, media, theater and dance, and literature. The anthology served as the primary written record of workshops, collaborations, and conversations that founded the new fields of women's studies and women and development research programs across the decolonizing world. It seemed that almost every conference produced a feminist anthology, and nearly every Third World feminist volume was based in a major organizational meeting or transnational conference.

For example, the publication in 1988 of the anthology *Gender and Caribbean Development* marked the institutional establishment of the field of women's studies in the Caribbean. Edited by Caribbean feminist scholars Patricia Mohammed and Catherine Shepherd, the volume included research presented at the inaugural two-week seminar marking the creation of the Women and Development Group at the University of the West Indies in 1986.[74] The extended research seminar reflected the flourishing of Caribbean feminist research following the founding of the first transregional feminist research organization in the region across languages, the Caribbean Association for Feminist Research and Action (CAFRA), in 1985.[75] Funded by the Ford Foundation, the UN Development Fund for Women (UNIFEM), and the Institute of Social Studies in The Hague, in association with the government of the Netherlands, the anthology included essays from scholars across the Caribbean, the United States, and Europe and signaled the reach of the field of Caribbean women's and gender studies.

The Caribbean-wide volume opened with a preface by none other than Lucille Mathurin Mair, Jamaican feminist, chair of the second UN Conference for Women at Copenhagen, and longtime international collaborator on transnational ventures with the Center for Women's Development Studies (CWDS), an Indian feminist organization, and the transnational collective DAWN. The volume featured chapters on the development of women's studies, the UN Decade for Women, feminist theory, women's history, social scientific methods, women's work, Caribbean literature, and the place of women's organizations and feminist movements in Caribbean women's lives. Contributors linked the work of Caribbean women's studies to work around the world, from women's studies in India to the UN international conferences to the work of DAWN linking the study of women across regions.

The conference and the subsequent published volume on the study of women and gender in the Caribbean had a significant impact, resulting in the first comprehensive curriculum in women's studies in the region and the first research center in the English-speaking Caribbean across the multiple campuses of the University of the West Indies. In her framing remarks, Mair wrote of the infinite possibilities of this new field of women's studies, noting that there was no one way to understand questions of women and gender. Everything was new, and the essays presented in the volume provided an opening for an unprecedented field of inquiry—a novel search for studying the world through women. "The field of Women's Studies is still so relatively new . . . that there are no traditional groupings, no standard ways of presenting material, or even agreement about its definition," noted Mair. "A distinctive feature of this book is the range of material which is covered as we search for the tools to analyze and understand the relationship between gender and development in the region."[76]

The anthology was an experiment and a search for methods and tools for the new domain of research that was the study of women and gender. The framing remarks also point to a critical feature of the anthology: disagreement and debate, which were essential to the culture of the feminist conferences and intellectual projects that shaped the anthologies. By allowing a multiplicity of perspectives, approaches, and visions for the study of women, anthologies conveyed a partial account of the many differences that defined the life of feminist intellectual work.

Feminist anthologies were often years in the making. Influenced by a world of growing feminist movements, the collections offer a window into a world of feminist activism and its complex relationship to the rapidly changing domain of feminist research. They produce for the record a condensed archive of debates and ideas that shaped the proliferation of academic and policy conferences on women, gender, and sexuality.

Perhaps the most impactful volume on the history of women and gender in India, *Recasting Women,* first published in 1989 by Kali for Women and in 1990 by Rutgers University Press for an international audience, was first conceptualized at a national conference on women held in Delhi in 1981.[77] The editorial efforts for the volume were catalyzed by influential feminist protests that defined the next decade: actions for the reform of rape and customary laws, enactment of law against dowry murders, and mass movements for workers' rights. Influenced by these Indian feminist movements in the middle of the 1980s, the editors, feminist scholars Kumkum Sangari and Sudesh Vaid, directed authors to immerse themselves in the archives and reimagine the colonial histories of India by and through the analytic of gendered power. The goal of the anthology on the history of women and gender was to transform the project of postcolonial history writing itself by placing women and gender at the heart of the British colonial and Indian nationalist projects. For the authors, the project of gender history was urgent in the present, where historical claims to culture and religious pasts were used to justify the subjugation and killing of women. What resulted was a field-defining anthology featuring essays that critically engaged not only gendered histories of colonial power but the enduring patriarchal subjugation of women in nationalist thought and the many unfulfilled dreams of postcolonial liberation for women.

Like so many genres of feminist writing in the Third World, the multidisciplinary feminist anthology was seen by editors as a critical pedagogical tool for the burgeoning field of women's and gender studies. Functioning as "readers" for students exploring the field, these texts combined wide-ranging disciplinary approaches and areas of social science research with literature, testimony, and government reports in one text for teaching and research. Although there was no one canon in the study of women, there were foundational texts that became classics by virtue of being published and republished in these collections across regions and languages.

In 1991, Pakistani feminists created the most comprehensive reader on Pakistani women for students and scholars, *Finding Our Way: Readings on Women in Pakistan*. Brought together by an editorial board of five women under the auspices of ASR, including feminist scholars Fareeha Zafar, Samina Rehman, Neelam Hussain, Farida Shaheed, and Shahnaz Kazi, the collection featured multiple genres of writings on women in English and Urdu. As Zafar explains in the preface, the volume resulted from a UNESCO regional meeting on the social and human sciences in Asia that assessed the rise of women's sciences in the social sciences in Pakistan.[78] This UNESCO meeting recommended the creation of a curriculum in women's studies in Pakistani universities as well as a comprehensive set of teaching materials for use by students and instructors.

In 1989, just one year after massive feminist protests against Sharia laws and the mysterious death of General Zia in a plane crash in 1988, the new government under Prime Minister Benazir Bhutto, the country's first woman leader, established five Centres of Excellence for Women's Studies at universities across cities in Pakistan. Although the project not only was the result of a UNESCO regional meeting on social science and new government initiatives to institutionalize women's studies but also was funded by UNESCO, the editorial collective insisted on the autonomy of the intellectual project in the *Finding Our Way* anthology: "Financial support for the compilation of this book was provided by UNESCO . . . however, UNESCO is not responsible in any way for the choice and presentation of material, and for the facts given, interpretation offered, and opinions expressed in this publication."[79] The statement distanced UNESCO from any responsibility for the contents, but also asserted that the anthology reflected an autonomous domain of independent Pakistani feminist research.

Finding Our Way reached across social scientific research, creative forms that expressed "women's voices" and feminist theories of patriarchy, women's oppression, and religion and gendered power. The anthology featured policy papers and social scientific studies on topics seen across other volumes from other regions—women and the law, women and health, women and development, and images of women in media and popular culture. The collection then turned to the importance of women's perspectives and "voice," with wide-ranging contributions, from a first-person testimonial of a poor peasant woman to extracts from a novel, short stories, and poetry in Urdu, including "We Sinful Women" and "To a Girl" by prominent Pakistani feminists Kishwar Naheed and Fahmida Riaz, respectively. Finally, on women's voices, the collection included an extract from the once-banned 1985 status of women in Pakistan report that was commissioned and then suppressed by General Zia; its publication now signaled a moment of promise after years of authoritarian military dictatorship. The collection ended with feminist theory about patriarchy and women and Islam alongside statistical information about the demographics of women.

The publication of the Pakistani feminist anthology was an epistemic event that argued for the field of women's studies to combat the unequal production of social scientific knowledge. Fareeha Zafar staged this intervention in the introduction to the anthology. In Zafar's view, the establishment of women's studies in universities institutionalized the truth that the field was "a legitimate separate body of knowledge which is multidisciplinary in character." The field of women's studies was not simply about the study of women; it was "a struggle to show that both the content and the form of existing knowledge is related to the unequal distribution of social power relations between men and women."[80] The field laid bare the unjust structures that shaped the very production of social knowledge and demonstrated how women's studies transformed the very methods and possibilities for all social scientific inquiry.

Despite extensive policymaking and international attention on the status of women, research on women "failed to make any substantial impact on the major institutions undertaking social science research, as the universities have not picked up this new trend in knowledge."[81] This new epistemological field required many types of texts and approaches: the social scientific analysis of women and work, the first-person testimonials of everyday working-class women, and the evocative poetry of feminists like Kishwar Naheed declaring that it was "we sinful women" who raised the "banner of truth" against the police barricades of authoritarian states.[82] The women's studies reader for a university student required social scientific data and analysis, personal accounts of the experiences of women, and the many genres of affective politics in feminist protest.

These collections across Third World feminist projects represent but a small selection of the many feminist anthologies published in this moment. The volumes reflect the ambitions of feminists in the politically tumultuous period of the 1980s and early 1990s. As women experienced profound discontent with the failed promises of citizenship and women's rights and flooded the streets in protest against virulently misogynistic nationalist authoritarian politics, feminist editors and writers again and again advocated for the liberatory possibilities of collective writing and editing for the movement. The genre of the anthology established the writing of Third World women by Third World women as a novel area of research and publication.

At the heart of these projects was a feminist commitment to understanding the contradictions of womanhood in the past and present. As girls and women were held up as the paradigmatic symbol of cultural purity and nationalist majoritarianism, in reality, they faced cruel conditions of sexual and gendered violence, labor exploitation, and basic threats to their survival. For editors and contributors, there was revolutionary potential in the genre-defying feminist anthology as a critical resource against the simultaneous idealization, objectification, and erasure of women.

Women Writing Their Worlds

In 1986, Kali for Women, in association with the London-based progressive press Zed Books, published the first monograph on the history of Third World women, *Feminism and Nationalism in the Third World*.[83] Written by visionary Sri Lankan feminist sociologist Kumari Jayawardena and grounded in extensive research in the collections of women's writings held at the Women's Archives in Amsterdam, *Feminism and Nationalism in the Third World* was a major intervention into feminist thought, a reclamation of lost histories of feminism across the growing divisions between feminism and nationalist movements in regions across the modern decolonizing world.

Jayawardena founded the Social Scientists Association in Sri Lanka and produced pathbreaking works on colonialism, feminism, and critiques of ethnic violence and war. Initially drafted during a visiting research position at the International Institute of Social Studies in the Netherlands, *Feminism and Nationalism in the Third World* was the result of Jayawardena's efforts to create comprehensive curricular material for the institute's Women and Development Program and a response to the lack of curriculum or texts that adequately addressed the many Third World feminist movements and ideas that defined the politics of feminism in most of the world. The work is a critical example of Third World women's projects that returned to archives to compile, translate, and reclaim the writings and histories of women of the world.

For Jayawardena, the Third World feminism of the 1980s emerged in the wake of long-standing fractures in the alliance between movements for women's rights and the anti-colonial nationalist cause.[84] The study documented, over geographies and time, the profound transformations in the decolonizing world brought about by feminist movements, focusing on regions in an expansive geography that Jayawardena broadly names "Asia." Asia was not a Cold War region, but a geopolitical space that linked the spaces of the Muslim world, the Indian Ocean, and the Pacific—what today might be called West Asia and the Indo-Pacific. Jaywardena's project connected regions across a transnational geography of feminisms at a time of anti-colonial nationalism and anti-imperial modernization efforts, with chapters that encompassed Egypt, Iran, Turkey, India, Afghanistan, Sri Lanka, Japan, Korea, the Philippines, Vietnam, Indonesia, and China. For Jayawardena, the study required nuanced understandings of the specificity of place and history alongside the common internationalism that defined this moment across geographies. While ideas of Third Worldism offered an idea of collective political alliance against imperialism, Third World feminism required careful attention to social and historical differences alongside the anti-colonial political alliances that linked geographies. As she argued for women's central role in anti-colonial movements, Jayawardena revealed the intersecting problems of patriarchal exclusion at the heart of anti-colonial nationalism and the misogyny and gender inequity that permeated postcolonial modernization projects.

Jayawardena's novel theory of feminisms at a time of anti-colonial nationalism was based on two key arguments that defined the epistemological intervention of Third World feminisms. First, as Jayawardena suggested, the book was a radical reclamation of a longer history of feminism and women's rights that transformed the colonized and Western-dominated Third World for over a century, ideas that received little attention in history writing: "Many people in the Third World are not aware that their countries have a history of active feminism, or of early movements for women's emancipation, that were supported both by women and men reformers."[85] The critical genealogies of feminism at the height of empire that the book offered revealed the crucial role of women in revolutionary and democratic visions of anti-colonial liberation.

Second, Jayawardena spoke directly to the reactionary politics of the postcolony, arguing against nationalist condemnations of feminism as a foreign ideology that stood against the norms of traditional cultures and societies. Postcolonial political movements built on the subjugation of women dismissed and disappeared the long non-Western genealogies of feminist thought and action. Combating this historical erasure, Jayawardena produced a definitive history of feminism that centered the ideas of colonized women as foundational to the anti-colonial struggle. *Feminism and Nationalism in the Third World* established that there could be no decolonization without a commitment to the radical equity that, for more than a century, feminists had called for across the colonial and postcolonial worlds.

Feminism and Nationalism in the Third World was a game-changing title for the young Kali for Women press; the book found multiple audiences beyond South Asia through its distribution across Europe, the United States, and other parts of the world by Zed Press. Thus far in this chapter, we have encountered a few of the many unprecedented books from Kali for Women's unparalleled catalog, including the popular manual on the body, *Sharir ki Jankaari*, published in Indian languages, and the anthology *Recasting Women*, which was field defining for colonial histories of gender and garnered a significant Western audience through its republication by Rutgers University Press. While Kali for Women became famous as the main venue for feminist writing and exchange in India, its editors were committed Third World feminists who saw the work of the press as urgently transnational in scope and multidisciplinary in range. As Ritu Menon declared at the second International Feminist Book Fair in 1986, Third World women's movements and epistemologies could not be built and sustained if they were wholly dependent on the whims of First World publishers and their reductive understandings of the lives of most women of the world.

As speakers had proclaimed at the International Feminist Book Fair, Third World women needed their own network of autonomous feminist presses that aligned with the politics of a feminism in opposition to neocolonialism, authoritarianism, and occupation.

Autonomous feminist publishing was essential because of the complex and rapidly changing terrain of feminist movements in the postcolony, which worked both with and in opposition to the state. Editor Urvashi Butalia described the careful engagement of women's movements and writing with state power in the 1970s and early 1980s, when early women's movements were still advocating for women's equality and rights within the language of the state. Feminists held the postcolonial state to its promises of radical equality but also took to the streets in massive protests that condemned state complicity with sexual violence, dowry killings, and class oppression: "We continue to confront the State, but we also continue to collaborate with it, to negotiate with it."[86] It was this push and pull of feminist contestations and collaborations with the state, working within state processes for reform and against violent state-sanctioned structures of policing, militarism, and patriarchal law, that animated the world of autonomous feminist publishing. In its early years, Kali for Women served as a primary platform for articulating the reform-oriented liberal feminist projects of upper-caste elite women, although there were notable exceptions in the first years of publication. Yet, with the fracturing of mainstream middle-class feminisms amid the resurgence of anti-caste movements and majoritarian violence in the early 1990s, Kali for Women and other presses began to expand their lists to reflect the rise of radical anti-state and revolutionary anti-caste, anti-Hindu majoritarian feminist movements.

Kali for Women published numerous acclaimed books in the first decade after its founding in 1984, establishing its reputation as the leading feminist press in South Asia and one of the most highly regarded and infrastructurally sound feminist presses in the world.[87] It was the first of many important feminist presses in India and served as a model for feminist presses in the Third World. After nearly two decades, in 2003, the co-editors of Kali for Women parted ways and established their own feminist imprints, Zubaan and Women Unlimited. The reach of the books produced by Kali for Women over its long life was impressive, the result of the efforts of editors Butalia and Menon, who made strategic alliances with international authors and publishers at feminist and Third World book fairs and international conferences and through their own research and writing. Butalia had long-established relationships from her time working as an editor at presses in London. These relationships became critical alliances for the circulation of Kali titles, which reached global audiences through publishing collaborations with key progressive and feminist publishers like Zed Books and Women's Press, both based in London, as well as Oxford University Press in London, India, and Pakistan, and Florence Howe and the Feminist Press. Over two decades, the editors traveled to international conferences across the world while maintaining their close relationships with feminist activists and movements on the ground.[88]

Internationalism in publishing was a politics, according to Ritu Menon: "It was precisely these kinds of accidental things that had a ripple effect. That's why we published with so many feminist presses . . . this is what we were all doing, and this is what we wanted to do, and this was the kind of collaborative work that seemed to have great significance."[89] She described vividly the rare opportunities made possible by the sociality of international events like the International Feminist Book Fair, which established long-term transnational collaborations that shaped feminist publishing. Kali for Women books found a global audience through the republication of its many titles around the world, while women's writings and memoirs were carefully edited by the press and circulated among receptive international audiences. For the editors, the act of feminist publishing across Third World geographies, languages, and genres was a radical act of alliance and a politics.

Reflecting on the reach of Kali for Women's publications across form and geography, Menon argued that the commitments of feminist publishers in the 1980s had little to do with markets. The politics, the ideas, the relationships—those were what was urgent:

> That's why we published with so many publishers. It is an act of solidarity, that people took for granted. You did things out of solidarity. You weren't really thinking, should it be done or not, who is going to read it, is there going to be an audience, is it relevant in India or in Africa or in Lebanon? It was an act of solidarity, so you did it. That's what we don't have now. The feminist book fair was the ground on which this solidarity was so possible.[90]

Across its many books, Kali for Women published women's writing from across South Asia and all over the world. The defiantly internationalist commitment of the editors can be found in their shepherding of the coauthored feminist theory text of Kamla Bhasin and Pakistani feminist Nighat Said Khan, the first monograph published by the press. This commitment to internationalism resulted in a sustained commitment by the editors to publish the works of Third World women from across geographies in their new imprints; for instance, in solidarity with the cause of women living under occupation, Menon collaborated with Palestinian feminists, hosting Palestinian women writers for book events across cities in India.[91]

Transnational collaboration was made possible through Kali for Women publications that featured feminists from across the world, including the critical writings on violence and war by Sri Lankan feminists Kumari Jayawardena and Malathi de Alwis; the historical and theological studies of women and Islam of Moroccan feminist Fatima Mernissi; and the feminist writings of Egyptian feminist Nawal El Saadawi. Ritu Menon recounted how, when Kali for Women published Mernissi's *Women in Muslim Paradise* in 1988, the author asked for her royalties to be paid to her in the form of glass bangles from the markets in Delhi where she had visited.[92] Menon recalled a revelatory moment with Mernissi: "Writing, Fatima said to us, is a subversive activity in patriarchal societies."[93]

While primarily working as editors for Kali for Women, Butalia and Menon were moved to write their own books because of the political urgency of feminist research. They each produced essential histories of women, gender, and violence that have transformed the field of women's studies in India. The collaborations with feminists across South Asia also had an impact on the editors as they worked on their own research and writing projects across the India-Pakistan border, particularly the workshops of ASR and key Pakistani feminists who brought Indian feminists to Lahore for transnational conferences. They embarked on field-changing independent research projects and collaborations that explored the histories of the Partition of India by and through their own family genealogies that linked India to Pakistan. Their histories of the political and social world of women's experiences of sexual and gendered violence and displacement during the Partition and its aftermath have shaped a generation of new scholarship.

In the press's list built over almost two decades, one finds every major genre of feminist thought from across decolonizing spaces. These titles reflect wide-ranging genres of nonfiction and scholarly works, including anthologies and feminist research monographs, popular manuals and guidebooks, and textbooks. As the editors sought out authors and editors of anthologies, poetry, fiction, and textbooks for a new market for women's writing, they also asserted their commitment as a press to documenting the Indian feminist movement.

In the press's first decade, one finds different approaches to feminist writing. An early Kali publication, *Women and Struggle* (1988), published the report of Nari Mukti Sangharsh Sammelan, a rural low-caste and Dalit women's organization.[94] Kali for Women published prominent feminist ecological activist and scientist Vandana Shiva's *Staying Alive: Women, Ecology, and Survival in India* (1988), a critical work of ecological feminism that examined the impact of environmental crises and exploitation on women; it would be the first of many books by Shiva published by the press.[95] Direct actions by women in the 1970s and 1980s are vividly reflected in Radha Kumar's expansive account of the Indian women's direct actions in *The History of Doing*, published by Kali for Women in 1993.[96] More than thirty years later, *A History of Doing* remains in publication; in this essential account, women's movements in the 1970s and 1980s are brought to life through a rich archive of photographs and archival images that animate the many direct actions of women across class and caste lines. The great historian of ancient India Romila Thapar, upon the occasion of the tenth anniversary celebrations of Kali for Women, wrote and published her famous study *Sakuntala* (1995) with Kali for Women, which followed the famous tale of Sakuntala from the ancient epic the *Mahabharata* to her resurgence as a mythic ideal in modern Indian nationalism.[97]

Beyond anthologies, book-length studies, and criticism, the press distinguished itself as a leading publisher of Third World feminist literature by and through the publication of women's literary writings in multiple languages and in translation. One of the first publications undertaken by the press was a compilation of short stories in English by prominent women writers titled *Truth Tales* (1986), followed by multiple short story collections and novels that featured Indian women in translation.[98] Kali for Women published the works of Ismat Chughtai and Qurrutalain Hyder in translation, and these novels were subsequently translated and published around the world. The press's diverse collections of research studies, journalistic reporting, short stories, and feminist theory from the region found new audiences in their republication in association with multiple partners, including Florence Howe and the US-based Feminist Press.

Howe had built a lifelong connection to the rich and expanding world of Indian feminisms through her many trips to India and the UN international conferences for women. This long engagement with Indian feminism produced books and volumes that expanded the readership of Indian feminisms worldwide and made Indian feminist literature and scholarship among the most circulated of all writings on women from around the decolonizing world. As we learn in Chapter 3, Howe traveled to India for the first time at the invitation of Vina Mazumdar and developed long-term collaborations with organizations like CWDS and Kali for Women. Preserved among her personal papers and the papers of the Feminist Press at Brown University are Howe's detailed notes and photocopies of the papers at the first-ever national women's studies conference in India, in 1981. The collection includes her audio recordings of early CWDS workshops (perhaps the only audio recordings available of these important events). Howe and Mazumdar had worked closely together to establish *Women's Studies International*, which fostered an international turn in Feminist Press titles.

Along with her many collaborations with Mazumdar, between 1985 and 1993 Howe collaborated with India-based feminist academics, activists, and editors Susie Tharu and K. Lalita to document women's writings across genres and across centuries. Tharu and Lalita were scholars and founders of the feminist organizing collective Anveshi; they would soon be curating and editing many collections of women's writings that continue to serve as essential sourcebooks and works of translation. The collaboration between Howe, Tharu, and Lalita led to the Feminist Press's first-ever sourcebook of global women's writings over centuries, funded in part by a small grant from the Ford Foundation.

Tharu and Lalita's edited two-volume classic, *Women Writing in India* (volume 1 was published in 1991, volume 2 in 1993), republished by Oxford University Press India, was a landmark collection of women's writings from South Asia over the centuries. Today it remains the single most comprehensive archive of translations of women's writings in multiple Indian languages across premodern and modern India, spanning more than a millennium, from 600 BCE to the late twentieth century. It has been the standard sourcebook for courses on women, literature, and politics in India, the United States, and around the world for over three decades.

Critically, the volumes' titles referenced women *writing* in India, using the verb form, to represent the act of writing as a form of political practice for women across communities, though it primarily focuses on elite upper-caste Hindu women who had access to literacy. The collection was formed through multiple workshops held over many years. The writing of women was discovered, translated, and annotated by nine research groups at workshops across regions and in multiple languages over four years.[99] As

Tharu described them, these collaborative sessions yielded multiple forms and genres that revealed women in the act of writing, producing "songs, prayers, letters, shared memories, unfinished fragments, documents from other collections, medical records, testimonies, statements before judicial or administrative authorities, marginal notes in books they had read, citations in other texts." She noted that "even exercise books could yield significant material."[100] The question of women writing their worlds extended beyond the act of women writing with the pen to create a theory of women's authorship that moved beyond text to constitute novel practices of archival reading and compilation. The collection included "oral composition, private communication, official testimony (before a judge or an administrator) and even brushed against the grain of dismissal to try and capture what was being dismissed."[101] Book reviews argued that the publication of *Women Writing in India* was a signal event for the writing of Indian history, as the collection demonstrated the persistent presence of women's archives and compelled historians to read and engage women writers across time and language.[102]

Women Writing in India reflected the social hierarchies of caste, class, race, and religion that shaped access to and the status of publishable women's writings. Its two volumes, while written in the 1980s, were published at a moment when "the Indian women's movement" was increasingly under scrutiny for claiming a singular movement for Indian women. By the early 1990s, the idea of "the movement" had fractured as upper-caste, urban-based feminist organizers and researchers were critiqued by diverse groups for silencing lower-caste and Dalit women, excluding early LGBT organizing, and perpetuating majoritarian upper-caste perspectives that marginalized Muslim women.

The volumes were produced in spite of a complete lack of resources and remuneration for editorial and translation work. International foundations were wholly unwilling to financially support the *Women Writing* project in India, according to Howe. While editors Lalita and Tharu received some royalties, the hundreds of women who had worked on *Women Writing in India* received nothing but copies of the two volumes.[103] Howe described working nights and weekends to edit the volume, and the costs of typesetting and printing, she noted, had put the Feminist Press in debt.[104] The acts of writing and publishing were urgent for so many women, yet the work involved—writing, translating, annotating, editing—became a complicated terrain of unremunerated work by women. A labor of love perhaps, but labor nonetheless that received no remuneration and little credit for the many forms of intellectual work involved.

Women Writing in India, with its pathbreaking editorial work as well as its shortcomings and deficits, served as the foundation and impetus for later important collections of writings. These included a collection from 2000 by former *Manushi* co-editor and queer scholar Ruth Vanita and medieval historian and queer activist Saleem Kidwai, *Same Sex Love in India*, as well as multiple collections of Dalit women's writings, such as edited collections by Tharu and Lalita. It was also the inspiration and initial model for the multi-year, global pan-Africanist project that became the massive four-volume *Women Writing Africa*.[105]

Florence Howe recounted that at the Modern Language Association conference in 1990 she was asked to speak for five minutes on a panel and comment on "Books That Changed My Life." For that panel, she invited Susie Tharu to travel from India to help publicize the volume at the conference. They stood together in front of the room and held up the galleys of the first edition of *Women Writing in India*. Twenty years after the founding of the Feminist Press, Howe exclaimed, she never thought she could publish a book with "twenty-six hundred years of women's writings in India."[106]

At the conference, Tuzyline Jita Allan, a scholar of African feminist literature at Baruch College, approached Howe. Spurred by the discussion of the *Women Writing in India* collection, Allan asserted that African feminist scholars wished to pursue parallel volumes of women writing in Africa.[107] What followed was a nearly two-decade effort to document the many acts of women writing in Africa, a far more extensive project than *Women Writing in India*. Remembering the nearly impossible conditions of the experience of the India project—little funding and unremunerated labor—Howe was reluctant to take it on. When the second volume of *Women Writing in India* appeared, Howe took copies to the Ford Foundation offices in New York City, and program officer Alison Bernstein responded, "Thanks, Florence, and, of course, Africa is next."[108] Howe refused to do the project because of the difficulty of obtaining funding, but relented after Bernstein reassured her that Ford would be willing to support the project, starting with a $40,000 seed grant. The Feminist Press staff, alongside Allan and Abena Busia, a feminist scholar of the African continent at Rutgers University, consulted with Tharu about her experiences with the India volume and began planning for the first conference for the volume, held in Ghana in 1994.

Following this initial seed grant, Howe and the African feminist editorial collective applied to the Ford Foundation for $200,000 in 1995 for what they imagined would be a two- or three-volume project parallel to *Women Writing in India*. In a letter to the Ford Foundation, Howe made a powerful plea for funding the work of recuperating the lost voices of women: "Why have women writers been 'lost'—not only in India and Africa, but in North America, in Europe, and elsewhere in the world? That loss of history makes for further losses: without a history, young women may find it impossible to imagine a future that contains them."[109] The grant theorized the vast possibilities of women writing across different frameworks on the continent through the concepts of physical, political, historical, linguistic, and cultural geography.[110] Howe made a dramatic and persuasive argument for the collection: at stake in this massive undertaking of African feminist collecting was the very future of women.

Women Writing Africa faced many struggles in securing financial support for the volumes as well as infrastructural issues with finding and publishing women's writings. The project extended to almost two decades, with the last volume published by the Feminist Press in 2009. The press's archives include application after application from Howe to fund internationalist projects like *Women's Studies International* and *Women Writing Africa*. This time, using funds from Ford, the project established bank accounts on the continent under the name "Women Writing Africa" from which they paid scholars and translators. Ultimately, though, the massive four-volume collection, like *Women Writing in India*, was produced through the voluntary, largely unpaid labor of contributors, editors, and project directors. No woman worked full-time on the *Women Writing Africa* project. All members of the editorial collective and the contributing author network had full-time jobs as well as extensive caregiving responsibilities to their families.[111]

Women Writing Africa, while grounded in the writings, voices, and intellectual visions of African women, was published by an American publisher, an issue that spurred extended discussion and debate among the editors, who expressed concern about an ethics of feminist knowledge production dependent on First World publishing.[112] At the urging of an editorial collective composed entirely of African women, Howe tried to find local publishers to partner in the publication of the volumes, yet it was nearly impossible to find any single African publisher. She came to realize that the material infrastructure and access to print in India far surpassed anything on the African continent: "When the project began, I imagined that, as in India, the volumes would be widely distributed by an African publisher. I could not have imagined how isolated publishers were in Africa."[113] The books published in East Africa had no circulation in southern regions, while books from the south were not available in the western, eastern, or northern parts of the continent.

Then, of course, there was the problem of colonial language inheritance. The Feminist Press relied on a French publisher in Paris whose business model included Francophone Africa to publish French translations of the collections. However radical its vision of women in print, *Women Writing Africa* was trying to do the important work of reclaiming women's lives in an impossibly unequal world of publication. More than a decade after the Third World women's panels at the International Feminist Book Fair in the mid-1980s, the conditions for the autonomous publication of Third World texts in the Third World remained nearly impossible.

Despite these challenges, this momentous effort by hundreds of women across the African continent, the United States, and Europe achieved a remarkable result: four volumes covering geographic regions of North, South, East, and West Africa, the first three over five hundred pages and the fourth and final volume on North Africa reaching almost seven hundred pages. The *Women Writing Africa* project was overseen and guided by codirectors Tuzyline Jita Allan and Abena Busia alongside Howe, who secured extensive funding, codirected workshops, and oversaw the production work for the volumes. Allan and Busia had broad training in the literatures of Africa and the African diaspora. Each volume featured editors with expertise in the region. Contributors included teachers, artists, historians, anthropologists, archivists, and librarians working in English, French, and Indigenous languages. The editors sent hundreds of query letters to writers, scholars, activists, artists, and archivists across regions asking for their expertise in contributing to the volume as authors and editors and in other roles: "We are writing to introduce you to Women Writing Africa . . . we are looking for African publishers to produce the volumes locally, and we are also seeking libraries and archives where we may deposit and protect these valuable materials, which contain stories and voices from the African past that would otherwise not be heard."[114]

Reflecting their editorial vision of *Women Writing Africa* as an endeavor across disciplines, genres, and forms, the editors insisted that the work of scholarly curation for African women required both empirical rigor and a poetic sensibility.[115] The title of the collection foregrounded the actions of women who wrote their worlds, as Busia argues, animating the experiences of women through "the intangible heritage of African women, expressed in our literature and orature, through presenting songs, letters, journals, diaries, legal depositions, and other significant historical texts, as well as fiction, drama, and poetry."[116]

Ultimately, over almost twenty years, the anthology of women writing created a new network of feminist thinkers across the African continent. It was the most concerted effort to advocate for the many endangered subaltern archives and histories of women on the continent. It remains the most significant source of writings on African women in English and French.

Afterlives: "To Make Place in This World. For My Book."

Nawal El Saadawi opened her 1999 memoir by describing the revelatory experience of writing her "first words": "It was my mother who taught me how to read and write. The first word I wrote was my name, Nawal. I loved the way it looked. It meant a 'gift.' "[117]

Over the course of this chapter, we have seen that many women struggled to do the work of writing words. They viewed writing as not only a catalyst for political struggle but also, as El Saadawi framed her life, a gift. Third World feminist writing and publication took many novel forms: monographs, women's bibliographies, white papers, policy reports, essays, novels, short stories, children's books, open letters, poems, oral testimonials, and songs. These many genres were curated in the collective endeavors of Third World women in new feminist newspapers and journals, anthologies, and critical source collections.

At the urging of feminist editor Urvashi Butalia, Vina Mazumdar wrote her memoir, *Memories of a Rolling Stone*, at the age of eighty-one to reflect on her remarkable career and life. Published by Butalia's imprint Zubaan in 2010, the book is a testament to this moment of women furiously meeting, researching, writing, and publishing. Mazumdar opens her book with a tribute to the many people who changed her life: "As for the 10,000 plus women who became my gurus from the 1970s onwards—India's forgotten majority—I have tried to fight their battles through the twin movements of Women and Women's Studies."[118] The twinned women's movement and women's studies movement no doubt produced writings that created entire intellectual fields and sparked political visions for Third World feminisms that have endured. For Mazumdar, the memoir served as testimony and proof of a collective historical moment of epistemological change—a time when the world of ideas was suddenly transformed through the study of women and gender.

The feminist memoirs of the many women who animate this chapter, captured in autobiographies, life histories in interviews, and oral testimonials, are critical sources for my argument that Third World feminism is a novel form of feminist politics that centered epistemology. Third World feminist writing and publishing was a powerful political domain in the 1970s and 1980s that transformed the way we understand everything from development to democracy and human rights. These life histories of women in the Third World often focus less on the interiority of the individual and instead write women in their worlds, providing some of the best documentation of a rapidly changing terrain of political movements and the epistemological revolutions precipitated by the study of women as a field of inquiry. These texts and oral histories also testify to the precarity that loomed large as women gained access to print in the early 1990s, a time of neoliberal economic reform and ongoing debt programs across the decolonizing world. The memoir is perhaps the greatest repository of histories of this extraordinary epistemological revolution, when feminist writing became an act of political dissent in the decolonizing world and the pen was wielded so prolifically and so suddenly by thousands of women in pursuit of a new democratic politics of radical equity and justice.

By writing their worlds, this generation of feminist writers and intellectuals created a rich historical archive of underexplored institutional memories and histories and of social and political events that would otherwise have remained undocumented. Their accounts offer insights into a truly remarkable generation of women who formed feminist collectivities that made possible new epistemologies of rights and justice.

Reading their accounts today, however, we realize that this story of the urgency of feminist writing is a generational story of networks and collectives of women who are largely no more. Their work could not always be sustained by the generations that followed. The efforts of women to create enduring institutions and structures for deep and careful study of women and gender, while momentous, were not sufficient in the face of enduring material deprivation, gendered labor exploitation, and the ongoing political marginalization of feminist movements in the increasingly authoritarian spaces of the Third World.

Today, almost forty years after the International Feminist Book Fair in Oslo where El Saadawi urged women to refuse to be silenced by taking up the pen, it is strange to imagine a world of writing and publishing in print and online without the voices of women from around the world. While they remain the least represented authors and editors in global publishing, women of color and Third World women from the decolonizing spaces of Asia, the Middle East, and Africa are now published by mainstream academic and publishers in ways that would have never been imagined by Third

World women in the 1970s and 1980s. The rapid expansion of global feminist publishing in the 1970s by and through autonomous Third World research organizations, collectives, and feminist presses had permanently changed the landscape of publishing by the 1990s. Today increased access to literacy around the world, the proliferation of print in multiple languages, and new media online have made the idea of women writing commonplace for a younger generation of readers, writers, and activists. Mainstream academic and trade publishers have capitalized on the idea of an audience for women's writings; every major press has at least some titles by women, albeit often in individualized, commoditized genres and forms, and some mainstream forums publish feminist texts.

Although mainstream academic and trade publishers continue to publish some global women's writings, what distinguishes the present is the almost total obliteration of formal infrastructures of autonomous research and writing for women as a result of the total retraction of state funding for universities, the dismantling of all research infrastructures and institutes built over decades, and the dramatically inward turn of American and European institutions like the Ford, Mellon, and Carnegie Foundations, away from international projects and research. In the face of ongoing threats to their work by the ruling government, the Ford Foundation decided to close its India office in 2016 and, in its haste to leave, disposed of *all* its archives for the region—the documents of more than half of a century of work in India. Though an earlier grant from Ford was approved to create a digital library, the archivists, students, and feminist scholars of a major feminist research organization in India sit waiting for the arrival of funds to preserve their endangered archives. It has been and will continue to be a wait with no resolution, as organizations stop work as they seek approval from the state to accept basic funds to pay staff and students. Bureaucratic holds, delays, and new paperwork mandates have now made accessing basic resources for preservation and research nearly impossible.

The collapse of the meager streams of funding for feminist research and writing in much of the world has been punctuated by the end of feminist publishing as we know it. Ritu Menon mourned the total collapse of the world of feminist publishing in the early 2000s in her 2020 memoir *Address Book*, from the disappearance of the many feminist presses that animated the stalls of the International Feminist Book Fair to the closure of allied publishers like Zed Books, which closed its doors in 2020. "Earlier, in the 1980s and 1990s there were more than two dozen," Menon recounts, "together with feminist bookshops (not a single one of the originals around anymore), magazines, reviewing periodicals, librarians, typesetters, designers, printers, even—all part of the Women in Print movement, all reinforcing each other's work."[119] She later describes the project of writing and publishing as a politics of solidarity. "Books and writing and the women's movement are what connected us, across the world. As they evolved, we began to understand that sisterhood may not be global, that deep schisms exist, deep divides of inequality between and among us, but we can still express solidarity."[120]

The collective energy and joy surrounding the expanding world of autonomous feminist writing and publishing that made the book fairs possible in the 1980s may be no more. Forty years after the first International Feminist Book Fair, the promises of radical democratization through feminist media have largely gone unfulfilled, co-opted by the reality of a new media landscape dominated by marketing and influential patriarchal authoritarians on social media who deploy virulent, misogynistic populist language and imagery on media to threaten and silence feminist dissent.

Yet, despite the loss of feminist infrastructures for writing and publishing and the increasingly precarious conditions of research, women and sexual minorities still have an urgent desire to write their worlds—to write like life depends on it.

5

The Protest, or What if We Took to the Streets?

It began with dozens of women walking together, carrying signs as they marched in twos and threes.[1] In their hands were posters and pickets, as well as copies of a petition contesting a newly proposed revision of the Law of Evidence that would make a woman's testimony in court worth only half that of a man.

The demonstration on February 12, 1983, started on Mall Road in Lahore. Women young and old gathered for the very first public protest expressing opposition to the military rule of General Muhammed Zia-ul-Haq, Pakistan's president. They walked peacefully down the main thoroughfare, which had been built during British rule as the road to the colonial governor's house, with Mughal monuments and shrines dotting each side of the path. The central street was a featured road in the heart of the city, carefully curated with trees lining the boulevard. As the women marchers approached the courthouse, they were soon confronted with barricades and dozens of police. They continued on, defying the authority in front of them. They staged a sit-in before the barriers near the court, with speakers proclaiming equal rights for women and protesting the draconian revision of a law that would dispossess women of their right to full citizenship.[2] The public protest paralleled transnational women's demonstrations and protests held by women across the decolonizing world who were staging nonviolent actions with transnational symbols—like the petition that contested sweeping legal reforms intent on subordinating women.

What followed was total chaos and violence.[3] Photographs from the protest paint a picture of the brutal scene as it unfolded.[4] Dozens of police hold their *lathis* (batons) high over the people as they sit peacefully, then hit them indiscriminately. The images convey the stark contrast that animated the event: a peaceful, nonviolent protest led by middle- and upper-class women wearing salwar kameez, holding one another as they huddle under attack from police officers clad in berets and tan uniforms and wielding *lathis*. Crowds flee the street as tear gas canisters release billowing smoke, poisoning the air. Women hold their hands out in protest while supporting a woman bleeding from the head, while another person attends to an injured woman lying on the street, surrounded by a crowd. The back of a police truck overflows with women arrested at the demonstration. The overt, indiscriminate acts of violence by the police contrast profoundly with the peaceful scene around them. Women, under attack, cast looks of pain, shock, and, most of all, defiance.

One image stands out among the photographs of the demonstration. A police officer, reinforced by policemen behind him, brazenly draws his *lathi* while pushing a young woman, Zhila Shah, in a crowd of women who

FIGURE 5.1: Chaos as police charge on women protesting Pakistan's proposed revision of the Law of Evidence, February 12, 1983. Photograph by Rahat Ali Dar, February 12, 1983.

are seated and standing. What catches the viewer's eye immediately is the woman's expression of agony and struggle as she falls, her face in total focus, in contrast with the blurred movement of the people around her. Her distress is difficult to see, but hard to look away from.

The protest had been called by the Punjab Women Lawyers' Association in collaboration with Women's Action Forum (WAF). It included women who would rise to prominence as leading intellectuals, lawyers, and human rights advocates: the famed feminist lawyer and human rights leader Asma Jahangir; her sister and fellow pro-democracy lawyer Hina Jilani; sociologist and Shirkat Gah director Farida Shaheed; and artist, teacher, and activist Lala Rukh.[5] What spurred the historic protest was a technical change to the law whose implications required legal and religious expertise to parse. Yet what these lawyers, scholars, and activists understood, based on their years of research and transnational exchange on women and postcolonial law, was that the state was dangerously conspiring to subjugate women under the law beyond Pakistan's severe Muslim family code, targeting the very evidentiary procedures that defined the basic rights of citizens.

The proposed revision of the Law of Evidence would revoke the colonial-era Law of Evidence Act, section 144 of the Pakistan Penal Code, originally passed in 1872, which had been incorporated into Pakistani law at independence in 1947. In its place, Zia's government presented the revised Qanun-e-Shahadat (law of evidence) based on patriarchal interpretations of Sharia structures of testimony in legal cases. Proposed before the appointed members of an undemocratic parliament in early 1983, the change would essentially make the testimony of two women equivalent to that of one man, justified by a distorted interpretation of Muslim legal guidance on the number of witnesses required for a particular accusation of crime.

Remarkably, this was the first major public protest to truly rock the new government. Before the Law of Evidence protest, years of state policy in Pakistan had expanded policies that subordinated women to men in all realms of legal, social, and political life. The rise of Zia and his Islamicization of laws in 1979 brought dramatic legal changes that enshrined in law the secondary citizenship of women and their subjugated status as legal subjects. By 1983, Zia's Hudood Ordinances, passed in 1979 and instituted widely in 1981, had driven the mass prosecution and imprisonment of women accused of adultery and making false charges of rape. The alarming proposal to repeal the secular British colonial Law of Evidence meant that in the face of authoritarian laws used to prosecute women and absolve men of gender and sexual violence, women would have essentially no voice in court cases.

The petition against this revision of the law carried by women of the Punjab Women Lawyers' Association and WAF on the day of the protest was symbolic, invoking a long tradition of petitioning that had thrived in the colonial world for centuries. From precolonial petitions submitted to shrines and Mughal authorities to the powerful histories of formal anti-colonial movements in the actions of the Indian National Congress and leaders like Mohandas Gandhi, petitioning had been essential in politics in spaces like South Asia as the primary means of contesting state authority. By one account, British colonial subjects sent more than a million petitions to the British colonial office during the long nineteenth century, and the number of petitions increased in the first decades of the twentieth century.[6] The petition as an instrument of anti-colonial action was well established by the time of independence.

It was this deep transnational history that prompted the alliance of highly educated women—lawyers, scholars, and other visible public figures, including actors and journalists—to turn once again to the petition in 1983. They believed it would allow them to stake a claim to their constitutionally enshrined rights as citizens and explicitly summon a long-standing anti-colonial genealogy of protest in the face of domination and state violence. The paper petition in the Law of Evidence protest symbolized the powerful and intimate relationship between expert claims to legal interpretation and the mass mobilization of women in the streets in a visible wave of anti-authoritarian politics against the military dictatorship.[7] The petition was at once a highly technical form of legal contestation and a genre with radical democratic promise, accessible to all who wished to make explicit demands upon the state. In the post-Partition subcontinent, the legal system became a primary domain for marginalized and oppressed communities to make claims on the state.[8]

The petition was a powerful tool of anti-authoritarian movements and actions in postcolonial states that represented the universal rights of citizenship for all that had been promised at the moment of independence. The Law of Evidence protest was followed by more and more petitions against parallel laws and thousands of pages of writing by women contesting the very premise of the Law of Evidence as well as the wide range of strict religious laws enacted after 1979. The demonstration was one of many mobilizations in South Asia in which women claimed expertise and knowledge for themselves.

In this chapter, I argue that Third World feminist protest in the 1980s was, at its heart, a project of transnational feminist knowledge. Global research on women shaped the rise of a novel wave of women's protest that emerged across geographies. Conversely, the highly public street protests of women catalyzed a vast global knowledge economy focused on women's democratic rights and citizenship that would shape knowledge production about transnational women's rights for decades to come. I analyze key early public actions by women as they protested postcolonial authoritarianism and argued for women's equal democratic rights and citizenship during the late 1970s and early 1980s, including large-scale movements against patriarchal religious laws, policing and militarism, and state-sanctioned gendered violence. Women's transnational research was foundational for women's public acts of dissent in mass mobilizations in the streets. A vast domain of knowledge shaped women's direct action and produced women's protests as world historical events.

In focusing on protest as a site for Third World women's knowledge production, I argue that Third World women's protest culture of the 1980s shaped a transnational *feminist hermeneutical politics*. The claim to the right of interpretation, based in expert readings of authoritative texts, catalyzed women's public political action for rights. Women across geographies focused on their right to interpret and reform civil, criminal, and customary law. They utilized a vast transnational apparatus of women's research to critique the technical language used in policy and procedure and to make a claim to equal citizenship under multiple, overlapping systems of law. In multiple postcolonial spaces, women worked to dismantle deeply patriarchal laws inherited in the aftermath of colonialism and to revoke the many new postcolonial customary laws that subjugated women under men's claims to traditional religious authority.

Indeed, the conundrum of the relationship between constitutional democracy and customary law was a unifying problem for women in postcolonial Asia and Africa. Women researchers and activists probed the often incoherent relationship between civil and customary law. Postcolonial governance structures were intended to hold together multiple religious, ethnic, racial, and political minorities long pitted against one another in divide-and-rule policies of colonial governance. Women looked to transnational norms of constitutionalism and feminist legal reform to shape their protests and mobilizations in multiple postcolonial geographies. They utilized transnational symbols of nonviolent protest to stake a claim to women's fundamental rights as postcolonial states worked to strike a balance between the ideas of tradition, culture, and religion and the universalism promised by radically inclusive constitutional democracies. In doing so, women turned to a transnational feminist hermeneutics that linked women's claims to constitutional citizenship and revolutionary textual reading practices.

Many new civil and criminal codes, alongside cultural codes of conduct based on sex segregation in regions like South Asia, the Middle East, and North Africa, forbade public demonstrations of any kind, thus prohibiting women from appearing or speaking out in public, particularly in opposition to the state. Women fought to abolish these customary and legal spatial strictures by building women's transnational research collectives (like WLUML), claiming their right to the public, and demonstrating in the streets for their citizenship.

This chapter pivots around International Women's Day (IWD), March 8, and documents its growing significance for women's protest cultures across the decolonizing world in the 1970s and 1980s. IWD had long symbolized the power of feminist internationalism underlying feminist claims to democratic rights, but the day came to have new meaning in this moment. With origins in revolutionary politics in the United States and Europe in the first decades of the twentieth century, IWD was adopted and celebrated by a wide range of socialist countries and movements that followed, expanding to the Soviet Union, China, Trinidad and Tobago, and Afghanistan.[9] In 1975, the United Nations officially recognized March 8 as International Women's Day. By 1977, the UN General Assembly had proclaimed International Women's Day the "United Nations Day for Women's Rights and International Peace." The declaration marked a new era of women's internationalism and the expanding distance of IWD from its origins in socialist women's movements.

The day came to symbolize a new UN-based women's internationalism with its emphasis on women's rights and peace. But International Women's Day in its many iterations had potent political possibilities beyond its symbolic meaning at the UN. March 8, as a transnational symbol, took on new meaning for feminists in the decolonizing world who used the holiday to demonstrate against rising authoritarianisms in an urgent appeal to transnational women's rights that transcended the failed postcolonial state. In 1979, women in Iran initiated massive protests against pending conservative reforms that would dramatically restrict women's dress and public life through new legal codes and forms of surveillance and policing.[10] In the 1980s, across South Asia, West Asia and North Africa, the African continent, Latin America, and beyond, IWD became critical as women organized, published, and protested on March 8 against patriarchal authoritarianism and military dictatorships.

The occupation of public space was thus critical to the feminist knowledge project. Women's research and writing lay at the heart of women's anti-authoritarian popular politics, defining the trajectory of protests and public actions in opposition to state policy and authority. Over the course of this chapter, I reflect on these questions of protest and epistemology through highly visible public protest events organized by women. In postcolonial spaces, feminist research was a politics that traveled from the page to the streets in pursuit of justice and equality.

The Protest as Iconography

The 1983 protest against the revised Islamist Law of Evidence exemplifies the intimate connection between public acts of dissent and the rise of transnational feminist research. As women staked a claim to citizenship through the written page of the petition, a new politics came to life—a popular movement against authoritarianism that asserted both women's expert knowledge of the law and their freedom to take up space in the streets. What followed the violent aftermath of the protest was an entire domain of research and writing on women and law that defined a politics of dissent for decades to come.

"We have wisdom, we have knowledge and strength."[11] So proclaimed Habib Jalib, the famed progressive Pakistani poet and activist who had opposed martial law for decades, as he spoke in front of the courthouse in Lahore in February 1983. Jalib was not just speaking to this crowd of women sitting in front of the police barricades but was reciting a poem. On the first anniversary of the establishment of WAF, Jalib had marked the occasion in a poem, translated from Urdu into English as "Poem Written for Women's Action Forum's First Anniversary." Jalib's recitation of the poem a year later at the Law of Evidence demonstration was endowed with even more meaning and urgency.

Jalib's poem refused the dogmatic oppression of women, declared the right of women to knowledge, and proclaimed their endless pursuit of free will. It condemned the hypocrisy of dogmatic fundamentalism, asserted the power of women to claim self-determination, and declared women's right to dignity in the face of patriarchal violence. An English translation of the Urdu poem by feminist Jugnu Mohsin, WAF member and later a journalist, circulated widely in the media after the protest.

> No more a friendless world as it once used to be
> No more of wretched helplessness or weak dependency

We know when we prosper or suffer at your hands,
And yet you believe that we still cannot see!
We can now be arbiters of our lives as we will,
No more a need to cower but to control our destiny.
As tyrants, you cannot remain enshrined in our hearts
For we are not your worshipers but partners in equality
No more are we supplicants dependent on your whims,
We have wisdom, we have knowledge and strength, tenacity.
No more backward dogma or self-appointed priests,
All respect to the message of human dignity.

—HABIB JALIB, TRANSLATED FROM URDU BY JUGNU MOHSIN[12]

It was this poem that Jalib was reciting on that fateful day as women staged a sit-in around him. Soon after Jalib began his remarks at the demonstration, the police descended upon the crowd. Jalib, who had been demonized, jailed, and persecuted by military dictators many times over his fifty years of life, was hit directly by a police *lathi*. The violent act is preserved in a photograph in which Jalib, with no means to defend himself, closes his eyes and raises his arms in a defensive position. The stick strikes him across the

FIGURE 5.2: The poet Habib Jalib being beaten with a police baton during the protest against the Law of Evidence, February 12, 1983. Photograph by Azhar Jafri for *DAWN* (1983).

arms. Featured prominently in the image are his hands, close to the camera, lifted in a gesture of peace and nonviolence.

Jalib's verses were a just a few among the many protest poems and songs that shaped women's street protests in Pakistan. Poetry was regularly recited in public performance and as collective chants at public demonstrations. Verses declaring women's free will and rights to bodily and political autonomy were memorialized in the many publications of women's organizations that emerged during this tumultuous moment. The poetry of Jalib and others was a mainstay of WAF publications alongside testimonials, statistics, and research studies on women.

Years later, Jalib's pivotal recitation of his poem was memorialized in a WAF publication from 1985 that publicized the acts of defiance by the people who marched that fateful day.[13] In the newsletter, a sketch of Jalib reciting poetry at the protest appears next to the verses of his poem in Urdu. He holds pages of his writing in one hand. His other arm is raised as he speaks the powerful lines declaring the free will of all people. The hand of the poet of the people raised in defiant performance contrasts with his vulnerability captured in the photograph from the moment in the February 1983 protest when he lifted his arms to protect himself under the violent *lathi* charge of the police.

As news of the protest and the violent police response spread quickly to international venues, many local national newspapers condemned the women of the Punjab Women Lawyers' Association and WAF for touting women's rights in public and transgressing the bounds of the private, as many of the women were unveiled. International news and transnational women's organizations celebrated the protest as well as the women involved for their defiance in the face of blunt force and their nonviolent tactics. For the larger Movement for the Restoration of Democracy in Pakistan, the Law of Evidence protest was a signal event that revealed the profound cruelty of the unjust policing and military violence that fortified Zia's rule and laid bare a neofascist Pakistan under Zia for the world to see.

The protest was more than a one-day event—it led to months of direct mobilizations of women in new public actions and a massive proliferation of knowledge for years to come. It became an iconic moment symbolizing a new era of democratic aspiration. Beyond the immediate media reaction to the events of February 1983, the Law of Evidence protest was the most visible declaration of a new era of women's rights led by educated people with expertise in law, human rights, social science, and the arts. The protest solidified the WAF's role in catalyzing a new women's movement in Pakistan

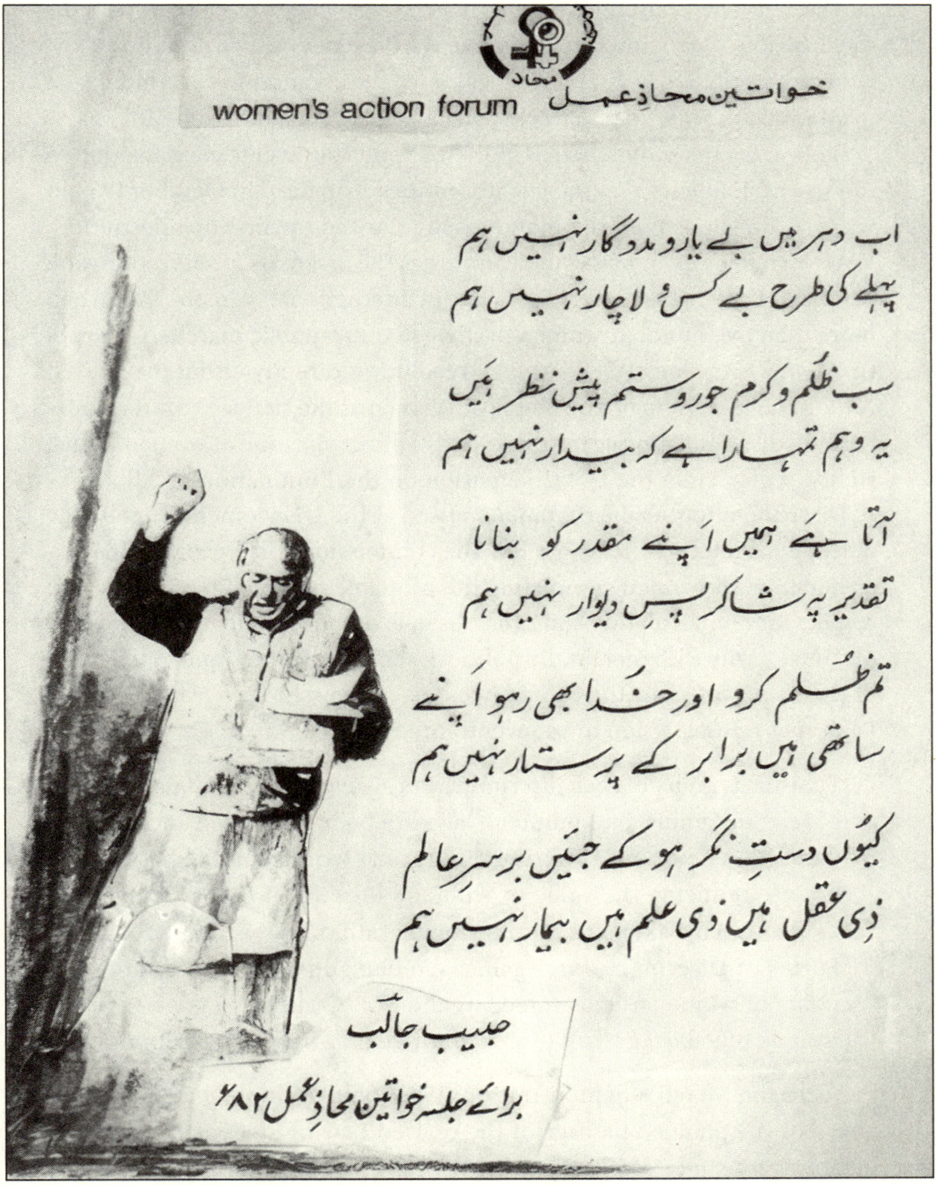

FIGURE 5.3: Habib Jalib's "Poem Written for Women's Action Forum's First Anniversary" (1985). ASR/Nighat Said Khan Archival Collection.

and brought the Pakistani Women Lawyers' Association into public view for the first time. Suddenly, attendance at WAF events swelled as hundreds of women across class and communities joined the organization and mobilized to continue the push against Zia's patriarchal laws against women.[14]

Following the protest, WAF mobilized multiple events in opposition to the Law of Evidence. Yet the law was ultimately passed in October 1984 in watered-down form. In the months that followed the first demonstration, WAF organized eight mass public protests. The first mass mobilization took place on March 8, 1984, on the occasion of International Women's Day, when more than five hundred women participated in a public march. As part of that demonstration, WAF issued a resolution directly citing the United Nations Commission on the Status of Women as the standard for recognizing legal discrimination against women as a direct violation of women's equal rights. It also cited the UN Convention on the Elimination of All Forms of Discrimination Against Women, passed at the UN women's conference in Copenhagen three years earlier. The commission had "recognise[d] discrimination of women as violating the principles of equality of rights and respect for human dignity and as an obstacle to the participation of women on equal terms with men in the political, social, economic and cultural life of their countries." At the conference, the commission had also addressed Pakistan's refusal to sign the convention:

> Pakistan is guilty of such discrimination against women. Under the garb of religion, unjust and inhuman laws are being proposed and promulgated which not only discriminate against women on the basis of sex but are reducing the value of women's life to half that of a man. We demand that Pakistan sign the Convention on the Elimination of all Forms of Discrimination Against Women and uphold the status and rights of women as guaranteed by the 1973 Constitution. We urge the women of Pakistan to unite and continue the struggle for their rights.[15]

After the March 8 demonstration, WAF held multiple public protests ahead of the planned passage of the revised Law of Evidence.[16] The next demonstration and sit-in against the law took place on April 11, 1984. WAF followed up with another demonstration on May 21. Then just six days later, on May 27, which multiple women's organizations had declared a "Black Day," hundreds of women gathered on the Mall in the center of Lahore in opposition to the proposed Law of Evidence. On August 7, two hundred women gathered at the Mall and submitted a petition against the Law of Evidence. On August 9, a protest meeting was held in front of the Lahore High

Court. On October 26, despite the many actions of women's organizations, Zia signed the Law of Evidence. After it became law, on November 10, 1984, WAF publicly demonstrated in the streets, stopping traffic for over an hour as members distributed leaflets explaining that the Law of Evidence was unjust and against the spirit of Islam.[17] Despite the law's passage, these women still claimed the right to knowledge *and* the right to be present in the streets.

Artist and teacher Lala Rukh was arrested alongside many of WAF's founding members at the first demonstration in February 1983. Lala Rukh was a visual artist and professor at the National College of Art in Lahore, where she later founded Pakistan's first master of fine arts program in visual art. As a key member of WAF, she was responsible for highly influential visual art and photography depicting the mass mobilization of women in the months and years following the first Law of Evidence protest. As WAF's membership expanded rapidly and the group planned regular agitations against government policies, Lala Rukh created posters, pamphlets, and newsletters to promote WAF's work and the cause of women's rights. In these many genres, she invented a new iconography for the Pakistani women's movement that not only helped it build momentum but also memorialized WAF's achievements in creating a new domain of radically anti-authoritarian politics.

Soon after her arrest, Lala Rukh began to create flyers, posters, and visual art for the movement, but she found that printers and publishers in Pakistan were unwilling to print publications and posters for women as they mobilized for demonstrations and organizational meetings. When she found that no one would reproduce her images, Lala Rukh taught herself the art of screen printing and then, in her backyard, began to make her own reproductions and prints for distribution.

Among Lala Rukh's many visual art pieces from this era, a striking cover image for a 1985 WAF newsletter shows the women of WAF in protest, walking atop an annual calendar. The art served as the cover for WAF's sixth official newsletter. The newsletters documented the many protests, demonstrations, and marches held by women in opposition to the Law of Evidence and Zia's continued authoritarianism.

The piece, "Women's Action Forum Calendar," uses an iconic photograph of a WAF women's protest from 1984. In the image, women are superimposed on the grid of a calendar for the year 1985, laid down in perspective like the ground or street upon which women march.[18] In Lala Rukh's artistic rendering, women march in protest atop the grid in anticipation of a year of public protest. In contrast, the 1977 cover image (which opens chapter 2

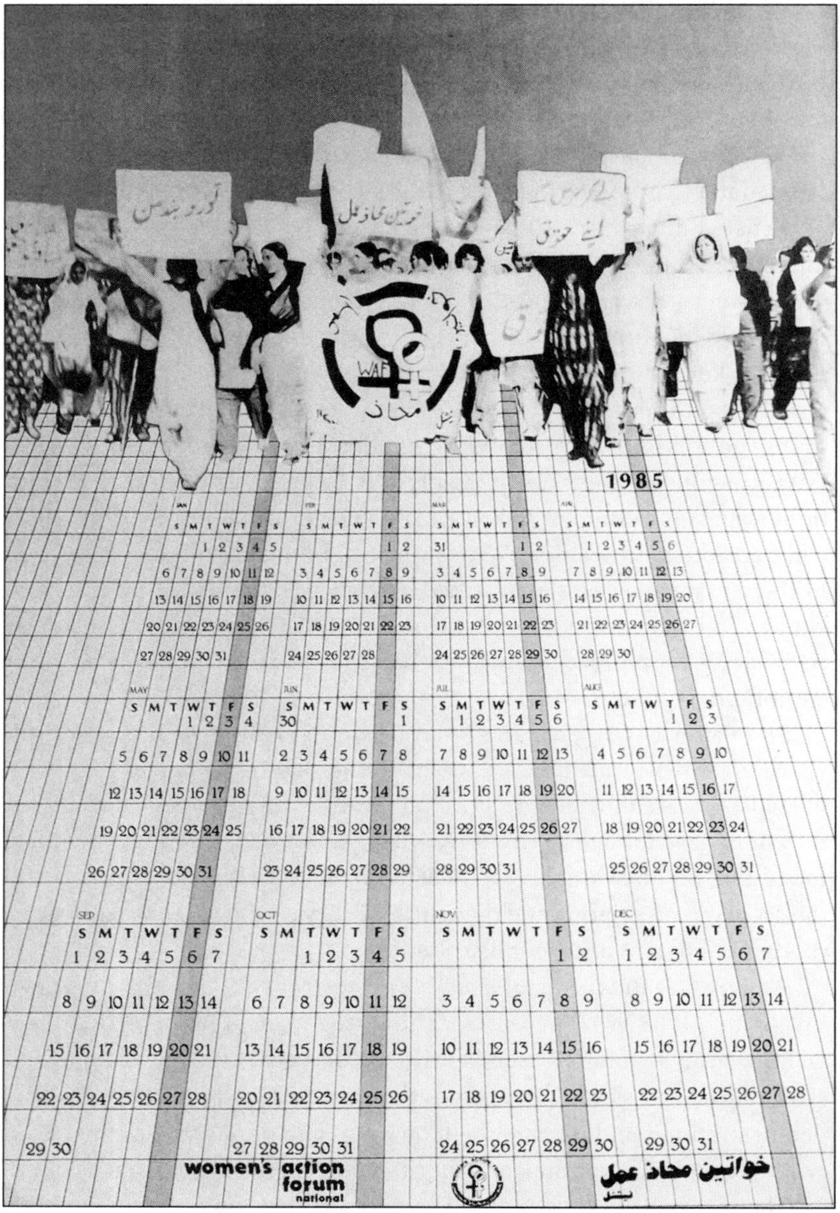

FIGURE 5.4: Cover of *WAF Newsletter* 6 (January 1985). ASR/Nighat Said Khan Archival Collection. Courtesy of the estate of Lala Rukh.

of this book) depicts a graph of the declining status of women in India with sketched figures of women passively looking on. The 1985 image builds on this feminist iconography contrasting people with the empty spaces and grids of graphs and charts.

The people who populate the crowd on the poster come from a real photograph, probably taken by Lala Rukh herself, who regularly documented the WAF protests as a skilled photographer and artist. In the image, women hold signs declaring women's equal rights and proclaiming that women are breaking the chains of patriarchy. At the center of the image is the circular symbol of two intersecting Linnean symbols for women, one black and the other white. The symbol invokes a global iconography of women's rights that had come to dominate public demonstrations, conferences, and publications on women in the decade before. Next to the symbol for woman is the English acronym WAF—the organization leading the charge for women's rights.

In another poster for WAF created during the same period in 1985, Lala Rukh offered a new answer to the question of *how* to archive violence perpetrated against women. Amassing a visual representation of the endemic violence facing women, Lala Rukh's poster features a bold title, "Crimes Against Women," made from cut-out newspaper letters. Next to the title, more than a dozen dates from 1983 and 1984 testify to the widespread violence that women faced across Pakistan. At the center of the poster is a massive collage of dozens of newspaper articles reporting violence enacted upon women, including the murder of a young girl, the public flogging of a woman, and the murder of women at the hands of their husbands. This poster uses powerful multilingual aesthetics to boldly abstract the documentary impulse and archival practices of feminist clipping and compilation. Indeed, Third World women's organizations were already creating archives as a foundation for feminist research (see chapter 3). In her collage of newspaper clippings, Lala Rukh radically envisioned the archive as a testimonial itself to the everyday violence women faced and the continual threat to women's survival. The poster places the endemic nature of gendered violence in full view, with piles of newspaper clippings laid in every direction in a chaotic collage that is stunning and painful to view.

Lala Rukh's original printing technique became the basis of her 1987 self-published book *In Our Own Backyard*, a guidebook on screen printing that explained print techniques for movements across the subcontinent that wanted to create posters, images, and print publications for oppositional activism and grassroots mobilization.[19]

FIGURE 5.5: Lala Rukh, "Crimes against Women" (1985), poster for a WAF campaign. ASR/Nighat Said Khan Archival Collection. Courtesy of the estate of Lala Rukh.

Later, Lala Rukh also led workshops on screen printing in her backyard.[20] She, alongside other feminists, founded the Simorgh Women's Resource and Publication Centre to create an explicit research arm for the women's movement. As Lala Rukh recounted in an interview, the work of research and printing was also advocacy and training: "There was a need for research work on the issues of women, and no one was doing it. It was a resource and publication center. We did a lot of grassroots work, that was my role—training in screen-printing . . . it served to bring women together to discuss their issues and find solutions through poster making, stuff like that."[21]

The Law of Protest

Among the organizers of the Law of Evidence protest in February 1983 was a young lawyer who had established her position as an advocate against authoritarianism when she was just eighteen. As a young woman, Asma Jahangir (née Jilani) filed a case against the state for arresting her father, Malik Ghulam Jilani, who had been detained under the military dictatorship of Ayub Khan in 1971. The case, *Asma Jilani v. Province of Punjab* (1972), would reach Pakistan's Supreme Court and become the vehicle for a landmark rebuke of the military dictatorship by the judiciary.[22]

Jahangir and her younger sister Hina Jilani went on to become lawyers and were active in the Punjab Women Lawyers' Association. In the broader struggle against the Hudood Ordinances, the sisters formed the legal vanguard, directing the writing and serving of hundreds of legal briefs, petitions, and notices to the Supreme Court. The definitive book-length study of and argument against the Hudood Ordinances that Jahangir and Jilani eventually produced would directly shape legal reform under the 2006 Protection of Women Act.[23] As president of the Punjab Women Lawyers' Association, Jilani pledged on April 25, 1982, "full cooperation to the WAF in the endeavors to enhance the status of women in Pakistan."[24] An important aspect of this support was the Free Legal Aid Centre, which the law firm started in January 1983. It provided women with legal representation and guidance and offered pro bono support in all courts, including the Supreme Court.

The vast majority of the cases adjudicated by women lawyers focused on domestic and sexual violence cases. Under the Hudood Ordinances passed under Zia, the testimony of women alone was deemed insufficient to legally determine whether an alleged rape had taken place. In fact, girls and women could prove they had been raped only if they could produce witness testimony from four men who had directly witnessed the crime. But if they had no witnesses and still maintained the accusation of rape, then, seemingly paradoxically, they could be *charged* with a crime. Using new provisions within the Hudood legal policy, the police could charge the victim with adultery—a crime governed by punishments based in public humiliation and shame and carrying the harsh sentence of public flogging. Under Zia's new laws, women faced a system that used deeply patriarchal religious interpretations to justify the total subjugation of women.

Jahangir consistently pushed back against the legal basis of the Hudood Ordinances, questioning their reliance on a distorted understanding of Islamic jurisprudence. Like women contesting Muslim law across different geographies in the postcolonial world, she and other feminist scholars in Pakistan maintained that Zia's new system of Muslim law passed was a false interpretation of Islamic jurisprudence based in deliberate misinterpretation and patriarchal readings of scripture and tradition. Jahangir, Jilani, and others thus invested the feminist project with deep research and training in the technical expertise of multiple legal systems, from secular postcolonial law to Sharia to international human rights law.

In doing so, Jahangir publicly asserted her right as a woman to read and interpret the Qur'an, like so many of her feminist colleagues working on issues of women and law across postcolonial societies facing patriarchal legal reforms in the aftermath of the Iranian Revolution in Iran, India, Algeria, and Senegal. This hermeneutical political work was done in petitions and legal briefs in which the equality of women was asserted from the theological juridical literature, often with direct citations from the Qur'an. In the prevailing political climate, in which orthodox religious men dominated society as the sole interpreters of religious (and civic) life, Jahangir and other feminist legal scholars challenged their hegemonic authority by performing their own exegetical and hermeneutic interventions in the public sphere, pointing out the centrality of equality between men and women in Islam.

In reaction to her protests and what it regarded as subversive readings of Muslim law, the religious and political right accused Jahangir of blasphemous conduct, including sacrilegious speech against Islam. This purposefully threatening accusation posed a danger to the lives of Jahangir and her family. In 1986, she was charged with disrespecting the Prophet under a newly amended law passed by Zia's government that made blasphemy a punishable offense carrying a life sentence or death.[25] While she had been imprisoned numerous times before (in September 1983, for instance), this extreme charge laid bare how legal manipulation had led to the total collapse of constitutional rights in Pakistan. The charge, the threat to her survival, and the imprisonment galvanized Jahangir to found Pakistan's Human Rights Commission in 1986, which cemented her lifetime commitment to fighting blasphemy charges for women and minorities.

As lawyers came together to create new associations and defend women under the punitive system of the Hudood Ordinances, other direct action women's organizations emerged to fight the laws imposed by Zia. WAF emerged from a broad constellation of organizations that had long advocated for women's rights, rooted in women's organizing in colonial India. These organizations included the All Pakistan Women's Association, the Pakistan Women Lawyers' Association, and the research organization Shirkat Gah. While the movement was composed primarily of political organizations working for democratic rights, it was rooted in deep research on women. WAF's organizing committee was composed of women from educated urban families who were steeped in the histories of anti-colonial and anti-authoritarian protest for democratic rights. Many had been directly involved in actions against the military dictatorship of Ayub Khan (1958–1969). And even as the movement in the early 1980s was constituted by many young women who had come into feminist organizing under Zia, their families and parents had participated just two decades earlier in the failed electoral campaign of Fatima Jinnah and worked to pass the Muslim Family Law Ordinance of 1961.

From its inception, WAF had cast itself as a "pressure group" in the political system with a broad-based agenda of *bedari* (consciousness-raising) for the women of Pakistan. These issues were directly articulated in WAF's manifesto, approved on April 12, 1982, which declared: "W.A.F., as a pressure group is committed to protecting and promoting the fundamental rights of women by resisting and fighting all forms of oppression and educating women regarding their rights."[26] The manifesto laid out five basic goals for the organization: asserting equality between men and women, fighting for the rights of women as citizens, affirming the right of women to control their destiny, pushing for the right to education for girls and women, and declaring WAF's commitment to feminist internationalism through its adherence to "fundamental human rights for women and men as laid down by the UN charter."[27]

WAF defined what it meant by "consciousness-raising" in its charter document under the heading "Methods for Realizing the Aims of WAF: Through the Media, Meetings, Seminars, Workshops, Signature Campaigns, Distribution of Relevant Information."[28] While it did employ all these means, the street protest became the key mode for WAF women to target the broadest public and an international audience by speaking directly to the holders of power (the judiciary, the bureaucracy) and to the national and international media (newspapers). WAF's meetings produced a public resolution, which was then converted into a statement and often a legal petition. The petition would then be delivered to the relevant authority during a public march or demonstration. These public actions were carefully choreographed alongside key activities such as press releases, position papers, and public news conferences. Finally, the actions were memorialized in WAF's quarterly newsletters alongside detailed research articles about women, legal subordination, and violence against women. The newsletter was available as a free mail subscription to people across the country.

A representative list illustrates the genres of protest organized by WAF, from public statements to resolutions to petitions to marches. In an emergency meeting of the Working Committee of WAF Lahore on September 28, 1983, members expressed "grave concern over the arbitrary way in which women in Lahore today, Sep 24, were arrested while expressing their views on the current situation in the country."[29] A resolution passed by WAF's general body on October 3, 1983, "unanimously condemned the public flogging of Lal Mai in Liaquatpur, Bhalwapur."[30] The resolution stated that such brutal public acts made a "mockery of the status of women in Islam" and that WAF was "enraged at turning punishments into public spectacles, particularly degrading for women in a country which professes to uphold and protect their honor." From February 1983 on, WAF mobilized again and again, making resolution after resolution condemning violence against women under the Zia state. It organized direct actions and multiple public marches that distributed research for the broader public about the condition of women and the unjust and incorrect interpretation of Muslim law touted by Zia's government.

The production of knowledge around actions was swift and public. For example, WAF issued an emergency call for a demonstration on April 11, 1984, "against the discrimination on the basis of sex in the proposed laws of Qisas and Diyat (Law of Evidence)." Six women's organizations responded with twenty-four hours' notice, and forty-five women gathered at the Regal Chowk at 2:00 p.m. The women, carrying placards and black flags, marched along the busy throughfare toward the Lahore High Court building. Along the way, "leaflets were distributed to the public" to explain the prejudicial structures of the law and its misuse of Muslim jurisprudence. Once they reached the court, "press statements were given to the Reporters of all major newspapers."[31] The press release that followed the demonstration seven days later, dated April 18, 1984, condemned the "heinous crimes committed against women in recent weeks," which the release enumerated as "marching women naked in the streets of Nawabpur, repeated criminal assault on two women over a period of ten days," and "barbaric and savage killing of Mehvish Bashir aged three years and Hina Rafiq aged four years in Chiniot." The press release indicted the hypocrisy of the law and invoked the international rights of women, arguing that "the proposed laws of Qisas and Diyat and the Law of Evidence are creating an atmosphere whereby women are not considered as human beings and are therefore being subjected to inhuman and degrading crimes."[32]

The press releases were followed by specific research papers that illuminated the basis of the protests. The research study "Law of Qisas and Diyat as Proposed by the Council of Islamic Ideology [CII]" was released in February 1984. Mounting its critique from a historicist perspective, WAF argued that "the CII draft law on Qisas and Diyat does not quote a single verse from the Holy Quran in support of its draft, for the simple reason that it cannot." The refutation of CII was done through a careful exegetical analysis of the Qur'an and the tradition of the Prophet. First, using Surah 9, verse 71, the study established that men and women are considered equals under law, and then followed with other references to scripture that asserted the lack of any theological basis for the proposed law. The WAF study of Qisas and Diyat concluded that "the draft proposal of the CII be rejected as unIslamic."[33]

WAF's newsletters publicized the organization's work as well as the emerging research on women. For example, the WAF newsletter published in January 1985 curated a list of the resolutions, protests, and press releases alongside an essay on the Law of Evidence, poetry by Habib Jalib, and women's protest songs.[34] The newsletters linked the struggle for women in Pakistan to global feminist actions, describing movements for women's rights in different parts of the world. In the featured sections "Women in Protest" and "Women for Life on Earth," WAF described women's protests around the world, from Algeria to South Asia, and ongoing international feminist efforts for nuclear disarmament since 1981. In the "Spreading Information" section, the newsletter detailed seminars held at WAF on female labor in Pakistan. Research seminar proceedings were available for readers and held at the WAF headquarters in cities across Pakistan. WAF newsletters ended with a call to the readership to submit everything from letters to poems, stories, research, and reports on women's organizations for publication in the circular.[35]

WAF's mission was always internationalist. As an organization, it mobilized women and created new visions of international solidarity by distributing international news and research and by mounting demonstrations that invoked international women's and human rights and linked women's actions in Pakistan to the movements of women around the world. The internationalism of the movement was symbolized in the annual demonstrations of women in Pakistan for International Women's Day held on March 8. In its newsletters and press releases, WAF highlighted the importance of the annual celebration of international women's rights and the broader connections of WAF to movements against authoritarianism and laws that disenfranchised women. For example, WAF's seventh newsletter, published in April 1985, detailed a WAF seminar in celebration of International Women's Day that connected Pakistani women's rights to the origins of women's movements around the world.[36]

Thus, the annual mobilization on International Women's Day combined the many genres of protest featured in WAF's strategies for political contestation, from the informational flyer to the petition to the public protest with the attendant press releases and leaflets. Through these many forms of research and writing, WAF members created a political and aesthetic vision of women's liberation. Crucially, such mobilizations brought all these genres to life in the streets.

The Protest against Secrecy

On March 8, 1981, on International Women's Day, hundreds of women gathered at the University of Algiers. As would be the case two years later in Lahore, these women were organizing against a proposed "family code" that was secretly being debated by the legislature. The previous year, undisclosed regulations had been introduced to ban the movement of all women out of Algeria. Next, rumors circulated that an anti-democratic code was being drafted that would make women second-class citizens.

And so, on the occasion of IWD, women came together en masse to discuss a plan of action. The women in attendance came from multiple communities and represented worker's unions, women's organizations, and different political parties. Together, they planned a variety of actions to fight the many changes led by men, who sought to deny them access to basic democratic rights and participation in the legislative process.[37]

At the meeting, rumors of the secret code spread throughout the crowd. A group of women surreptitiously circulated fifty copies of a leaked draft of the proposed family code. While passing around documents at an organizational meeting might seem like a regular occurrence, the very act of making the draft public was radically defiant. As one woman told French journalist and sociologist Marie-Victoire Louis in her investigative reporting on Algerian women's organizing in the early 1980s, distributing the few copies of the draft was less about informing people of the contents of the code and more about making a clear statement: "because with 50 copies, you cannot really inform," but it is possible "to denounce the antidemocracy of the regime with a concrete act."[38]

The circulation of these clandestine copies of the code allowed a select few women to glimpse the profound control over every aspect of women's bodies, movement, work, and lives that the proposed law would bring. The draft included articles that would require a woman to "obey her husband and show him consideration as head of the household," bear children without restriction and breastfeed all children, and respect all wishes of her husband's parents and family. It permitted polygamy at the discretion of the husband and mandated the total restriction of women's movements outside the familial home, with the exception of visiting her own parents. It gave men complete control over women's access to work. While men could seek divorce, women would have limited ability to initiate divorce and no right to any marital property or maintenance after divorce.[39] Despite the efforts of women to publicize the alarming proposal, no one knew the full content of the laws under deliberation by the state.

Just two decades earlier, an almost utopian vision of radical freedom for Algerian women had seemed like a real possibility. At the time, Algeria was the heart of the Third World liberationist project, and it occupies a central place in the twentieth-century histories of liberation and social and political thought. Algeria was a critical site of settler colonialism, anti-colonial revolution, and decolonization, and its anti-colonial resistance movement—and the violent suppression by French occupiers—had captured the world's attention in the 1950s and 1960s. Algeria's violent resistance transformed modern political imaginations of anti-colonial struggle and eventually succeeded in overthrowing French rule with the declaration of Algerian independence in 1962. The case of Algerian independence and decolonization was critical for key philosophical and political theories of the long effects of settler colonialism, racism, and violence and the possibilities and limits of decolonization, most famously in the writings of the Martinique-born doctor and philosopher Franz Fanon.

This betrayal by lawmakers twenty years after independence was especially bitter because women had been key symbols and actors in the Algerian liberation struggle. Algerian lawyer, resistance leader, and, later, politician

Zohra Drif, in her memoir *Inside the Battle of Algiers*, recounted the promise of the anti-colonial movement for women as well as their subsequent disillusionment and political marginalization in the decades that followed Algerian independence.[40] In the 1950s, as Drif documented, the political resistance against the French colonial state largely excluded the women of Algeria. Little by little, however, organizations like the FLN (Front de libération nationale) came to see women as an asset to the movement, though often in limited roles: "We wanted to be recruited by the fighters' 'secret organization' to mobilize in Algiers and, little by little, to convince them to dispatch us to the armed groups."[41] Drif and other women joined the FLN in 1955–1956 to undertake espionage, surveillance, and armed resistance against French colonial occupiers. They came to be known as *mujahidat* (freedom fighters) and served as critical symbols in early independent Algeria.

Drif imagined that the end of colonization would be a time of liberty and equality for women in Algeria: "We always believed that our *liberation* and our affirmation would come with the end of colonization. We had always considered it better to die with honor in the armed struggle for dignity and liberation than to survive in the disgrace of tolerating colonization—and by settlement, at that."[42] Yet the women of the movement understood that their resistance against colonial rule was also a struggle to transform "sociological and cultural realities" and to work against "all the taboos that had been drilled into us, even [to] break the ultimate taboo by going to live far from our families in mixed quarters with our brothers in arms. We were fully conscious of the risk that our society might condemn us for that."[43]

Still, by the mid-1950s, even as they met resistance from the main leaders of the FLN, women had become a critical part of anti-colonial organizing, following in a longer tradition of feminist organizing in Algeria from the 1920s onward.[44] Key women in the FLN who led major armed resistance efforts, including Drif as well as Samia Lakhdari and Djamila Bouhired, were chosen to present the Algerian question to the UN in January 1957.[45] On the international stage, these women submitted formal documentation outlining the injustices of the French settler occupation of Algeria and the Algerians' demands for independence. The anti-colonial struggle would continue until 1962. Many women like Drif, who was prosecuted and incarcerated between 1957 and 1962, remained critical to that struggle and the international coverage of Algeria.

Yet, postcolonial Algeria did not live up to the ideals promised by the liberation movement. Soon after independence, the nationalist party ceded ground to conservative movements, breaching the trust of women and the ideals of equal citizenship. Algeria's first constitution in 1976 formally recognized the equality of women.[46] Yet, by the late 1970s in Algeria, as in much of the Muslim world in the Middle East, North and West Africa, South Asia, and Southeast Asia, equal rights for women became a target of the resurgent Islamicist religious right. The rise to power of Islamist Chadli Bendjedid in 1978 inaugurated a new era marked by calls for the reform of Algerian law to bring it into adherence with authoritarian religious movements across the region from Iran to Pakistan. For women in Algeria who had led a globally transformative anti-colonial struggle, the liberation movement held extraordinary promise. By 1980, however, women had to confront the tragic betrayal of Algerian sovereignty as they were suddenly denied the basic rights of citizenship.

Ideas about women's equality and liberation among women's research organizations and international networks were not the only ideas moving across borders and nation-states at this time. The aftermath of the Iranian Revolution in 1979 saw a massive explosion of transnational Islamist movements that promoted right-wing ideologies of power based in the patriarchal control of women. These authoritarian political visions insisted that state sovereignty was to be achieved solely through cultural nationalism, which was predicated on the total subjugation of women under Muslim law. For example, the arguments against women's equality used in making the Hudood Ordinances in Pakistan in the 1970s were influential in Algeria as men authored and finalized the Algerian Family Code—especially the work of Pakistani Islamist ideologue Abul a'la Maududi. Maududi led right-wing Islamist political movements and gained massive popularity in the 1970s. He pushed for Sharia laws that would regulate women's reproduction, mandate the total veiling of women, ensure the complete subordination of women in patriarchal marriage, and deny women access to public space. The leading thinker in the creation of anti-minoritarian legislation and the Hudood Ordinances in Pakistan, Maududi was a "founding father" of modern-day Islamist politics based in the total subjugation of women and the relegation of women to the status of minors under the law.[47]

Women had taken to the streets against these regulations a year earlier, on March 8, 1980, to protest restrictions on their physical movement and migration from Algeria. In 1981, women faced police and barricades as they protested.[48] The ban on women's movement prompted feminists to organize a mass demonstration for International Women's Day.[49] The government relented on the travel ban, but news soon broke that a commission had been formed to write the Code sur le statut personnel (Personal Status Code), known in English as the Family Code, which would be presented to the People's National Assembly (APN), the lower house of the Algerian parliament. The women staged a sit-in in front of the offices of the National Union of Algerian Women, demanding to see the text of the code. This public struggle continued throughout 1980 and into 1981. Yet, despite the many public protests led by women—at great risk to themselves and their families—the text of the draft code was kept secret.[50]

Women's public protests were met with more and more suppression and policing from the government. There was an almost total media blackout on women's protests, for fear of government repression of the press and state violence. In September 1981, Algeria's national newspaper, *El Moudjahid*, announced the government's plan to adopt the complete Family Code that had been circulated in parts during that fateful meeting on International Women's Day in March 1981. Although fifty copies of parts of the draft text had been circulated among a few people who opposed the code, none of the contents had been confirmed, and the full draft of the law was entirely unknown to almost all people in Algeria.

The women responded with a damning petition against the state, invoking the very same mechanisms of protest used by women's movements linked across the postcolonial world. On September 28, 1981, women submitted the following to members of the APN:

> *El Moudjahid* of September 21, 1981, announced the approval by the Council of Ministers of a text entitled: "*Code sur le statut personnel.*" . . . As soon as it is adopted, it will have the force of law. This "personal status" is in fact nothing other than the resurgence of the draft family code that women have been fighting for years. It is thanks to their struggle that this text could not be submitted to the APN in 1979. This family code, as its name indicates, must codify relations within the family unit and govern the daily life of each of us. It will transform the nature of the social relations of an entire people. It therefore concerns our entire national community. Whatever the content of this text, we denounce the silence that surrounded its preparation and the absence of any popular consultation. A project developed without the knowledge of the people can only satisfy a minority. We cannot accept, we do not accept that our future is decided without us. We refuse the APN vote on a text that the people cannot view themselves since they have been excluded from the decision-making process. We demand that on this issue, the people can decide freely and democratically. This is why we are signing this petition

en masse and calling for it to be taken together to the headquarters of the APN.[51]

As the petition argued, the Algerian government's secrecy was fundamentally anti-democratic, and the code would undermine the foundational tenets of Algerian society. The petition against the rumored draft of the Family Code was circulated across the country. A coalition of women under the umbrella of the National Union of Algerian Women composed and gathered signatures for the petition against the code, garnering between seven and eight thousand signatures in a matter of days. The petition demanded that the code be rejected outright, as it would transform every aspect of social and political life in Algeria without the say of the people.

In October 1981, about one hundred women marched in the streets in opposition to the Family Code. Their appearance in public in opposition to the state was met with condemnation in an article in *El Moudjahid*, which labeled the protesters "bad women."[52] Catalyzed by the publicity and public debate—and in spite of the state's silence on their petition and the widespread public shaming of women for appearing in public space—women mobilized again, this time in a larger protest. On November 16, 1981, women took to the floor of the APN to protest the secret debate on the proposed code. Strategically, this time the organizers of the demonstration ensured that the *mujahidat* generation, symbols of nationalist liberation, stood publicly at the front of this struggle, now visibly supporting the rights of women in opposition to the nationalist party in power. Here stood key veteran women who had once been imprisoned for their anti-colonial resistance publicly defying their own comrades, who now served in the ruling government. Among them were Zohra Drif and Djamila Bouhired, who had been "heroines" of the nation in the early post-independence period and had represented the FLN and the cause of Algerian independence on the international stage almost twenty-five years before.[53]

The protesting women chanted slogans like "No to the Family Code," "No to Silence, Yes to Democracy!" and "No to the Betrayal of the Ideals of November 1, 1954!" Their demands were sixfold: "Women should reach the age of legal marriage at the same time as men, they should have unconditional right to work, they should enjoy equality in marriage and in divorce, polygamy should be abolished, common inheritances should be equally distributed, and single mothers [should] have legal status."[54] The police arrived on the scene and began to photograph the women. Soon the police escalated their repression and arrested three women leaders of the protest. Though the protesters initially dispersed, they soon reassembled, despite the police crackdown, and continued to chant in opposition to the Family Code.[55]

Under pressure, the Algerian government withdrew the code from legislative debate. However, the state, using the authoritarian tactics of governments across the decolonizing world, soon made an example of the women's demonstrations by imprisoning the main leaders of the protest in December 1983. Ongoing debates about the most effective approach to preventing the passage of the code followed, with key women standing in total opposition to any aspect of the code and other reformist factions pushing for a revision of the code to appease different political and religious factions.

While women who opposed the code outright fought their prison sentences and threats to their lives, the Algerian Family Code was passed by the parliament in June 1984.[56] Ultimately, the Family Code was finalized in a closed secret session of the one-party government; there was little revision, and the provisions mandating women's obedience to men remained intact. The framers of the code used claims of total authority over the interpretation of the Qur'an to argue for repressive laws that controlled and dispossessed women.[57] The major tenets of the Family Code that passed in 1984 subordinated women to men through familial structures and denied women the right to work. The Family Code remains the rule of law in Algeria today.

Hermeneutics as Protest

This moment of transnational feminist protest took many shapes, from large-scale mobilizations of people marching in the streets with legal petitions in hand to lectures and research studies that, based on close textual readings of codes, refuted postcolonial laws that subjugated women. From postcolonial spaces in South Asia to the spaces in North Africa, women argued that the very act of interpretation, whether of secular law or religious text, was a critical form of protest against new methods of patriarchal control justified through claims of culture and tradition. Perhaps the most renowned feminist thinker to argue for women's fundamental right to textual interpretation on the international stage was the famed Moroccan sociologist, political scientist, and feminist writer Fatima Mernissi.

Mernissi narrated her own defiant protest during a public confrontation at a scholarly conference in Malaysia in 1984 in her pathbreaking book, *The Veil and the Male Elite*, originally published in Arabic and translated into English in 1991.[58] By the early 1980s, Mernissi was a highly regarded expert on women's lives and work in Muslim societies. At the conclusion of a scholarly talk on women in Muslim history, she was verbally assaulted by a hostile Pakistani man who was then the editor of a London-based scholarly journal on Islam. The editor, in a dramatic act of public denunciation, contested Mernissi's liberatory reading of the life of a woman descended from the Prophet, Sukayna. He insisted that Mernissi's interpretation was not simply a misinterpretation of Muslim pasts but a dangerous and condemnable narrative that threatened Islam. He denied her expertise in Muslim history and insisted that her knowledge of the tenets of Islam was suspect and without authority. As Mernissi recounted, during the question-and-answer session, the man declared himself the absolute authority on women's subordination in Muslim societies, despite his inability to read Arabic and his lack of basic knowledge of the many texts that Mernissi cited in her study. The man not only screamed in public and mocked her ideas but went further, denying her the right to speak by trying to "snatch the microphone away from me in a vindictive rage."[59]

The exchange with the editor, and Mernissi's refusal to cede ground to a man's physical and epistemic assault, epitomized the decades-long work of people like Mernissi and Asma Jahangir, as well as the work of women's networks like Women Living Under Muslim Laws, who challenged the distorted claims of authorities to a patriarchal Muslim past to justify the subjugation of women in the present. Mernissi powerfully reframed the public confrontation as a structural critique, arguing that the man's dramatic and violent reaction to her public speech was not exceptional. His actions exemplified something bigger and more widespread: the common authoritarian reactions of postcolonial men to women who accessed and produced knowledge. As Mernissi declared, "That verbal aggression that I was subjected to and that attempt to obliterate the memory of Sukayna by a modern Muslim man who only accepts his wife as veiled, crushed, and silent remains for me an incident that symbolizes the whole matter of the relationship of the Muslim man to time—of amnesia as memory, of the past as warping the possibilities of the present."[60] This single interaction symbolized the illogical reality of patriarchal authoritarianism in the postcolony that perpetuated manipulations of religious authority to supersede democratic rights.

The confrontation between Mernissi and the hostile man at the scholarly talk was an assault on the right of women to knowledge itself. In the moment, and throughout her many speeches and publications over several decades, Mernissi insisted on her place as an expert in textual hermeneutics and asserted the critical role of women as authoritative interpreters of the past and present of Muslim societies. In doing so, she rejected the basic idea that Islam inevitably subjugated women and argued that this misconception had been perpetuated by centuries of colonial orientalist depictions of the Muslim world that served as the basis for nationalist chauvinism among postcolonial authorities. According to Mernissi, Islam had become a tool of patriarchal authority in the postcolonial world, politicized in structures of law and custom that distorted the diverse traditions of Muslim societies.

For Mernissi, women's access to education and knowledge was the primary avenue for dissent against dogmatic originalist readings that relied on the past to control women. Her defiant description of ongoing confrontations with authoritarian men featured her signature optimism and narrative flare. Women like her were producing knowledge and claiming the domain of textual interpretation to contest key justifications of patriarchy in the postcolony. It was women's intellectual work that would transform the world: "The present is always fabulous, because there everything is possible—even the end of always looking to the past and the beginning of confidence, of enjoying in harmony the moment that we have."[61]

Even before the 1984 confrontation, Mernissi was one of the most visible Third World feminists in the 1970s and 1980s and a key member of transnational feminist research initiatives that transformed the domain of research on women and gender across the decolonizing world.[62] Mernissi completed her master's degree in political science at the Sorbonne and her doctorate in sociology at Brandeis University. She established herself in 1975 as a leading postcolonial feminist thinker with her first book, *Beyond the Veil*, and went on to publish over a dozen books that were translated into multiple languages around the world.[63]

Mernissi's defiant voice and vibrant visions of women's freedom animate the archives of Third World feminist projects again and again across different modes of feminist research. Her writings defied norms of social scientific empiricism by bringing together wide-ranging methods: qualitative research, including surveys and sociological interviews, as well as political theory, textual hermeneutics, literary storytelling, and memoir. She appears across the archives of Third World feminist research in sources ranging from women's organizational papers to foundation and UN reports. She was a key figure in feminist exchanges not only on the African continent but in South and Southeast Asia, Europe, and the United States.

Mernissi was a prominent voice at UN women's conferences and workshops, in Third World research organizations, and in feminist books and anthologies. As I explore in chapter 1, during and after the International Women and Development Conference at Wellesley College in 1976 she became a vocal critic of the burgeoning field of women's development research, which she argued was devoid of the perspectives and visions of Third World women. Mernissi coauthored a powerful critique of the dangers of Western development research that replicated an imperial "maternalism" and did little to represent or improve the life-worlds of women.[64] Mernissi attended all the UN conferences on women, and through many conferences and workshops she built sustained and productive relationships with feminists across the African continent, the Middle East, and South and Southeast Asia and among women of color in Europe and the United States.

By the mid-1970s, she was a well-known expert on women and Islam and was regularly cited by scholars, activists, UN officials, and NGOs. In 1976, Ford Foundation officer Adrienne Germain suggested that Ford support Mernissi's travel to meet with women organizers in Pakistan and circulated copies of *Beyond the Veil* to foundation experts in the United States and Pakistan, an early suggestion that laid the foundations for a long-term exchange between Mernissi and South Asian feminists.[65] Mernissi visited India in 1984, traveling from Delhi to Bangalore and meeting with feminist editors, activists, and scholars. She was a founding member of DAWN and built close relationships with international feminists at the Bangalore meeting in late 1984. That same year, alongside prominent international feminists from across the world, Mernissi was a key contributor to Robin Morgan's volume *Sisterhood Is Global*, and she attended the Sisterhood Is Global Institute alongside many women she had engaged at Wellesley and the UN conferences. A decade after the Wellesley conference and two years after her public confrontation with the Pakistani editor, in 1986, Mernissi became one of the first authors published by the Indian feminist press Kali for Women. She maintained a close relationship for years with the press's editors, Urvashi Butalia and Ritu Menon. She also published her work with the feminist collective Simorgh in Pakistan. Mernissi was widely read, translated, and cited in scholarship from across South Asia, as well as in the writings of women researchers across the Middle East and Africa.[66]

As the many influential speeches and publications in just one decade of her life show, Mernissi's project of feminist protest was based in deep textual hermeneutics and historical research that was transnational at heart, with connections to women scholars and activists across the decolonizing world. For example, in her ambitious 1993 account of women leaders in the history of Muslim societies, *The Forgotten Queens of Islam*, Mernissi linked the stakes of her radical feminist readings of Muslim religious texts to women's contestations against authoritarian politics in Pakistan.[67] She set the stage of her hermeneutical project through the dramatic and controversial ascent to power of Benazir Bhutto. The first woman prime minister of Pakistan, Bhutto was elected following the death of military dictator Muhammad Zia-ul-Haq. According to the opposition party and multiple conservative Islamist factions, her election was against Islam. These reactionary men insisted that never, over the centuries, had a woman ruled a Muslim state. They argued that Bhutto's democratic election as prime minister of Pakistan, an Islamic republic, was an act of blasphemy and an illegal and prosecutable offense according to the laws passed under Zia.[68]

As Mernissi claimed, her own transgressive history of Muslim women's powerful lives—this "simple idea of daring, as a woman, to question history"—would be condemned by authoritarian powers as a "troubling blasphemy," akin to women like Asma Jahangir and Benazir Bhutto daring to publicly interpret the law and claim political power.[69] Mernissi's critique of the logic deployed by conservative men was pointed: against every basic tenet of an electoral democracy and the UN's Universal Declaration of Human Rights, authoritarian men used the claim of tradition to distort and invent Muslim pasts in order to condemn women as illegitimate. This authoritarian threat to women's will and political rights claimed sole power over religious tradition and piety. But men's depictions of Muslim pasts devoid of women were a lie. Countering these distortions with careful textual exegesis and historiographic authority, Mernissi outlined the lives of fifteen Muslim queens who had governed over political states. As Mernissi insisted, hers was not a project of historical recuperation for the sake of romantic nostalgia about women's history, but rather a direct critique of present authoritarian politics and institutions that distorted religious tenets and history to justify women's political subordination and exclusion in the present.

Even as she was adamantly transnational in her feminist commitments and scholarly reach, the heart of Mernissi's expansive work as a feminist activist, scholar, and public intellectual was her beloved Morocco. The politics of postcolonial authoritarianism in Morocco and parallel spaces in North Africa shaped Mernissi's internationalist critiques of women's subjugation. Yet Morocco's deep history of learning and transnational exchange animated the vivid landscape of Mernissi's visions for a radically liberated future for women. Morocco had achieved independence and reunification in 1956, but it faced decades of authoritarian rule and inflicted some of the worst human rights violations on the continent. Women and sexual minorities suffered profoundly under new laws that enshrined the patriarchal household and dispossessed and criminalized their social and sexual autonomy. In a pathbreaking collection of interviews with Moroccan women conducted in the late 1970s and early 1980s, *Doing Daily Battle,* Mernissi condemned the structure of law that implemented these regulations, the Moroccan Family Code, which was enacted soon after independence.[70]

Mernissi argued that the legal system perpetuated fictions about the segregated and subjugated roles of women in society, codifying into religious law the patriarchal desires of men. According to Mernissi, a "wide gulf" separated the reality of women's lives and experiences from the Family Code, which reduced women to the position of subordinate wives, dependent on men. "It is interesting to note that the Moroccan Family Law was drafted solely by men," Mernissi declared.[71]

The contradictions of the real experiences of women—described in Mernissi's careful qualitative interviews with women—and the patriarchal ideologies of Morocco's newly established sovereignty based on the control of women's bodies and labor were a profound tragedy: "At the dawn of Moroccan independence, the nationalist leaders, who had undergone torture in prison so that equality and democracy could reign, designed the future Moroccan family without consulting the central element of that family—women."[72]

Postcolonial nationalism perpetuated grave distortions of women's roles in society, through the law and beyond, threatening women's lives and livelihoods and denying them the basic tenets of democratic rights. That nationalist promise of equality was replaced by the nightmare of inequality under the guise of culture and religiosity. Men dictated the symbolic world by claiming total authority over tradition in an effort to prevent women from defining the meaning of ideas. For Mernissi, they did so through "terrorist tactics" built on the negation and humiliation of women as legitimate interpreters and producers of knowledge. These authoritarian acts attempted to silence her as an expert: "As a Moroccan woman who has had access to writing and an advanced education . . . I have learned to distinguish the varieties of terrorist tactics that men, who monopolise the symbolic values of our society, use to stop me from expressing myself, or to denigrate what I say."[73]

According to Mernissi, authoritarian men deployed two techniques of public humiliation to dismiss women intellectuals. First, they insisted that "'what you are talking about is an imported idea,' and, secondly, they accuse women of lacking expertise by insisting that 'what you are talking about is not representative' (referring to access to science)."[74] Mernissi systematically broke down these two public "terrorist" techniques used by men to dispute the intellectual and political rights of women, arguing that these claims set men up as the sole guardians of knowledge, "the legitimate and exclusive interpreter of the cultural heritage and its content," who excluded women from accessing any authority to history or heritage.[75]

These twin modes of disappearing women's ideas and rights were critical mechanisms for postcolonial authoritarianism. The common accusation from postcolonial men that feminism was an "imported idea" was not simply about denying the legitimacy of women's equal rights—it was about refusing women the *possibility* of autonomous thought by dismissing their ideas as foreign, as influenced by Western feminism. Mernissi argued that men not only condemned women but endangered their lives by accusing them of betraying the national project: "He accuses you of the worst crime in his book—treason to the national cause. You are an agent of foreign enemies."[76] But conservative accusations against outspoken women went further. Alongside the accusation that advocacy of women's rights was a dangerous foreign ideology, authorities accused women intellectuals not only of being treasonous but of having no intellectual capacity to access or comprehend knowledge related to religious or political authority. "The person speaking sets himself up as the general guardian of scientific truth. He has a monopoly on scientific truth, and it is in the name of that scientific truth that he intimates that you should hold your tongue."[77]

Public dissent was a way of life. In a speech critiquing the dominance of men at the UN population conference in Cairo in 1994, Mernissi insisted on the rights of women to act publicly, in defiance of authority, in defense of their fundamental human rights.[78] She argued that in a world where both postcolonial reactionary forces and international authorities like UN experts claimed total authority over ideas of culture and religion, women had little choice but to undo the logic of absolute subjugation by asserting their humanity in protests, speeches, and research on law and religion. These dissident acts were essential for women's survival in the world: "I want to share with you something I am coming to understand, which is *le model de heresy*, heresy as a model."[79]

For Fatima Mernissi, the feminist heretic—exemplified in her own acts of defiant speech and public protest, proliferative research and writing, and transnational Third World feminist solidarity and alliance-building across postcolonial geographies—was critical for the functioning of democracy itself: "Women are builders of civil society. We are the ones who are going to build it. You know why? We have no choice. Either you shut up and you are humiliated, or you do what I'm doing. You scream."[80]

The Protest as Anti-Policing

As we have already seen in the many protests across the decolonizing world, International Women's Day was foundational for the political and intellectual mobilization of women who claimed the domain of internationalism to argue for women's rights. One of the most iconic International Women's Day protests in South Asia was held on March 8, 1980, in Delhi, India, the culmination of months of women's protests demanding new state interventions for endemic violence against women. Women in Algeria mobilized the same day against draconian laws that limited their movement and autonomy. In India, the mass mobilization of women aimed to confront the Supreme Court of India and the Government of India for the grave miscarriage of justice in rape cases, particularly the symbolic case of Mathura, a girl who had been raped in police custody in western India eight years earlier.

The 1980 International Women's Day protest in Delhi took place three years before the first major mobilization against the Law of Evidence in Pakistan, garnering international attention, and took place months after massive agitations across India against "dowry murders," the killing of women as a result of disputes over marital dowry. The March 1980 protests created an iconography that traveled across regions and became headline news for national and international media outlets. Like so many feminist movements of the era in the postcolonial world, the event was rooted in a technical reading of the law and the careful research, petitioning, and advocacy of the feminist researchers and legal experts who ignited the movement.

On September 16, 1979, four lawyers and professors of law released an open letter addressed to the justices of the Supreme Court of India to provoke public debate about the court's verdict in the 1978 case *Tuka Ram v. State of Maharashtra*. The four letter writers had emerged as leaders in an era of legal reform. They included the famed jurist and scholar Upendra Baxi; feminist lawyer, scholar, and key author of the Indian status of women report Lotika Sarkar; legal scholar Raghunath Kelkar; and public litigation advocate and scholar Vasudha Dhagamwar. In the letter, the lawyers reminded the court of its responsibility to protect democracy and human rights, especially following the failures that came with the declaration of the Emergency by Indira Gandhi. Mathura, the minor girl at the heart of the famous case, which was also known as the Mathura Rape Case, was a member of the Adivasi (tribal) community who was raped by two policemen while being forcibly held at a police station after she was the subject of an abduction case in rural Maharashtra in western India seven years earlier, in 1972.[81]

The policemen were first acquitted of the crime at the lower court level in a case initiated in 1974, then convicted by the Bombay High Court in a decision that was appealed to the Indian Supreme Court. In September 1978, the three Supreme Court justices overturned the Bombay High Court's decision to convict and instead voted to acquit the two policemen. In the Supreme Court judgment, the justices asserted that there was no medical evidence to prove that Mathura had been raped, as there were no marks or visible physical proof of resistance. According to the justices, Mathura was a promiscuous girl who had not struggled or raised her voice against the sexual acts, and "because she was used to sex, she might have incited the cops (they were drunk on duty) to have intercourse with her."[82]

The open letter engaged in a close reading of section 375 of the Indian Penal Code and disputed the justices' characterizations of the rape of a minor and consent through erroneous use of medical evidence as mandated under the Indian Evidence Act of 1872, the colonial-era law that was under dispute across borders. The letter condemned the ruling, carefully critiquing the structures of law used to justify the patriarchal judgment, and insisted that the Mathura case was representative of a grave miscarriage of justice happening in rape cases across India every day: "[A] case like this with its cold-blooded legalism snuffs out all aspirations for the protection of human rights of millions of Mathuras in the Indian countryside."[83]

When the open letter decrying the Mathura judgment was first released, no one was willing to publish it. Then, after months of getting no traction, the authors sent the letter to the premier Pakistani newspaper, *DAWN*, which, unlike its Indian media counterparts, was willing to print a document in opposition to the highest court in India.[84] The authors began to publicize the case and the letter among women's groups and lawyers. Only then did people begin to take notice of the Supreme Court's scandalous judgment and mobilize in coalitions.

A rich body of scholarship has addressed the significance of the Mathura Rape Case for mobilizing the women's movement against rape in India. These studies include Nivedita Menon's field-defining book on Indian feminist engagements with the law; Kalpana Kannabiran and Ritu Menon's study of the long history of protest against rape in India; Prabha Kotiswaran's research on rape cases and the increasing dominance of feminist engagements with the law and state power through the mobilization against rape in India; and Amartya Kanjilal's detailed legal study of the open letter, narratives of the Mathura case, and the aftermath of the case.[85] In the months following the release of the open letter, the Forum Against Rape, founded

FIGURE 5.6: Women protesting in front of the Supreme Court of India, Delhi, 1980. Courtesy of Keystone/Getty Images.

in 1980, began to mobilize mass protests in opposition to colonial-era rape laws and structures of evidence. The mobilization focused not only on the judiciary but also on the national parliament, the highest lawmaking body in India. For example, pathbreaking Indian feminist scholar Lata Mani (then a student) joined with a group of feminists involved with grassroots protest organizing through the Forum Against Rape and other emerging women's groups and movements to hold a demonstration and submit a petition to the Indian parliament calling for the total overhaul of the legal code governing rape law.

The Forum Against Rape, in coalition with wide-ranging women's groups in Delhi, organized a highly public protest in front of the Supreme Court of India to decry the problem of rape in India and call for the reopening of the Mathura Rape Case and a radical revision of colonial-era rape law.[86] Subsequent mobilizations were organized by a coalition of women's groups for International Women's Day on March 8, 1980. In the months that followed, a knowledge revolution took place that created a body of research and writing on the patriarchal core of colonial-era laws against rape that shaped the symbolic world of street protests, from signs to petitions.

Researchers began to address violence against women as a primary subject of research on Indian women for the first time. These research initiatives had direct policy implications and eventually led to a revision of the law in 1983 that declared custodial rape a criminal offense. On the other side of the border in Pakistan, the colonial-era Evidence Act had been replaced with a new law that claimed Muslim legal authority to relegate women to second-class rights in court. In contrast, in India, a progressive amendment made to the Indian Evidence Act revised the law to presume that if a victim said that she did not consent to an act of sexual intercourse, the court was compelled to take her expression of nonconsent as the presumptive truth and premise of the proceedings.

The Mathura Rape Case was symptomatic of a crisis of endemic violence and brutality against the most marginalized and poor people in India by multiple upper-caste Hindu and state authorities, especially at the hands of the police and Indian military. The open letter and subsequent mobilizations for changes to the law exposed the widespread corruption and cruelty of policing in India. Yet even in the face of movements for reform of the law in the early 1980s, sexual violence against girls and women, particularly by the police and military, continued unabated.

The year 1980 was a signal year in the mobilization against rape and violence against women in India. The mass mobilizations catalyzed by the open letter to the Supreme Court of India sparked an explosion of movements against rape, particularly custodial rape by the police. Radha Kumar's extraordinary illustrated and carefully documented account of feminist movements in India from 1993 accounts for the breadth of mobilizations against custodial rape. Feminist groups had mobilized against custodial rape two years earlier, in 1978, after Rameeza Bee was gang-raped by policemen and her husband, a rickshaw puller, was subsequently murdered for protesting the rape. The husband's rickshaw pullers' association led a mass action against the police, which led to massive policing and the eventual declaration of a curfew and an army presence. The protests continued until the state created a commission to investigate the rape and murder.[87]

Kumar recounts the many rapes and local actions that followed the International Women's Day protest in March 1980. Her account remains the most comprehensive study of feminist actions and demonstrations in India in the 1980s, including photographs and detailed engagements with the many types of feminist actions that took place as women argued for justice and a massive overhaul of the law.[88] In Kumar's telling, multiple local communities—often low-class, low-caste Muslim and Dalit communities—took to the streets to protest the endemic problem of sexual violence by the police and military. As she argues, protests against rape law and dowry murders frequently started in local, often rural and semi-urban areas, and were led by local workers' unions and activists from across communities. News coverage of these regional protests garnered the attention of women's groups in the cities, who took up the cause and mobilized to bring attention to rapes by the police and the need for reform.[89] Using the techniques of extensive empirical research and case reports, petitioning, press releases, and press conferences, these feminist organizations took their protests public and international. The news of the unjust acts of sexual violence spread widely, garnering international attention.

Yet, even as protest after protest brought attention to endemic issues of sexual and gendered violence, the question of authority remained, as so often the violence was committed by the police.

"Who will police the police?"[90] The question was provocatively asked in 1980 by Vasudha Dhagamwar, one of the four authors of the open letter in the Mathura Rape Case. In the wake of the Mathura case, Dhagamwar emerged as a critical voice in a growing movement against abusive policing and militarism in the early 1980s. She was on the law faculty at the University of Pune after studying economics at Oxford and receiving her PhD from the School of Oriental and African Studies in London. Known for her work in legal rights and her public interest litigation on behalf of tribal communities, especially cases of custodial violence and torture, she wrote research articles, books, and broader essays for the public on the hypocrisies and systemic exclusion of marginalized people in criminal justice systems in India.

In her public writing in the 1980s, Dhagamwar openly critiqued the police and called for a massive overhaul of policing and carceral systems in India. In her essay "Policing the Police," published in the annual issue of the journal *Mainstream* in 1980, she staged the stark reality of the violence of policing:

> Fear is the traditional Indian response to the police. Children grow up with the threat that the policeman will come and get them if they don't behave, ringing in their ears. Nor is the fear of the police-bogeyman dispelled by our adult experiences. They remain something to be avoided. It is thought better to suffer an assault—and certainly rape—than go to them. That is a way of adding to one's woes, a sure sign of lunacy. It is common knowledge that in our country the police routinely beat up and even torture suspects in their custody. Rape by policemen is also not a new phenomenon, although its ventilation is new, dating from the Open Letter to the Chief Justice of India in the Mathura case.[91]

The power of the police was completely unchecked. In her essay, Dhagamwar condemned the complicity of the Indian middle classes, who, she argued, perpetuated rape and violence against the working classes at the hands of the police by saying and doing nothing. The judiciary, lawyers, and poor people appearing in courts all depended on the benevolence of the police, which gave them extraordinary power not only to determine the outcome of cases but to abuse people under their supervision, both victims and people accused of crimes.[92]

One year after coauthoring the protest letter against the Indian Supreme Court's Mathura judgment and just a few weeks after the 1980 International Women's Day protests, Dhagamwar translated the work of protest into a feminist knowledge project. She, along with other feminist researchers, began to investigate the many incidents of rape across India. In a related documentary report from May 3, 1980, titled "The Lodipur Rape: After Mathura, What?" and published in *Mainstream*, Dhagamwar reported on the rape of an eighteen-year-old woman, Bachia, at the hands of the police in Patna, in Bihar in north India.[93] Dhagamwar recounted how she and other women lawyers heard of the custodial rape and came to write a report about the incident. Nothing had been done by any state or legal authority to take accounts of the police rape from the woman or her husband, a rickshaw driver, or to protect them. No one had called for any investigation except the husband's rickshaw pullers' union, which, as in previous cases, mobilized to seek justice through collective action. News of the woman's rape spread to her village, and she was cast out by her natal family and community for losing propriety.[94]

Dhagamwar decried the failure of women's movements for their singular focus on the Mathura case as if it were an exception, while hundreds of women were being similarly raped every day across India, even in the same region. Dhagamwar's account of these daily rapes by the police in nearby regions of Bihar and Uttar Pradesh is devastating. In January 1980 in the north Indian state of Uttar Pradesh, multiple people reported witnessing the mass rape of women by policemen. In February in the nearby state of Bihar, a newspaper reported the rape of a ten-year-old girl by a policeman as she was returning from the public lavatory in the morning. The girl had to be hospitalized for days after the rape. Afterward, she was given a measly 1,000 rupees by the state of Bihar for the crime. On March 19, 1980, a woman vegetable seller was raped by a policeman in another part of Bihar. In the five months prior to the Bachia case alone, there were multiple incidents of rape of girls and women by the police with no consequences, let alone public scrutiny or women's mobilizations against the crimes.

No lawyer, activist, or official seemed to have investigated or publicized the injustice of any of these incidents, and, as Dhagamwar pointed out, they were not subject to critiques or mass mobilizations by women's groups. Women lawyers had not gone to interview and collect evidence of the incidents. Even as women had protested publicly in key urban centers across India, no women's groups or NGOs had offered aid to these women in the conservative heartland of the country.

Dhagamwar offered an extensive report on the events that unfolded before, during, and after the rape of Bachia by the police. Then she outlined the need for parallel case studies of the thousands of rapes happening across India. For Dhagamwar, detailed case studies and empirical research that comprehensively and systematically accounted for rapes was necessary to expose the endemic issue of sexual violence across India. Protests calling solely for a change in the language of the law would do little to help these women. As Dhagamwar argued, detailed research and investigation of *all* rape cases was required beyond redefinitions of law, including the testimonies of "raped women, their well-wishers, neighbours, the police, even the rapist if he can be located."[95] Lawyers would have to publish these interviews and case studies with the names of the accused police officers as well as other authorities and communities to prevent impunity. Only then would there be any knowledge about the systemic problem of custodial rape at the hands of policemen. Dhagamwar concluded that justice was an elusive prospect for most women: "Mathura is a beginning. By itself it is no guarantee of justice to the countless women who have been raped, and who continue to be raped."[96]

In Dhagamwar's reporting on rape cases, we see how public protest, in the form of the open letter and mass mobilizations, translated directly into a critical knowledge project that documented the devastating experiences of women, not only in terrible acts of sexual violence but also in struggling against the failures of the police and in working to surmount the many barriers to justice. In her many writings in the early 1980s against the police, the military, and broader carceral corruption, Dhagamwar directly indicted and condemned state authority and the many different arms of the Indian state that abused and killed people under the guise of justice. Her essays demanded investigations of dire prison conditions, torture at the hands of authorities, and the cruel lack of due process as prisoners waited endlessly in prison to have a trial. She testified to the suffering of young children, particular low-caste and Dalit girls, who were forced to work in impossible conditions and treated with cruelty by people who considered them not just servants but actual property, as detailed in Dhagamwar's careful case research.

These critiques reflect the critical place of common, shared techniques of transnational feminist mobilization: empirical research, petitions, and detailed reports of the facts of gendered violence and corruption were essential to feminist critiques of policing in a time of feminist protests. Critiques of the authoritarian nature of the Indian state, particularly its practices of policing and militarism, reached an all-time high in the late 1970s and early 1980s. By then, even the middle and upper classes had experienced the reach of authoritarianism in Indira Gandhi's Emergency and had become disillusioned with the ruling party. The first large-scale women's protests in this moment focused on the law, and protests demanding legal reforms would endure as the defining action of mainstream Indian feminist movements.

Dhagamwar, along with her coauthors of the open letter, provoked lawyers, feminists, and a broader reading public in India to reflect on the unjust nature of policing, adjudication, and imprisonment in a supposedly democratic postcolonial state. Soon after writing these indictments of authority, Dhagamwar founded the public litigation advocacy organization MARG (Multiple Action Research Group). Built on Dhagamwar's vision of deep, situated research and research-based case reports, the organization focused on justice work across a wide cross-section of the poor and marginalized, including people in rural communities and tribal communities, women, children, unorganized workers, and displaced peoples.

While Dhagamwar's early anti-policing projects offered a powerful indictment of state authority, over the course of the next two decades, amid the rise of a powerful rhetoric of Hindu majoritarianism, Dhagamwar's perspectives shifted. Like many upper-caste Hindu feminists of the 1980s, she became an adamant defender of a uniform civil code for women's rights. Yet embedded within her commitment to secular structures of civil law were majoritarian Hindu ideas that dismissed intersectional issues of religious, political, and gender identity. In the years that followed her bold indictments of the police, she would become a direct apologist for state violence and right-wing Hindu majoritarian domination under the pretense of secular language and legal objectivity.

Her early writings against violent policing directly contradicted her later complicity with and apologist stance on police and right-wing state violence during the 1990s and 2000s. As a leading feminist lawyer, Dhagamwar was an official member of the state agency in charge of the study of women, the

National Commission for Women. In 2002, in the aftermath of the violent pogrom and mass killings of Muslims in Gujarat, carried out under the direct supervision of the state's chief minister, Narendra Modi (elected prime minister of India in 2014), Dhagamwar participated in an investigation into the conditions of Muslim women in refugee camps commissioned by that body. The commission's report offered no account of the suffering of women in systemic acts of rape and murder, particularly at the hands of the police and the state, or of the central role of Modi and local police authorities in anti-Muslim violence.[97]

As an author of the report, Dhagamwar wrote a two-part account of the Commission for Women's investigation for the Indian national newspaper *The Hindu*. Rather than analyze the systemic and state-sponsored nature of the acts of ethnic cleansing and violence against minorities, Dhagamwar blamed Muslim women for creating the conditions of their own oppression through their lack of collective action for legal and social reform within their communities.[98] Ignoring the widespread evidence of genocidal sexual violence by Hindus and the police in the Gujarat pogrom, she instead condescendingly critiqued the displaced Muslim women in refugee camps for not pressing for revisions to Muslim customary law or demanding a civil code to address community patriarchal violence. Ultimately, Dhagamwar laid the blame for the anti-Muslim pogrom squarely on what she characterized as Muslim women's incompetence in advocating for themselves. In response to Dhagamwar's editorials, multiple women's organizations, including the Delhi-based Saheli Women's Resource Centre, condemned the report and expressed their lack of faith in the National Commission for Women to protect the interests of all women.[99]

Dhagamwar's insistence that a uniform civil code was the only avenue for women's rights and her patronizing view that religious women lacked feminist consciousness was not uncommon among an early generation of Indian feminist scholars, who claimed that secularism, especially through the law, could resolve social and political differences. Many feminists from upper-caste Hindu families invested in the promise of pluralism under Indian democracy without publicly engaging the problem of majoritarian politics in India and considering the long-term effects of a bifurcated legal system that delimited political claims among minorities. In Dhagamwar's view, India's constitutional democracy was fully realized only through secular law, a structure that would naturally resolve the problem of women's rights for other religious and political minorities—including Muslim and Dalit, so-called Other Backward Classes, and tribal women.

These fissures in feminist organizing had long created divisions in feminist protests, most famously in the 1980s in the case of Shah Bano, a Muslim woman whose efforts to obtain maintenance from her ex-husband challenged the contradictions of Indian civil, criminal, and customary legal structures and led to a direct conflict between many feminists, Muslim legal authorities, and the Indian state.[100] Feminist movements have had to confront the continuously incongruous relationship of civil laws to customary legal structures as well as the general limits of formal legal reforms for creating sustainable gender justice on the ground.[101]

In their commitment to a uniform code, feminist scholars like Dhagamwar refused to recognize any difference among minorities. Rather, they looked to bluntly override the complicated tangle of secular and customary legal codes that had shaped Indian social and political life since the eighteenth century. Yet this seemingly neutral vision of the law for women did little to address the insidious ways in which upper-caste Hindu majoritarianism had been embedded in supposedly universal legal structures for marriage, divorce, inheritance, rape, and dowry. Indian feminist research of the 1980s, while it powerfully indicted the state for failures in policing and legal reform, offered little reflection on how majoritarian upper-caste structures of governance and policing enforced systems of religious and caste subjugation and policed these differences through gendered and sexual violence. By the early 1990s, with the triumphant rise of right-wing Hindu movements and the domination of the Bharatiya Janata Party in the decades that followed, Indian feminists had to contend with the failure of the idealization of secularism and universalism in a uniform code and the co-optation of the uniform code as the primary agenda of the Hindu right.

The result of this conflict between uniform civil law and the problem of minorities and oppressed peoples is a condition of perpetual irresolution that has created ongoing divisions in feminist ideas of justice in India. As women researchers and activists pursued universal liberal ideas of equal citizenship and rights for women, many of them had to confront the long-term effects of a colonial legacy of customary legal structures that permanently reshaped the nature of social power by and through religious law and transformed the workings of sovereignty in the postcolonial world. These vexing issues continue to plague feminist intellectuals today as they confront the increasing vulnerability of minorities and oppressed castes to violence and exclusion under the authoritarian projects of the majoritarian rule of the Hindu right.

The Afterlives of the Protest

In 2012, twenty-nine years after the brutal crackdown on women protesters in Lahore, February 12 was declared National Women's Day in Pakistan.[102] Finally, it seemed, the Pakistani state had symbolically recognized women's rights and the assimilation of women's mass mobilization in the streets against the Law of Evidence into a national narrative of progress. Yet the Qanun-e-Shahadat order of 1984 remains law today, and women's testimony continues to be worth half that of men in civil courts. Forty years after its enactment, the law is still the authority in procedures of evidence, despite decades of women's and international human rights activism to repeal the discriminatory act.

As for the broad Hudood Ordinances passed by General Zia's government in 1979, it took Pakistani activists, researchers, and lawyers nearly three decades of political movements and protests to change the basic structures of the ordinance, which subordinated the rights of women to men across civil and criminal law. In 2006, twenty-seven years after the passage of the law, Pakistan's National Assembly finally passed the Protection of Women Act under pressure from women's groups. This law was only a revision of the *zina* laws under the Hudood Ordinances, not a total repeal. These reforms, though they transformed some aspects of the legal structure, remain insufficient and continue to be subject to critiques from civil rights and human rights organizations.[103] Adultery and fornication remain offenses, and adultery is punishable by eighty lashes of the whip. The most important revision in this new act was the removal of rape from the domain of the ordinance, placing it under the Pakistan Penal Code.[104] Feminist organizations and lawyers continue to advocate for the revision of the structure of rape law under the penal code, most recently with the successful repeal in March 2021 of the use of prejudicial medical evidence of women's virginity in rape cases through an appeal to the constitutional right of dignity.[105]

The concerns raised by feminist protesters in the 1980s remain today. In 2018, multiple deaths shocked women in Pakistan. On January 4, 2018, a seven-year-old girl, Zainab Ansari, was raped and murdered. On February 11, Asma Jahangir, the tireless advocate for women's rights, passed away suddenly. These deaths, as well as the brutal murder of media influencer Qandeel Baloch in July 2016 and the global #MeToo movement beginning in 2017, were key catalysts for an alliance of feminist and women's organizations in Karachi (the Awami Workers Party, the Feminist Collective, the Women's Collective, Girls at Dhabas, and others) to announce a nationwide march on

International Women's Day that paralleled the many women's marches held across the world from 2017 onward. The rallies were held on March 8, 2018, in central locations in Karachi, Lahore, and Islamabad under the name Aurat March (women's march).[106] The women claimed public space for themselves as a collective and demanded an end to gender-based violence and honor killings, as well as equity for women in wage, labor, and workforce matters.

In the long history of women's protest, it is no surprise that the organizers of Aurat March planned the mass demonstration to be held on International Women's Day, invoking almost a century of women's internationalism that directly critiqued the nation-state for its failures to create true citizenship and rights for women. The Aurat March was held just a month after the sixth annual National Women's Day memorializing the Law of Evidence protest in February 1983. By holding the Aurat March on IWD on March 8, organizers refused the state co-optation of the domain of women's rights through the assimilation of the key moment of feminist dissent against the revised Law of Evidence as a state holiday. The Aurat March defied nationalist rituals that memorialized and selectively institutionalized the celebration of the women of WAF and the Pakistan Women Lawyers' Association while dismissing and erasing the critical anti-authoritarian foundations of the movement.

In 2020, thirty-six years after the publication of WAF's first manifesto, Aurat March organizers in Lahore released their own manifesto online for an international audience.[107] The Aurat Manifesto argued for economic, reproductive, and environmental justice; an end to police brutality; an accounting for the enforced disappearances of thousands of activists at the hands of the military; and an end to imperial wars that had transformed Pakistan for decades. As the march was called the Aurat March, the manifesto included a clear statement that trans people were included in the project from the start. The manifesto directly condemned ongoing police harassment of and brutality toward trans and gender-nonconforming people as a goal of the Aurat March.[108]

The marches, held in collaboration with a wide array of women's groups, were immediately condemned by right-wing politicians and the media for their signs and symbols declaring the will of women. The most contentious was a sign that proclaimed: "Mera Jism Meri Marzi" (my body, my will). For the Pakistani state and the religious right, this statement was the antithesis of good womanhood. The Aurat March was condemned for its acts of public obscenity (a punishable offense under the law), and authorities called the women who appeared in public, many without veils, "sexual deviants" and "anti-national traitors." Massive, carefully orchestrated campaigns of doxing and online harassment were soon launched against the organizers and participants in the Aurat March.

Despite these widespread campaigns to discredit the movement, the Aurat March as a movement has continued to grow and change. In the aftermath of the lockdowns in response to the COVID-19 pandemic, the 2021 manifesto reframed the health politics of the pandemic as a question of feminist rights. The disease that was most endemic was patriarchy: "Patriarchy is a ravaging illness, killing women every day. It is a femicide."[109] Most recently, the 2024 manifesto expressed solidarity with international liberation movements, including local struggles and queer and trans struggles in Pakistan and across the world.[110]

Like Pakistan's Law of Evidence passed in 1984, the Algerian Family Code of 1984 remains law today with few revisions, more than forty years after Algerian women took to the streets and organized by the thousands against the code. It endures despite decades of feminist organizing against state and militant violence against women. As the draconian civil laws outlined in the Family Code have remained law, women have continued to resist and protest. Throughout the 1990s and early 2000s, women's groups mobilized in street protests to fight patriarchal laws and terrorist acts of violence against women, including burnings and acid attacks that targeted women deemed aberrant and condemnable, from single mothers to defiant girls and women in public.[111] Women's organizations and feminist researchers have produced detailed research studies over many years that document violent acts against women by Islamist groups and advocate for the rights of Algerian women at UN women's and human rights conferences. The knowledge project to expose and make public the effects of a law shrouded in secrecy continues today as women document the dangerous effects of an authoritarian civil code that, in opposition to the Algerian constitution, denies women access to basic citizenship. The Family Code finally underwent a revision in 2005, more than twenty years after its initial passage; it repealed the article requiring total obedience of a wife to her husband but left the code largely intact.

In 2019, a wave of massive nonviolent protests, called the Hirak (the revolution of smiles), broke out against the anti-democratic rule of Algerian president Abdelaziz Bouteflika and led eventually to Bouteflika's resignation after twenty years of rule. Women were critical participants in the protests, taking to the streets en masse after decades of fear and patriarchal violence directed at women.[112] Algerian revolutionary Djamila Bouhired, by then eighty-four years old, took to the streets. Bouhired stood for rights once again, as she had for Algerian independence at the United Nations in the

1950s and the liberation of women against the Family Code in November 1981.[113] In the years that followed, protests and public actions for democratic governance and economic redistribution in Algeria continued. On International Women's Day on March 8, 2021, exactly forty years after the mass meeting of women on the first International Women's Day, women again marched against the Family Code as part of larger social mobilizations for democratic governance in Algeria.[114]

While many laws in Pakistan and Algeria remained largely intact, the early 1980s feminist mobilizations in India led to a massive reform of rape law by the Indian parliament in 1983. But tensions continued. While custodial rape by the police was now constituted as a specific crime under the criminal code, the Indian government refused to recognize rape by the Indian military as a criminal offense. Moreover, even after the 1983 reforms, the charge of rape continued to be gender-specific: only a "man" could rape a "woman" under the law. Rape was legally defined as forceful penetration of a vagina by a penis. In the decades after the Mathura Rape Case, many forms of prejudicial medical evidence of women's past sexual history and proof of women's virginity continued to be used in rape law. While feminists pushed for other reforms, they were unsuccessful in redefining rape to include marital rape, which remains legal under the Indian Penal Code to this day.

In Delhi in 2012, a young woman was gang-raped and murdered on private transportation. In response, hundreds of thousands of people took to the streets to protest conditions of endemic sexual violence against women and impossible living conditions in mega-urban spaces in India.[115] The case garnered international attention, causing cities across the country to shake with anger as people clashed in large-scale demonstrations. Large crowds dominated by men demanded the death penalty for the working-class men accused of the rape. Many feminist groups came out in vehement opposition to the death penalty, insisting that additional policing and carceral punishment would do little for women. Instead, feminists called for massive reforms to public safety for women and an overhaul of rape laws.

As the protests took over city streets, the Government of India again created a commission on the reform of rape law. The Verma Committee, headed by the former chief justice of the Supreme Court of India, J. S. Verma, released its report in 2013, thirty years after the government commission that reformed the law in response to the Mathura Rape Case protests of the early 1980s.[116] Ultimately, the government reformed rape law again. Rape remains an act defined by biological difference, and legal mandates for invasive and prejudicial medical evidence are largely unchanged.[117] Marital rape remains legal, and under the Armed Forces (Special Powers) Act, the Indian army continues to have total impunity in acts of sexual violence against women.

Even so, women challenged the increasingly authoritarian structures of the Indian state and took to the streets to demand their right to equal citizenship. In December 2019, a powerful women's protest emerged in reaction to the Citizenship (Amendment) Act (CAA), which proposed to create a National Register of Citizens that would exclude thousands of people. One key claimed space was at Shaheen Bagh in Delhi starting in December 2019.[118] A resistance organized and populated by multiple generations of Muslim women, sexual minorities, and students gathered in the Shaheen Bagh neighborhood of Delhi to occupy a public street with a sit-in that lasted months and blocked a major roadway. They sat together, sang, recited poetry, and welcomed people of different communities. There were readings of the preamble to the Indian Constitution, an invocation of a hermeneutics of constitutional justice that reminded the increasingly authoritarian Indian state of Muslim women's legally enshrined right to exist with dignity in a postcolonial India. The occupation at Shaheen Bagh was deeply local yet at the same time national and international. For over a hundred days—until the Government of India's COVID-19 lockdown of March 2020—protesters gave passionate speeches, sang songs, and sat together in solidarity, and recordings of these acts flooded the international news and social media. Yet, by 2024, despite mass mobilizations against the CAA, the Indian government implemented new exclusionary citizenship laws.

———

The street, where women claimed public space and discourse, was shaped by women's collective protests and a long tradition of women's hermeneutical politics across geographies, from Iran and Algeria to India and Pakistan. The knowledge systems that women have created since the early 1970s became a critical infrastructure for their public dissent. The conferences, working groups, commissions, reports, organizations, and research infrastructures of white papers and research studies establishing the "status of women" as a politics created spaces in which women could directly demand rights and full citizenship. Women scholars and activists remade feminist politics against authoritarianism through direct actions that raised the democratic possibility across Third World states. Women marched in the streets, carried placards, made public demands of the state, and submitted thousands of petitions. In so doing, they opened up new domains of political mobilization for all people, and certainly for the most marginalized and the dispossessed. Though they faced brutal crackdowns, state neglect, and ongoing threats of gendered violence, women pursued structural changes across the decades, creating a new lexicon and domain of research to build an independent political future. These innovations in the streets had a profound impact on the domain of research on women, catalyzing more substantive change than hundreds of reports, conferences, and studies on the condition of women. Women's protests transformed the status of women from a social scientific measure into a mass politics for democratic rights.

While draconian laws that delimit the rights of women endure, women have testified and continue to protest subjugation. Moreover, they are still demanding democratic representation by conducting transnational research; submitting petition after petition; publishing newsletters, research papers, books, and press releases; invoking feminist internationalism with massive public marches on International Women's Day; and occupying the streets. In the past fifty years, women have again and again insisted on their right to interpret texts and ideas and claim internationalism in the face of patriarchal nationalism. They speak and share their anti-authoritarian ideas in public, placing their bodies in the way of multiple authorities, in front of the shield and barricade, and in defiance of the police *lathi* charge.

Afterword, or We're Still Here

Just two months after the violent events of September 11, 2001, celebrated Black American feminist poet, essayist, and activist June Jordan decried the calls for vengeance and war that had rung out in the weeks that followed 9/11. Speaking in November 2001 at Barnard College in New York City—seven months before she would die of cancer—Jordan reflected on the challenges of the present and future in the aftermath of violence:

> Indeed some of us did not die.
> And what shall we do, we who did not die?
> What shall we do now? How shall we grieve, and cry out loud
> and face down despair?[1]

Just a few weeks earlier, the feminist network Women Living Under Muslim Laws (as noted in the introduction) had also urgently implored the United States to not resort to violence as they warned of the long-term effects of US military interventions for women around the world. For June Jordan, as for WLUML, the events that unfolded in the aftermath of 9/11 were a tragic result of the global inequality and proxy wars that had fostered strife and fundamentalism from the 1970s through the 1990s, perpetuating violence against the world's most vulnerable people.

This ongoing danger of retributive violence was familiar and deeply felt for Jordan. After all, by 2001 she had devoted more than three decades to exposing the devastating effects of and reactions to state violence, particularly for the world's women. Jordan was perhaps the most widely published Black intellectual of the twentieth century, and in her many writings the Third World loomed large. She insisted on a politics of solidarity among marginalized people around the world. She wrote against apartheid, offered a devastating critique of the complicity of the United States in the bombings in Beirut in the 1980s, expressed grief at the experiences of Palestinian refugees, and reported firsthand on the suffering of Nicaraguans as a result of US military intervention.[2]

Long before 2001, Jordan had developed a vision of Black liberation inextricable from Third World solidarity, internationalism, and feminism.[3] In 1968, she wrote of the assassination of Martin Luther King Jr. in a poem that eulogized his life, insisting that his death symbolized supremacist fears about the growing waves of freedom worldwide.[4] In the 1970s, she conceptualized a new politics of refusal against white supremacist speech, instead insisting on the fundamental value of "particular, Black, and Third World lives."[5] As Jordan declared: "Our lives are not debatable."[6] Inverting the logic of global hierarchy, she asserted that most of the world had been "mistakenly termed the Third World,"[7] a misnomer for Black and Third World people who "constitute the majority of life on this planet" and thus were the true First World.[8]

Jordan's expression of grief and search for future promise in 2001 reflects the long and hard struggle of women to theorize the lives of everyday people and their right to a future, despite the often totalizing destruction of war and violence. Across her extraordinary oeuvre of essays, poems, and speeches, Jordan envisioned a politics based in the perseverance and generative visions of marginalized people. In front of the UN General Assembly in 1978, in the midst of the UN Decade for Women, Jordan decried South Africa's apartheid state for women, recalling that more than forty thousand women made a "deliberate defense of life" against apartheid in the 1950s. As she declared in the present tense, in language that anticipated a radically different future for women after the end of apartheid, "*we are the ones we have been waiting for*."[9]

Many women of this generation have looked back on their own lives to document the many movements and research networks that they led in order to claim their place in history. Their recollections come to us in different forms—in autobiographies and memoirs as well as in the many popular interviews, collective stories, and comprehensive oral histories of Third World women documented years later by a younger generation of feminist activists and scholars. These life writings serve as critical sources for understanding the history of internationalism and the unrealized promises and failures of decolonization.

Women's memoirs and oral histories are an essential archive of this moment of internationalism, offering a window into the political optimism that shaped feminist work. The very idea of feminism was an epiphany for West Indian sociologist and feminist activist Peggy Antrobus. In her reflective interviews, Antrobus described her experience, as a young woman, of the cruel effects of endemic patriarchal violence among the Caribbean communities, including the death of two sisters as a result of horrific acts of domestic violence. Transnational feminist research changed everything and shaped Antrobus's life's work: "Academics and activists from Africa, Asia, and Latin America gave me the kind of theoretical and intellectual understanding of what I was actually experiencing."[10] West African feminist and founding member of AAWORD Filomina Steady vividly describes in her memoir the thrill of the experience of solidarity of Third World women at the Wellesley International Women and Development Conference in 1976: "I walked down the aisle looking very pregnant and determined . . . I then announced that the Africa Group had a statement."[11] That statement, declaring the right of African women to write themselves in research, would form the foundations of the principles of the pathbreaking radical research organization AAWORD.

Yet feminist memoirs and life histories also reveal the challenges to Third World feminist research and activism caused by the privatization of global capital and the professionalization of feminism. In her memoir structured around the names in her address book, Indian feminist publisher Ritu Menon remembers the resolute goals and expansive reach of the autonomous domain of women's publishing. "Everyone thought we were mad when we said we would publish everything from pamphlets to PhDs," she recounts. "Our focus was women, and if this called for engaging with everything from activist material to academic research, we would do so."[12] Feminist writing had the unique ability to travel, making "national borders dissolve."[13]

But by 2020, as she wrote the memoir during the COVID-19 pandemic lockdown, that moment of progressive publishing was gone. As Menon mourns, "These days, I can count the number of feminist publishers in the world on the fingers of one hand."[14] For Pakistani sociologist, feminist activist, and archivist Nighat Said Khan, while authoritarian dictators fostered fear, in response, women developed a real sense of intimacy, creativity, and pleasure in the work of feminist dissent: "I remember those years of very intense and close friendships in the women's movement before we all settled into our careers. I remember the earnest political and personal discussions and the openness to explore and grapple at something. I remember there was a sadness when this started going away."[15] Decades later, that optimism and possibility had been foreclosed: "I think we've forgotten how to laugh. I've forgotten."[16]

Third World women recount an expanding domain of global feminist research and movements in the rich and complicated life stories they tell. While full of nostalgia for the pure political promise of feminist writing, few women in their memoirs address the biases and conflicts that fractured feminist efforts, the differences in political views and hierarchies of access, class, race, caste, and education that shaped this moment of Third World feminism. When not celebrating the moment, women's life writings most often bemoan the rhetoric of fear and suspicion that has come to dominate the politics of international women's and gender rights since 9/11.

Yet, in spite of the challenges to the revolutionary promise of feminist writing in the decades that followed, these women most often close their memoirs with determination, arguing that the work continues. Even as women have claimed their past and their own histories, they have also always insisted on their right to transform the future.

At the heart of the many ideas of Third World women explored across this book, like Jordan's poignant expression of outrage, is a plea for an *epistemology of survival* in the face of crisis. Here was the essence of the anti-authoritarian stance of wide-ranging Third World women: in order to counter the politics of domination and annihilation, women insisted on the rights of the most vulnerable to create knowledge about the realities they faced in order to live more freely. Women had the right to study their histories, write transformative policy for the present, and build research infrastructures for a better future. This framework of feminist research worked to confront the realities of women's lives, bear witness to the many hardships women faced, and dissent against a Cold War geopolitics fueled by war, mass displacement, and global capitalist exploitation. In their insistence that the world's women had the fundamental right to live, Third World women expressed a determination and radical optimism that resonate today and offer insights (and perhaps some reprieve) in the face of the disaffection and defeatism of the present moment.

There are many lessons to be learned from this history. First, Third World feminism was anti-authoritarian at its heart, expressly so, not only in its commitment to mass social and political movements but also through the transnational production of feminist knowledge. Third World feminist theories of anti-authoritarianism diagnosed neocolonialism as an enduring project of epistemological domination fueled by the systemic subjugation of women and sexual minorities. To counter these neocolonial structures of knowledge, Third World women insisted on the rights of women to sovereignty, both epistemic and bodily, and the boundless possibilities of writing women into existence through situated research.

Second, this history reveals that radical change for Third World women was catalyzed through transnational collectivity that brought people together across differences and borders. Feminist internationalism offered a trenchant critique of the dangers of postcolonial nationalism and authoritarianism through new models of cross-border solidarity and networks. It provokes us to reflect on the past and future of collaboration and collective thinking, even as transnational alliances are increasingly foreclosed today in a world of anti-migration policies, increasingly draconian border regimes, and the massive defunding of development programs and scientific research and education.

And third, this history teaches us how fragile systems of minoritized knowledge were and remain today. Seemingly resilient infrastructures for global research on women have been and continue to be dismantled by increasingly authoritarian states, foundations, reactionary think tanks, and universities in crisis. Through this history, we confront the epistemological limits of feminist research in its reliance on social scientific empiricism and its complicated reliance on state power and become better able to account for the widescale material collapse of research architectures for researching women and sexual minorities in the first decades of the twenty-first century. Through these histories, we begin to recognize and undo the reductive logic of the quantitative indices and measures that are naturalized today and continue to dominate the material foundation for global research on women, gender, and sexuality. We must account for the history of infrastructures of research to understand what exactly is being dismantled with the rise of authoritarianism in our present in threats to true free speech, the weaponization of the language of national security to gut nongovernmental organizing, and the systematic bureaucratic starvation of feminist research.

Now, as then, we need a resilient project of disciplinary dissent to reimagine and build new domains of knowledge for the twenty-first century, one that centers an epistemology of survival.

Fifty years ago, women fought for a new vision of liberation in a time of disenchantment and disillusionment with the nationalist project and pursued a radical vision of worldmaking as they came together at global conferences, wrote new studies, reports, and books, created research networks, and protested in the streets. They pursued the difficult work of decolonizing knowledge despite increasingly impossible conditions of inequality and displacement all around them. They insisted on their right to build a future through knowledge despite the cruelty, devastation, and disappointment with the project of postcolonial sovereignty. With determination, women continued to write themselves into the world, pushing against the widespread cynicism, pessimism, and dread that surrounded them—a disaffection not unlike our own today.

The personal papers of June Jordan reflect the determination that characterizes this history of feminist research and writing. When I engaged Jordan's proliferative archives more than two decades after her death, I was far removed from her moving call to action and the decades-long struggle of Third World women who worked to transform international debates by centering the freedom of women and building a world of feminist knowledge. And yet the urgency of her words, carefully preserved in the pages of her archive, resonates in our present. Here was the same resolve—to keep doing the work, in spite of it all—inscribed with devastating clarity by June Jordan in 2001, on the page, in her own handwriting.

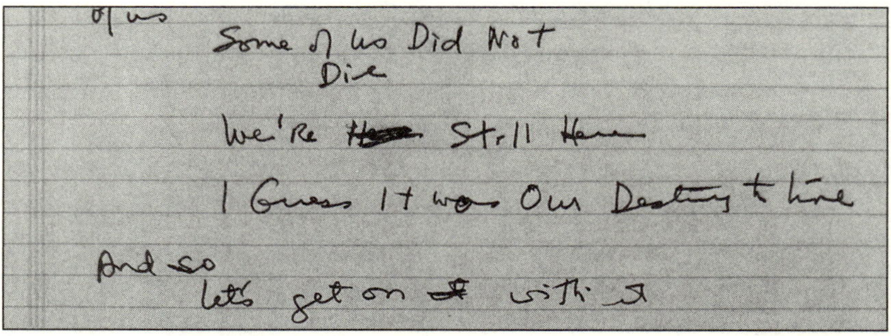

FIGURE A.1: June Jordan handwritten notes, 2001. Papers of June Jordan, Schlesinger Library on the History of Women in America. Copyright Christopher D. Meyer, 2001. Reprinted by permission of the Frances Goldin Literary Agency.

Some of Us Did Not
    Die.
We're Still Here.
I Guess It Was Our Destiny to live
And so
    let's get on with it.[17]

ACKNOWLEDGMENTS

First and foremost, my deepest thanks to the many women who took time to share their life histories and expertise with me. It has been one of the great privileges of my life to learn from you.

I wrote most of this book while serving as caregiver to my amazing mother, Rupa. I thank her for her love, laughter, and brilliance, and for always being proud of me. I am so, *so* lucky to be her daughter. Thank you. The stories and lives I explore here have offered a beautiful escape from the anxieties of the past several years—the stressful environment of painful procedures in hospital rooms, grueling travel, and the profound exhaustion of never-ending worry. I am grateful to a network of chosen family who gave us food and love during times of profound duress. Researching and writing a book about the efflorescence of transnational feminist ideas during a global pandemic, a time when people were unable to gather together or travel to be in collective gave me the opportunity to reflect on how we might imagine a better world, radically different from the desperation and uncertainty of the present. It has been a privilege to dwell in these rich histories and bear witness to the extraordinary lives of these women.

Thank you to many people who helped guide this project by teaching me about their pathbreaking research and remarkable lives in formal interviews, including Peggy Antrobus, Nighat Said Khan, Evelynn Hammonds, Ritu Menon, Rounaq Jahan, Martha Chen, Uma Chakravarti, the late Nirmala Banerjee, and Filomena Steady.

Thank you to Manan Ahmed Asif for modeling how to think and write with radical humanity and love. Thank you for your profound clarity of mind and ideas, for talking, walking, affirming my ideas, mapping arguments, reading, editing, and reading again (and again).

Thank you to my students. I wrote this book for you. I am in awe of your ethical vision and creative approach to ideas. May we work together to create sustainable knowledge infrastructures for a better world.

My thanks to TZ, Genevieve Clutario, Lauren Kaminsky, and Ju Yon Kim for making lockdown and the years that have followed full of joy, laughter, and collective risk analysis. Thank you to Genevieve for always, always showing up. Thank you to Dwaipayan Banerjee and Kareem Khubchandani for joyous friendship and intellectual comradery. Thanks to all of my family, especially dearest Jessica Schmidt, my forever bestie, and my cousin Bipasha Ray, for your love and many insights that shaped this book.

Thank you to the two anonymous readers of this manuscript for their wonderful feedback and guidance and to the generous readers who engaged with the full manuscript during my workshop: Rohit De, Joanne Meyerowitz, and David Engerman. Thank you to Ben Platt for your supportive and insightful editorial guidance and for believing in this project.

Thank you to Jennifer C. Nash for big hugs and intellectual companionship. Thank you to my dear friend Rohit De for shared curiosity in transnational histories and long-lasting friendship. Thank you to Anjali Arondekar for all of the laughter and feminist dreams. Thank you to Sarah Haley, Shana Redmond, and Robeson for love and solidarity. Thank you to Jocelyn Olcott and Durba Ghosh for your generosity and collaborative spirit. Thank you to Judith Surkis for careful feedback on the manuscript. Thank you to Esmat Elhalaby for companionship in the history of ideas. Thank you to Parimal Patil, Jane Kamensky, Maya Jasanoff, Kirsten Weld, Robert Reid-Pharr, Jinah Kim, Robin Bernstein, Sarah Richardson, Mary Lewis, Evelynn Hammonds, and Jocelyn Viterna for your guidance. Thank you to so, so many who have made my work possible and who have offered feedback on this project, brilliant feedback, diverse expertise, and vital support. Thank you to Brandon M. Terry for the shared love of ideas. Thank you to my treasured feminist mentees Tara Suri, Poorna Swami, Chrystel Oloukoi, Sana Naeem, and Jordan Villegas. Thank you to Robyn Wiegman, Lorgia Garcia-Pena, AB Huber, Pete Sigal, Lisa Lowe, Mary John, Maha Ahmed, Nadim Massad, Kavi Ahmed, Kitty Ahmed, Sarah Pinto, Jyoti Puri, Banu Subramaniam, Elora Chowdhury, Gowri Vijayakumar, Jessica Namakkal, Elizabeth Ault, Caroline Light, Linda Schlossberg, Michael Bronski, Imani Perry, Afsaneh Najmabadi, Shahnaz Rouse, Lucy Burns, Annabel Kim, Hannah Frydman, Camille Robcis, Katrina Forrester, Rosie Bsheer, Partha Chatterjee, Rashid Khalidi, Mona Khalidi, Mira Nair, Mahmood Mamdani, Gabeba Baderoon, Adom Getachew, Jinah Kim, Martha Selby, Vishal Khandelwal, Vivek Bald, Vijay Iyer, Hannah Marcus, Victor Seow, Andrew Gordon, Kavita Sivaramakrishnan, Gyan Prakash, Divya Cherian, Robert Travers, Kelvin Ng, Sara Kang, Eli Nelson, Kirin Gupta, Phoebe Suh, Aditya Balasubramaniam, Emma Heaney, Kadji Amin, Jules Gill-Peterson, Jasbir Puar, Samantha Pinto,

Nurfadzilah Yahaya, Sandipto Dasgupta, Ali Raza, Vivek Bald, Aziza Ahmed, Premilla Nadasen, Omnia El Shakry, Carolyn Dean, Mrinalini Sinha, Ishita Pande, Rachel Berger, Indrani Chatterjee, Douglas Haynes, Deborah Coen, Heather Love, Regine Michelle Jean-Charles, Corinne Field, Evren Savci, Chandan Reddy, Riley Snorton, Ajantha Subramaniam, Vince Brown, Walter Johnson, Alison Frank Johnson, Richard Thomas, Elliott Powell, Ali Karjoo-Ravary, Beeta Bhaghoolizadeh, Delara, Soraya, Tamika Samuel, Glenn Lopez, Larson Hogstrom, Ethan, Yuna, Hero. Thanks to everyone at the Hungarian Pastry Shop, including Ida, Noreen, James, and Philip.

Thank you to Professor David Bell and the wonderful fellows at the Shelby Cullom Davis Center and the faculty in the Princeton University Department of History; and to Dean Tomiko Brown-Nagin and the Harvard Radcliffe Institute for support for the research and writing of this book. Thank you to all of the staff at the Schlesinger Library on the History of Women in America, including Tamar Gonen Brown, Jenny Gotwal, Mimosa Shah, and John Jayo. Thanks to the Weatherhead Center for International Affairs and Harvard for research and manuscript workshop support. Thank you to Jessica Taylor for research support, to Poorvi Bellur, Heer Cheema, and Mahnoor Jalal for research assistance, and to Audra Wolfe for editorial feedback. Thank you to the many amazing people at archives and libraries across the world who made research possible during a pandemic, including the UN archives, ASR, Shirkat Gah, Government College Lahore, the Center for Women's Development Studies in Delhi, Harvard Library, Princeton Library, the Rockefeller Foundation archives, Abby Stewart and the Global Feminisms Project at the University of Michigan, Smith College special collections, Brown University special collections, Duke University special collections, Wellesley College special collections, and the countless staff and workers who have digitized materials and made them publicly accessible across geographies. Thanks to Princeton University Press for all of their intellectual and material support, including the global equity grant. Thank you to my fierce editor Priya Nelson and thanks for the editorial support of Thalia Leaf, Emma Wagh, Cynthia Buck, and Theresa Liu.

Thank you to many colleagues who generously invited me to share work in progress and offered insightful feedback for this project: Jennifer C. Nash and Jocelyn Olcott and the Duke Feminist Theory Workshop, the Duke Franklin Humanities Center, and Duke Gender, Sexuality, and Feminist Studies; Vanessa Ogle, Lauren Benton, Samuel Moyn, and faculty and students at the International and Global History Workshop, Department of History, Yale University; Rohit De, David Engerman, Kasturi Gupta, and the wonderful participants in the "Traveling Expertise in South Asia" workshop in Kathmandu; Rovel Sequeira and Seda Saluk and their Global South Gender and Sexuality Collective at the University of Michigan; the Cold War Media Group, New York University; "Law and Humanities in/ from the Global South" and Sharika Thiranagama at Stanford University; George Chauncey, Camille Robcis, and Denise Cruz, the Columbia Research Initiative on the Global History of Sexualities, Columbia University; South Asian Studies and Naisargi Dave, University of Toronto; Wallace Best and the Princeton University Program in Gender and Sexuality Studies; and David Bell, Natasha Wheatley, Angela N. H. Creager, and the Davis Center seminar in the Department of History at Princeton University.

Chapter 2, "The Report," appears in an earlier version in Durba Mitra, "The Report, or, Whatever Happened to Third World Feminist Theory?," *Signs: Journal of Women in Culture and Society* 48, no. 1 (Spring 2023): 557–84. Some language from my essays "Feminism for the Living" in *Feminism against Cisness*, edited by Emma Heaney (Durham, NC: Duke University Press, 2024), 241–50, and "Sisterhood Is X: On Solidarity Then and Now" in *South Atlantic Quarterly* 122, no. 3 (2023): 431–52, is included in revised form in the introduction. A brief excerpt of my editorial introduction to "Outraged/ Enraged: The Rage Special Issue," *Signs: Journal of Women in Culture and Society* 46, no. 4 (Summer 2021): 785–800, appears in revised form at the end of chapter 5, "The Protest."

APPENDIX

Short Bios of Selected Women Who Animate *The Future That Was*

Peggy Antrobus (1935–) is a West Indian activist, civil servant, and scholar who transformed the trajectory of research on women in the Caribbean. The first adviser on women's affairs in Jamaica and cofounder of the first research unit on women at the University of the West Indies, Antrobus is widely celebrated as a generous and charismatic feminist scholar and organizer who created connections between Caribbean feminists and global feminist networks. Dr. Antrobus completed a degree in economics at Bristol University and earned a master's degree in social work from the University of Birmingham (United Kingdom) and a PhD in education from the University of Massachusetts Amherst. Antrobus was a direct mentee of Lucille Mathurin Mair, ambassador, diplomat, and feminist writer. She is the founding member of several key women research networks, including Development Alternatives with Women in a New Era (DAWN), the Women and Development Unit (WAND) at the University of the West Indies, and the Caribbean Association for Feminist Research and Action (CAFRA).

Kamla Bhasin (1946–2021) was an Indian political scientist, feminist activist, poet, and writer who founded Sangat, an Indian feminist network and advocacy organization, and led transnational feminist networks that reached across South Asia. Bhasin was well known for her work popularizing ideas of women's rights through accessible poetry, children's books, and popular textbooks and pamphlets that were translated across dozens of languages and published widely across South Asia. Educated at state colleges in Rajasthan, Bhasin went on to complete a PhD in the sociology of development at the University of Münster in Germany. She worked at the Food and Agricultural Organization of the United Nations for years. In the 1980s and 1990s, she worked closely with Nighat Said Khan, Pakistani feminist scholar and activist, to build a transnational network of feminist scholars and artists. Through Sangat, Bhasin created accessible feminist literature and held workshops to foster feminist ideas of human rights and sustainable development. During the COVID-19 pandemic, Bhasin produced dozens of speeches and readings of her writing on women's rights, poetry, and children's books on YouTube.

Urvashi Butalia (1952–) is a feminist publisher, editor, scholar, and cofounder with Ritu Menon of the pathbreaking feminist press Kali for Women, which was among the longest-lasting feminist presses anywhere in the world. Butalia went on to found her own feminist imprint, Zubaan, in 2003. She is the author of key feminist studies of Indian history and society, including the field-defining study of the Partition of India, *The Other Side of Silence* (Kali for Women, 1998). She completed an undergraduate degree from Miranda House, Delhi University, a master's in literature at Delhi University, and a master's in South Asian studies at the University of London. Butalia has written widely on issues of women, gender, and sexuality, majoritarianism, and the critical role of independent media in democratic societies.

Vasudha Dhagamwar (1940–2014) was an Indian feminist lawyer, writer, and activist who founded the Multiple Action Research Group (MARG), a legal advocacy organization. Dhagamwar completed a degree at the Law College of the Indian Law Society in Pune and then completed a bachelor of law from Mumbai University, a degree in economics and politics at Oxford University, and a PhD in legal history from the School of Oriental and African Studies. In 1979, Dhagamwar was one of the four authors of the famous open letter from legal scholars on the Mathura Rape Case that catalyzed feminist movements on women's rights and gender violence in India. Her work with MARG centered public interest litigation with a focus on displaced people, torture in tribal communities, and prison reform. Dhagamwar worked with the Government of India as part of the National Commission for Women and coauthored a contested report of the NCW on the experience of minority women during the Gujarat pogrom in 2002.

Florence Howe (1929–2020) was an American feminist publisher, writer, and scholar who founded the Feminist Press and was a key thinker in American feminist and international feminist movements from the 1970s onward. Howe completed degrees in English from Hunter College and Smith College and coursework in a PhD program in art history and literature at the

University of Wisconsin–Madison. As a faculty member at Goucher College in Maryland, Howe published research on education, desegregation, and women's rights. In 1970, she founded the Feminist Press, one of the longest-running feminist publishers in the world and a critical center for innovative feminist research and writing during the American and international feminist movements of the 1970s through the 1990s. Through her work as founder of the Feminist Press, Howe collaborated with women around the world, traveling to Asia, Africa, the Middle East, and Latin America to foster feminist research and writing across geographies.

Rounaq Jahan (1944–) is a Bangladeshi political scientist, interdisciplinary feminist scholar, and international expert on women and gender. A founding figure in the fields of women's studies and feminist development research in Bangladesh, Jahan completed a bachelor's degree in Dhaka, master's degrees in political science from the University of Dhaka and Harvard University, and a PhD in government from Harvard University. She served as a faculty member at the University of Dhaka from 1970 to 1993, when she joined the faculty at Columbia University. She is founder of the groundbreaking feminist research collective Women for Women, which produced the first comprehensive published research on women in newly established Bangladesh in 1973. Jahan has served as an adviser and expert for the government of Bangladesh and the United Nations on many issues, including education, gender justice, and development strategies and policy. She has served as a consultant to the United Nations on development, population, women, and children. Jahan has published extensively on issues of gender, development, and democratic governance in Bangladesh.

Asma Jahangir (1952–2018) was Pakistan's leading human rights lawyer, feminist legal scholar, and fierce international law advocate. She founded the first legal aid organization in Pakistan and was a key legal thinker in Pakistan and on the international stage, serving as president of Pakistan's Supreme Court Bar Association and chairperson of the Human Rights Commission of Pakistan, which she cofounded in 1986. Jahangir completed a bachelor's in law at Punjab University. An expert in constitutional law and Muslim family law in comparative perspective, she passionately advocated for women, children, poor people, and religious minorities throughout her career. She was a founding member of Women's Action Forum and a key leader in major movements against militarism and authoritarianism, from protests against the Law of Evidence in the 1980s to the Lawyers' Movement in 2007. She authored multiple books and reports on women's rights and prejudicial customary law, human rights around the world, and the suffering of children.

Devaki Jain (1933–) is an Indian feminist economist, civil servant, and international development expert. Jain completed undergraduate studies in mathematics and English at Mysore University. She then attended St. Anne's College at the University of Oxford, where she also completed a PhD in the interdisciplinary field of philosophy, politics, and economics. She began her career as faculty at Miranda House, University of Delhi, and then founded and directed the Institute of Social Studies Trust in New Delhi. Jain was a longtime consultant and expert for the United Nations on issues of development and women's issues. She was editor of the first curated volume on women in postcolonial India and founding member of Development Alternatives for Women in a New Era (DAWN). She is author of multiple books and studies on women and economic development.

Hina Jilani (1953–) is a Pakistani lawyer, feminist scholar, and leading expert in international human rights. Educated in law at Punjab University, Jilani is best known for her work alongside her sister Asma Jahangir in multiple domains of law, including their work cofounding the first legal aid organization in Pakistan and pathbreaking protests, advocacy, and scholarly research against draconian family laws in Pakistan. Jilani is an advocate of the Supreme Court in Pakistan, a role she has held since 1992. She was a special representative of the Secretary-General on Human Rights Defenders at the United Nations from 2000 until 2008 and has served as a consultant and expert in human rights law at the United Nations for decades.

Nighat Said Khan (1946–) is a Pakistani feminist sociologist, writer, and activist, as well as a key archivist of the Pakistani feminist movement. She founded the feminist organization ASR (Applied Socio-economic Research) and collaborated with feminist scholars, artists, and activists from across South Asia to build a rich domain of intellectual life for women across borders for over three decades. Khan completed a bachelor's degree at Columbia University and worked toward a PhD in sociology at the University of Manchester under the direction of Hamza Alavi. She is a founding member of Women's Action Forum and a longtime collaborator with Indian feminist Kamla Bhasin, including through their coauthored book on key feminist ideas, *Some Questions on Feminism and Its Relevance in South Asia*

(1986), as well as through numerous collaborative projects and conferences on wide-ranging issues, from social science research on women to feminist conferences on dance, theater, and music across the India-Pakistan border.

Lala Rukh (1948–2017) was a Pakistani visual artist, teacher, and activist. A founding member of Women's Action Forum and founder of the master's program in visual art at Punjab University, Lala Rukh shaped the visual iconography of feminism in Pakistan and across South Asia and beyond. Educated in fine arts at Punjab University and then the University of Chicago, Lala Rukh was on the faculty of Punjab University for over thirty years. A visual artist who worked across media, her posters and artwork were exhibited across the world, including at the Metropolitan Museum of Art in New York City, the Tate Modern in London, and documenta 14 in Kassel, Germany. As a key feminist organizer and artist for the movement, Lala Rukh produced powerful images and essays for newsletters, pamphlets, signs, and posters in support of the movement.

Lucille Mathurin Mair (1924–2009) was a Jamaican historian, ambassador, diplomat, and international women's rights expert. She was the first woman to serve as under secretary-general of the United Nations in 1982, secretary-general for the second World Conference of the United Nations Decade for Women in Copenhagen in 1980, and secretary-general of the United Nations Conference on Palestine. Mathurin Mair completed a degree in history at London University and a PhD in history from the University of the West Indies. Her 1974 dissertation, published in 2006 as a book, was a pathbreaking work of research as the first history of women in Jamaica, and the work set the stage for the field of research on the history of women and slavery in the Caribbean. Known for her even temper and extraordinary diplomacy, Mair was a founding thinker and institution-builder for research on women and gender in the Caribbean and a key mentor to many Black Caribbean feminist thinkers. Mair was well known for her transnational feminist institution-building. Beyond her major roles in Jamaica's Ministries of Women's Affairs, Information Service, and Foreign Affairs, she served as Jamaica's permanent representative to the United Nations and also as ambassador to Cuba. Mair cofounded the Women and Development Unit at the University of the West Indies, collaborated with feminist organizations across the Caribbean, the United Kingdom, Asia, and Africa, and was a founding member of Development Alternatives with Women for a New Era (DAWN).

Vina Mazumdar (1927–2013) was a scholar, civil servant, and activist whose research and institution-building transformed the trajectory of the study of women in India and the wider domain of international women's studies. She completed a bachelor's degree at the University of Oxford in 1951 and then served as faculty in political science at the University of Patna. Mazumdar went on to receive a PhD in political science from Oxford, which she completed while living there alone with her two small daughters. She was the secretary of India's Status of Women Commission, which produced the pathbreaking *Towards Equality* report (1974) on the status of women in India, a text that would shape research on women across the postcolonial world. She went on to support the development of the field of women's studies through her position at the Indian Council of Social Science Research. Mazumdar cofounded the Center for Women's Development Studies in 1980 as well as the Indian Association for Women's Studies in 1982. Described again and again as fearless and a force of nature, Mazumdar shaped the global trajectory of women's studies through her institution-building and collaborations with feminist thinkers from across the world, including founder and editor of the American publisher Feminist Press, Florence Howe.

Ritu Menon (1949–) is an Indian feminist publisher, scholar, and writer who cofounded the pathbreaking feminist press Kali for Women in 1984 with Urvashi Butalia and then founded her own feminist publishing house Women Unlimited. Her research, writing, and editorial work have been foundational to the study of women and the Partition of India. She has written across genres about women and gendered violence, the persecution of religious minorities, and women's writing in South Asia. She is the coauthor, with Kamla Bhasin, of *Borders and Boundaries: Women in India's Partition* (Delhi: Kali for Women, 1998), among other pathbreaking books.

Fatima Mernissi (1940–2015), one of the most visible global feminist intellectuals of the twentieth century, was a prominent Moroccan feminist sociologist, a feminist writer across fiction and nonfiction, and an international activist. Mernissi completed a degree in political science at the Sorbonne and a PhD in sociology at Brandeis University. She was professor of sociology at the Mohammed V University in Rabat, Morocco. A prolific and foundational scholar of women, Islam, and democracy, she published multiple pathbreaking studies of women and their critical roles in premodern and modern Muslim societies. Among her many publications, her first study, *Beyond the Veil* (1975), defined the field of research on Muslim women and global politics, and her literary memoir, *Dreams of Trespass* (1994), which was translated into dozens of languages, recounted her girlhood experiences and imagined the possibility of freedom for girls and women. Mernissi was also a founding member of the Moroccan Organization for Human Rights and a key advocate for a feminist human rights framework.

Nawal El Saadawi (1931–2021) was an Egyptian doctor, feminist writer, and activist, and became one of the most visible global feminist activists and thinkers in the twentieth century. El Saadawi was trained as a doctor at Cairo University, graduating with a medical degree in 1955. She later attended Columbia University, where she completed a master's degree in public health. Cofounder of the Arab Women's Solidarity Association and the Arab Association for Women's Rights, Saadawi was a visible advocate for women's rights on the global stage and a leading voice for Third World women at conferences for the UN Decade for Women and at Beijing. She served at the Ministry of Health in Egypt and later as a UN adviser for women in Africa and the Middle East. Saadawi was the author of numerous books on women, sexuality, and Islam, including her first book, *Women and Sex* (1972), which resulted in her firing from prominent positions at the Ministry of Health and loss of membership in Egyptian medical associations. Her outspoken work as a feminist writer and speaker led to her incarceration, her political exile until her return to Egypt in 1996, and her later activism in political movements in Egypt in 2011.

Lotika Sarkar (1923–2013) was an Indian feminist legal scholar who shaped feminist research in India through her participation in India's Status of Women Commission and her institution-building work to develop women's studies in India. She transformed feminist engagements with the law over many decades through her work on the 1974 *Towards Equality* report on the status of women in India and also in her key role in the open letter dissenting from the Supreme Court decision in the famous Mathura Rape Case in 1979. Sarkar was the first Indian woman to graduate with a doctorate from the University of Cambridge, which she completed in the field of law. She was the first woman to join the faculty of law at the University of Delhi and spent many years as a law professor at the Indian Law Institute in the later 1980s and 1990s. She cofounded the CWDS with Vina Mazumdar in 1980, and in 1981, alongside Mazumdar, Neera Desai, and others, she co-organized the first national conference on women's studies in India. In memorials and the reflections of colleagues and students, Sarkar was described as a quiet, deeply learned woman who was ceaselessly generous with resources and time.

Marie-Angélique Savané (1947–) is a Senegalese feminist sociologist and public intellectual. A leading feminist thinker in Africa, Savané completed her graduate studies in sociology in France. She was cofounder of multiple key feminist organizations, including the Association of African Women for Research and Development (AAWORD) and Development Alternatives with Women for a New Era (DAWN), and the editor of the journal *Famille et Développement.* She has served as a consultant and international expert on research on women and population for the United Nations. She has written extensively on family law and women in Senegal, feminist movements in Senegal and the broader African continent, women's labor, and agrarian development.

Farida Shaheed is a feminist sociologist and activist, a civil servant, and a longtime representative to the United Nations. A prolific writer and international gender expert, Shaheed has been critical to the trajectory of the study of women as the author and editor of foundational texts on the history of feminism and women's rights in Pakistan, including a volume she coauthored with Khawar Mumtaz, *Two Steps Forward, One Step Back? Women of Pakistan* (1986). She completed a bachelor's degree in sociology at the University of Geneva and a master's degree in sociology at Leeds University. She is the founder and longtime director of Shirkat Gah Women's Resource Centre in Lahore, a research institute focused on women's rights and gender justice in Pakistan. She is a founding member of Women's Action Forum and Women Living Under Muslim Laws. She served as the first special rapporteur of cultural rights to the United Nations and was appointed special rapporteur on the right to education at the United Nations in 2022.

Filomina Steady (1941–), a key feminist scholar of African and African Diasporic women, worked for decades to expand the domain of research on the continent and beyond. Dr. Steady received a PhD in anthropology from the University of Oxford. She is an expert on global gender issues and a pathbreaking scholar of Black women, with a special focus on race and power in Africa and the African Diaspora. She spent many years as a professor at Wellesley College and is a founding member of the pathbreaking Association of African Women for Research and Development (AAWORD). Steady has served in multiple roles as a researcher and expert, including as consultant to national and international organizations, the United Nations, and US specialized agencies.

Zenebework Tadesse is an Ethiopian sociologist and women's rights activist. She was a founding member of the Association of African Women for Research and Development (AAWORD), and as its first executive director, she fostered comparative research on women across the African continent. Tadesse completed degrees in sociology and international relations at Binghamton University in New York. Later she moved to Chicago, where she became involved with internationalist student politics and the Black Panther Party. Following her work fostering feminist research in Africa through AAWORD, Tadesse worked for many years to build gender research at the Council for the Development of Social Science Research in Africa (CODESRIA), cofounded the Forum for Social Sciences in Ethiopia, and cofounded the transnational feminist research collective Development Alternatives with Women for a New Era (DAWN). Tadesse is an author of multiple research publications on gender, agrarian politics, land rights, and democracy in Africa and has served at the United Nations as an expert on women, development, and democracy in Africa.

NOTES

Introduction, or What Is the Future We Yearn For?

1. I reflect on the idea of yearning for global unity through the words of Toni Morrison, who uses the term "yearnings" to describe global solidarity for decolonization in contrast to the cynicism of later ideas of "one world" in an era of privatization and globalization in the 1990s. She marks the end of a language of solidarity and alliance across decolonizing geographies, where ideas like global unity and universalism were "less like categories of historical trends than yearnings" (Morrison, *The Source of Self Regard*, 6). I address Morrison's ideas in further detail in Mitra, "Sisterhood Is X."

2. In contrast to the utopian and idealistic ideas of unity of early Third Worldism—what Vijay Prashad has described as the Third World as a dream of solidarity rather than a specific geography in the world—Third World feminism reimagined the Third World through the idea of a coalition against authoritarianism that confronted how neocolonial structural adjustment and authoritarianism shaped the realities of women's struggles in postcolonized spaces. On this idealized conception of the Third World project, see Prashad, *The Darker Nations*. On the Third World project as a utopian dream, see Prakash and Adelman, *Inventing the Third World*.

3. The women I write about at length in this book explicitly identify as feminists in their writings and in oral histories. The term "feminist" is an emic category used by women in diverse archives from this period, when women described themselves as both Third World women and Third World feminists. While a few women were initially reluctant to use the category, most Third World women I study actively claimed the concept of feminism as central to their research projects by the end of the UN Decade for Women. The term "feminist" is a site of wide-ranging thought among women of color and internationalists. Through the 1980s, there were important critical engagements among Black women and Indigenous, Latin American, Asian, African, and other Third World women about the perceived limitations of second wave feminism and its exclusion of women of color. These critiques generated new concepts like "womanism," centered in the perspectives and life-worlds of Black women, as coined by writer Alice Walker in 1979 and described as "womanist prose" in *In Search of Our Mothers' Gardens*.

4. On the intimacy in shared histories of exploitation and geographies of global capital, see Lowe, *The Intimacy of Four Continents*.

5. For productive oral histories of revolutionary feminisms and women's experiences in the Global North and South that engage these complicated relationships with and against the state, see Bhandar and Ziadah, *Revolutionary Feminisms*.

6. Or, in the language of historian Ranajit Guha in his framing text for subaltern studies, "it is the study of this historic failure of the nation to come to its own." The project of subaltern history writing emerged in the pivotal years of 1979–1983, contemporaneous with the massive expansion of research that took women as subjects of history and the present. See Guha, "On Some Aspects of the Historiography of Colonial India," 7.

7. There is a rich and growing literature critiquing the United Nations and international law as domains of political aspiration and negative governance over women, building on the foundational interventions of scholars like Sally Engle Merry in *Human Rights and Gender Violence* and *The Seductions of Quantification*. Tani Barlow frames the dual role of the UN as a site that both enables and disables women's liberatory politics in her essay "Asian Women in Reregionalization," while Laura Hyun Yi Kang, in *Traffic in Asian Women*, offers a powerful analysis of the global "traffic" in Asian women as vulnerable subjects in international domains that both expand carceral logics of governance and obfuscate ongoing feminist struggles for reckoning and repair after histories of war and violence. Kang builds on Barlow's essay on the enabling and disabling nature of the UN (*Traffic in Asian Women*, 265). See also Rana Jaleel's book *The Work of Rape*, which examines the place of international law in perpetuating colonial structures of knowledge in the redefinition of rape as a war crime.

8. Lila Abu-Lughod warned of this logic just after 9/11 in her canonical essay "Do Muslim Women Really Need Saving? Anthropological Reflections on Cultural Relativism and Its Others." Elizabeth Bernstein offers a critical diagnosis of the complicated collusion between American feminists and right-wing movements and states in her essay "Militarized Humanitarianism Meets Carceral Feminism: The Politics of Sex, Rights, and Freedom in Contemporary Antitrafficking Campaigns." The co-optation of the language of gender and women's rights by the state through women's collusion with state power has been conceptualized through the idea of "governance feminisms" in the introduction of Janet Halley, Prabha Kotiswaran, Rachel Rebouché, and Hila Shamir in their book *Governance Feminism*. There is a substantial and growing literature on neoliberal feminisms and security; see, for example, Bina D'Costa's "Gender Justice and (In)security in Pakistan and Afghanistan" and "Securitizing Women's Rights and Gender Equality" by Natalie Hudson. On the neoliberalization of women's and queer rights and the work of feminism under neoliberalism, see Roy, *Changing the Subject*.

9. Sarah Bellows-Blakely offers an account of the rise of African women's research on girl-focused education programs in the 1990s catalyzed by the lead-up to Beijing and the rapid marginalization of African women's research on the international stage in her book *Girl Power?*

10. On US policy that worked to define women in the Third World as the "deserving poor" and the resulting systems of perpetual indebtedness, see Meyerowitz, *A War on Global Poverty*.

11. Saba Mahmood in *Politics of Piety* cautions against parallel binary thinking in her field-defining critique of Western liberal assessments of Muslim women's agency and conceptions of freedom.

12. Sylvanna Falcon argues that feminists strategically engaged intersectional issues of gender and racism at the UN, particularly at the 2001 conference in Durban, South Africa. On the intersection of feminism and anti-racism at Durban, see Falcon, *Power Interrupted*. Anti-caste and Dalit feminist writing and research proliferated after the late 1980s publication of the Mandal Commission's report and appeared from the 1990s on the international stage, starting at the Beijing Women's Conference in 1995 and in large numbers at the World Conference Against Racism, Racial Discrimination, Xenophobia, and Related Intolerance in Durban, South Africa, from August through early September of 2001. See Narang, "Caste at Durban," and Natrajan and Paul, *Against Stigma*, particularly the chapter by V. Geetha on the limited place of Dalit women and other hierarchies in the movement at Durban in her chapter entitled "Durban: The Local Contexts of a Global Moment."

13. Women Living Under Muslim Laws (WLUML), "In Search of Justice," 268.

14. WLUML, "In Search of Justice," 268.

15. WLUML, "In Search of Justice," 269.

16. Shaheed, "Controlled or Autonomous," 1014.

17. Colonization also never ended, and indeed, new forms of colonialism emerged in the time of decolonization. The UN began to declare International Decades for the Eradication of

Colonialism during the lead-up to the end of apartheid, with the first decade in 1990–2000. These decades continue today: the current Decade for the Eradication of Colonialism is set to conclude in 2030. For an overview, see United Nations, "International Decades for the Eradication of Colonialism," https://www.un.org/dppa/decolonization/en/history/international-decades (accessed April 14, 2024).

18. The 1956 Suez Canal Crisis marked a critical turning point for the global reach of the anti-colonial struggle, catalyzing liberation movements in Asia and on the African continent that took many decades to achieve formal sovereignty. See Louis and Owen, *Suez 1956*.

19. Chatterjee, "The Legacy of Bandung," 657.

20. An articulation of the now-classic phrase "the darker nations of the world" comes from the 1915 essay by W.E.B. Du Bois, "The African Roots of War," in which he calls for the end of racial prejudice and imperial domination around the world.

21. Most studies of women's movements in the postcolonial world remain bound by national borders and nationalist histories. Some key studies and collections offer complex histories of transnational feminist collaboration in the first half of the twentieth century in imperial geographies, including Rupp, *Worlds of Women*; Sinha, Guy, and Woollacott, *Feminisms and Internationalism*; and Burton, *Burdens of History*. On the place of feminism in early twentieth-century internationalism, see Sluga, "Women, Feminisms, and Twentieth-Century Internationalisms." On Latin American transnational feminist organizing in the first half of the twentieth century, see Marino, *Feminism for the Americas*. On key transnational feminist conferences, see Nijhawan, "International Feminism from an Asian Center," and Elisabeth Armstrong's comprehensive study of trans-Asian alliance and early ideas of revolutionary feminist transnationalism, *Bury the Corpse of Colonialism*. On the place of women's movements in anti-colonial efforts and in the period after decolonization, see, for example, the rich scholarship on women's movements in colonial and postcolonial India, including Sinha, *Specters of Mother India*, and, more recently, "A Country of Her Making: Women's Negotiations of Society and Politics in Post-Colonial India," a special issue of *South Asia: Journal of South Asian Studies* edited by Anjali Bhardwaj Datta, Uditi Sen, and Mytheli Sreenivas; see Datta, Sen, and Sreenivas, "Introduction: A Country of Her Making." On Black women internationalists from the twentieth century, see Higashida, *Black Internationalist Feminism*; Umoren, *Race Women Internationalists*.

22. On the significance of Bandung and non-alignment for the revision of internationalism in relation to a politics of women's health, see Ahmed, "Bandung's Legacy."

23. Ministry of Foreign Affairs, Republic of Indonesia, "Final Communiqué of the Asian-African Conference." On Bandung and women's movements of the period, see Salsabila Putri Noor Aziziah, "Unmasking Memories of Feminist Anti-Imperialist Movement." I discuss the Asia-African women's conferences referred to in Aziziah at length in chapter 1.

24. There is an extensive and rich literature that situates the importance of Bandung and considers this moment in relation to broader political ideas of non-alignment and Third World alliance. See, for example, Lee, *Making a World after Empire*; Eslava, Fakhri, and Nesiah, *Bandung, Global History, and International Law*; Lewis and Stolte, "Other Bandungs."

25. As we learn from the work of political theorist Adom Getachew, Black anti-colonial thinkers from across the Atlantic world refashioned the platforms of the UN and internationalism through novel visions of world-making based in radical principles of egalitarianism against domination. Getachew, *Worldmaking after Empire*. See also Mazower, *No Enchanted Palace*; Mazower, *Governing the World*. On the intertwined histories and interdependence of nationalism and internationalism, see Sluga, *Internationalism in the Age of Nationalism*.

26. Thinking with Adom Getachew and her theory of UN worldmaking in *Worldmaking after Empire*.

27. The declaration cited the official Charter of the UN to "promote social progress and better standards of life in larger freedom"; see "1710 (XVI). United Nations Development Decade:

A Programme for International Economic Co-operation (I) 16," December 19, 1961, p. 17, in UN, *Resolutions Adopted on the Reports of the Second Committee,* UN Archives, A/RES/1710 (XVI).

28. Egyptian Marxist economist and political theorist Samir Amin's field-defining work in the 1970s and 1980s theorized global capitalism in the postcolonial world as predicated on the center's exploitation of the periphery, the Third World, a foundational framework for dependency theory and other critiques of development economics. Amin's theorization of unequal development was critical for political theories that centered economic analysis to understand failed democratic state formation and authoritarianism in postcolonies. See Amin, *Unequal Development.*

29. Mottahedeh, *The Mantle of the Prophet.*

30. On the colonial origins of the use of the state of emergency for authoritarian rule, see Hussain, *The Jurisprudence of Emergency*. On the use of the "emergency" in the making of postcolonial authoritarian governance in spaces like India, see, for example, Tarlo, *Unsettling Memories*; Prakash, *Emergency Chronicles.*

31. Eqbal Ahmad wrote three consecutive essays that conceptualized the postcolonial state in crisis and were published in *Arab Studies Quarterly*. See Ahmad, "From Potato Sack to Potato Mash"; Ahmad, "Post-Colonial Systems of Power"; Ahmad, "The Neo-Fascist State."

32. These frameworks are offered in two essays by Ahmad, "Post-Colonial Systems of Power" and "The Neo-Fascist State." Ahmad builds upon the work of Pakistani sociologist Hamza Alavi, who offers a transformative theory of the postcolonial state as a "military-bureaucratic oligarchy" created through the complicated legacy of largely intact colonial state structures inherited by postcolonial states and the dramatic realignment of class and elite social structures in the postcolony made possible through structures of equal development and global capitalism. The state that results is authoritarian in multiple domains, including hierarchies of class power made possible through development-enduring authoritarian colonial state legal frameworks and novel structures of elite social and political domination built on militarism and bureaucracy. See Alavi, "The State in Post-Colonial Societies."

33. The definitive account of the first conference marking International Women's Year is Olcott, *International Women's Year*. On the UN Decade for Women and Second World connections, see Ghodsee, *Second World, Second Sex*. In *Sisters in the Mirror*, Elora Shehabuddin offers a long history of Muslim women's activism and solidarity in the twentieth century. On body politics and the Commission on the Status of Women from the 1940s through the early 1970s, leading up to the International Women's Year and Decade for Women, see Russo, *Women, Empires, and Body Politics.*

34. For a clear overview of the trajectory across these frameworks, see Meyerowitz, *A War on Global Poverty*, 170–79, specifically the rooting of WID in key International Labour Organization (ILO) thinkers. On women and the ILO, see Eileen Boris's definitive study of the ILO and women, *Making the Woman Worker.*

35. Joanne Meyerowitz offers a critical intervention about the way feminists, especially Third World feminists, engage the new international economic order (NIEO) in reconceptualizing frameworks of women and development and centering economic geopolitics in women's internationalism; see Meyerowitz, "A Feminist NIEO?" On the role of 1990s paradigms of violence against women in shaping debates about trafficking, rape, and women's engagement with the politics of harm and international human rights, see Kang, *Traffic in Asian Women*, and Jaleel, *The Work of Rape.*

36. Here I am thinking with historian Camille Robcis's history of the "war" on gender in the 1990s. Robcis traces how gender developed as a key theoretical concept in feminist theory alongside feminist internationalism, shaping new domains of critical theory from the mid-1980s into the 1990s. Gender, as a theoretical idea, was distorted and quickly demonized by religious authorities (especially the Catholic Church) invested in the fortification of the heterosexual reproductive family. See Robcis's forthcoming book, *The War on Gender.*

37. American feminist Charlotte Bunch was critical in reshaping women's rights through the rhetoric of human rights, and her statement on this reframing marked a turning point in women's rights internationalism. See Bunch, "Women's Rights as Human Rights." Inderpal Grewal offers a key critique of this turn in her article " 'Women's Rights as Human Rights.' " Sally Engle Merry's key study describes the mechanisms of this turn to human rights through the lens of gender violence in *Human Rights and Gender Violence*. See also Samuel Moyn's definitive history of human rights, *The Last Utopia*, although he does not address the dominant role of women's rights in the rise of human rights.

38. On Black women's internationalism in SNCC and the origins of the Third World Women's Alliance, see Blackwell, "Triple Jeopardy"; Kannan, "The Third World Women's Alliance"; Romney, *We Were There*; Wilson, "The Making of Triple Jeopardy."

39. Combahee River Collective, "The Combahee River Collective Statement." On the Combahee River Collective and its transnational reach, see *How We Get Free*, edited by Keeanga-Yamahtta Taylor. For a detailed overview of Combahee meetings, see Brown, "Rigorous Loving." Angela Davis reflects on the key influence of the Third World Women's Alliance in *Angela Davis: An Autobiography*. Herbert Marcuse's *A Study on Authority* (1936) offers a foundational critique of ideas of authority in Enlightenment philosophy and the enduring and contradictory life of authoritarian ideas in liberatory social and political thought. Marcuse was a key thinker for Angela Davis, who studied with the German philosopher and linked him to the early development of her Third World anti-authoritarian and abolitionist feminist thought.

40. By the early 1980s, there was a veritable industry in First World women's writings on the suffering of Third World women and the need for development. See, for example, Huston, *Third World Women Speak Out*; Fisher, *Women in the Third World*.

41. Mohanty, "Under Western Eyes."

42. This reclamation and link between Third World women and feminism was made explicit at Chandra Talpade Mohanty's own conference held in 1983 and co-organized with Ann Russo, "Common Differences: Third World Women and Feminist Perspectives." See the archive of the program and photographs from the conference at the website of the Center for the Study of Global Gender Equity, "1983 Common Differences Conference." The conference was the genesis of the widely influential 1991 volume by Mohanty, Russo, and Torres, *Third World Women and the Politics of Feminism*.

43. Gayatri Chakravorty Spivak was a key theorist of these ideas. In the early 1980s, she theorized Third World women in multiple venues, including the 1983 "Common Differences" conference. Spivak makes a critical intervention by powerfully staging the central impossibility of colonial histories of subalternity through her exegesis on the critical impossibility of the Third World woman. See Spivak, "Can the Subaltern Speak?"

44. The rich efflorescence of US-based Black and women of color feminisms from the late 1970s and 1980s created new genres and epistemologies of feminist thought that linked the struggles of US women of color feminists to those of Third World women. Key texts in this genealogy of women of color and Black feminist thought that engage Third Worldism include, for example, Bambara, *The Black Woman*; Combahee River Collective, "The Combahee River Collective Statement"; hooks, *Feminist Theory*; Lorde, *Sister Outsider*; multiple essays in the collected works of Audre Lorde in Byrd, Cole, and Guy-Sheftall, *I Am Your Sister*; Anzaldúa and Moraga, *This Bridge Called My Back*; Mohanty et al., *Third World Women and the Politics of Feminism*; Jordan, *Civil Wars*; Jordan, *Some of Us Did Not Die*. See also the afterword, where I address these themes in Jordan's writing.

45. Foundational work conceptualizing the emergence of transnational feminisms includes the key interventions of Inderpal Grewal and Caren Kaplan in their collection *Scattered Hegemonies* and in Alexander and Mohanty, *Feminist Genealogies*. See also Bernal and Grewal, *Theorizing NGOs*. On coalition-building among women of color and Third World women, see Chowdhury, "Locating Global Feminisms Elsewhere."

46. Nkrumah, *Neo-Colonialism.*

47. In my oral interview with Dr. Rounaq Jahan, I learned of her engagement with the Ford Foundation to conduct research on Bangladeshi women as early as 1971 while she was in Dhaka before fleeing the war for the United States. Jahan later returned to Dhaka and began to conduct research on the status of Bangladeshi women. Dr. Rounaq Jahan, interview 1 with the author, May 18, 2021. The Ford Foundation archives reveal the early investment in research on women in Bangladesh during the war and just after independence in late 1971. See, for example, early Ford reports on women in Bangladesh written during and after the war, including Jahan's important research on Bangladeshi women: Rounaq Jahan, *Women in Bangladesh,* February 1974, file 002185; Sandra and Laura Zeidenstein, *Observations on the Status of Women in Bangladesh,* May 1973, file 005779; and Elinor Barber, "Women in Bangladesh: Memo," November 7, 1973, file 007846; all in Ford Foundation Archives. See also Jahan, *Women in Bangladesh* (Dhaka: Ford Foundation, 1974). On the broader history of women's activism and solidarity in Bangladesh in relation to other women in the Muslim world, see Shehabuddin, *Sisters in the Mirror.*

48. Robyn Wiegman's study of the institutionalization of academic women's studies and other minoritized fields in the US academy is instructive as an example for a global history of women's studies and the rise of neoliberal educational institutions, an inquiry undertaken in the postcolonial world long before it was in US institutions. See Wiegman, *Object Lessons.*

49. On the complicated relationship of feminists to and against the state during this critical period of deindustrialization, see Forrester, " 'In and against the State.' " My thanks to Katrina for many productive conversations across shared research interests on this 1970s–1980s moment in feminist thought.

50. For a contested critique of Black feminist claims to moral certitude through claims to "intersectionality," see Nash, *Black Feminism Reimagined.* On the critique of the valorization of trans women as paradigmatic radicals, see Gill-Peterson, *A Short History of Trans Misogyny.*

51. See also Merry, *The Seductions of Quantification.*

52. Murphy, *The Economization of Life*; see also Murphy, "Against Population, towards Alterlife." I engage in an extended discussion of these themes in relation to the production of "cis feminisms" in Mitra, "Feminism for the Living." This knowledge economy that uses demographic data to extract use value dates back centuries, from the enumerative calculus of the Atlantic slave trade to Malthus's viral understanding of overpopulation, to the colonial census and settler colonial ethnology, all of which deployed and institutionalized biological sex difference and the control of reproduction and sexuality as primary categories of social measure and capitalist production. For an analysis of this project of calculated enumeration and commodification of women and reproduction in relation to structures of knowledge that shape the archives of slavery, see Morgan, *Reckoning with Slavery.* For more on the history of enumeration and the census in relation to categories of feminized sexuality in the colonial world, see Mitra, *Indian Sex Life.* On the resultant reduction of women from the Third World to their use value, see Tadiar, *Remaindered Life.*

53. On the complicated trajectory of family planning and the rise of feminisms in India, see Sreenivas, *Reproductive Politics and the Making of Modern India.* On the important intervention linking family planning, feminism, and the work of state development, see Sreenivas, "Feminism, Family Planning, and National Planning." There is a rich global history on birth control movements. See, for example, Connolly, *Fatal Misconception*; Ahluwalia, *Reproductive Restraints*; Hodges, *Contraception, Colonialism, and Commerce*; Bashford, *Global Population.* On reproductive control and the new authoritarian ideas of girl children as objects of protection, see Tambe, *Defining Girlhood in India.*

54. On critiques of this obfuscation and the critical place of gender in the politics of caste, see Anupama Rao's edited collection, *Gender and Caste.* On the long history of complicated representations of caste and gender and the obfuscation of caste subjection through historical

representation, see Gupta, *The Gender of Caste*. On critiques by communist women of the disappearance of class in revolutionary feminist movements, see Loomba, *Revolutionary Desires*.

55. I am thinking here with Mary John, who alerts us to the possibilities and limits of comparative thinking across Third World geographies in "Feminisms and Internationalisms." There is a rich literature on women's movements and feminist ideas in postcolonial India. A wide range of accounts critically engage the Indian feminist movement in terms of the promise (and at points limitations) of the movement, including Ray, *Fields of Protest*; Sunder Rajan, *The Scandal of the State*; Puri, *Woman, Body, Desire in Post-Colonial India*; Menon, *Recovering Subversion*.

56. Everyone from Milton Friedman to Amartya Sen utilized India as the paradigmatic exemplar for development economic arguments toward a "free economy," specifically citing the poor condition of women and their possible mobility in the promise of a free economy as "freedom." More broadly, South Asia serves as a critical space for late twentieth-century development economics. In *Apostles of Development*, David Engerman documents the rise of development economics through a history of elite South Asian men who have redefined the field of development economics and who rely extensively on exemplars from postcolonial South Asian societies.

57. Forbes, *Women in Modern India*; Kumar, *The History of Doing*.

58. Basu, *Women's Movements in the Global Era*.

59. For important comparative contexts, see, for example, on Third World and women of color feminisms in the United States, Hong, *Death beyond Disavowal*; Olcott, *International Women's Year*; Okihiro, *Third World Studies*. On transnational and international feminisms centered in Second and Third World feminisms, see Marino, *Feminism for the Americas*; Ghodsee, *Second World, Second Sex*; Kim, "Cold War Feminisms in East Asia"; Kim, *Among Women across Worlds*.

60. On the rise of human rights in the 1970s, see Moyn, *The Last Utopia*. On the limits of human rights (and international law) in a time of inequality, see Moyn, *Not Enough*.

61. Nithila Kanagasabai and Shilpa Phadke discuss the importance of this conference in the making of cross-border friendships among feminists across regions of South Asia in "Forging Fraught Solidarities."

62. This book derives its title from Urmila Haksar's 1972 memoir of her childhood, *The Future That Was*, published in Bengali as *Nijeke Niye*. Haksar was an advocate for women's issues in post-independence India, a key member of the Commission on the Status of Women in India, and coauthor of *Towards Equality*, a 1974 report on the status of women in India; see Government of India, *Towards Equality*. The autobiography focuses on her upbringing and life experiences before marriage. She later wrote on life with her husband, Parmeshwar Narayan Haksar, who was principal secretary under Indira Gandhi and first chancellor of Jawaharlal Nehru University. An analysis of her autobiography can be found in Harish, *Indian Women's Autobiographies*, 93–100.

63. See Mitra, "Sisterhood Is X," 451–52.

1. The Conference, or What if Gathering Together Liberated Us?

1. "Third World Women Speak Out: A Workshop at Forum '85. Speakers discuss the primary concerns of women in their countries: poverty, literacy, prejudice, women's rights, and teen pregnancy, among others," 1985, box 2, Vt-99, reel 8, Women's Video Collective Africa Project, videotape collection, Schlesinger Library on the History of Women in America, Harvard Radcliffe Institute, Harvard University.

2. According to official UN estimates, the NGO Forum at Nairobi had at least twelve thousand participants. See United Nations, "Conferences: Women and Gender Equality."

3. In figure 1.2, an illustration in a 1986 publication of the International Women's Tribune Centre depicts the 1985 Nairobi conference at KICC as the Tower of Babel, revising an image

originally published in *Xilonen* for the 1975 conference in Mexico City. My thanks to Jocelyn Olcott for making this curious connection and sharing her extensive archival knowledge. See the original image in *Xilonen: The Daily Newspaper of the International Women's Year Tribune,* June 27, 1975, 5. See International Women's Tribune Centre, *Images of Nairobi,* 15.

4. The Women's Video Collective Africa Project, based in Cambridge, Massachusetts, has the most detailed documentation of the pavilion space, including eighteen minutes of coverage of the outdoor areas of the NGO Forum at the Nairobi conference, which took place at KICC and the University of Nairobi. See "Scenes from the Quad," 1985, box 2, Vt-99, reel 8, Women's Video Collective Africa Project, videotape collection.

5. Gyan Prakash and Jeremy Adelman have offered an important framework for understanding the history of the idea of the Third World in their edited volume, *Inventing the Third World.* There they describe "Third World" as an anachronistic term that today represents both "failed dreams and forgettable nightmares." Yet, despite its negative valence today, it was once an idea rooted in a radical vision of anti-colonialism in a time of decolonization (7).

6. Zinsser, "From Mexico to Copenhagen to Nairobi."

7. Legg, *Roundtable Conference Geographies*; and Legg et al., *Placing Internationalism.*

8. Mukherjee, "The All-Asian Women's Conference 1931."

9. See Asian Relations Organization, *Report of the Proceedings and Documentation of the First Asian Relations Conference,* 208–34; Stolte, "The Asiatic Hour"; Thakur, "An Asian Drama"; and Karia's visualization of the conferences in "Forgotten Femissaries."

10. See Armstrong, "Before Bandung."

11. On the diverse romantic visions of anti-colonialism and the new world order of the Afro-Asian moment, a collection of contributed essays explores a wide range of Afro-Asian connections in the 1950s and 1970s. See Lewis and Stolte, *The Lives of Cold War Afro-Asianism,* 7–20. On the Afro-Asian women's conferences, particularly their relationship to the politics of resistance, see Gupta, "Femme Fatale."

12. Armstrong, "Before Bandung," 305.

13. There is a significant literature on the Bandung conference and the larger Bandung moment, which saw the proliferation of meetings, workshops, and conferences spurred by new networks of non-alliance and Second and Third World collaboration. See, for example, Tan and Acharya, *Bandung Revisited*; Lee, *Making a World after Empire*; Eslava, Fakhri, and Nesiah, *Bandung, Global History, and International Law*; Shimazu, "Diplomacy as Theatre"; Liu and Zhou, "Bandung Humanism and a New Understanding of the Global South"; Phillips, "Beyond Bandung;" Lewis and Stolte, "Other Bandungs." On the Afro-Asian writers at the intersection of Second and Third Worldism, see Djagalov, *From Internationalism to Postcolonialism.* On women's movement alliances across Soviet and African spaces and the significance of Second World politics in the UN Decade for Women, see Ghodsee, *Second World, Second Sex.*

14. Afro-Asian Women's Conference, *The First Afro-Asian Women's Conference,* 1.

15. With thanks to Kirin Gupta for discussions of the conferences and her dissertation research on these key events in the history of women and decolonization. See Gupta, "Towards a Decolonial Democracy" and "Femme Fatale."

16. Afro-Asian Women's Conference, *The First Afro-Asian Women's Conference,* 1.

17. Afro-Asian Women's Conference, *The First Afro-Asian Women's Conference,* 2.

18. Afro-Asian Women's Conference, *The First Afro-Asian Women's Conference,* 4–8.

19. Central Intelligence Agency (CIA), *The Afro-Asia Peoples Solidarity Organization.*

20. CIA, *The Afro-Asia Peoples Solidarity Organization,* 13.

21. CIA, *The Afro-Asia Peoples Solidarity Organization,* 13–14.

22. CIA, *The Afro-Asia Peoples Solidarity Organization,* 11.

23. Afro-Asian People's Solidarity Organization (AAPSO), *Documents of the Second Afro-Asian Women's Conference*, 27.

24. AAPSO, *Documents of the Second Afro Asian Women's Conference*, 31, 27–65.

25. AAPSO, *Documents of the Second Afro Asian Women's Conference*, 67, 80.

26. AAPSO, *Documents of the Second Afro Asian Women's Conference*, 103.

27. AAPSO, *Documents of the Second Afro Asian Women's Conference*, 107. See also the discussion of Afro-Asian women's conference statements that emphasized both national liberation and women's equality in Gupta, "Towards a Decolonial Democracy."

28. AAPSO, *Documents of the Second Afro Asian Women's Conference*, 109.

29. AAPSO, *Documents of the Second Afro Asian Women's Conference*, 112.

30. AAPSO, *Documents of the Afro-Asian Symposium on Social Development of Women*, 7.

31. AAPSO, *Documents of the Afro-Asian Symposium on Social Development of Women*, 33.

32. AAPSO, *Documents of the Afro-Asian Symposium on Social Development of Women*, 37–38.

33. AAPSO, *Documents of the Afro-Asian Symposium on Social Development of Women*.

34. This discontent is elegantly staged by David Scott in *Conscripts of Modernity* as the tragic mode that distinguished this period of disillusionment in the face of postcolonial failure.

35. UN General Assembly, Resolution 3275 (XXIX), "Resolutions Adopted on the Reports of the Third Committee," December 10, 1974, UN Archives.

36. Olcott, *International Women's Year*.

37. Meyerowitz, *A War on Global Poverty*, 116–17.

38. On the Barnard conference and the tensions between activists and scholars on the place of feminist ideas, see Corbman, "The Scholars and the Feminists."

39. The Center for Research on Women at Wellesley was funded by private philanthropic foundations like Carnegie and later Ford. See "Wellesley College Proposal to the Carnegie Corporation for Establishment of the Wellesley Center," 1973, Wellesley College Archives.

40. Margaret J. Hay, "Letter to African Studies on Women and Development," 1975, Conference on Women and Development Planning folder, box 99, Wellesley College Archives.

41. Women and Development Planning Committee, " 'Women and Development' Prospectus for a Conference to Be Held at the Center for Research on Women," June 1976, p. 1 (of fourteen pages), Conference on Women and Development Planning folder, box 99, Wellesley College Archives.

42. Women and Development Planning Committee, "Prospectus," 1.

43. Women and Development Planning Committee, "Prospectus," 2.

44. On USAID financial support for the Wellesley conference, see Meyerowitz, *A War on Global Poverty*, 117.

45. Women and Development Planning Committee, "Prospectus," 9.

46. See the special Autumn 1977 issue of *Signs* that resulted from the Wellesley conference, "Women and National Development: The Complexities of Change," including the subsection on "implications," with five brief and limited reflections on the conference's successes and challenges. Wellesley Editorial Committee, "Women and National Development."

47. "Women and Development Conference Program," p. 3, General (June 1976), file 1 of 2, box 100, Wellesley College Archives.

48. Government of India, *Towards Equality*. In an oral history interview about the conference, Filomina Steady spoke extensively about the specific interactions between Asian and African feminists at what she called the "rebel" conference and noted that everyone was inspired by the Indian feminist report. Dr. Filomina Steady, interview 1 with the author, May 19, 2022. Vina Mazumdar recounts similar understandings of her experiences in her memoir, *Memories of a Rolling Stone*.

49. Steady, interview 1 with the author.

50. Steady, interview 1 with the author. Steady later went on to work for the United Nations and took on the position of tenured professor at Wellesley College in Africana studies.

51. African Women's Collective, "African Women Take a Stand." My thanks to Rudo Madiwa for our exchange on this statement on the International Women and Development Conference.

52. African Women's Collective, "African Women Take a Stand."

53. African Women's Collective, "African Women Take a Stand."

54. Several different iterations of this essay exist. The first version appeared as "A Critical View of the Wellesley Conference" in the Winter 1978 issue of *Quest*; later, in 1997, it was published in a longer form in the *Nawal El Saadawi Reader* as "Women and Development: A Critical View of the Wellesley Conference."

55. Mohanty, "Under Western Eyes."

56. El Saadawi, Mernissi, and Vajrathon, "A Critical View of the Wellesley Conference," 143.

57. Meyerowitz, *A War on Global Poverty*, 119.

58. El Saadawi, Mernissi, and Vajrathon, "A Critical View of the Wellesley Conference," 143.

59. UN, *Report of the World Conference of the International Women's Year: Mexico City, 19 June–2 July 1975* (E/CONF.66/34), 1976, UN Archives.

60. Olcott, *International Women's Year*, 5.

61. UN Secretary General, *Measures Taken to Implement the World Plan of Action and Related Resolutions of the World Conference of the International Women's Year and to Initiate Procedures for the Review and Appraisal of the Plan* (A/31/220), October 14, 1976, p. 11, UN Archives.

62. UN, *Report of the World Conference . . . Copenhagen.*

63. UN, *Report of the World Conference to Review and Appraise the Achievements of the United Nations Decade for Women . . . Nairobi, 15–26 July 1985* (A/CONF.116/28/Rev.1), 1986, UN Archives.

64. UN, *Report of the Fourth World Conference on Women, Beijing 4–15 September 1995* (A/CONF/177/20/Rev.1), 1996, UN Archives. See also my overview of the UN women's conferences: Durba Mitra, *Solidarity! Transnational Feminisms Then and Now*, exhibition at Lia and William Poorvu Gallery, Schlesinger Library on the History of Women in America and Digital Curation, Harvard Radcliffe Institute, Harvard University, March 27 to October 23, 2023, https://www.radcliffe.harvard.edu/event/2023-solidarity-exhibition (accessed March 1, 2024).

65. UN General Assembly, Resolution 3275 (XXIX), "Resolutions Adopted on the Reports of the Third Committee," December 10, 1974, UN Archives.

66. Key exceptions include the field-defining work of Sally Engle Merry, who has sought to conceptualize the transformative place of global women's rights in the making of measures for late twentieth-century policymaking. Seem for example, Merry, *The Seductions of Quantification*; see also Meyerowitz on women, microloans, and policy shifts away from redistribution toward global indebtedness in *A War on Global Poverty*.

67. With thanks to feminist historian Judith Surkis for her insights on the gendered nature of the trajectory of UN politics and women's issues. The UN uses the language of "feminization" to characterize poverty as specifically a women's issue. See the discussion of women as heads of households, microcredit, and poverty in UN Department of Information, "The Feminization of Poverty: Fact Sheet 1," UN Women, 2000, https://www.un.org/womenwatch/daw/followup/session/presskit/fs1.htm (accessed February 27, 2024).

68. UN, *Report of the World Conference . . . Mexico City*, 73.

69. UN Secretary General, *Measures Taken to Implement the World Plan of Action . . .* (A/31/220), 11.

70. UN Secretary General, *Measures Taken to Implement the World Plan of Action . . .* (A/31/220), 13.

71. UN Secretary General, *Measures Taken to Implement the World Plan of Action . . .* (A/31/220), 14.

72. UN Secretary General, *Measures Taken to Implement the World Plan of Action . . .* (A/31/220), 16–17.

73. UN Secretary General, *Measures Taken to Implement the World Plan of Action . . .* (A/31/220), 15.

74. UN, "United Nations Decade for Women, 1976–1985," *Bulletin* no. 6 (1982): 3–4, World Conference of the UN Decade for Women—Follow Up folder, March 2, 1982–November 11, 1983, S-1028-0007-10, UN Archives.

75. UN Women, *The Legacy of INSTRAW in Promoting the Rights of Women*, 8.

76. UN Women, *The Legacy of INSTRAW in Promoting the Rights of Women*, 22.

77. UN, "Notes Concerning the International Training and Research for Women," November 1, 1977, p. 1, Women—1972–1977 folder, S-0971-011-15, UN Archives.

78. UN, "Notes Concerning the International Training and Research for Women," November 1, 1977, p. 2, UN Archives. On the initial discussions of the pledge by Iran, see George F. Davidson, "Memorandum, George F. Davidson, Under Secretary-General for Administration and Management to the UN Secretary General, March 22, 1976," Women—1972–1977 folder, S-0971-011-15, UN Archives. See also UN Women, *The Legacy of INSTRAW in Promoting the Rights of Women*, 25.

79. UN, "Notes Concerning the International Training and Research for Women," 2.

80. UN Women, *The Legacy of INSTRAW in Promoting the Rights of Women*, 85. On the particular training in statistics, see "Training and Advisory Services," Conference to Review and Appraise the UN Decade for Women, January 30–November 14, 1986 folder, S-1028-17-5, UN Archives.

81. UN, "Press Release: International Women's Television Series Holds Final Meeting," 1–2, World Conference to Review and Appraise the UN Decade for Women, January 18–December 10, 1984 folder, S-1028-0007-08, UN Archives.

82. Jain did not name Myrdal directly in the memoir but said that the perpetrator was a prominent Swedish economist writing a magnum opus on Asian economies. See Jain, *The Brass Notebook*, 118–22. This allegation was widely reported with the publication of Jain's memoir. See, for example, Wenzel, "Nobel Prize Economist Gunnar Myrdal Accused of Sexual Assault."

83. Budgets for research consultants abound in the UN archives. See, for example, a consultancy budget of around $200,000 for technical research over a year with "in-depth technical review of key issues relating to the concerns of women" that could "identify targets and strategies for action" in relation to a Nairobi preparatory meeting in 1984. UN, "Proposed Programme Budget for the Biennium 1984–1985," p. 6, World Conference to Review and Appraise the Achievements of the UN Decade for Women, January–December 18, 1983 folder, S-1028-0007-08, UN Archives.

84. International Research and Training Institute for the Advancement of Women, *Training Manual for Users and Producers*.

85. *Women News*, no. 7 (September 1986): 1–4, Conference to Review and Appraise the UN Decade for Women January 30–November 14, 1986 folder, S1028-17-5, UN Archives.

86. *Women News*, no. 7 (September 1986): 4–5.

87. Boris, *Making the Woman Worker*.

88. *Women News*, no. 7 (September 1986): 4–6.

89. For example, UNESCO held research seminars on women as early as the 1960s and systematized the research by the middle of the 1970s. It held numerous transnational regional conferences on women's studies and social science—for example, a conference on women's studies and social science in Asia in New Delhi in 1981 and one on women's studies and social science in the Arab world in Tunis in 1982.

90. A partial list of UNESCO comparative research studies on women between 1980 and 1986 can be found in *Women News*, no. 7 (September 1986): 5.

91. Getachew, *Worldmaking after Empire*.

92. UN, *Report of the World Conference . . . Mexico City*, 74.

93. On the debates and process that led to the adoption and passing of Resolution 32 as part of the Declaration of Mexico—with eighty-nine votes in favor, one opposed (Israel), and fourteen abstentions—see Olcott, *International Women's Year*, 210–13, 218.

94. This connection was reiterated in official resolutions at Copenhagen, but especially by Third World feminists at the NGO Forums in 1980 and 1985. See "We Are Fighting for Equality among Human Beings and Independence," *FORUM 80*, July 16, 1980, 8.

95. UN, *Report of the World Conference . . . Mexico City*, 110, underlined in original.

96. UN, *Report of the World Conference . . . Mexico City*, 110, underlined in original.

97. UN, *Report of the World Conference . . . Mexico City*, 111.

98. See UN, Resolution 3379, "Elimination of All Forms of Racial Discrimination," November 10, 1975, which cites Resolution 3151 from the UN General Assembly in 1973 in its condemnation of the "unholy alliance between South African racism and zionism."

99. Zina Harman, "Letter Dated 27 June 1975 to the President of the World Conference of the International Women's Year from the Head of the Delegation of Israel" (E/CONF.66/24), June 27, 1975, UN Archives.

100. The walkout was reported in "Many Exit as Mrs. Rabin Speaks at Conference," *New York Times*, June 26, 1975, 2. Peggy Antrobus, the head of Jamaica's Women's Bureau and a new representative at the conference, described the walkout by an alliance of Third World delegations and her excitement and ambivalence at formal UN politics. Dr. Peggy Antrobus, interview 1 with the author, April 30, 2021. The Afro-Asian women's conferences reflected an earlier period of solidarity across Third World women. Direct connections and transregional alliances between Arab and Indian feminists dated back to the early twentieth century and were at their peak through the 1930s and 1940s. See Elhalaby, *Parting Gifts of Empire*.

101. Moynihan, *The Negro Family*. The report was published by the Department of Labor's Office of Policy Planning and Review. At the time, Moynihan was the assistant Labor secretary.

102. Davis, "Reflections on the Black Woman's Role in the Community of Slaves."

103. Buckley, "Brawler at the UN."

104. Buckley, "Brawler at the UN," 34.

105. Buckley, "Brawler at the UN," 34.

106. This position became particularly clear in his complicated use of racial language in his response to the passing of UN Resolution 3379. See Moynihan, "Response to the Passing of United Nations Resolution 3379," November 10, 1975, https://www.americanrhetoric.com/speeches/danielpatrickmoynihanun3379.htm (accessed November 15, 2023).

107. Buckley, "Brawler at the UN," 34, 107.

108. See Economic Commission of Western Asia (ECWA), *Effects of the Israeli Occupation of Palestinian Women*.

109. ECWA, *Effects of the Israeli Occupation of Palestinian Women*, program of action, paragraph 16; program of action, point A.

110. ECWA, *Effects of the Israeli Occupation of Palestinian Women*, paragraphs 1, 2, and 3.

111. ECWA, *Effects of the Israeli Occupation of Palestinian Women*, paragraph 16.

112. ECWA, *Effects of the Israeli Occupation of Palestinian Women*, paragraph 16.

113. ECWA, *Effects of the Israeli Occupation of Palestinian Women*, paragraph 18; program of action, points A, B, and D.

114. ECWA, *Effects of the Israeli Occupation of Palestinian Women*, paragraph 19; program of action, points N and O.

115. ECWA, *Effects of the Israeli Occupation of Palestinian Women*, paragraph 27; program of action, points A and E.

116. Yehuda Z. Blum, "Letter Dated 6 May 1980 from the Permanent Representative of Israel to the United Nations Addressed to the Secretary-General" (A/35/220), May 13, 1980, p. 1, S-0913-0020-04, UN Archives.

117. "'It's a Diversion,' Israelis Charge," *FORUM 80*, July 25, 1980, 8.

118. Blum, "Letter Dated 6 May 1980," 1–2.

119. Blum, "Letter Dated 6 May 1980," 2.

120. UN, "World Conference of the United Nations Decade for Women, July 14–30 1980, Copenhagen, Denmark," World Conference for United Nations Decade for Women 1978–1980 folder, S-0913-0020-05, UN Archives.

121. UN, "Press Release: World Conference for the Decade for Women, Copenhagen, August 1, 1980," p. 13, World Conference for United Nations Decade for Women July 7, 1980–November 18, 1980 folder, S-0913-0020-05, UN Archives.

122. UN, *Report of the World Conference . . . Copenhagen*, 5.

123. "India Comes to the Rescue," *FORUM 80*, July 25, 1980, 8; UN, "Press Release: World Conference for the Decade for Women, Copenhagen," 1; UN, *Report of the World Conference . . . Copenhagen*, 50–51.

124. UN, *Report of the World Conference . . . Copenhagen*, 49–50.

125. UN, *Report of the World Conference . . . Copenhagen*, 50.

126. UN, *Report of the World Conference . . . Copenhagen*, 50–51.

127. N. Krishnan, "Letter Dated 3 June 1985 from the Permanent Representative of India to the UN Addressed to the Secretary General" (A/40/365), June 11, 1985, Conference to Review and Appraise the UN Decade for Women January 1985–June 1985 folder, S-1028-14-12, UN Archives.

128. "Report of the Ministerial Conference of Non-Aligned and Other Developing Countries on the Role of Women in Development, Held at New Delhi on 10 and 11 April 1985" (A/40/365), p. 7, Conference to Review and Appraise the UN Decade for Women January 1985–June 1985 folder, S-1028-14-12, UN Archives.

129. "Report of the Ministerial Conference of Non-Aligned and Other Developing Countries. . . ," 11.

130. "'Arab Women and Children under Israel's Administration: A Paper in Rebuttal of Document A/CONF.116/6,' Transmitted by the Letter Dated 19 March 1985 from the Chargé d'Affaires a.i. of the Permanent Mission of Israel to the United Nations Addressed to the Secretary-General" (A/40/188), Conference to Review and Appraise the UN Decade for Women January 4–June 28 1985 folder, S-1028-14-12, UN Archives.

131. "'Arab Women and Children under Israel's Administration,'" 22–31, 42–47.

132. "Women to Rally for March Today," *FORUM 85*, July 19, 1985, 1, emphasis added.

133. "Women to Rally for March Today," 1.

134. "World Conference to Review and Appraise Achievements of UN Women's Decade Opens in Nairobi" (WOM/324), July 16, 1985, World Conference to Review and Appraise the UN Decade for Women July 1–October 3, 1985 folder, S-1028-15-1, UN Archives.

135. "Arabs Walked Out," *FORUM 85*, July 23, 1985, 1.

136. "UN Women's Conference Drops Reference to Zionism as Racism," *New York Times*, July 27, 1985, 1.

137. "UN Women's Conference Drops Reference to Zionism as Racism."

138. "UN Women's Conference Drops Reference to Zionism as Racism."

139. "UN Women's Conference Drops Reference to Zionism as Racism."

140. UN, *Report of the World Conference to Review and Appraise the Achievements of the United Nations Decade for Women*, 26.

141. UN, *Report of the World Conference . . . Nairobi*, 62.

142. "UN Women's Conference Drops Reference to Zionism as Racism."

143. UN, *Report of the World Conference . . . Nairobi*, 17.

144. UN, *Report of the World Conference . . . Nairobi*, 27.

145. Kathleen Hendrix, "Analysis: Women's Conference Ends with Plans for the Future," *Los Angeles Times*, August 2, 1985.

146. Evelyn Hammond, interview 1 with the author, January 21, 2020.

147. Bush, "Mrs. Bush's Remarks on International Women's Day."

2. The Report, or Whatever Happened to Third World Feminist Theory?

1. Government of India, *Towards Equality*; Indian Council of Social Science Research, *Critical Issues on the Status of Women*.

2. The line drawings that appear widely in development publications alongside graphs and charts were promoted by the UN and UNESCO as a key form of communication for "illiterate" populations of states whose citizens lacked basic access to literacy. In combining data visualizations with line drawings and photographs to create artistic cover designs, the ICSSR covers for summary reports on women stand out in the images and graphic designs of the era.

3. For international women's rights in the Cold War–era "Second World," see Ghodsee, *Second World, Second Sex* (on the USSR) and Kim, "Cold War Feminisms" (on East Asia).

4. McKittrick, *Dear Science and Other Stories*, 44–45.

5. See chapter 1 for a discussion of the Moynihan Report. For reflections on Black feminist critiques of the Moynihan Report and its place in the history of Black feminist thought, see King, "Black 'Feminisms' and Pessimism."

6. Davis, "Reflections on the Black Woman's Role in the Community of Slaves," 2.

7. Spillers, "Mama's Baby, Papa's Maybe," 65–66.

8. Mohanty, "Under Western Eyes."

9. Partha Chatterjee's expansive "most of the world" from his book *Politics of the Governed*.

10. Notably, the wide-ranging studies on the growth of the human sciences during the Cold War overlook the massive industry of knowledge produced by and about women. Mark Solovey describes the broader "politics–patronage–social science nexus" that emerged during the Cold War in US-state-sponsored social science projects funded by the military. See Solovey, "Project Camelot and the 1960s Epistemological Revolution." See also Cooper and Packard, *International Development and the Social Sciences*, 1–42.

11. Chatterjee, "The Nationalist Resolution of the Women's Question."

12. On the critical place of the UN for claims of self-determination in decolonizing nations in Africa, see Getachew, *Worldmaking after Empire*.

13. Keguro Macharia powerfully assesses the dominant narrative conventions of contemporary NGO reports as "report realism"; see "Report Realism: Tentative Notes on Contemporary Kenyan Writing."

14. Mazumdar, *Memories of a Rolling Stone*, 3.

15. Dr. Rounaq Jahan, interview 1 with the author, May 18, 2021. Strikingly, Jahan used the phrase "immediate effects" several times to reflect the urgent commitments of women researchers to this work.

16. Dr. Peggy Antrobus, interview 1 with the author, April 30, 2021.

17. Menon, *Recovering Subversion*; Sunder Rajan, *The Scandal of the State*; and Tamale, *Decolonization and Afro-Feminism*.

18. Halley et al., *Governance Feminism.*

19. Roy, "Melancholic Politics and the Politics of Melancholia"; and Roy, "Politics, Passion, and Professionalization."

20. Mohanty et al., *Third World Women and the Politics of Feminism*, ix.

21. Sen, *Development as Freedom.*

22. Murphy, *The Economization of Life*; Tadiar, *Remaindered Life*; and Wynter, "Unsettling the Coloniality of Being/Power/Truth/Freedom."

23. Olcott, *International Women's Year*, 5.

24. Antrobus, "Equality, Development, and Peace."

25. Antrobus, *The Global Women's Movement.*

26. Mitra, *Indian Sex Life.*

27. Murphy, *The Economization of Life.*

28. Meyerowitz, *A War on Global Poverty.*

29. Tambe, *Defining Girlhood in India.*

30. League of Nations, *Status of Women.*

31. Laville, "A New Era in International Women's Rights?"

32. UN Women, *A Short History of the Commission on the Status of Women*, 6.

33. United Nations Section on the Status of Women and UNESCO, "The United Nations Commission on the Status of Women," June 1956, file 179820, UNESCO Archives.

34. Ward, *Women in the New Asia.*

35. United Nations, *The Status and Role of Women in East Africa.*

36. UN Women, *A Short History of the Commission on the Status of Women*, 7.

37. Lee, "Law and the Status of Women," 6.

38. Gruberg, "Official Commissions on the Status of Women," 140.

39. Royal Commission on the Status of Women in Canada, *Report of the Royal Commission on the Status of Women in Canada*, ix–x.

40. Kennedy, "Policy Ideas and Commissions of Enquiry," 42.

41. During International Women's Year in 1975, Trinidad and Tobago produced a comprehensive status of women report authored by barrister Stephanie Daly. Peggy Antrobus recounted to me how the Trinidad and Tobago commission resented the directives of the Canadians, who had been sent to dictate the contours of the status of women report based on their own Canada report. Dr. Peggy Antrobus, interview 1 with the author, April 30, 2021.

42. Piccini, "'Women Are a Colonised Sex,'" 309.

43. Adrienne Germain traveled widely to report on the status of women, with consultation in Bangladesh, India, Pakistan, Indonesia, the Philippines, Ghana, and Kenya; subsequent reports between 1973 to 1979 can be found in the Ford Foundation archives. See Adrienne Germain, "Final Report: Consultancy on Women in Bangladesh, Memorandum to George Zeidenstein," December 17, 1975, file 002881, Ford Foundation; Adrienne Germain, "Consultancy on Women's Status and Roles in India," interoffice memorandum, March 23, 1976, file 004249, Ford Foundation; Adrienne Germain, "Women in Development: Final Consultancy Report," memorandum, April 2, 1976, file 004250, Ford Foundation; Adrienne Germain, Sidney Jones, and Elisabeth Booz, "Food, Employment, and the Role of Women in Indonesia," 1978, file 004647, Ford Foundation; Adrienne Germain, "Women's Role in Development: Pakistan Consultancy Report," August 1976, file 005004, Ford Foundation; Adrienne Germain and Audrey Smock, "The Status and Roles of Ghanaian and Kenyan Women: Implications for Fertility Behavior," September 1, 1974, file 005009, Ford Foundation; Adrienne Germain, "Summary of Interviews on the Status of Women in the Philippines," June 15, 1973, file 005796, Ford Foundation.

44. Adrienne Germain, "Poor Women: A New-Feminist View," May 1, 1975, file 005008, Ford Foundation.

45. Franklin A. Thomas, "Memorandum to the Staff," January 8, 1980, p. 1, file 005697, Ford Foundation.

46. Soha Abdel Kader, "The Status of Egyptian Women, 1900–1973," September 1973, file 003591, Ford Foundation; Rounaq Jahan, "Women in Bangladesh," February 1974, file 002185, Ford Foundation; "Women for Women," 1975, Ford Foundation.

47. Thanks to Dr. Evelynn M. Hammonds (interview 1 with the author, January 21, 2020) for these insights about American Black feminists and their relationship with Ford regarding travel to the UN women's conference in Beijing in 1995. The Ford Foundation's interest in women of color feminisms expanded throughout the 1980s and 1990s. See Aileen C. Hernandez, "National Women of Color Organizations: A Report to the Ford Foundation," 1991, file 017199, Ford Foundation.

48. Sipilä, "Foreword," 1.

49. Lee, "Law and the Status of Women," 4.

50. Linner, "Status of Women and Law in Sweden," 289.

51. Dagadzi, "Law and the Status of Women in Togo," 295.

52. Luckham, "Law and the Status of Women in Ghana," 69.

53. Cortes, "Philippine Law and Status of Women," 230.

54. Sadjadi and Hedin-Pourghasemi, "Law and the Status of Women in Iran," 141.

55. I have written at length about how a parallel and related project of global commensurability shaped the internationalist language of sisterhood for a set of American women invested in the empirical comparative project of indicators and quantitative measures of women's oppression, which I describe as a closely related project of equivalence and commensurability that linked movement politics to UN frameworks. See my extended discussion of Robin Morgan's deployment of commensurability and equivalence in her "sisterhood" projects in Mitra, "Sisterhood Is X."

56. Government of India, *Towards Equality.*

57. John, "Thinking about Politics and State Power."

58. Agnihotri and Mazumdar, "Changing Terms of Political Discourse," 1870.

59. Government of India, *Towards Equality*, xiii.

60. Government of India, *Towards Equality*, i–ii.

61. Stewart, Lal, and McGuire, "Expanding the Archives of Global Feminisms."

62. Government of India, *Towards Equality*, 8.

63. Government of India, *Towards Equality*, 8.

64. Government of India, *Towards Equality*, 355–57.

65. Government of India, *Towards Equality*, 356.

66. John, "Thinking about Politics and State Power"; Prakash, *The Emergency Chronicles.*

67. Jahan, *Women for Women*, 1.

68. Jahan, *Women for Women*, 1.

69. Acharya, *The Status of Women in Nepal*, 1.

70. Acharya, *The Status of Women in Nepal*, cover.

71. Fussell and Haaland, *Communicating with Pictures.*

72. Contemporary feminist curators and intellectuals have transformed this history through a series of exhibits and publications, radically reimagining the history of photography and visualizations of Nepali women amid the long struggle for women's liberation and rights in relation to other political movements in twentieth- and twenty-first-century Nepal. My thanks to Diwas Raja Kc for introducing me to their contemporary rethinking of the status legacy. Diwas Raja Kc and NayanTara Gurung Kakshapati's exhibit "The Public Life of Women: A Feminist Memory Project," shown at the Nepal Picture Library and internationally in multiple exhibit spaces, demonstrated the extensive work and campaigns to preserve and document the landscape of feminisms in Nepal, juxtaposing the photographs of research like the status of women project with images of mass mobilizations as well as family albums and intimate portrayals of women

in portraits and in political spaces. The exhibit and more extensive research can be found in their publication on the archives of visuals of women in Nepal, Kc and Kakshapati, *The Public Life of Women*.

73. Desai, "The Making of a Feminist," 315.

74. Carolyn D. Spatta, "An Inventory of Women's Studies Programs and Women's Research Centers in Asia, Africa, the Middle East and Latin America" February 1980, file 007683, Ford Foundation; see also Imam, "Gender Analysis and African Social Sciences in the 1990s."

75. Spatta, "An Inventory of Women's Studies Programs"; and Imam, "Gender Analysis and African Social Sciences in the 1990s."

76. For reflections on revolutionary epistemologies in feminist thought from the 1970s, see Bhandar and Ziadah, *Revolutionary Feminisms*.

77. John, "Thinking about Politics and State Power."

78. Mumtaz and Shaheed, *Women of Pakistan*, 63–64.

79. Mumtaz and Shaheed, *Women of Pakistan*, 64.

80. See the table of contents in Pakistan Women's Rights Commission, *Report of the Pakistan Women's Rights Commission*.

81. Pakistan Commission on the Status of Women, *Report of the Pakistan Commission on the Status of Women*.

82. Pakistan Commission on the Status of Women, *Report*, ii.

83. Shirkat Gah Women's Resource Centre, *Towards a Better Tomorrow*, 5.

84. Decades after the publication of *Towards Equality*, Mazumdar explicitly addressed the obfuscation of caste, religious difference, and minoritized status in the report and the increasingly present issue of Hindu upper-caste majoritarianism. See Bagchi, "Towards Equality," 14.

85. Yogesh Atal, "Preface," in Rahimi, *Status of Women: Afghanistan*, i.

86. Rahimi, "Afghanistan," in UNESCO, *Social Sciences in Asia II*, 7–22.

87. Rahimi, *Status of Women: Afghanistan*, 5.

88. Thanh, *Status of Women: Vietnam*, 12–13.

89. Wei, *Status of Women: China*, 10–12.

90. Dr. Peggy Antrobus, interview 2 with the author, May 7, 2021.

3. The Organization, or What if We Collaborate across Borders?

1. "The Nairobi Manifesto," 44. The manifesto was originally published as an AAWORD occasional paper in 1985.

2. "The Nairobi Manifesto," 46.

3. "The Nairobi Manifesto," 44. On the manifesto and the possibilities for women's rights "beyond Nairobi," see Staudt and Glickman, "Beyond Nairobi," 4–6.

4. "The Nairobi Manifesto," 46.

5. "The Nairobi Manifesto," 46.

6. There is a substantial historiography of early twentieth-century internationalist women's movements built through colonial networks. See, for example, Rupp, *Worlds of Women*; Sinha, *Specters of Mother India*; and Armstrong, *Bury the Corpse of Colonialism*.

7. There is a vast literature on feminist engagements with the rise of NGOs. See, for example, Hodžic, "Feminist Bastards"; Alvarez, "Beyond NGO-ization?"; Roy, "The Indian Women's Movement"; and Nazneen and Sultan, "Struggling for Survival and Autonomy." On the mode of NGO reproduction by and through the perpetuation of an economy of "projects," see Krause, *The Good Project*.

8. For feminist scholars Victoria Bernal and Inderpal Grewal, the sudden widespread presence of NGOs helps explain the lack of reflexive scholarly research on their rapid rise: "The NGOs

remain poorly understood despite their ubiquity, or perhaps partly because of their rapid proliferation and diversification." See Bernal and Grewal, "Introduction: The NGO Form," 1.

9. Partha Chatterjee's theorization of "political society" in *Politics of the Governed* discusses the mediation of state and civil society. Elsewhere, Chatterjee with Kalyan Sanyal argues that state mediators perpetuate structures of primitive accumulation among rural agricultural laborers through government welfare programs that guarantee state support by creating permanent dependencies of communities living in a peasant economy. See Chatterjee, "Rethinking Postcolonial Capitalist Development."

10. As reported by Feminist Press editor Florence Howe in "Women's Studies International at Copenhagen," 10.

11. As Mamdani argued, the harsh structural adjustment divestment in higher education ended the expansion of the promise of the African university. See Mamdani, "University Crisis and Reform," 10.

12. Multiple sources cite the 1976 Wellesley International Conference on Women and Development as critical to the formation of AAWORD, as recounted to me in my oral interview with Sierra Leonian feminist Filomina Steady, founding member of AAWORD and later a faculty member at Wellesley College. Interview 1 with the author, May 19, 2022.

13. Association of African Women for Research and Development (AAWORD), "The Experience of the Association of African Women for Research and Development," 110.

14. Zenebework Tadesse, interview by Negar Esfandiary, January 14, 2013, Track 4, Women's Leadership Partnership Oral History Collection, Women's Leadership Partnership, Bethesda, Maryland.

15. AAWORD, "The Experience of the Association of African Women for Research and Development," 103.

16. Steady, "Research Methodology and Investigative Framework for Social Change," 13.

17. Steady, "Research Methodology and Investigative Framework for Social Change," 12.

18. Steady, "Research Methodology and Investigative Framework for Social Change," 13.

19. Steady, "Research Methodology and Investigative Framework for Social Change," 15.

20. Savané, "International Interview," 19.

21. On the critical place of dynamic, usable research on women to contest social scientific depictions of Africa as "primitive" and unchanging, see AAWORD, "The Experience of the Association of African Women for Research and Development," 105–106. On the social sciences of women in Africa, see Parpart, "Women's Rights and the Lagos Plan of Action." On pan-Africanism and feminism, see Tamale, *Decolonization and Afro-Feminism*, 369–83.

22. For an excellent comprehensive analysis of CODESRIA's work, including a chapter on the relationship between its gender initiatives and the work of AAWORD, see Hoffman, "The Knowledge Commons, Pan-Africanism, and Epistemic Inequality."

23. Nimi Hoffman addresses the important role of African feminism in CODESRIA in "The Knowledge Commons," 202–51, including the impact of AAWORD on the trajectory of feminist research and the complicated relationship of AAWORD to the later dominance of CODESRIA in the social scientific study of the African continent.

24. Imam, "Gender Analysis and African Social Sciences in the 1990s," 251.

25. Fall, "Introduction," 4.

26. Fall, "Introduction," 3n1.

27. See, for example, some of AAWORD's many publications of edited materials, including Imam, Chelli, and Abdel-Kader, *Women and the Mass Media in Africa*; AAWORD, *Women and Reproduction in Africa*; Khasiani and Njiro, *The Women's Movement in Kenya*; Mukabi-Kabira, Adhiambo-Odoul, and Nzomo, *Democratic Change in Africa*; AAWORD, *Programme de leadership pour les jeunes*; Tamboura-Diawara, *Gender, Economic Integration, Governance, and Methods of Contraceptives*; Tamboura-Diawara, *Gender and HIV/AIDS in Africa*; Tamboura-Diawara, *Women*

and Violence in Africa; AAWORD, *Genre et politiques neoliberales*; AAWORD, *The Perceptions and Representations of African Men and Women.*

28. Nkrumah, *Neo-Colonialism.*

29. Devaki Jain, "A View from the South," unpublished draft in Devaki Jain's personal papers, shared with the author, 10.

30. Tambe and Trotz, "Historical Reflections on DAWN," 215.

31. Sen and Grown, *Development, Crises, and Alternative Visions.*

32. Institute of Social Studies Trusts, "Report of DAWN Delhi Workshop Convened," unpublished report, p. 11, CD-75, Center for Women's Development Studies (CWDS) Archives, Delhi.

33. Bleie and Lund, "Proceedings from DAWN's Bergen Meeting," 3.

34. Bleie and Lund, "Proceedings from DAWN's Bergen Meeting," 4.

35. Devaki Jain, "The Decade's Full-Circle Implications for an Asian Agenda," theme paper, Sixth General Meeting, Association of Development Research and Training Institutes of Asia and the Pacific, June 1985, p. 5, CD-75, CWDS Archives.

36. Mair, "Women: A Decade Is Time Enough," 590.

37. Mair, "Women: A Decade Is Time Enough," 592.

38. Mair, *International Women's Decade.*

39. Mair, *International Women's Decade*, 1–2, 13.

40. See, for example, Kumud Sharma's citation of Mair in "Gender Concerns in Development Debate: Emerging Perspectives," paper presented at the Association of Development, Research and Training Institutes of Asia and the Pacific, June 1985, p. 3, file CD-65, CWDS Archives.

41. Neera Desai, Vina Mazumdar, and Kamalini Bhansali, "From Women's Education to Women's Studies: A Long Drawn Struggle for Legitimacy and Influence," paper delivered at the UGC Workshop on Publication of Volume on Women's Studies, 1999, pp. 10–12, CD-653.2, CWDS Archives.

42. Mazumdar, *Memories of a Rolling Stone*, 1.

43. John, *Women's Studies in India*, 5.

44. Kumud Sharma, "Being in a Discourse: Women's Studies, Institutions, and Critical Pedagogy—A Case Study of CWDS," unpublished paper, p. 2, file 653.2, CWDS Archives.

45. Societies Registration Act, India, https://www.mca.gov.in/Ministry/actsbills/pdf/Societies_Registration_Act_1860.pdf (accessed March 15, 2024).

46. CWDS 1980 Programme Brochure, quoted in Sharma, "Being in a Discourse," 2–3.

47. Sharma, "Being in a Discourse," 3.

48. Vina Mazumdar, quoted in Desai, Mazumdar, and Bhansali, "From Women's Education to Women's Studies," 17.

49. *Samya Shakti*, July 1983, 5, quoted in Sharma, *Changing the Terms of the Discourse*, liii.

50. The first conference in 1982 of the Indian Association for Women's Studies had multiple objectives for expanding and institutionalizing women's studies in India. The goals of the conference were to create an agenda for research in the field; create a bibliography and resources to help researchers doing work in the field; discuss methods and theories in the field; design course material and develop curricula based in the field of women's studies; and support the work of women academics, women's institutions, and women's organizations. See Kusum Dutta, "Note on the First National Conference on Women's Studies, April 20–24, 1981," p. 1, Indian Association of Women's Studies, https://www.iaws.co.in/ncws/1ST_CONFERENCE_ON_WS_1981/NCF01.2_Note_on_Ist_Conference_1981.pdf (accessed June 28, 2023).

51. Gore, *Education for Women's Equality*, 20–23.

52. For an in-depth study of Vida Tomšič and Yugoslavian feminist alliances with Third World women, including her correspondence with Vina Mazumdar and visit to India, see Bonfiglioli, "Women's Internationalism and Yugoslav-Indian Connections."

53. Tomšič, *Women, Development, and the Non-Aligned Movement*, 12–16.

54. Tomšič, *Women, Development, and the Non-Aligned Movement*, 28–29.

55. Tharu and Lalita, *Women Writing in India*, vol. 1; Tharu and Lalita, *Women Writing in India*, vol. 2.

56. Howe, *Promises to Keep*, 4.

57. Howe, *Promises to Keep*, 13.

58. Howe, *Promises to Keep*, 4.

59. Howe, *Promises to Keep*, 4–5.

60. CWDS has too many publications to name here, but I offer some titles to reflect the wide range of research that took place under the auspices of CWDS. The "partnership series" addressed workshops conducted in rural India: CWDS, *The Seeds of Change*; CWDS, *Perspectives on Rural Women and Development*; and CWDS, *Partners in Grassroots Democracy*. Other publications demonstrate the expansive reach of the social scientific research as well as the primary work of serving as a resource for research on women and publishing bibliographic information and key documents for the purpose of research and teaching: Mehra and Saradomoni, *Women and Rural Transformation*; CWDS, *Women's Work and Employment*; Mazumdar, *Emergence of Women's Question and the Role of Women's Studies*; Kelkar, *Women's Work and Agricultural Technology*; CWDS, *Rural Women's Claim to Priority*; CWDS, *Bibliography: Women and Participatory Development*; Sarkar, *National Specialised Agencies and Women's Equality*; Mazumdar, *Khadi and Village Industries Commission*; Vyas and Asija, *Women and Law: An Annotated Bibliography*; Vyas and Usmani, *Women: An Annotated Bibliography of Bibliographies*; CWDS, *Confronting Myriad Oppressions*; Vyas, *Voices of Resistance, Silences of Pain*; Mazumdar, *Peasant Women Organise for Empowerment*; Mazumdar and Krishnaji, *Enduring Conundrum*.

61. See, for example, Sarkar, Sharma, and Kasturi, *A Pathmaker*; Sarkar, Sharma, and Kasturi, *Between Tradition, Counter Tradition, and Heresy*; Sharma, *Memory Frames*; Sharma, *Changing the Terms of the Discourse*. See also the special collection of essays on Vina Mazumdar edited by Mary E. John in the February 2017 issue of the *Indian Journal of Gender Studies*.

62. John, *Women's Studies in India*, 12.

63. See Shirkat Gah's declaration on the "Mission" page of its website (https://shirkatgah.org/our-mission/).

64. Mumtaz and Shaheed, *Women of Pakistan*, 67.

65. For a comprehensive overview of women's movements in Pakistan from the earliest forms of organizing in post-independence Pakistan, as well as an overview of the political transformations that shaped women's movements, with careful interviews with WAF members, see Khan, *The Women's Movement in Pakistan*.

66. Ayub, *Women in Pakistan and Other Islamic Countries*, 1.

67. Ayub, *Women in Pakistan and Other Islamic Countries*, 2.

68. Mumtaz and Shaheed, *Women in Pakistan*, 67.

69. Shirkat Gah's founding document, the Memorandum of Association, quoted in Mumtaz and Shaheed, *Women in Pakistan*, 67.

70. Shaheed, "Maintaining Momentum in Changing Circumstances," 166.

71. Nighat Said Khan, interview 1 with the author, January 26, 2023.

72. Nighat Said Khan, interview 1 with the author, January 26, 2023.

73. See, for example, the folders of photographs of an early ASR workshop with women in Sindh in 1986, ASR Archives, Lahore University of Management Sciences (LUMS), Lahore, Pakistan.

74. The ASR Archives have saved and cataloged all textbook and reference texts in English and Urdu produced by ASR in the 1980s and 1990s to disseminate knowledge about women's issues to a wider public. See "List of ASR Publications, First Decade 1983–1993," ASR Archives. These publications include everything from children's texts for girl's empowerment to English and Urdu accounts of women's rights written for a broad public.

75. See folders for "South Asia Theater Workshop, Lahore, 1988," "South Asian Peoples Theater Festival, 1989," and "South Asian Theater Festival, Lahore, 1992," in Photographs, ASR Archives.

76. Several interviewees spoke about these workshops and conversations across South Asia specifically. Nighat Said Khan, interview 1 with the author, January 26, 2023; Ritu Menon, interview 1 with the author, August 5, 2022; Uma Chakravarti, interview 1 with the author, May 10, 2023.

77. On friendship as a critical praxis for feminist organizing in South Asia, see Kanagasabai and Phadke, "Forging Fraught Solidarities."

78. Nighat Said Khan, interview 1 with the author, January 26, 2023.

79. Chhachhi and Abeysekera, "Forging a New Political Imaginary," 553–77, cited in Kanagasabai and Phadke, "Forging Fraught Solidarities," 9–10.

80. The ASR Archives contain a file of photographs of the Bangladesh conference in 1986. Khan described this workshop for me, as well as another declaration of apology by Pakistani feminists at the March 2001 ASR workshop. Nighat Said Khan, interview 1 with the author, January 26, 2023.

81. Khan and Bhasin, "Educating Each Other on Women's Development."

82. See, for example, online events held by Women's Action Forum Lahore, "Herstory/Ourstory: The Women's Movement in Pakistan 1947–2021," February 21, 2021, https://youtu.be/1M0U_N6cHww?feature=shared (accessed January 25, 2025); Women's Action Forum Lahore, "Kaun Azad Hua? Looking Back on 74 Years of India and Pakistan," https://youtu.be/qFiT_tUtQLY?feature=shared (accessed January 25, 2025).

83. Dr. Uma Chakravarti, interview 1 with the author, May 10, 2023.

84. Farida Shaheed, "The Women's Movement," "A Making of Meaning Conference," March 2001, Lahore, Pakistan, Video Recordings Collection, ASR Archives, available at https://youtu.be/9DArFTOceKE (accessed July 10, 2023).

85. WLUML, "In Search of Justice," 268. On WLUML in the aftermath of 9/11, see Balchin, "Women Living Under Muslim Laws."

86. WLUML, "In Search of Justice," 268.

87. WLUML, "In Search of Justice," 269.

88. Shaheed, "Controlled or Autonomous"; and Moghadam, "Women Living Under Muslim Laws."

89. Shaheed, "Controlled or Autonomous," 997.

90. Shaheed, "Controlled or Autonomous," 997–98.

91. WLUML, "Information of Interest," 15, 4.

92. Moghadam, *Globalizing Women*, 147–48.

93. Shaheed, "Controlled or Autonomous," 1014.

94. Shaheed, "Controlled or Autonomous," 998.

95. Shaheed, "Controlled or Autonomous," 1006.

96. See *WLUML Dossier* 1 (1986) and its table of contents at https://www.wluml.org/1986/02/06/dossier-1/ (accessed October 2023).

97. Badri, "African Women Speak on Female Circumcision."

98. Rahman, "Female Sexuality and Islam."

99. Helie Lucas and Laws, "Bound and Gagged by the Family Code."

100. Zenebework Tadesse, interview by Negar Esfandiary, January 14, 2013, Track 4, Women's Leadership Partnership Oral History Collection.

4. The Book, or How Can We Seize the Means of Knowledge Production?

1. Kaufmann, "A World of Writers," 13.

2. Kaufmann, "A World of Writers," 13–14.

3. Kaufmann, "A World of Writers," 14.

4. Kaufmann, "A World of Writers," 14.

5. On the feminist book fair in the broader context of the feminist book trade and bookshops, see Careless, "Mapping Feminist Book Fortnight."

6. Menon, "Dismantling the Master's House," 175.

7. Ritu Menon, interview 1 with the author, August 5, 2022.

8. Feminist Book Fair Group, *259: An Introduction to a World of Women's Books.*

9. Goldsmith, "1st International Feminist Book Fair."

10. Butalia, "On the Absence (So Far) of Feminist Book Publishing in India," 18.

11. There is a rich literature on the rise of women's print cultures in the colonial world. See, for example, on the Middle East and North Africa, Beth Baron's important early study, *The Women's Awakening in Egypt*; Winckler, "Between 'Central' and 'Marginal.'" On South Asia, see Orsini, *Print and Pleasure*; Nijhawan, *Women and Girls in the Hindi Public Sphere*; Ghosh, *Power in Print*; Alam, *Women, Islam, and Familial Intimacy in Colonial South Asia.* On African feminist print traditions, see the four-volume *Women Writing Africa* from the Feminist Press. On Black women's print cultures in Francophone diasporas, see Mulira, "'We Were but Women.'"

12. See, for example, Ford Foundation, Center for Women's Development Studies (CWDS) Files 1981–1987, Ford Field Office File, file 08250637.

13. Vina Mazumdar, "Vina Mazumdar, Director, CWDS Grantee Letter to Ford Foundation, January 8, 1982," file 08250637, Ford Foundation.

14. Ford Foundation, "Grant Letter to Centre for Women's Development Studies, April 1, 1982," file 08250637.

15. Nighat Said Khan, interview 1 with the author, January 26, 2023.

16. Nighat Said Khan, interview 1 with the author. Khan has worked to preserve ASR's papers and the record of ASR's work to publish research and hold international workshops. The archives of ASR's research are preserved at the library of Lahore College for Women University. In 2023, ASR transferred its organizational papers and multimedia archive for preservation to the Saida Waheed Gender Institute at Lahore University of Management Sciences.

17. Shaheed, *The Women of Pakistan.*

18. Shaheed, *The Women of Pakistan*, i.

19. Shaheed, *The Women of Pakistan*, iv.

20. Shaheed, *The Women of Pakistan*, iv.

21. Imam and Mama, "The Role of Academics in Limiting and Expanding Academic Freedom." See also Imam, Mama, and Sow, *Engendering African Social Sciences*; Ampofo et al., "Women's and Gender Studies in English-Speaking Sub-Saharan Africa."

22. Dr. Filomina Steady, interview 1 with the author, May 19, 2022.

23. Dr. Rounaq Jahan, interview 1 with the author, May 18, 2021.

24. See, for example, discussions of the challenges of meeting family responsibilities while conducting feminist research and writing in feminist memoirs like Mazumdar, *Memories of a Rolling Stone*; Jain, *The Brass Notebook.*

25. Vina Mazumdar, "The Role of Research on Women in Development: The Indian Experience," unpublished paper presented at the ESCAP Regional Preparatory Conference for the World Conference of United Nations Decade for Women, New Delhi, India, November 5–9, 1979, p. 6, Center for Women's Development Studies (CWDS) Library Archives, Delhi, India.

26. Mazumdar, "The Role of Research on Women in Development," 6.

27. These are some of the many manual titles included in Shaheed's comprehensive bibliography; see Shaheed, *The Women of Pakistan.*

28. "Transcript of Urvashi Butalia Interview, conducted by Jayati Lal," November 5, 2004, p. 23, Global Feminisms Comparative Case Studies of Women's Activism and Scholarship, University of Michigan.

29. Puri, *Woman, Body, Desire in Post-Colonial India*, 39–40.

30. Pancholi and Vohra, "How We Wrote a Sex-Ed Book in 80s India."

31. Pancholi and Vohra, "How We Wrote a Sex-Ed Book in 80s India."

32. "Transcript of Urvashi Butalia Interview," 21–22.

33. Pancholi and Vohra, "How We Wrote a Sex-Ed Book in 80s India."

34. Bhasin, *Ulti Sulti Meeto*.

35. Bhasin, *Ulti Sulti Meeto*.

36. Interview with Kamla Bhasin, "Song, Humour, and Indian Pakistani Feminism," YouTube, https://www.youtube.com/watch?v=au6AquXWG6 (accessed January 2, 2024).

37. A coalition of queer, trans, Dalit, and dominant feminists critiqued Bhasin's remarks and linked her exclusionary rhetoric to a long history of exclusion that defined upper-caste Hindu women's approaches to feminist coalition and thought. For queer, nonbinary, and trans communities like the Feminist Futures Collective, long marginalized by feminist movements, it was time for feminists to account for their failures and purposeful structures of domination and exclusion. As they argued, Bhasin's comments were not exceptional, but rather a reflection of broad and long-standing tensions between the goals of a mainstream elite feminist project directed at the state and the many working-class, worker, Dalit and Bahujan, and queer and trans movements that were critical of the early goals of liberal reform feminisms that perpetuated caste domination and heterosexism. See Feminist Futures Collective, "Call for Accountability in Feminist Circles."

38. See Kamla Bhasin's YouTube channel at https://www.youtube.com/@kamlabhasinofficial1581 (accessed December 29, 2023).

39. On the alliance's impact on the wide-ranging intersectional feminist projects that followed, see Kannan, "The Third World Women's Alliance." On the alliance as a Black feminist project that was explicitly transnational in reach and Third Worldist in its commitments, see Romney, *We Were There*.

40. Third World Women's Alliance, "Women in the Struggle," 8.

41. Third World Women's Alliance, "Women in the Struggle," 8.

42. Third World Women's Alliance, "Women in the Struggle," 9.

43. Levin, "Introducing *Manushi*," 31.

44. "Transcript of Ruth Vanita Interview, Conducted by Jayati Lal," April 23, 2004, p. 8, Global Feminisms Comparative Case Studies of Women's Activism and Scholarship, University of Michigan.

45. "Transcript of Urvashi Butalia Interview," 10.

46. "Transcript of Ruth Vanita Interview," 8.

47. "Transcript of Ruth Vanita Interview," 20.

48. *Manushi*, no. 3 (July/August 1979): front matter.

49. "Sharing Our Problems," *Manushi*, no. 4 (December 1979/January–February 1980): front matter.

50. "Sharing Our Problems."

51. *Manushi*, no. 10 (1982): 38.

52. *Manushi*, no. 3 (December 1979/January 1980): 39.

53. Rich, "Reaching Out to Our Sisters," 39.

54. *Viva* Editors, "Letter to the Editors," 39–40.

55. Williams, " 'Call Us Ms.' "

56. On *Agenda* and *Feminist Africa*, see Tamale, *Decolonization and Afro-Feminism*, 53, 55–57.

57. The full article is available via the digitization and curation efforts of Mia Guzina and Dylan Tomlins, "Public Debates on Women's Issues in Postcolonial Kenya: Selections from *Viva*," Illinois Library, updated November 10, 2021, https://iopn.library.illinois.edu/scalar/public-debates-on-womens-issues-in-postcolonial-kenya-selections-from-viva/the-source---divorce-controversy-letters-to-the-editor?path=index (accessed January 10, 2024).

58. Patel, "'Call Me Ms.,'" 11.

59. Howe, "Women's Studies International at Copenhagen," 7–11.

60. Howe, "Women's Studies International at Copenhagen," 9.

61. Howe, "Women's Studies International at Copenhagen," 10.

62. Howe and Mazumdar, "Women's Studies International," 2.

63. Howe and Mazumdar, "Women's Studies International," 2.

64. Jain, *Indian Women*, xii.

65. Pinto and Nash, "Then and Now," 18. Pinto and Nash were writing in 2022.

66. On the complicated relationship between oppositional politics and the market of publishing, with a focus on Kitchen Table Press, see Murray, "'Books of Integrity.'"

67. Anzaldúa, "Speaking in Tongues," 168.

68. Anzaldúa, "Speaking in Tongues," 169.

69. Anzaldúa, "Speaking in Tongues," 173.

70. Mohanty, "Under Western Eyes."

71. See the extensive list of country studies of women in the table of contents in Morgan, *Sisterhood Is Global.*

72. See the title of Morgan's introduction to the volume and her framing remarks in "Planetary Feminism: The Politics of the Twenty-First Century," in *Sisterhood Is Global*, 1–37.

73. I have written at length about the concept of sisterhood and Robin Morgan's comprehensive sisterhood volumes as projects of neocolonial aggregate comparison. In such projects, comparison functions as a key mechanism to reinforce universalist and biologically determinist ideas of womanhood across space and time. See Durba Mitra, "Sisterhood Is X."

74. Mohammed and Shepherd, *Gender and Caribbean Development.*

75. Reddock, "Women's Organizations and Movements in the Commonwealth Caribbean," 63.

76. Mair, "Preface," xiv.

77. Sangari and Monapatra, "Kumkum Sangari Looks Back at *Recasting Women*."

78. ASR, *Finding Our Way*, preface (unpaginated).

79. ASR, *Finding Our Way*, front matter.

80. ASR, *Finding Our Way*, viii.

81. ASR, *Finding Our Way*, viii.

82. ASR, *Finding Our Way*, 259.

83. Jayawardena, *Feminism and Nationalism in the Third World.*

84. De Mel, *At the Cutting Edge*, xvi.

85. Jayawardena, *Feminism and Nationalism in the Third World*, ix.

86. "Transcript of Urvashi Butalia Interview," 14.

87. The organizational and financial papers of Kali for Women, which span more than two decades, have been acquired by Ashoka University in Sonipat, Haryana, and are currently being cataloged and remain in processing. For a testament to the growth of feminist publishing in the Third World as recounted at the height of Kali for Women, see Butalia and Menon, *Making a Difference.*

88. Ritu Menon, interview 1 with the author.

89. Ritu Menon, interview 1 with the author.

90. Ritu Menon, interview 1 with the author.

91. Ritu Menon discusses these many collaborations through an innovative memoir of her work in publishing and writing through her relationships with the names in her address book. See Menon, *Address Book.*

92. Menon, *Address Book*, 63; Mernissi, *Women in Moslem Paradise.*

93. Menon, *Address Book*, 63.

94. Omvedt and Kelkar, *Women and Struggle.*

95. Shiva, *Staying Alive.*
96. Kumar, *The History of Doing.*
97. Thapar, *Sakuntala.*
98. Kali for Women, *Truth Tales.*
99. Howe, *A Life in Motion*, 405.
100. Tharu, "*Women Writing in India* Reconsidered," 50.
101. Tharu, "*Women Writing in India* Reconsidered," 51.
102. Howe, *A Life in Motion*, 397.
103. Howe, *A Life in Motion*, 405.
104. Howe, *A Life in Motion*, 406.
105. Daymond et al., *Women Writing Africa*, vol. 1; Addy and Diaw, *Women Writing Africa*, vol. 2; Lihamba et al., *Women Writing Africa*, vol. 3; Sadiqi et al., *Women Writing Africa*, vol. 4.
106. Howe, *A Life in Motion*, 404.
107. Howe, *A Life in Motion*, 404.
108. Howe, *A Life in Motion*, 405.
109. Florence Howe, "Letter from Florence Howe, The Feminist Press, to Janice Petrovich and Alison Bernstein, The Ford Foundation Re: Women Writing Africa: Archival Collections and Bibliographical Resources," March 30, 1995, FH208 (African Projects and Conferences) (c. 1993–1999), Feminist Press Papers, Brown University Special Collections, Providence, Rhode Island.
110. Howe, "Letter from Florence Howe to Janice Petrovich and Alison Bernstein."
111. Howe, *A Life in Motion*, 430.
112. Busia, "Creating the Archive of African Women's Writing," 236.
113. Howe, *A Life in Motion*, 432.
114. Tuzyline Jita Allan, Abena P. A. Busia, and Florence Howe, "Form Letter to Solicit Contributors to *Women Writing Africa*," January 27, 1997, FH208 (African Projects and Conferences) (c. 1993–1999), Feminist Press Papers.
115. "Abena Busia Interview by Negar Esfandiary," March 18, 2016, Track 2, Women's Leadership Partnership Oral History Collection, Women's Leadership Partnership, Bethesda, Maryland.
116. Busia, "Creating the Archive of African Women's Writing," 236.
117. El Saadawi, *A Daughter of Isis*, 1.
118. Mazumdar, *Memories of a Rolling Stone*, 2–3.
119. Menon, *Address Book*, 47.
120. Menon, *Address Book*, 136.

5. The Protest, or What if We Took to the Streets?

1. Interview with Farida Shaheed in chapter 3 of Women's Action Forum, part of the interactive history project led by Ali Usman Qasmi and his students in the course "Walking in the City: Mapping Everyday Life in Lahore" at Lahore University of Management Sciences; see Women's Action Forum, "Chapter 3: Resistance against the Law of Evidence," https://archive.lums.edu.pk/interactives/womens-action-forum/chapter3slide2 (accessed May 15, 2024).
2. Saigol, "Remembering February 12, 1983." See also Women's Action Forum, "Chapter 3: Resistance against the Law of Evidence."
3. Neelam Hussain, a founding member of Women's Action Forum, reflected on the brutality of the police and shared her memory of getting hit on the head and cut during the protest as she was forced into the back of a police truck. See JPP's Torture Watch, "The Women's Movement in Pakistan: An Era Foregone."
4. On the significance of feminist anti-authoritarian protests against the rise of Islamist movements and martial law in Pakistan, see Asif, *Disrupted City*, 265–67.

5. Khan, *The Women's Movement in Pakistan*, 87–88.

6. Huzzey and Miller, "Colonial Petitions, Colonial Petitioners, and the Imperial Parliament," 262.

7. De and Travers, "Petitioning and Political Cultures in South Asia," 9–10.

8. On everyday use of the legal system in postcolonial India, see De, *A People's Constitution*.

9. Kaplan, "On the Socialist Origins of International Women's Day."

10. On Iranian feminist actions in March 1979, see Esfandiari, *Reconstructed Lives*. On the aftermath of the 1979 actions and the Iranian revolution exiles in diaspora, see Moradian, "Iranian Diasporic Possibilities."

11. Habib Jalib, "Poem Written for Women's Action Forum's First Anniversary," English translation by Jugnu Mohsin published in *WAF Newsletter* 6 (January 1985), ASR Archives, Lahore University of Management Sciences, Lahore, Pakistan.

12. Jalib, "Poem Written for Women's Action Forum's First Anniversary."

13. Habib Jalib, "Poem Written for Women's Action Forum's First Anniversary," original Urdu text published in *WAF Newsletter* 6 (January 1985), ASR Archives.

14. See WAF papers dated between 1983 and 1985, including newsletters, research studies, and meeting proceedings, in the ASR Archives.

15. WAF, "Some Statements 1981–1991," p. 19, ASR Archives.

16. WAF divided into two organizational structures in 1983, WAF (National) and WAF (Democratic), which came together to collaborate in these demonstrations against the Law of Evidence.

17. *WAF Newsletter* 6 (January 1985), ASR Archives.

18. *WAF Newsletter* 6 (January 1985). The designer of the calendar upon which Lala Rukh superimposed her art was Sajid Masood.

19. Dhar, "Celebrating Artist, Activist and Teacher Lala Rukh on International Women's Day."

20. Lookman, "Interviews, Past and Present: Lala Rukh by Mariah Lookman." See also Lala Rukh, *In Our Own Backyard*, description of item, Metropolitan Museum of Art, https://www.metmuseum.org/art/collection/search/815506 (accessed May 19, 2024).

21. Lookman, "Interviews, Past and Present: Lala Rukh by Mariah Lookman."

22. Many obituaries memorializing Jahangir in 2018 recounted the story of her petitioning the court on behalf of her jailed father. See, for example, Ijaz, "Asma Jahangir: Lawyer, Activist, Fighter."

23. Jahangir and Jilani, *The Hudood Ordinances: A Divine Sanction?*

24. Hina Jilani, "Letter from Punjab Women Lawyers' Association to Women's Action Forum," April 25, 1982, ASR Archives.

25. Ahmed, "A Brief History of the Anti-Blasphemy Laws."

26. "Women's Action Forum Manifesto," April 12, 1982, ASR Archives.

27. "Women's Action Forum Manifesto."

28. "Methods for Realizing the Aims of WAF: Through the Media, Meetings, Seminars, Workshops, Signature Campaigns, Distribution of Relevant Information," April 1982, ASR Archives.

29. "WAF Statement," September 28, 1983, ASR Archives.

30. "General Resolution of WAF," October 3, 1983, ASR Archives.

31. "WAF April 11, 1984 Demonstration," April 18, 1984, ASR Archives.

32. "WAF Press Release, April 11th Demonstration," April 18, 1984, ASR Archives.

33. WAF, "Law of Qisas and Diyat as Proposed by the Council of Islamic Ideology," February 1984, ASR Archives.

34. *WAF Newsletter* 6.

35. *WAF Newsletter* 6.

36. *WAF Newsletter* 7 (April 1985), ASR Archives.

37. Louis, "Les Algériennes, la lutte."

38. Louis, "Les Algériennes, la lutte."

39. In her report on the organizing efforts against the proposed family code, Louis included a comprehensive list of articles that had been circulated in draft form that day in March 1982. See Louis, "Les Algériennes, la lutte."

40. Drif, *Inside the Battle of Algiers.*

41. Drif, *Inside the Battle of Algiers*, 47.

42. Drif, *Inside the Battle of Algiers*, 104.

43. Drif, *Inside the Battle of Algiers*, 191.

44. On women's rights advocacy in early twentieth-century Algeria and its importance as part of social reform and modernization movements that addressed women in the interwar period, see Rahnama, *The Future Is Feminist.*

45. Drif, *Inside the Battle of Algiers*, 199–200.

46. Salhi, "Algerian Women, Citizenship, and the 'Family Code,'" 28.

47. For more on Maududi, see Nasr, *Mawdudi and the Making of Islamic Revivalism*; Asif, *Disrupted City*, 261–67.

48. Salhi, "Algerian Women, Citizenship, and the 'Family Code,'" 30–31.

49. Messaoudi and Schemla, *Unbowed*, 48–49.

50. Louis describes the efforts against lawmakers' secrecy in her 1982 report from the period in "Les Algériennes, la lutte."

51. The original draft of the petition in French is quoted in full by Louis in "Les Algériennes, la lutte."

52. Louis quotes from anonymous sources on this article on the "bad women" of the October 1981 protest in "Les Algériennes, la lutte."

53. Louis, "Les Algériennes, la lutte"; see also Messaoudi and Schemla, *Unbowed*, 50.

54. Messaoudi and Schemla, *Unbowed*, 50.

55. Louis, "Les Algériennes, la lutte."

56. The full text of the code can be found at https://ihl-databases.icrc.org/en/national-practice/family-code-1984 (accessed June 11, 2024).

57. Messaoudi and Schemla, *Unbowed*, 55.

58. Mernissi, *The Veil and the Male Elite.*

59. Mernissi, *The Veil and the Male Elite*, 193.

60. Mernissi, *The Veil and the Male Elite*, 194.

61. Mernissi, *The Veil and the Male Elite*, 194.

62. One of the most extensive engagements with Mernissi's thought and life in English can be found in the exceptional volume edited by Minoo Moallem and Paola Bacchetta, *Fatema Mernissi for Our Times.* As the editors note, Mernissi personally preferred to spell her first name with an "e," as "Fatema." I have chosen to retain the spelling of her name as it appeared in her publications (Fatima) for the purpose of consistency.

63. Mernissi, *Beyond the Veil.*

64. El Saadawi, Mernissi, and Vajrathon, "A Critical View of the Wellesley Conference."

65. Adrienne Germain, "Women's Role in Development: Pakistan Consultancy Report," p. 10, September 23, 1976, file DAP-769-804, 005004, Ford Foundation Archives.

66. See, for example, Ritu Menon's recollections of Mernissi's charisma and deep commitment to feminist collaboration across borders. Mernissi was an early supporter of Kali for Women, publishing the study *Women in Moslem Paradise* in 1986, one of the first scholarly monographs published by the feminist press. For that book, Mernissi refused to take a commission, instead insisting that her only compensation be in bangles. Menon also recounted how often Mernissi was heckled and attacked in public and her books banned across the Arab world during her career. See Menon, *Address Book*, 62–63, 66–68.

67. Mernissi, *The Forgotten Queens of Islam.*

68. Mernissi, *The Forgotten Queens of Islam*, 5.

69. Mernissi, *The Forgotten Queens of Islam*, 9.

70. Mernissi, *Doing Daily Battle.*

71. Mernissi, *Doing Daily Battle*, 2.

72. Mernissi, *Doing Daily Battle*, 2.

73. Mernissi, *Doing Daily Battle*, 14.

74. Mernissi, *Doing Daily Battle*, 14.

75. Mernissi, *Doing Daily Battle*, 14.

76. Mernissi, *Doing Daily Battle*, 14.

77. Mernissi, *Doing Daily Battle*, 14.

78. Video recording of Fatima Mernissi as part of the panel on "First Dialogue on Religion, Culture, and Women's Human Rights in the Muslim World," organized by the Sisterhood Is Global Institute and the Center for the Global South, American University, Washington, DC, 1994, https://youtu.be/v7FJMSvakr4?feature=shared (accessed May 30, 2024).

79. Recording of Mernissi, "Dialogue on Religion, Culture, and Women's Human Rights."

80. Recording of Mernissi, "Dialogue on Religion, Culture, and Women's Human Rights." A CBC obituary for Mernissi quotes from her speech "'Women Are Builders of Civil Society': A Speech by the Late Fatima Mernissi," CBC Radio, November 30, 2015, https://www.cbc.ca/radio/asithappens/as-it-happens-monday-edition-1.3343703/women-are-builders-of-civil-society-a-speech-by-the-late-fatima-mernissi-1.3343714 (accessed May 30, 2024).

81. Prabha Kotiswaran offers a comprehensive overview of the reform of rape laws based on mobilizations following the Mathura Rape Case in "Governance Feminism in the Postcolony." On the details of the case, the law professors' open letter, and its aftermath, see Kanjilal, "Narrating Legal Reform."

82. *Tuka Ram vs. State of Maharashtra*, September 15, 1978, 1979 AIR 185 1979 SCR (1) 810 1979 SCC (2) 143, https://main.sci.gov.in/jonew/judis/4992.pdf (accessed May 15, 2024).

83. Baxi et al., "An Open Letter to the Chief Justice of India," 23.

84. Kanjilal, "Narrating Legal Reform," 203.

85. Sunder Rajan, *The Scandal of the State*; Menon, *Recovering Subversion*; Kannabiran and Menon, *From Mathura to Manorama*; Kotiswaran, "Governance Feminism in the Postcolony"; Kanjilal, "Narrating Legal Reform." On feminist engagements with the law in relation to rape cases in the courts, see Baxi, *Public Secrets of Law.*

86. Kumar, *The History of Doing*, 127–42.

87. Kumar, *The History of Doing*, 128.

88. Kumar, *The History of Doing*, 127–42.

89. Kumar, *The History of Doing*, 131.

90. Vasudha Dhagamwar published a collection of her public essays and opinion pieces from the early 1980s. See Dhagamwar, *Criminal Justice or Chaos?*, 9.

91. Dhagamwar, *Criminal Justice or Chaos?*, 9.

92. Dhagamwar, *Criminal Justice or Chaos?*, 9–16.

93. Dhagamwar, *Criminal Justice or Chaos?*, 42–57.

94. Dhagamwar offered a detailed account of this investigation into the rape case, the findings, and the lack of attention on the crime in *Criminal Justice or Chaos?*, 44–53.

95. Dhagamwar, *Criminal Justice or Chaos?*, 53.

96. Dhagamwar, *Criminal Justice or Chaos?*, 57.

97. National Commission for Women, India, *Report of the Committee . . . to Assess the Status and Situation of Women and Girl Children in Gujarat.*

98. Dhagamwar, "The Women in Gujarat's Camps–I" and "The Women in Gujarat's Camps–II."

99. Saheli Women's Resource Center, "A Letter from Saheli Women's Resource Centre."

100. A rich literature examines the case of Shah Bano and the conflicts between personal law, women's rights, and state power over minorities. See, for example, Engineer, *The Shah Bano Controversy*; Sunder Rajan, *The Scandal of the State*; Parashar, *Women and Family Law Reform in India*. On the case in Indian media, see Mody, "The Press in India."

101. On the limits of legal reform for feminist movements in India, see Menon, *Recovering Subversion*; on the shifting feminist perspectives on Muslim personal law and the reform of law for gender justice, see Menon, "A Uniform Civil Code in India."

102. Goulding, "International Women's Day and Women's Rights in Pakistan."

103. Lau, "Twenty-Five Years of Hudood Ordinances."

104. Lau, "Twenty-Five Years of Hudood Ordinances," 1314.

105. Tahir, "Supreme Court of Pakistan Delivers Landmark Judgement on Sexual Violence."

106. Saeed, "Aurat March 2018: Freedom over Fear."

107. Aurat March, "Aurat March Lahore: Manifesto for 2020."

108. Aurat March, "Aurat March Lahore: Manifesto for 2020," 4.

109. Ahmed, "'Aurat March' 2021 Presents Feminist Healthcare Manifesto in Pakistan."

110. Aurat March, "Aurat March Lahore Unveils 2024 Manifesto."

111. Salhi, "Algerian Women, Citizenship, and the 'Family Code.'"

112. Bendimerad, "Algerian Women Embrace a Spirit of Resilience and Revolution."

113. Hierons, "Liberation Betrayed?"

114. Rédaction Africanews, "Algerian Women Protest Demanding Equal Rights."

115. Arya, "Nirbhaya 10 Years On."

116. Verma, Seth, and Subramanium, *Report of the Committee on Amendments to Criminal Law*.

117. Mitra and Satish, "Testing Virginity, Evidencing Rape."

118. I engage Shaheen Bagh as a mode of feminist protest in my introduction to Kaplan, Haley, and Mitra, "Outraged/Enraged: The Rage Special Issue," 791–92.

Afterword, or We're Still Here

1. June Jordan, "Untitled speech, address to the Barnard Center for Research on Women, 2001: preliminary notes, outline, handwritten draft of speech, contract, correspondence, itinerary, publicity; adaption printed as the introduction to *Some of Us Did Not Die*." Papers of June Jordan, 1936–2002 (inclusive), 1954–2002, Schlesinger Library, Harvard Radcliffe Institute.

2. Jordan, *Directed by Desire*.

3. Jordan's visions linking civil rights, women's rights, and anti-colonial struggles emerged from a long tradition of Black women's internationalism. On Black women as central thinkers in Black internationalism, see, for example, Higashida, *Black Internationalist Feminism*. On a foundational period of Black women's internationalism in the first decades of the twentieth century, see Umoren, *Race Women Internationalists*.

4. Jordan, "In Memoriam: Martin Luther King, Jr."

5. Jordan, *Civil Wars*, 91.

6. Jordan, *Civil Wars*, 94.

7. Jordan, *Civil Wars*, 118.

8. Jordan, *Civil Wars*, 143. With thanks to Esmat Elhalaby, who engages Jordan's Third Worldism in the introduction to his book on the decolonization of knowledge across Arab and Indian thought, *Parting Gifts of Empire*.

9. Jordan, "Poem for South African Women," 279.

10. Rowley and Antrobus, "Feminist Visions for Women in a New Era," 68.

11. Steady, *Woman in Action*, 223.

12. Menon, "Ritu Menon: A Life in Feminist Publishing."

13. Menon, "Ritu Menon: A Life in Feminist Publishing."

14. Menon, *Address Book*, 47.

15. Khan, "I Remember—Nighat Said Khan."

16. Khan, "I Remember—Nighat Said Khan."

17. Jordan, "Untitled speech, address to the Barnard Center for Research on Women, 2001: preliminary notes, outline, handwritten draft of speech, contract, correspondence, itinerary, publicity; adaption printed as the introduction to *Some of Us Did Not Die*." Papers of June Jordan, 1936–2002 (inclusive), 1954–2002, Schlesinger Library, Harvard Radcliffe Institute.

BIBLIOGRAPHY

Archival Records

ASR Archives, Nighat Said Khan Archival Collection, Lahore University of Management Sciences (LUMS), Lahore, Pakistan

Center for Women's Development Studies Library Archives, Delhi, India

Charlotte Bunch Papers, Schlesinger Library on the History of Women in America, Harvard Radcliffe Institute, Harvard University, Cambridge, Massachusetts

Feminist Press Papers, Brown University Special Collections, Providence, Rhode Island

Ford Foundation Archives, Rockefeller Archive Center, Sleepy Hollow, New York

Global Feminisms: Comparative Case Studies of Women's Activism and Scholarship, University of Michigan, Ann Arbor, Michigan

International Labour Organization Archives, Geneva, Switzerland

International Women's Tribune Centre Papers, Sophia Smith Collection of Women's History—Special Collections, Smith College, Northampton, Massachusetts

June Jordan Papers, Schlesinger Library on the History of Women in America, Harvard Radcliffe Institute, Harvard University, Cambridge, Massachusetts

Peggy Antrobus Papers, Princeton University Special Collections, Princeton University, Princeton, New Jersey

Poster Collection, Schlesinger Library on the History of Women in America, Harvard Radcliffe Institute, Harvard University, Cambridge, Massachusetts

Robin Morgan Papers, Duke University Special Collections, Duke University, Durham, North Carolina

Robin Morgan Papers, Schlesinger Library on the History of Women in America, Harvard Radcliffe Institute, Harvard University, Cambridge, Massachusetts

Sound and Picture Archives for Research on Women (SPARROW), Mumbai, India

United Nations Archives, New York, New York

United Nations Educational, Scientific, and Cultural Organization (UNESCO), Paris, France

Wellesley College Archives, Wellesley, Massachusetts

Women's Leadership Partnership Oral History Collection, Bethesda, Maryland

Women's Video Collective Africa Project, videotape collection, Schlesinger Library on the History of Women in America, Harvard Radcliffe Institute, Harvard University, Cambridge, Massachusetts

Newspapers and Periodicals

DAWN

FORUM 80

FORUM 85

Los Angeles Times
Manushi
New York Times
Viva: The Magazine for Kenyan Women
WAF Newsletter
Xilonen

Interviews

Peggy Antrobus, April 30, 2021; May 7, 2021
Nirmala Banerjee, August 5, 2022
Uma Chakravarti, May 10, 2023
Martha Chen, October 31, 2019
Evelynn M. Hammonds, January 21, 2020
Rounaq Jahan, May 18, 2021
Nighat Said Khan, January 26, 2023
Ritu Menon, August 5, 2022
Filomena Steady, May 19, 2022

Primary and Secondary Sources

Abu-Lughod, Lila. "Do Muslim Women Really Need Saving? Anthropological Reflections on Cultural Relativism and Its Others." *American Anthropologist* 104, no. 3 (2002): 783–90.

Acharya, Meena. *The Status of Women in Nepal*, vol. 1, *Background Report*. Kathmandu: Tribhuvan University Press, 1979.

Addy, Esi Sutherland, and Aminata Diaw, eds. *Women Writing Africa: The West and the Sahel*, vol. 2. New York: Feminist Press, 2003.

African Women's Collective. "African Women Take a Stand." *African Affairs* 6 (September/October 1976): 29.

Afro-Asian People's Solidarity Organization (AAPSO). *Documents of the Afro-Asian Symposium on Social Development of Women, Published on the Occasion of the International Women's Year*. Cairo: Permanent Secretariat of the Afro-Asian People's Solidarity Organization, 1975.

Afro-Asian People's Solidarity Organization. *Documents of the Second Afro-Asian Women's Conference*. Cairo: Permanent Secretariat of the AAPSO, 1973.

Afro-Asian Women's Conference. *The First Afro-Asian Women's Conference, Cairo, January 14–23, 1961: Reports, Messages, Speeches, Resolutions*. Cairo: Amalgamated Press of Egypt, 1961.

Agnihotri, Indu, and Vina Mazumdar. "Changing Terms of Political Discourse: Women's Movement in India, 1970s–1990s." *Economic and Political Weekly* 30, no. 29 (1995): 1869–78.

Ahluwalia, Sanjam. *Reproductive Restraints: Birth Control in India, 1877–1947*. Urbana: University of Illinois Press, 2010.

Ahmad, Eqbal. "From Potato Sack to Potato Mash: The Contemporary Crisis of the Third World." *Arab Studies Quarterly* 2, no. 3 (1980): 223–34.

Ahmad, Eqbal. "The Neo-Fascist State: Notes on the Pathology of Power in the Third World." *Arab Studies Quarterly* 3, no. 2 (1981): 170–80.

Ahmad, Eqbal. "Post-Colonial Systems of Power." *Arab Studies Quarterly* 2, no. 4 (1980): 350–63.

Ahmed, Asad. "A Brief History of the Anti-Blasphemy Laws." *Herald*, October 31, 2018. https://herald.dawn.com/news/1154036 (accessed May 2, 2024).

Ahmed, Aziza. "Bandung's Legacy: Solidarity and Contestation in Global Women's Rights." In *Bandung, Global History, and International Law: Critical Pasts and Pending Futures*, edited by

Luis Eslava, Michael Fakhri, and Vasuki Nesiah, 450–64. Cambridge: Cambridge University Press, 2017.

Ahmed, R. Umaima. "'Aurat March' 2021 Presents Feminist Healthcare Manifesto in Pakistan." *Global Voices*, March 21, 2021. https://globalvoices.org/2021/03/14/aurat-march-2021-presents-feminist-healthcare-manifesto-in-pakistan/ (accessed May 24, 2024).

Alam, Asiya. *Women, Islam, and Familial Intimacy in Colonial South Asia*. Leiden: Brill, 2021.

Alavi, Hamza. "The State in Post-Colonial Societies." *New Left Review* 74 (1972): 59–81.

Alexander, Jacqui M., and Chandra Talpade Mohanty, eds. *Feminist Genealogies, Colonial Legacies, Democratic Futures*. New York: Routledge, 1997.

Alvarez, Sonia. "Beyond NGO-ization? Reflections from Latin America." *Development* 52, no. 2 (2009): 175–84.

Amin, Samir. *Unequal Development: An Essay on the Social Formation of Peripheral Capitalism*. New York: Monthly Review Press, 1976.

Ampofo, Akosua Adomako, Josephine Beoku-Betts, Wairimu Ngaruiya Njambi, and Mary Osirim. "Women's and Gender Studies in English-Speaking Sub-Saharan Africa." *Gender & Society* 18, no. 6 (2004): 685–714.

Antrobus, Peggy. "Equality, Development, and Peace: A Second Look at the Goals of the UN Decade for Women." Paper presented at the Associated Country Women of the World Conference, Vancouver, Canada, June 1983.

Antrobus, Peggy. *The Global Women's Movement: Origins, Issues, and Strategies*. New York: Zed Books, 2004.

Anzaldúa, Gloria. "Speaking in Tongues: A Letter to Third World Women Writers." In *This Bridge Called My Back: Writings by Radical Women of Color*, edited by Gloria Anzaldúa and Cherríe Moraga, 165–74. New York: Kitchen Table Press, 1983.

Anzaldúa, Gloria, and Cherríe Moraga, eds. *This Bridge Called My Back: Writings by Radical Women of Color*. New York: Kitchen Table Press, 1984.

Applied Socio-economic Research (ASR). *Finding Our Way: Readings on Women in Pakistan*. Lahore: ASR and UNESCO, 1991.

Armstrong, Elisabeth. "Before Bandung: The Anti-Imperialist Women's Movement in Asia and the Women's International Democratic Federation." *Signs: Journal of Women in Culture and Society* 41, no. 2 (2016): 305–31.

Armstrong, Elisabeth. *Bury the Corpse of Colonialism: The Revolutionary Feminist Conference of 1949*. Berkeley: University of California Press, 2023.

Arya, Divya. "Nirbhaya 10 Years On: The Lives the Delhi Gang Rape Changed." BBC, December 5, 2022. https://www.bbc.com/news/world-63817388 (accessed May 23, 2024).

Asian Relations Organization. *Report of the Proceedings and Documentation of the First Asian Relations Conference, New Delhi, March–April, 1947*. New Delhi: Asian Relations Organization, 1948.

Asif, Manan Ahmed. *Disrupted City: Walking the Pathways of Memory and History in Lahore*. New York: New Press, 2024.

Association of African Women for Research and Development. "The Experience of the Association of African Women for Research and Development (AAWORD): A Workshop Report Prepared for the High-Level Meeting on the Review of Technical Cooperation among Developing Countries." *Development Dialogue* 1982, nos. 1/2: 101–13.

Association of African Women for Research and Development. *Genre et politiques neoliberales*. Rabat: AAWORD, 2006.

Association of African Women for Research and Development. *The Perceptions and Representations of African Men and Women of the Equality between Men and Women*. Dakar: AAWORD, 2007.

Association of African Women for Research and Development. *Programme de leadership pour les jeunes*. Dakar: AAWORD, 2001.

Association of African Women for Research and Development. *Women and Reproduction in Africa*. Occasional Paper Series 5. Dakar: AAWORD, 1992.

Aurat March. "Aurat March Lahore: Manifesto for 2020." Eqbal Ahmad Centre for Public Education. https://eacpe.org/app/wp-content/uploads/2020/03/Aurat-March-Lahore-2020-Manifesto.pdf (accessed January 10, 2024).

Aurat March. "Aurat March Lahore Unveils 2024 Manifesto." *Hum News*, February 26, 2024. https://humenglish.com/latest/aurat-march-lahore-unveils-2024-manifesto/ (accessed May 24, 2024).

Ayub, Nighat, ed. *Women in Pakistan and Other Islamic Countries: A Selected Bibliography with Annotations*. Karachi: Shirkat Gah, 1978.

Aziziah, Salsabila Putri Noor. "Unmasking Memories of Feminist Anti-Imperialist Movement: Where Were the Women in Bandung Conference?" *Focus on the Global South*, April 17, 2025. https://focusweb.org/unmasking-memories-of-feminist-anti-imperialist-movement-where-were-the-women-in-bandung-conference/ (accessed July 5, 2025).

Badri, Babiker. "African Women Speak on Female Circumcision: Reports from the Workshop Khartoum (October 21–25, 1984)." *WLUML Dossier* 3 (1987): 48–66.

Bagchi, Jasodhara. "Towards Equality." *Social Scientist* 41, nos. 11/12 (2013): 11–23.

Balchin, Cassandra. "Women Living Under Muslim Laws: The Challenges Facing a Transnational Gender Network in the Post 11 September Context." *International Feminist Journal of Politics* 6, no. 4 (2004): 679–83.

Bambara, Toni Cade, ed. *The Black Woman: An Anthology*. New York: Simon & Schuster, 1970.

Barlow, Tani E. "Asian Women in Reregionalization." *positions: asia critique* 15, no. 2 (2007): 285–318.

Baron, Beth. *The Women's Awakening in Egypt: Culture, Society, and the Press*. New Haven, CT: Yale University Press, 1994.

Bashford, Alison. *Global Population: History, Geopolitics, and Life on Earth*. New York: Columbia University Press, 2014.

Basu, Amrita, ed. *Women's Movements in the Global Era: The Power of Local Feminisms*. Boulder, CO: Westview Press, 2010.

Baxi, Pratiksha. *Public Secrets of Law: Rape Trials in India*. New Delhi: Oxford University Press, 2014.

Baxi, Upendra, Lotika Sarkar, Ragunath Kelkar, and Vasudha Dhagamwar. "An Open Letter to the Chief Justice of India." *Supreme Court Cases* 4, no. J17 (1979): 17–23.

Bellows-Blakely, Sarah. *Girl Power? A History of Girl-Focused Development from Nairobi*. Chicago: University of Chicago Press, 2025.

Bendimerad, Rym. "Algerian Women Embrace a Spirit of Resilience and Revolution," *Al Jazeera*, March 12, 2020. https://www.aljazeera.com/features/2020/3/12/algerian-women-embrace-a-spirit-of-resilience-and-revolution (accessed January 20, 2025).

Bernal, Victoria, and Inderpal Grewal. "Introduction: The NGO Form." In *Theorizing NGOs: States, Feminisms, and Neoliberalism*, edited by Victoria Bernal and Inderpal Grewal, 1–18. Durham, NC: Duke University Press, 2014.

Bernal, Victoria, and Inderpal Grewal, eds. *Theorizing NGOs: States, Feminisms, and Neoliberalism*. Durham, NC: Duke University Press, 2014.

Bernstein, Elizabeth. "Militarized Humanitarianism Meets Carceral Feminism: The Politics of Sex, Rights, and Freedom in Contemporary Antitrafficking Campaigns." *Signs: Journal of Women in Culture and Society* 36, no. 1 (2010): 45–71.

Bhandar, Brenna, and Rafeef Ziadah, eds. *Revolutionary Feminisms: Conversations on Collective Action and Radical Thought*. London: Verso, 2020.

Bhasin, Kamla. *Ulti Sulti Meeto*. Delhi: Kali for Women, 1988; Lahore: ASR Publications, 1988.

Blackwell, Maylei. "Triple Jeopardy: The Third World Women's Alliance and the Transnational Roots of Women-of-Color Feminism." In *Provocations: A Transnational Reader in the History of Feminist Thought*, edited by Susan Bordo, M. Cristina Alcalde, and Ellen Rosenman, 280–89. Berkeley: University of California Press, 2015.

Bleie, Tone, and Ragnhild Lund. "Proceedings from DAWN's Bergen Meeting." Working Paper A343, Development Research and Action Programme, April 1985.

Bonfiglioli, Chiara. "Women's Internationalism and Yugoslav-Indian Connections: From the Non-Aligned Movement to the UN Decade for Women." *Nationalities Papers* 49, no. 3 (2021): 446–61.

Boris, Eileen. *Making the Woman Worker: Precarious Labor and the Fight for Global Standards, 1919–2019*. Oxford: Oxford University Press, 2019.

Brown, Camara. "Rigorous Loving: Black Women, Black Feminism, and Friendship in the United States, 1970–1996." PhD diss., Harvard University, 2025.

Buckley, Tom. "Brawler at the UN." *New York Times*, December 7, 1975.

Bunch, Charlotte. "Women's Rights as Human Rights: Toward a Re-Vision of Human Rights." *Human Rights Quarterly* 12, no. 4 (1990): 486–98.

Burton, Antoinette. *Burdens of History: British Feminists, Indian Women, and Imperial Culture, 1865–1915*. Chapel Hill: University of North Carolina Press, 2000.

Bush, Laura. "Mrs. Bush's Remarks on International Women's Day at the United Nations." The White House, March 8, 2002. https://georgewbush-whitehouse.archives.gov/news/releases/2002/03/20020308-15.html (accessed July 1, 2025)

Busia, Abena P. A. "Creating the Archive of African Women's Writing: Reflecting on Feminism, Epistemology, and the Women Writing Africa Project." *Meridians: Feminism, Race, Transnationalism* 17, no. 2 (2018): 233–45.

Butalia, Urvashi. "On the Absence (So Far) of Feminist Book Publishing in India." In Feminist Book Fair Group, *259: An Introduction to a World of Women's Books*. London: Feminist Book Fair Group, 1985.

Butalia, Urvashi, and Ritu Menon. *Making a Difference: Feminist Publishing in the South*. Oxford: Bellagio Publishing Network, 1995.

Byrd, Rudolph P., Johnnetta Betsch Cole, and Beverly Guy-Sheftall, eds. *I Am Your Sister: Collected and Unpublished Writings of Audre Lorde*. Oxford: Oxford University Press, 2009.

Careless, Eleanor. "Mapping Feminist Book Fortnight: Regional Activism and the Feminist Book Trade in 1980s Britain." *Women: A Cultural Review* 33, no. 3 (2022): 280–313.

Center for Women's Development Studies. *Bibliography: Women and Participatory Development*. New Delhi: CWDS, 1986.

Center for Women's Development Studies. *Confronting Myriad Oppressions: Voices from the Women's Movement in India*. New Delhi: CWDS, 1994.

Center for Women's Development Studies. *Partners in Grassroots Democracy*. New Delhi: CWDS, 1990.

Center for Women's Development Studies. *Perspectives on Rural Women and Development*. New Delhi: CWDS, 1988.

Center for Women's Development Studies. *Rural Women's Claim to Priority: A Policy Debate*. New Delhi: CWDS, 1985.

Center for Women's Development Studies. *The Seeds of Change: Role of Grassroots Rural Women's Organisations in Development*. New Delhi: CWDS, 1987.

Center for Women's Development Studies. *Women's Work and Employment: Struggle for a Policy*. New Delhi: CWDS, 1983.

Central Intelligence Agency. *The Afro-Asia Peoples Solidarity Organization from April 1960–April 1961*. Washington, DC: CIA, 1961.

Chatterjee, Partha. "The Legacy of Bandung." In *Bandung, Global History, and International Law: Critical Pasts and Pending Futures*, edited by Luis Eslava, Michael Fakhri, and Vasuki Nesiah, 657–74. Cambridge: Cambridge University Press, 2017.

Chatterjee, Partha. "The Nationalist Resolution of the Women's Question." In *Recasting Women: Essays in Colonial History*, edited by Kumkum Sangari and Sudesh Vaid, 233–53. Delhi: Kali for Women, 1989.

Chatterjee, Partha. *Politics of the Governed: Reflections on Popular Politics in Most of the World*. New York: Columbia University Press, 2004.

Chatterjee, Partha. "Rethinking Postcolonial Capitalist Development: A Conversation between Kalyan Sanyal and Partha Chatterjee." *Comparative Studies of South Asia, Africa, and the Middle East* 36, no. 1 (2016): 102–11.

Chhachhi, Amrita, and Sunila Abeysekera. "Forging a New Political Imaginary: Transnational South Asian Feminisms." In *The Oxford Handbook of Transnational Feminist Movements*, edited by Rawwida Baksh and Wendy Harcourt, 553–77. Oxford: Oxford University Press, 2015.

Chowdhury, Elora. "Locating Global Feminisms Elsewhere: Braiding US Women of Color and Transnational Feminisms." *Cultural Dynamics* 21, no. 1 (2009): 51–78.

Combahee River Collective. "The Combahee River Collective Statement." April 1977.

Connolly, Matthew. *Fatal Misconception: The Struggle to Control World Population*. Cambridge, MA: Harvard University Press, 2010.

Cooper, Frederick, and Randall M. Packard. *International Development and the Social Sciences: Essays on the History and Politics of Knowledge*. Berkeley: University of California, 1998.

Corbman, Rachel. "The Scholars and the Feminists: The Barnard Sex Conference and the History of the Institutionalization of Feminism." In "Institutional Feelings: Practicing Women's Studies in the Corporate University," edited by Jennifer C. Nash and Emily A. Owens. Special issue, *Feminist Formations* 27, no. 3 (2015): 49–80.

Cortes, Irene R. "Philippine Law and Status of Women." *Columbia Human Rights Law Review* 8, no. 1 (1976): 229–62.

Dagadzi, Véronique. "Law and the Status of Women in Togo: Discrimination against Women in Togo." *Columbia Human Rights Law Review* 8, no. 1 (1976): 295–310.

Datta, Anjali Bhardwaj, Uditi Sen, and Mytheli Sreenivas. "Introduction: A Country of Her Making." In "A Country of Her Making: Women's Negotiations of Society and Politics in Post-Colonial India." Special issue, *South Asia: Journal of South Asian Studies* 44, no. 2 (2021): 218–27.

Davis, Angela. *Angela Davis: An Autobiography*. New York: Random House, 1974.

Davis, Angela. "Reflections on the Black Woman's Role in the Community of Slaves." *Black Scholar* 3, no. 4 (1971): 2–15.

Daymond, Margaret J., Dorothy Driver, Sheila Meintjes, Leloba Molema, Chiedza Musengezi, Margie Orford, and Nobantu Rasebotsa, eds. *Women Writing Africa: The Southern Region*, vol. 1. New York: Feminist Press at CUNY, 2003.

D'Costa, Bina. "Gender Justice and (In)security in Pakistan and Afghanistan." *Postcolonial Studies* 19, no. 4 (2016): 409–26.

De Mel, Neeloufer, and Selvy Thiruchandran, eds. *At the Cutting Edge: Essays in Honor of Kumari Jayawardena*. Delhi: Women Unlimited in Association with Kali for Women, 2007.

De, Rohit. *A People's Constitution: The Everyday Life of Law in the Indian Republic*. Princeton, NJ: Princeton University Press, 2018.

De, Rohit, and Robert Travers, eds. "Petitioning and Political Cultures in South Asia." Special issue, *Modern Asian Studies* 53, no. 1 (2019): 1–20.

Desai, Neera. "The Making of a Feminist." *Indian Journal of Gender Studies* 25, no. 2 (2018): 307–18.

Dhagamwar, Vasudha. *Criminal Justice or Chaos?* Delhi: Har Anand Publications, 1997.

Dhagamwar, Vasudha. "The Women in Gujarat's Camps–I." *The Hindu*, May 22, 2002, 10.

Dhagamwar, Vasudha. "The Women in Gujarat's Camps–II." *The Hindu*, May 23, 2002, 10.

Dhar, Jyoti. "Celebrating Artist, Activist, and Teacher Lala Rukh on International Women's Day." Ruya Maps, March 8, 2020. https://www.ruyamaps.org/2protest-art/international-womens-day-lala-rukh (accessed May 28, 2024).

Djagalov, Rossen. *From Internationalism to Postcolonialism: Literature and Cinema between the Second and the Third Worlds*. Montreal: McGill-Queen University Press, 2020.

Drif, Zohra. *Inside the Battle of Algiers: Memoir of a Woman Freedom Fighter*. Chicago: Just World Books, 2017.

Du Bois, W.E.B. "The African Roots of War." *Atlantic* 115, no. 5 (May 1915): 707–14.

Economic Commission of Western Asia (ECWA). *Effects of the Israeli Occupation of Palestinian Women Inside and Outside the Occupied Territories: Special Measures of Assistance to the Palestinian Woman*. Copenhagen: United Nations, 1980.

Elhalaby, Esmat. *Parting Gifts of Empire: Palestine and India at the Dawn of Decolonization*. Berkeley: University of California Press, 2025.

El Saadawi, Nawal. *A Daughter of Isis*. Translated by Sherif Hetata. London: Zed Books, 1999.

El Saadawi, Nawal, Fatima Mernissi, and Mallica Vajrathon. "A Critical View of the Wellesley Conference." *Quest* 4, no. 2 (1978): 101–7.

El Saadawi, Nawal, Fatima Mernissi, and Mallica Vajrathon. "Women and Development: A Critical View of the Wellesley Conference." In *Nawal El Saadawi Reader*, edited by Adele Newson-Horst, 143–53. New York: Zed Books, 1997.

Engerman, David C. *Apostles of Development: Six Economists and the World They Made*. Oxford: Oxford University Press, 2025.

Engineer, Ashgar Ali, ed. *The Shah Bano Controversy*. Mumbai: Orient Longman, 1987.

Esfandiari, Haley. *Reconstructed Lives: Women and Iran's Islamic Revolution*. Baltimore: Johns Hopkins University Press, 1997.

Eslava, Luis, Michael Fakhri, and Vasuki Nesiah, eds. *Bandung, Global History, and International Law: Critical Pasts and Pending Futures*. Cambridge: Cambridge University Press, 2017.

Falcon, Sylvanna. *Power Interrupted: Antiracist and Feminist Activism inside the United Nations*. Seattle: University of Washington Press, 2016.

Fall, Yassine. "Introduction: Gender Equality and Women's Struggles in the Global Age." In *Africa: Gender, Globalization, and Resistance*, edited by Yassine Fall, 1–5. Dakar: Association of African Women for Research and Development, 1999.

Feminist Book Fair Group, *259: An Introduction to a World of Women's Books*. London: Feminist Book Fair Group, 1985.

Feminist Futures Collective. "Call for Accountability in Feminist Circles." Medium, May 20, 2021. https://feministfuturescollective.medium.com/call-for-accountability-in-feminist-circles-4b0ae9846787 (accessed January 2, 2024).

Fisher, Maxine P. *Women in the Third World*. New York: Franklin Watts, 1989.

Forbes, Geraldine. *Women in Modern India*. Cambridge: Cambridge University Press, 1996.

Forrester, Katrina. "'In and against the State': Revolutionary Feminism during Deindustrialisation." Quentin Skinner Lecture delivered at the University of Cambridge, June 22, 2023. https://youtu.be/qIFIbJ3ciPo?feature=shared.

Fussell, Diana, and Ane Haaland. *Communicating with Pictures: Report of a Study Conducted by National Development Service (NDS) and UNICEF*. Kathmandu: UNICEF, 1976.

Geetha, V. "Durban: The Local Contexts of a Global Moment." In *Against Stigma: Studies in Caste, Race, and Justice since Durban*, edited by Balmurli Natrajan and Paul Greenough, 204–28. Delhi: Orient Blackswan, 2009.

Getachew, Adom. *Worldmaking after Empire: The Rise and Fall of Self-Determination*. Princeton, NJ: Princeton University Press, 2019.

Ghodsee, Kristin. *Second World, Second Sex: Socialist Women's Activism and Global Solidarity during the Cold War*. Durham, NC: Duke University Press, 2019.

Ghosh, Anindita. *Power in Print: Popular Publishing and Politics of Language and Culture in a Colonial Society*. New Delhi: Oxford University Press, 2006.

Gill-Peterson, Jules. *A Short History of Trans Misogyny*. London: Verso, 2024.

Goldsmith, Penny. "1st International Feminist Book Fair." *Kinesis* (October 1984): 22.

Gore, M. S. *Education for Women's Equality: Fifth J. P. Naik Memorial Lecture*. New Delhi: Center for Women's Development Studies, 1988.

Goulding, Kristine. "International Women's Day and Women's Rights in Pakistan: Interview with Farida Shaheed." United Nations Research Institute for Social Development, March 6, 2012. http://213.219.61.110/UNRISD/website/newsview.nsf/(httpNews)/D3A2E88D6F1458BFC12579B90068ECBB?OpenDocument (accessed May 12, 2024).

Government of India. *Towards Equality: Report of the Committee on the Status of Women in India*. New Delhi: Ministry of Education and Social Welfare, Department of Social Welfare, 1974.

Grewal, Inderpal. "'Women's Rights as Human Rights': Feminist Practices, Global Feminism, and Human Rights Regimes in Transnationality." *Citizenship Studies* 3, no. 3 (1999): 337–54.

Grewal, Inderpal, and Caren Kaplan, eds. *Scattered Hegemonies: Postmodernity and Transnational Feminist Practices*. Minneapolis: University of Minnesota Press, 1994.

Gruberg, Martin. "Official Commissions on the Status of Women: A Worldwide Movement." *International Review of Education* 19, no. 1 (1973): 140–47.

Guha, Ranajit. "On Some Aspects of the Historiography of Colonial India." In *Subaltern Studies I: Writings on South Asian History and Society*, edited by Ranajit Guha, 1–8. New Delhi: Oxford University Press, 1982.

Gupta, Charu. *The Gender of Caste: Representing Dalits in Print*. Seattle: University of Washington Press, 2016.

Gupta, Kirin. "Femme Fatale: Women Terrorists in Twentieth Century British Empire." PhD diss., Harvard University, 2025.

Gupta, Kirin. "Towards a Decolonial Democracy: Rageful Hope in the 1961 and 1972 Afro-Asian Women's Conferences." In *Feeling Democracy: Emotional Politics in the New Millennium*, edited by Sarah Tobias and Arlene Stein, 167–191. New Brunswick, NJ: Rutgers University Press, 2024.

Haksar, Urmila. *The Future That Was: An Autobiography*. Bombay: Allied Publishers, 1972.

Haksar, Urmila. *Nijeke Niye*. Calcutta: Ananda Publishers, 1974.

Halley, Janet, Prabha Kotiswaran, Rachel Rebouché, and Hila Shamir. *Governance Feminism: An Introduction*. Minneapolis: University of Minnesota Press, 2018.

Harish, Ranjana. *Indian Women's Autobiographies*. New Delhi: Arnold Publishers, 1993.

Helie Lucas, Marie-Aimée, and Sophie Laws. "Bound and Gagged by the Family Code." *WLUML Dossier* 5 (1988): 32–37.

Hierons, Charlie. "Liberation Betrayed? Algerian Feminism in the 21st Century." London School of Economics Middle East Center Blog, March 13, 2020. https://blogs.lse.ac.uk/mec/2020/03/13/liberation-betrayed-algerian-feminism-in-the-21st-century/ (accessed January 20, 2025).

Higashida, Cheryl. *Black Internationalist Feminism: Women Writers of the Black Left*. Urbana: University of Illinois Press, 2011.

Hodges, Sarah. *Contraception, Colonialism, and Commerce: Birth Control in South India, 1920–1940*. London: Ashgate, 2008.

Hodžic, Saida. "Feminist Bastards: Toward a Posthumanist Critique of NGOization." In *Theorizing NGOs: States, Feminisms, and Neoliberalism*, edited by Victoria Bernal and Inderpal Grewal, 221–47. Durham, NC: Duke University Press, 2014.

Hoffman, Nimi. "The Knowledge Commons, Pan-Africanism, and Epistemic Inequality: A Study of CODESRIA." PhD diss., Rhodes University, 2017.

Hong, Grace Kyungwon. *Death beyond Disavowal: The Impossible Politics of Difference*. Minneapolis: University of Minnesota Press, 2015.

hooks, bell. *Feminist Theory: From Margin to Center*. Boston: South End Press, 1984.

Howe, Florence. *A Life in Motion*. New York: Feminist Press, 2011.

Howe, Florence. *Promises to Keep: Trends in Women's Studies Worldwide—Tenth J. P. Naik Memorial Lecture*. New Delhi: Center for Women's Development Studies, 1994.

Howe, Florence. "Women's Studies International at Copenhagen: From Idea to Network." *Women's Studies Quarterly* 9, no. 1 (1981): 7–11.

Howe, Florence, and Vina Mazumdar. "Women's Studies International: Copenhagen to Montreal and Beyond." *Women's Studies Quarterly* 10, no. 2 (1982): 2.

Hudson, Natalie Florea. "Securitizing Women's Rights and Gender Equality." *Journal of Human Rights* 8, no. 1 (2009): 53–70.

Hussain, Nasser. *The Jurisprudence of Emergency: Colonialism and the Rule of Law*. Ann Arbor: University of Michigan Press, 2019.

Huston, Perdita. *Third World Women Speak Out: Interviews in Six Countries on Change, Development, and Basic Needs*. New York: Praeger, 1979.

Huzzey, Richard, and Henry Miller. "Colonial Petitions, Colonial Petitioners, and the Imperial Parliament, ca. 1780–1918." *Journal of British Studies* 61, no. 2 (2022): 261–89.

Ijaz, Saroop. "Asma Jahangir: Lawyer, Activist, Fighter." *The Wire*, February 11, 2018. https://tinyurl.com/2hkanwdh (accessed May 1, 2024).

Imam, Ayesha. "Gender Analysis and African Social Sciences in the 1990s." *Africa Development* 15, nos. 3/4 (1990): 241–57.

Imam, Ayesha, Mounira Chelli, and Soha Abdel-Kader, eds. *Women and the Mass Media in Africa*. Dakar: Association of African Women for Research and Development, 1992.

Imam, Ayesha, and Amina Mama. "The Role of Academics in Limiting and Expanding Academic Freedom." In *Academic Freedom in Africa*, edited by Mamadou Diouf and Mahmoud Mamdani, 73–108. Dakar: CODESRIA, 1994.

Imam, Ayesha, Amina Mama, and Fatou Sow. *Engendering African Social Sciences*. Dakar: CODESRIA, 1997.

Indian Council of Social Science Research (ICSSR). *Critical Issues on the Status of Women: Employment, Health, Education: Suggested Priorities for Action*. Delhi: ICSSR, 1977.

International Research and Training Institute for the Advancement of Women (INSTRAW). *Training Manual for Users and Producers in Compiling Statistics and Indicators on Women in Development*. New York: United Nations, 1987.

International Women's Tribune Centre. *Images of Nairobi: Reflections and Follow Up*. New York: IWTC, 1986.

Jahan, Rounaq, ed. *Women for Women*. Dhaka: Women for Women Research and Study Group with University Press Limited, 1975.

Jahan, Rounaq. *Women in Bangladesh*. Dhaka: Ford Foundation, February 1974.

Jahangir, Asma, and Hina Jilani. *The Hudood Ordinances: A Divine Sanction?* Lahore: Niaz Ahmad Sang-e-Meel Publications, 2003.

Jain, Devaki. *The Brass Notebook: A Memoir on Feminism and Freedom*. New York: New Press, 2020.

Jain, Devaki, ed. *Indian Women*. Delhi: Government of India, 1975.

Jaleel, Rana. *The Work of Rape*. Durham, NC: Duke University Press, 2021.

Jalib, Habib. "Poem Written for Women's Action Forum's First Anniversary." *WAF Newsletter* 6 (January 1985).

Jayawardena, Kumari. *Feminism and Nationalism in the Third World*. London: Zed Books, 1994 [1986].

John, Mary E. "Feminisms and Internationalisms: A Response from India." *Gender & History* 10, no. 3 (1998): 539–48.

John, Mary E., ed. Special collection of essays on Vina Mazumdar. *Indian Journal of Gender Studies* 24, no. 1 (2017): 71–125.

John, Mary E. "Thinking about Politics and State Power with Vina Mazumdar." *Indian Journal of Gender Studies* 24, no. 1 (2017): 111–25.

John, Mary E., ed. *Women's Studies in India: A Reader*. New Delhi: Penguin Books, 2008.

Jordan, June. *Civil Wars*. Boston: Beacon Press, 1981.

Jordan, June. *Directed by Desire: The Complete Poems of June Jordan*. Port Townsend, WA: Copper Canyon Press, 2005.

Jordan, June. "In Memoriam: Martin Luther King, Jr." In *Directed by Desire: The Collected Poems of June Jordan*, 29–30. Port Townsend, WA: Copper Canyon Press, 2005.

Jordan, June. "Poem for South African Women." In *Directed by Desire: The Complete Poems of June Jordan*, 279. Port Townsend, WA: Copper Canyon Press, 2005.

Jordan, June. *Some of Us Did Not Die: New and Selected Essays*. New York: Civitas Books, 2002.

JPP's Torture Watch. "The Women's Movement in Pakistan: An Era Foregone." November 4, 2015. https://jpptorturewatch.wordpress.com/2015/11/04/the-womens-movement-in-pakistan-an-era-foregone/ (accessed May 10, 2024).

Kali for Women. *Truth Tales: Contemporary Writing by Indian Women*. New Delhi: Kali for Women, 1986.

Kanagasabai, Nithila, and Shilpa Phadke. "Forging Fraught Solidarities: Friendship and Feminist Activism in South Asia." *Feminist Encounters: A Journal of Critical Studies in Culture and Politics* 7, no. 1 (2023): 1–13.

Kang, Laura Hyun Yi. *Traffic in Asian Women*. Durham, NC: Duke University Press, 2020.

Kanjilal, Amartya. "Narrating Legal Reform: The Open Letter and the Anti-Rape Movement." *Indian Journal of Gender Studies* 29, no. 2 (2022): 199–221.

Kannabiran, Kalpana, and Ritu Menon. *From Mathura to Manorama: Resisting Violence against Women in India*. New Delhi: Women Unlimited, 2007.

Kannan, Vani. "The Third World Women's Alliance: History, Geopolitics, and Form." PhD diss., Syracuse University, 2018.

Kaplan, Carla, Sarah Haley, and Durba Mitra, eds. "Outraged/Enraged: The Rage Special Issue." Special issue, *Signs: Journal of Women in Culture and Society* 46, no. 4 (Summer 2021): 785–800.

Kaplan, Temma. "On the Socialist Origins of International Women's Day." *Feminist Studies* 11, no. 1 (Spring 1985): 163–71.

Karia, Garima. "Forgotten Femissaries: Women's Diplomacy in the Afro-Asian World (1945–1975)." McGill University. https://www.mcgill.ca/arts-internships/files/arts-internships/aria_final_poster_garima_karia.pdf (accessed February 29, 2024).

Kaufmann, K. "A World of Writers." *Women's Review of Books* 4, no. 1 (1986): 13–14.

Kc, Diwas Raja, and NayanTara Gurung Kakshapati. *The Public Life of Women: A Feminist Memory Project*. Kathmandu: Nepal Picture Library and photo.circle, 2023.

Kelkar, Govind. *Women's Work and Agricultural Technology*. Delhi: Center for Women's Development Studies, 1985.

Kennedy, Finola. "Policy Ideas and Commissions of Enquiry." *Studies: An Irish Quarterly Review* 103, no. 409 (2014): 35–44.

Khan, Ayesha. *The Women's Movement in Pakistan: Activism, Islam, and Democracy*. London: I. B. Taurus, 2018.

Khan, Nighat Said. "I Remember—Nighat Said Khan." *Friday Times*, October 9, 2006. https://imadahmed.com/2006/10/09/i-remember-nighat-said-khan/ (accessed January 1, 2025).

Khan, Nighat Said, and Kamla Bhasin. "Educating Each Other on Women's Development: Report of a Workshop on Women and Development in Pakistan." *Convergence* 21, no. 4 (1988): 35–44.

Khasiani, Shanyisa Anota, and E. I. Njiro, eds. *The Women's Movement in Kenya*. Nairobi: Association of African Women for Research and Development, 1993.

Kim, Suzy. *Among Women across Worlds: North Korea in the Global Cold War*. Ithaca, NY: Cornell University Press, 2023.

Kim, Suzy. "Cold War Feminisms in East Asia: Introduction." *positions: asia critique* 28, no. 3 (2020): 501–16.

King, Tiffany Lethabo. "Black 'Feminisms' and Pessimism: Abolishing Moynihan's Negro Family." *Theory & Event* 21, no. 1 (2018): 68–87.

Kotiswaran, Prabha. "Governance Feminism in the Postcolony: Reforming India's Rape Laws." In *Governance Feminism: An Introduction*, edited by Janet Halley, Prabha Kotiswaran, Rachel Rebouché, and Hila Shamir, 75–148. Minneapolis: University of Minnesota Press, 2018.

Krause, Monika. *The Good Project: Humanitarian NGOs and the Fragmentation of Reason*. Chicago: University of Chicago Press, 2014.

Kumar, Radha. *The History of Doing: An Illustrated Account of Movements for Women's Rights and Feminism in India, 1800–1990*. Delhi: Kali for Women, 1993.

Lala Rukh. *In Our Own Backyard*. Lahore: Lala Rukh, 1987.

Lau, Martin. "Twenty-Five Years of Hudood Ordinances—A Review." *Washington & Lee Law Review* 64 (2007): 1291–1314.

Laville, Helen. "A New Era in International Women's Rights? American Women's Associations and the Establishment of the UN Commission on the Status of Women." *Journal of Women's History* 20, no. 4 (2008): 34–56.

League of Nations. *Status of Women: Communications Received from Governments and Women's International Organisations since September 1936*. Geneva: League of Nations, 1937.

Lee, Christopher J., ed. *Making a World after Empire: The Bandung Moment and Its Political Afterlives*. Athens: Ohio University Press, 2010.

Lee, Luke T. "Law and the Status of Women: Introduction." *Columbia Human Rights Law Review* 8, no. 1 (1976): 3–8.

Legg, Stephen. *Roundtable Conference Geographies: Constituting Colonial India in Interwar London*. Cambridge: Cambridge University Press, 2023.

Legg, Stephen, Mike Heffernan, Jake Hedder, and Benjamin Thorpe. *Placing Internationalism: International Conferences and the Making of the Modern World*. London: Bloomsbury, 2021.

Levin, Tobe. "Introducing *Manushi*: An Indian Feminist Journal." *Women's Studies Newsletter* 8, no. 1 (1980): 30–31.

Lewis, Su Lin, and Carolien Stolte. "Other Bandungs: Afro-Asian Internationalisms in the Early Cold War." *Journal of World History* 30, nos. 1/2 (2019): 1–19.

Lihamba, Amandina, Fulata L. Moyo, Mugyabuso M. Mulokozi, and Naomi L. Shitemi, eds. *Women Writing Africa: The Eastern Region*, vol 3. New York: Feminist Press, 2007.

Linner, Birgitta. "Status of Women and Law in Sweden." *Columbia Human Rights Law Review* 8, no. 1 (1976): 263–94.

Liu, Hong, and Taomo Zhou. "Bandung Humanism and a New Understanding of the Global South: An Introduction." *Critical Asian Studies* 51, no. 2 (2019): 141–43.

Lookman, Mariah. "Interviews, Past and Present: Lala Rukh by Mariah Lookman" (interview conducted January 6, 2016). *Mousse*, March 29, 2023. https://www.moussemagazine.it/magazine/lala-rukh-mariah-lookman-2023/ (accessed May 28, 2024).

Loomba, Ania. *Revolutionary Desires: Women, Communism, and Feminism in India*. London: Routledge, 2019.

Lorde, Audre. *Sister Outsider: Essays and Speeches*. Berkeley, CA: Crossing Press, 1984.

Louis, Marie-Victoire. "Les Algériennes, la lutte." *Les temps modernes Algérie*, nos. 432/433 (July/August 1982): 152–93. https://www.marievictoirelouis.net/document.php?id=399&themeid=397 (accessed June 10, 2024).

Louis, Roger W. M., and Roger Owen, eds. *Suez 1956: The Crisis and Its Consequences*. Oxford: Oxford University Press, 1991.

Lowe, Lisa. *The Intimacy of Four Continents*. Durham, NC: Duke University Press, 2015.

Luckham, Yaa. "Law and the Status of Women in Ghana." *Columbia Human Rights Law Review* 8, no. 1 (1976): 69–94.

Macharia, Keguro. "Report Realism: Tentative Notes on Contemporary Kenyan Writing." *Gukira*, January 25, 2012. https://gukira.wordpress.com/2012/01/25/report-realism-tentative-notes-on-contemporary-kenyan-writing/ (accessed March 4, 2024).

Mahmood, Saba. *Politics of Piety: The Islamic Revival and the Feminist Subject*. Princeton, NJ: Princeton University Press, 2005.

Mair, Lucille Mathurin. *International Women's Decade: A Balance Sheet*. Delhi: Center for Women's Development Studies, 1984.

Mair, Lucille Mathurin. "Preface." In *Gender and Caribbean Development*, edited by Patricia Mohammed and Catherine Shepherd, xi–xii. Mona, Barbados: University of the West Indies, 1988.

Mair, Lucille Mathurin. "Women: A Decade Is Time Enough." *Third World Quarterly* 8, no. 2 (1986): 583–93.

Mamdani, Mahmood. "University Crisis and Reform: A Reflection on the African Experience." *Review of African Political Economy* 58 (1993): 7–19.

"Many Exit as Mrs. Rabin Speaks at Conference." *New York Times*, June 26, 1975.

Marcuse, Herbert. *A Study on Authority* [1936]. Translated by Joris De Bres. New York: Verso, 2008.

Marino, Katherine. *Feminism for the Americas: The Making of an International Human Rights Movement*. Chapel Hill: University of North Carolina Press, 2019.

Mazower, Mark. *Governing the World: The Making of an Idea*. New York: Penguin, 2012.

Mazower, Mark. *No Enchanted Palace: The End of Empire and the Ideological Origins of the United Nations*. Princeton, NJ: Princeton University Press, 2009.

Mazumdar, Vina. *Emergence of Women's Question and the Role of Women's Studies*. Delhi: Center for Women's Development Studies, 1985.

Mazumdar, Vina. *Khadi and Village Industries Commission: A Report*. Delhi: Center for Women's Development Studies, 1988.

Mazumdar, Vina. *Memories of a Rolling Stone*. Delhi: Zubaan, 2010.

Mazumdar, Vina. *Peasant Women Organise for Empowerment: The Bankura Experiment*. New Delhi: Center for Women's Development Studies, 1998.

Mazumdar, Vina, and N. Krishnaji. *Enduring Conundrum: India's Sex Ratio*. Delhi: Center for Women's Development Studies, 2001.

McKittrick, Katherine. *Dear Science and Other Stories*. Durham, NC: Duke University Press, 2021.

Mehra, Rekha, and K. Saradomoni. *Women and Rural Transformation: Two Studies*. Delhi: Center for Women's Development Studies and Indian Council of Social Science Research, 1983.

Menon, Nivedita. *Recovering Subversion: Feminist Politics beyond the Law*. Delhi: Permanent Black, 2004.

Menon, Nivedita. "A Uniform Civil Code in India: The State of the Debate in 2014." *Feminist Studies* 40, no. 2 (2014): 480–86.

Menon, Ritu. *Address Book*. Delhi: Women Unlimited, 2021.

Menon, Ritu. "Dismantling the Master's House . . . : The Predicament of Feminist Publishing and Writing Today." *Australian Feminist Studies* 16, no. 35 (2001): 175–84.

Menon, Ritu. "Ritu Menon: A Life in Feminist Publishing." *Punch*, March 8, 2021. https://thepunchmagazine.com/the-byword/non-fiction/ritu-menon-a-life-in-feminist-publishing (accessed January 1, 2025).

Mernissi, Fatima. *Beyond the Veil: Male-Female Dynamics in a Modern Muslim Society*. Cambridge, MA: Schenkman; New York: Halsted Press, 1975.

Mernissi, Fatima. *Doing Daily Battle: Interviews with Moroccan Women*. London: Women's Press, 1988.

Mernissi, Fatima. *The Forgotten Queens of Islam*. Cambridge: Polity Press, 1993.

Mernissi, Fatima. *The Veil and the Male Elite*. Translated by Mary Jo Lakeland. Reading, MA: Addison-Wesley, 1991.

Mernissi, Fatima. *Women in Moslem Paradise*. Delhi: Kali for Women, 1986.

Merry, Sally Engle. *Human Rights and Gender Violence: Translating International Law into Local Justice*. Chicago: University of Chicago Press, 2006.

Merry, Sally Engle. *The Seductions of Quantification: Measuring Human Rights, Gender Violence, and Sex Trafficking*. Chicago: University of Chicago, 2016.

Messaoudi, Khalida, and Elisabeth Schemla. *Unbowed: An Algerian Woman Confronts Islamic Fundamentalism*. Philadelphia: University of Pennsylvania Press, 1998.

Meyerowitz, Joanne. "A Feminist NIEO?" Paper presented at the conference on "The New International Economic Order: Lessons and Legacies 50 Years Later," Università Ca'Foscari Venezia and Berggruen Institute Europe, Venice, May 10–11, 2024.

Meyerowitz, Joanne. *A War on Global Poverty: The Lost Promise of Redistribution and the Rise of Microcredit*. Princeton, NJ: Princeton University Press, 2021.

Ministry of Foreign Affairs, Republic of Indonesia, ed. "Final Communiqué of the Asian-African Conference." In *Asia-Africa Speak from Bandung*, 161–69. Jakarta: Indonesia Ministry of Foreign Affairs, April 24, 1955.

Mitra, Durba. "Feminism for the Living." In *Feminism against Cisness*, edited by Emma Heaney, 241–50. Durham, NC: Duke University Press, 2024.

Mitra, Durba. *Indian Sex Life: Sexuality and the Colonial Origins of Modern Social Thought*. Princeton, NJ: Princeton University Press, 2020.

Mitra, Durba. "The Report, or, Whatever Happened to Third World Feminist Theory?" *Signs: Journal of Women in Culture and Society* 48, no. 1 (Spring 2023): 557–84.

Mitra, Durba. "Sisterhood Is X: On Solidarity Then and Now." In "Feminism's Bad Objects," edited by Jennifer C. Nash and Samantha Pinto. Special issue, *South Atlantic Quarterly* 122, no. 3 (2023): 431–52.

Mitra, Durba. *Solidarity! Transnational Feminisms Then and Now*. Exhibition at Lia and William Poorvu Gallery, Schlesinger Library on the History of Women in America and Digital Curation, Radcliffe Institute for Advanced Study, Harvard University, March 27 to October 23, 2023. https://www.radcliffe.harvard.edu/event/2023-solidarity-exhibition (accessed March 1, 2024).

Mitra, Durba, and Mrinal Satish. "Testing Virginity, Evidencing Rape: Medical Jurisprudence and Rape Adjudication in Colonial and Postcolonial India." *Economic and Political Weekly* 49, no. 41 (October 11, 2014): 51–58.

Moallem, Minoo, and Paola Bacchetta, eds. *Fatema Mernissi for Our Times*. Syracuse, NY: Syracuse University Press, 2025.

Mody, Nawaz B. "The Press in India: The Shah Bano Judgment and Its Aftermath." *Asian Survey* 27, no. 8 (1987): 935–53.

Moghadam, Valentine M. *Globalizing Women: Transnational Feminist Networks*. Baltimore: Johns Hopkins University Press, 2005.

Moghadam, Valentine M. "Women Living under Muslim Laws." In *The Oxford Encyclopedia of Islam and Women*, edited by Natana J. DeLong-Bas. Oxford: Oxford University Press, 2013.

Mohammed, Patricia, and Catherine Shepherd, eds. *Gender and Caribbean Development*. Mona, Barbados: University of the West Indies, 1988.

Mohanty, Chandra Talpade. "Under Western Eyes: Feminist Scholarship and Colonial Discourses." *boundary 2*, vol. 12, no. 3; vol. 13, no. 1 (1984): 333–58.

Mohanty, Chandra Talpade, Ann Russo, and Lourdes Torres, eds. *Third World Women and the Politics of Feminism*. Bloomington: Indiana University Press, 1991.

Moradian, Manijeh. "Iranian Diasporic Possibilities: Tracing Transnational Feminist Genealogies from the Revolutionary Margins." In *Global 1979: Geographies and Histories of the Iranian Revolution*, edited by Arang Keshavarzian and Ali Mirsepassi, 104–38. Cambridge: Cambridge University Press, 2021.

Morgan, Robin. *Reckoning with Slavery: Gender, Kinship, and Capitalism in the Early Black Atlantic*. Durham, NC: Duke University Press, 2021.

Morgan, Robin, ed. *Sisterhood Is Global*. New York: Feminist Press, 1984.

Morrison, Toni. *The Source of Self Regard: Selected Essays, Speeches, and Meditations*. New York: Alfred A. Knopf, 2021.

Mottahedeh, Roy. *The Mantle of the Prophet: Religion and Politics in Iran*. Oxford: Oneworld Publications, 2002.

Moyn, Samuel. *The Last Utopia: Human Rights in History*. Cambridge, MA: Harvard University Press, 2011.

Moyn, Samuel. *Not Enough: Human Rights in an Unequal World*. Cambridge, MA: Harvard University Pres, 2019.

Moynihan, Daniel Patrick. *The Negro Family: The Case for National Action*. Washington, DC: US Department of Labor, Office of Policy Planning and Research, 1965.

Mukabi-Kabira, Wanjiku, Jacqueline Adhiambo-Odoul, and Maria Nzomo, eds. *Democratic Change in Africa: Women's Perspective*. Nairobi: Association of African Women for Research and Development, 1993.

Mukherjee, Sumita. "The All-Asian Women's Conference 1931: Indian Women and Their Leadership of a Pan-Asian Feminist Organisation." *Women's History Review* 26, no. 32 (2017): 363–81.

Mulira, Sanyu Ruth. "'We Were but Women': Print Culture, Anti-Colonialism, and Activism amongst Black Women in the Francophone Diaspora, 1920–1976." PhD diss., New York University, 2023.

Mumtaz, Khawar, and Farida Shaheed. *Women of Pakistan: One Step Forward, Two Steps Back*. London: Zed Books, 1987.

Murphy, M. "Against Population, towards Alterlife." In *Making Kin, Not Population*, edited by Adele Clarke and Donna Haraway, 101–24. Chicago: Prickly Paradigm Press, 2018.

Murphy, M. *The Economization of Life*. Durham, NC: Duke University Press, 2017.

Murray, Simone. "'Books of Integrity': The Women's Press, Kitchen Table Press, and Dilemmas of Feminist Publishing." *European Journal of Women's Studies* 5, no. 2 (1998): 171–93.

"The Nairobi Manifesto." *Issue: A Journal of Opinion* 17, no. 2 (1989): 44.

Narang, A. S. "Caste at Durban: Why and How." In *Caste, Race, and Discrimination: Discourses in International Context*, edited by Sukhadeo Thorat and Umakant, 207–10. Jaipur: Rawat Publications, 2004.

Nash, Jennifer C. *Black Feminism Reimagined: After Intersectionality*. Durham, NC: Duke University Press, 2018.

Nasr, Seyyed Vali Reza. *Mawdudi and the Making of Islamic Revivalism*. Oxford: Oxford University Press, 1996.

National Commission for Women, India. *Report of the Committee Constituted by the National Commission for Women to Assess the Status and Situation of Women and Girl Children in Gujarat in the Wake of the Communal Disturbance*. Delhi: Government of India, 2002.

Natrajan, Balmurli, and Paul Greenough, eds. *Against Stigma: Studies in Caste, Race, and Justice since Durban*. Delhi: Orient Blackswan, 2009.

Nazneen, Sohela, and Maheen Sultan. "Struggling for Survival and Autonomy: Impact of NGO-ization on Women's Organizations in Bangladesh." *Development* 52 (2009): 193–99.

Nijhawan, Shobna. "International Feminism from an Asian Center: The All-Asian Women's Conference (Lahore, 1931) as a Transnational Feminist Moment." *Journal of Women's History* 29, no. 3 (2017): 12–36.

Nijhawan, Shobna. *Women and Girls in the Hindi Public Sphere: Periodical Literature in Colonial India*. New Delhi: Oxford University Press, 2012.

Nkrumah, Kwame. *Neo-Colonialism: The Last Stage of Imperialism*. London: Thomas Nelson & Sons, 1965.

Okihiro, Gary. *Third World Studies: Theorizing Liberation*. Durham, NC: Duke University Press, 2016.

Olcott, Jocelyn. *International Women's Year: The Greatest Consciousness-Raising Event in History*. Oxford: Oxford University Press, 2017.

Omvedt, Gail Chetna Gala, and Govind Kelkar. *Women and Struggle: A Report of the Nari Mukti Sangharsh Sammelan*. New Delhi: Kali for Women, 1988.

Orsini, Francesca. *Print and Pleasure: Popular Literature and Entertaining Fictions in Colonial North India*. Ranikhet: Permanent Black, 2009.

Pakistan Commission on the Status of Women. *Report of the Pakistan Commission on the Status of Women*. Karachi: Pakistan Law House, 1989.

Pakistan Women's Rights Commission. *Report of the Pakistan Women's Rights Commission*. Islamabad: Ministry of Law and Parliamentary Affairs, 1976.

Pancholi, Indira, and Paromita Vohra. "How We Wrote a Sex-Ed Book in 80s India: An Interview with Indira Pancholi; The Story behind 'Shareer ki Jankaari' and the Women behind It!" *Agents of Ishq*, March 7, 2023. https://agentsofishq.com/post/how-we-wrote-a-sex-ed-book-in-80-s-india-an-interview-with-indira-pancholi-6406db583264f (accessed May 29, 2024).

Parashar, Archana. *Women and Family Law Reform in India: Uniform Civil Code and Gender Equality*. New Delhi: Sage Publications, 1992.

Parpart, Jane L. "Women's Rights and the Lagos Plan of Action." *Human Rights Quarterly* 8, no. 2 (1986): 180–96.

Patel, Zarina. "Call Us Ms." *Viva*, July 1979, 11–14.

Phillips, Andrew. "Beyond Bandung: The 1955 Asian-African Conference and Its Legacies for International Order." *Australian Journal of International Affairs* 70, no. 4 (2016): 329–41.

Piccini, Jon. "'Women Are a Colonised Sex': Elizabeth Reid, Human Rights, and International Women's Year 1975." *Australian Historical Studies* 49, no. 3 (2018): 307–23.

Pinto, Samantha, and Jennifer C. Nash. "Then and Now: Women of Color Originalism and the Anthological Impulse in Women's and Gender Studies." *Feminist Studies* 48, no. 1 (2022): 13–23.

Prakash, Gyan. *Emergency Chronicles: Indira Gandhi and Democracy's Turning Point*. Princeton, NJ: Princeton University Press, 2017.

Prakash, Gyan, and Jeremy Adelman, eds. *Inventing the Third World: In Search of Freedom for the Postwar Global South*. London: Bloomsbury, 2023.

Prashad, Vijay. *The Darker Nations: A People's History of the Third World*. New York: New Press, 2007.

Puri, Jyoti. *Woman, Body, Desire in Post-Colonial India: Narratives of Gender and Sexuality*. New York: Routledge, 1999.

Rahimi, Wali M. "Afghanistan." In United Nations Educational, Scientific, and Cultural Organization, *Social Sciences in Asia II: Afghanistan, Indonesia, Japan, Republic of Korea, Nepal: Reports and Papers in the Social Sciences*, 7–22. Paris: UNESCO, 1977.

Rahimi, Wali M. *Status of Women: Afghanistan*. Bangkok: UNESCO, 1991.

Rahimi, Wali M. *Status of Women: Afghanistan*. Paris: UNESCO, 1989.

Rahman, Farhat. "Female Sexuality and Islam." *WLUML Dossier* 5 (1988): 30–31.

Rahnama, Sara. *The Future Is Feminist: Women and Social Change in Interwar Algeria.* Ithaca, NY: Cornell University Press, 2023.

Rao, Anupama, ed. *Gender and Caste.* New Delhi: Kali for Women, 2003.

Ray, Raka. *Fields of Protest: Women's Movements in India.* Minneapolis: University of Minnesota Press, 2000.

Rédaction Africanews. "Algerian Women Protest Demanding Equal Rights." *Africa News,* March 9, 2021. https://www.africanews.com/2021/03/09/algerian-women-protest-demanding-equal-rights// (accessed January 20, 2025).

Reddock, Rhoda. "Women's Organizations and Movements in the Commonwealth Caribbean: The Response to Global Economic Crisis in the 1980s." *Feminist Review* 59 (1998): 57–73.

Rich, Adrienne. "Reaching Out to Our Sisters." *Manushi* (December 1979/January 1980): 39.

Robcis, Camille. *The War on Gender.* Princeton, NJ: Princeton University Press, forthcoming.

Romney, Patricia. *We Were There: The Third World Women's Alliance and the Second Wave.* New York: Feminist Press, 2021.

Rowley, Michelle, and Peggy Antrobus. "Feminist Visions for Women in a New Era: An Interview with Peggy Antrobus." *Feminist Studies* 33, no. 1 (2007): 64–87.

Roy, Srila. *Changing the Subject: Feminist and Queer Politics in Neoliberal India.* Durham, NC: Duke University Press, 2022.

Roy, Srila. "The Indian Women's Movement: Within and Beyond NGOization." *Journal of South Asian Development* 10, no. 1 (2015): 96–117.

Roy, Srila. "Melancholic Politics and the Politics of Melancholia: The Indian Women's Movement." *Feminist Theory* 10, no. 3 (2009): 341–57.

Roy, Srila. "Politics, Passion, and Professionalization in Contemporary Indian Feminism." *Sociology* 45, no. 4 (2011): 587–602.

Royal Commission on the Status of Women in Canada. *Report of the Royal Commission on the Status of Women in Canada.* Ottawa: Information Canada, 1970.

Rupp, Leila J. *Worlds of Women: The Making of an International Women's Movement.* Princeton, NJ: Princeton University Press, 1997.

Russo, Giusi. *Women, Empires, and Body Politics at the United Nations, 1946–1975.* Omaha: University of Nebraska Press, 2023.

Sadiqi, Fatima, Amira Nowaira, Azza el Kholy, and Moha Ennaji, eds. *Women Writing Africa: The Northern Region,* vol. 4. New York: Feminist Press, 2008.

Sadjadi, Shahnaz, and Marianne Hedin-Pourghasemi. "Law and the Status of Women in Iran." *Columbia Human Rights Law Review* 8, no. 1 (1976): 141–64.

Saeed, Mehek. "Aurat March 2018: Freedom over Fear." *News Pakistan,* March 2018. https://www.thenews.com.pk/magazine/instep-today/290411-aurat-march-2018-freedom-over-fear (accessed May 22, 2024).

Saheli Women's Resource Center. "A Letter from Saheli Women's Resource Centre—New Delhi to the National Commission for Women." May 6, 2002. https://www.onlinevolunteers.org/gujarat/women/saheli-ltr.htm (accessed May 15, 2024).

Saigol, Rubina. "Remembering February 12, 1983." *The News,* February 12, 2017. https://www.thenews.com.pk/tns/detail/562695-remembering-february-12-1983 (accessed May 1, 2024).

Salhi, Zahia Smail. "Algerian Women, Citizenship, and the 'Family Code.'" *Gender and Development* 11, no. 3 (2003): 27–35.

Sangari, Kumkum, and Pragati Mohapatra. "Kumkum Sangari Looks Back at *Recasting Women*—The Landmark Book on Gender." Indian Cultural Forum, July 25, 2018. https://indianculturalforum.in/2018/07/25/kumkum-sangari-recasting-women/ (accessed May 29, 2024).

Sarkar, Lotika. *National Specialised Agencies and Women's Equality: Law Commission of India*. Delhi: Center for Women's Development Studies, 1988.

Sarkar, Lotika, Kumud Sharma, and Leela Kasturi, eds. *Between Tradition, Counter Tradition, and Heresy: Contributions in Honour of Vina Mazumdar*. New Delhi: Center for Women's Development Studies, 2002.

Sarkar, Lotika, Kumud Sharma, and Leela Kasturi, eds. *A Pathmaker: Tributes to Vina Mazumdar*. Delhi: Rainbow Publishers, 2002.

Savané, Marie-Angelique. "International Interview: Feminism in Senegal." *Off Our Backs* 17, no. 10 (1987): 19, 22.

Scott, David. *Conscripts of Modernity: The Tragedy of Colonial Enlightenment*. Durham, NC: Duke University Press, 2004.

Sen, Amartya. *Development as Freedom*. Oxford: Oxford University Press, 1999.

Sen, Gita, and Caren Grown. *Development, Crises, and Alternative Visions: Third World Women's Perspectives*. New York: Monthly Review Press, 1987.

Shaheed, Farida. "Controlled or Autonomous: Identity and the Experience of the Network, Women Living Under Muslim Laws." *Signs: Journal of Women in Culture and Society* 19, no. 4 (1994): 997–1019.

Shaheed, Farida. "Maintaining Momentum in Changing Circumstances." *Journal of International Affairs* 72, no. 2 (2019): 159–72.

Shaheed, Farida, ed. *The Women of Pakistan: A Selected Bibliography with Annotations*. Lahore: Shirkat Gah, 1992.

Sharma, Kumud, ed. *Changing the Terms of the Discourse: Gender Equality and the Indian State*. Delhi: Center for Women's Development Studies and Pearson, 2012.

Sharma, Kumud, ed. *Memory Frames: Oral Narratives of Four First Generation Women's Studies Scholars*. New Delhi: Center for Women's Development Studies, 2005.

Shehabuddin, Elora. *Sisters in the Mirror: A History of Muslim Women and the Global Politics of Feminism*. Berkeley: University of California Press, 2021.

Shimazu, Naoko. "Diplomacy as Theatre: Staging the Bandung Conference of 1955." *Modern Asian Studies* 48, no. 1 (2014): 225–52.

Shirkat Gah Women's Resource Centre. "Mission." https://shirkatgah.org/our-mission/ (accessed January 10, 2024).

Shirkat Gah Women's Resource Centre. *Towards a Better Tomorrow: The Report of the Commission of Inquiry for Women (1997); A Simplified Version*. Lahore: Shirkat Gah Women's Resource Centre, 1997.

Shiva, Vandana. *Staying Alive: Women, Ecology, and Development*. London: Zed Books; Delhi: Kali for Women, 1988.

Sinha, Mrinalini. *Specters of Mother India: The Global Restructuring of an Empire*. Durham, NC: Duke University Press, 2006.

Sinha, Mrinalini, Donna Guy, and Angela Woollacott, eds. *Feminisms and Internationalism*. Oxford: Blackwell, 1999.

Sipilä, Helvi. "Foreword." *Columbia Human Rights Law Review* 8, no. 1 (1976): 1–2.

Sluga, Glenda. *Internationalism in the Age of Nationalism*. Philadelphia: University of Pennsylvania Press, 2013.

Sluga, Glenda. "Women, Feminisms, and Twentieth-Century Internationalisms." In *Internationalisms: A Twentieth-Century History*, edited by Glenda Sluga and Patricia Clavin, 61–84. Cambridge: Cambridge University Press, 2017.

Solovey, Mark. "Project Camelot and the 1960s Epistemological Revolution." *Social Studies of Science* 31, no. 2 (2001): 171–206.

Spillers, Hortense. "Mama's Baby, Papa's Maybe: An American Grammar Book." *Diacritics* 17, no. 2 (1987): 64–81.

Spivak, Gayatri Chakravorty. "Can the Subaltern Speak?" In *Marxism and the Interpretation of Culture,* edited by Cary Nelson and Lawrence Grossberg, 271–313. Urbana: University of Illinois Press, 1988.

Sreenivas, Mytheli. "Feminism, Family Planning, and National Planning." *South Asia: Journal of South Asian Studies* 44, no. 2 (2021): 313–28.

Sreenivas, Mytheli. *Reproductive Politics and the Making of Modern India.* Seattle: University of Washington Press, 2021.

Staudt, Kathleen, and Harvey Glickman. "Beyond Nairobi: Women's Politics and Policies in Africa Revisited." *Issue: A Journal of Opinion* 17, no. 2 (1989): 4–6.

Steady, Filomina. "Research Methodology and Investigative Framework for Social Change: The Case for African Women." In *Seminar on Research on African Women: What Type of Methodology?*, 12–21. Dakar: Association of African Women for Research and Development, 1983.

Steady, Filomina. *Woman in Action: Autobiography of a Global African Feminist.* Gloucestershire, UK: Mereo Books, 2023.

Stewart, Abigail J., Jayati Lal, and Kristin McGuire. 2011. "Expanding the Archives of Global Feminisms: Narratives of Feminism and Activism." *Signs: Journal of Women in Culture and Society* 36, no. 4 (2011): 889–914.

Stolte, Carolien. "'The Asiatic Hour': New Perspectives on the Asian Relations Conference, New Delhi, 1947." In *The Non-Aligned Movement and the Cold War: Delhi—Bandung—Belgrade,* edited by Natasa Miskovic, Harald Fischer-Tiné, and Nada Boskovska, 57–75. London: Routledge, 2014.

Stolte, Carolien, and Su Lin Lewis, eds. *The Lives of Cold War Afro-Asianism.* Amsterdam: Amsterdam University Press, 2022.

Sunder Rajan, Rajeswari. *The Scandal of the State: Women, Law, and Citizenship in Postcolonial India.* Durham, NC: Duke University Press, 2003.

Tadiar, Neferti X. M. *Remaindered Life.* Durham, NC: Duke University Press, 2022.

Tahir, Rida. "Supreme Court of Pakistan Delivers Landmark Judgement on Sexual Violence." *LSE Blog,* May 11, 2021. https://blogs.lse.ac.uk/wps/2021/05/11/supreme-court-of-pakistan-delivers-landmark-judgement-on-sexual-violence/ (accessed May 29, 2024).

Tamale, Sylvia. *Decolonization and Afro-Feminism.* Ottawa: Daraja, 2020.

Tambe, Ashwini. *Defining Girlhood in India: A Transnational History of Sexual Maturity Laws.* Urbana: University of Illinois Press, 2019.

Tambe, Ashwini, and Alissa Trotz. "Historical Reflections on DAWN: An Interview with Gita Sen." *Comparative Studies of South Asia, Africa, and the Middle East* 30, no. 2 (2010): 214–17.

Tamboura-Diawara, Aicha, ed. *Gender and HIV/AIDS in Africa.* Dakar: Association of African Women for Research and Development, 2003.

Tamboura-Diawara, Aicha, ed. *Gender, Economic Integration, Governance, and Methods of Contraceptives.* Dakar: Association of African Women for Research and Development, 2002.

Tamboura-Diawara, Aicha. *Women and Violence in Africa.* Dakar: Association of African Women for Research and Development, 2005.

Tan, See Seng, and Amitav Acharya, eds. *Bandung Revisited: The Legacy of the 1955 Asian-African Conference for International Order.* Singapore: National University of Singapore Press, 2008.

Tarlo, Emma. *Unsettling Memories: Narratives of the Emergency in Delhi.* Berkeley: University of California Press, 2003.

Taylor, Keeanga-Yamahtta, ed. *How We Get Free: Black Feminism and the Combahee River Collective.* Chicago: Haymarket Books, 2017.

Thakur, Vineet. "An Asian Drama: The Asian Relations Conference, 1947." *International History Review* 41, no. 3 (2019): 673–95.

Thanh, Ngo Ba. *Status of Women: Vietnam*. Bangkok: UNESCO, 1989.

Thapar, Romila. *Sakuntala: Texts, Readings, Histories*. New Delhi: Kali for Women, 1999.

Tharu, Susie. "*Women Writing in India* Reconsidered." *Review of Development and Change* 22, no. 1 (2017): 45–55.

Tharu, Susie, and K. Lalita. *Women Writing in India: 600 BC to the Early Twentieth Century*, vol. 1. New York: Feminist Press, 1991.

Tharu, Susie, and K. Lalita. *Women Writing in India: The Twentieth Century*, vol. 2. New York: Feminist Press, 1993.

Third World Women's Alliance. "Women in the Struggle." *Triple Jeopardy*, no. 1 (1971): 8.

Tomšič, Vida. *Women, Development, and the Non-Aligned Movement: Fourth J. P. Naik Memorial Lecture*. New Delhi: Center for Women's Development Studies, 1988.

Umoren, Imaobong D. *Race Women Internationalists: Activist-Intellectuals and Global Freedom Struggles*. Berkeley: University of California Press, 2018.

United Nations. "Conferences: Women and Gender Equality." https://www.un.org/en/conferences/women (accessed February 26, 2024).

United Nations. *Report of the World Conference to Review and Appraise the Achievements of the United Nations Decade for Women: Equality, Development, and Peace, Nairobi, 15–26 July 1985*. New York: United Nations, 1986.

United Nations. *The Status and Role of Women in East Africa*. New York: United Nations, 1967.

United Nations Educational, Scientific, and Cultural Organization (UNESCO). *Social Sciences in Asia II: Afghanistan, Indonesia, Japan, Republic of Korea, Nepal: Reports and Papers in the Social Sciences*. Paris: UNESCO, 1977.

UN Women. *The Legacy of INSTRAW in Promoting the Rights of Women: A Historical Record of the Institute between 1976 and 2010*. Santo Domingo: UN Women Training Center, 2016.

UN Women. *A Short History of the Commission on the Status of Women*. New York: UN Women, 2019.

"UN Women's Conference Drops Reference to Zionism as Racism." *New York Times*, July 27, 1985.

US Commission on the Status of Women. *American Women: Report of the US Commission on the Status of Women*. Washington, DC: US Government Printing Office, 1963.

Verma, J. S., Leila Seth, and Gopal Subramanium. *Report of the Committee on Amendments to Criminal Law*. Delhi: Government of India, 2013.

Viva Editors. "Letter to the Editors." *Manushi* (December 1979/January 1980): 39–40.

Vyas, Anju. *Voices of Resistance, Silences of Pain: A Resource Guide on Violence against Women*. New Delhi: Center for Women's Development Studies, 1996.

Vyas, Anju, and Sunita Asija. *Women and Law: An Annotated Bibliography*. Delhi: Center for Women's Development Studies, 1988.

Vyas, Anju, and Meena Usmani. *Women: An Annotated Bibliography of Bibliographies*. Delhi: Center for Women's Development Studies, 1989.

Walker, Alice. *In Search of Our Mothers' Gardens: Womanist Prose*. New York: Harvest/Harcourt Brace Jovanovich, 1983.

Ward, Barbara E., ed. *Women in the New Asia: The Changing Social Roles of Men and Women in South and South-east Asia*. Paris: UNESCO, 1963.

Wei, Zhangling. *Status of Women: China*. Bangkok: UNESCO, 1989.

Wellesley Editorial Committee, ed. "Women and National Development: The Complexities of Change." *Signs: Journal of Women in Culture and Society* 3, no. 1 (1977): 1–338.

Wenzel, Robert. "Nobel Prize Economist Gunnar Myrdal Accused of Sexual Assault." *Economic Policy Journal*, October 4, 2020. https://www.economicpolicyjournal.com/2020/10/gunnar-myrdal-accused-of-sexual-assault.html (accessed July 5, 2025).

Wiegman, Robyn. *Object Lessons*. Durham, NC: Duke University Press, 2012.

Williams, Beth Ann. "'Call Us Ms.': *Viva* and Arguments for Kenyan Women's Respectable Citizenship 1975–80." *Women's History Review* 26, no. 3 (2017): 414–32.

Wilson, Tiana U. "The Making of Triple Jeopardy." *Women's Studies Quarterly* 51, nos. 1/2 (2023): 201–7.

Winckler, Barbara. "Between 'Central' and 'Marginal': Three Syrian Women's Journals of the 1920s, Beirut and Damascus." *Journal of European Periodical Studies* 9, no. 1 (2024): 49–70.

Women Living Under Muslim Laws (WLUML). "Information of Interest: International Women Living Under Muslim Laws." *Women's International News*, October 1, 1989, 15, 4.

Women Living Under Muslim Laws. "In Search of Justice, Human Rights, and a Just Peace by Women Living Under Muslim Laws (WLUML)." *Meridians: Feminism, Race, Transnationalism* 2, no. 2 (2002): 268–70.

Wynter, Sylvia. "Unsettling the Coloniality of Being/Power/Truth/Freedom: Towards the Human, after Man, Its Overrepresentation—An Argument." *CR: The New Centennial Review* 3, no. 3 (2003): 257–337.

Xilonen: The Daily Newspaper of the International Women's Year Tribune, June 27, 1975.

Zinsser, Judith P. "From Mexico to Copenhagen to Nairobi: The United Nations Decade for Women, 1975–1985." *Journal of World History* 13, no. 1 (2002): 139–69.

NAME AND PLACE INDEX

Page numbers in italics refer to figures.